I0649798

Great Illustrated Classics

TITAN EDITIONS

Benvenuto Cellini. He was described by his contemporary, the artist and architect Giorgio Vasari, as "in all his doings of high spirit, proud, lively, very quick to act and formidably vehement; a person who knew only too well how to speak his mind to princes."

The AUTOBIOGRAPHY of
BENVENUTO CELLINI

Translated by Robert Hobart Cust

with eight full-page illustrations

and an introduction by

Raimondo Legame

DODD, MEAD & COMPANY

NEW YORK

Introduction

BENVENUTO CELLINI was born in Florence, Italy, in November, 1500, a half century later than the great Leonardo da Vinci and a quarter century after the most influential of the Florentine artists, Michaelangelo. In the opening pages of his autobiography, he relates that, following the birth of a daughter, his parents had already decided that their second child would also be a girl. When the midwife had washed the new baby and wrapped it in the fairest white linen, she brought it to the waiting father. "I am bringing you a fine present such as you did not anticipate," she said. "What God gives me is always dear to me," replied the father and, seeing that the child was a boy, added "Let him be Welcome—Benvenuto," and by that name the child was baptized.

The young boy was taught to play the flute and to sing by note but had an inexpressible dislike for both. As a result he was placed in the workshop of a local goldsmith and later, at the age of fifteen, on his own initiative, put himself to the goldsmith's trade with an excellent craftsman known as Marcone. From that time on the career in music was largely forgotten, although the young Benvenuto continued to make progress in what he called the "accursed art" of the cornet and flute.

When he was about sixteen years old and as a result of a quarrel with a younger brother who had stolen his clothes, the young Cellini left Florence for Pisa where he remained for a year with a goldsmith named Uliveri, returning to Florence only when he fell ill of a fever. In a short while he was on the road again, this time to Rome where, after various experiences in the employ of local goldsmiths, he finally secured Pope Clement VII as patron.

Cellini was present in Rome during the attack on the city by the Constable of Bourbon and, by his own admission, was of great service in its defense. From this point, and indeed earlier, Cellini's life is a series of art commissions, brawls, imprisonments and escapes, casual assignations—and endless inventions in the design of works in gold and silver and in the perfection of his sculpture which reached its highest point found in the Perseus. He moved continually from Florence to Rome to Paris and sojourned repeatedly in Venice, Naples, Bologna, Pisa and elsewhere in Italy. Among his achievements in medals during these years, the most distinguished is his "Hercules and the Nemean Lion." Perhaps his best known work, second only to the "Perseus Holding the Head of Medusa," is his celebrated salt cellar made for Francis First. Many of the objects described at length in the Autobiography, such as the chalice designed for Pope Clement VII, have perished.

The famous autobiography was begun in 1558 and was for the most part dictated to an amanuensis, to which fact much of the vigor and raciness of the style may be attributed. The closing reference in the book is to the death of the Cardinal de Medici in 1562. Cellini was to live on until 1571 when he died in Florence and was buried there in the Church of the Annunziata. The first printing of the autobiography took place in 1730 in Naples.

Of the autobiography, John Addington Symonds has written, "At one and the same time the most perfect extant monument of vernacular Tuscan prose, and also the most complete and lively source of information we possess regarding manners, customs, ways of feeling and modes of acting in the sixteenth century. It is the first book which a student of the Italian Renaissance should handle in order to obtain the right direction for his more minute researches. It is the last book to which he should return at the close of his exploratory voyages. Nowhere else, to my mind, do we find the full character of the epoch so authentically stamped. That is because this is no work of art or of reflection, but the plain utterance of a man who lived the whole life of his age. He touched the life of that epoch at more points than any person who has left a record of his doings. He was the first goldsmith of his time, an adequate sculptor, a restless travel-ler, an indefatigable workman, a Bohemian of the purest water, a turbulent bravo, a courtier and companion of princes; finally, a Florentine who used his native idiom with incomparable vivacity of style. These qualities combined in a single personality, strongly marked by specific characteristics, yet peculiar to the sixteenth cen-tury in Italy, render him unique as a guide through the labyrinth of that brilliant but perplexing epoch."

Robert Henry Hobard Cust, translator of the present edition, was born in 1861 and was educated at Eton and at Trinity College, Cam-bridge, and Magdalen College, Oxford. His translation of the Cellini Autobiography was completed in 1910. In view of the many popular editions of Mr. John Addington Symonds's translation and the con-tinuance of the long-accepted translation of Mr. Thomas Roscoe and that of Miss Anne Mcdonell, an explanation seems a fitting preface to this unparaphrased, unexpurgated edition.

Like Cellini's friend, the historian Benedetto Varchi, Mr. Cust has appreciated the fact that the force and brilliance of the work itself far outweigh all questions of style and grammar; and to cor-rect it into anything like conventional form would remove from the original its most salient and delightful characteristics. Esteeming the fine, polished language of Mr. Symonds's paraphrasing of the text, Mr. Cust in this translation has tried rather to recapture the energy, directness and racy animation of the original Italian manuscript. In the words of Mr. Cust, he has tried "to demonstrate the theory that the force and vividness of the original narrative are heightened rather than diminished by the wild confusion of detailed thought in the thread of it, by the very inconsequence of the sentences as regards one another, and by the utterly unstudied rattle of the narrator, as he pours out his reminiscences *pêle-mêle,* with the speed and spontaneity of the genuine *improvisatore.* One can picture the elderly and somewhat embittered—perhaps even dyspeptic—craftsman: once the favorite of popes, cardinals, kings and princes: who had lived in courts and camps, and swaggered about the world with boon companions of the best and the worst alike: setting himself down to dictate to his humble little fourteen-year-old scribe all the wonderful events of his past life, made the more incredible by the glamor of distance. One can fancy the rate at which his thoughts must have traveled: too fast even for his tongue, and much too fast for the unhappy young amanuensis, who must have often paused breathless, awe-struck and bewildered at some adventure of more than ordinarily striking character. No wonder that grammar halted, spelling collapsed, and orthography became more and more involved."

In presenting an unexpurgated translation of this classic, Mr. Cust has pointed out that to omit these touches of reality would argue an ignorance of history, especially of the sixteenth century, and that what some readers will consider coarse and disagreeable stories are in point of fact really Tenieresque or Hogarthian touches completing the realism of the whole.

Raimondo Legame

New York City

Contents

Contents

Illustrations

xi

LETTER OF BENVENUTO CELLINI TO
BENEDETTO VARCHI

To the most excellent (and) talented MR Benedetto and my most greatly honored (friend).

SINCE your Lordship tells me that this simple discourse regarding my life satisfies you much more in this plain fashion than if it were repolished and retouched by another hand, the which thing would not seem so like the actual truth as what I have written: for I have taken care not to say anything about those things whereon my memory is uncertain; rather I have related the plain truth, leaving out a great portion of certain remarkable chances regarding which others who had done such things would have made much capital: but since I have had to relate so many great matters, and in order not to make too great a volume, I have left out a large portion of the small ones. I send my servant in order that you may give him my saddle-bag and the book, and since I think that you will not have been able to finish reading all of it, so as not to weary you with so insignificant a matter, and since I have received what I desired of you and am most satisfied by it, with all my heart I thank you. Now I pray you, that you do not trouble to read further, but to send it back to me, keeping my *Sonnet,* for that I particularly desire, that it may experience the polish of your wondrous file: and from now onwards I will come to visit you, and serve you gladly as much as I know how and can.

Keep yourself in good health, I beseech you, and preserve me in your good favor.

In Florence. This day 22nd May 1559.

When Your Lordship may fancy that you are able to give some small assistance to this little friar of mine, together with those (members of the) Agnioli (family), I shall hold myself greatly obliged by it. (I am) always most ready to the commands of Your Lordship.

BENVENUTO CELLINI.

(On the back.)

To the most Magnificent and most Excellent Mr Benedetto Varchi, my most honored (friend).

SONNET AND DECLARATION

This my laborious life I here indite,
  Thanking the God of Nature, who my soul
  Gave unto me, and keeps in His Control;
  Strange deeds I wrought, and lofty, by His Might.
Vainly with me did Fate relentless fight.
  Glory and Life and Beauty were the goal
  Of my desires; of these I gained the whole
  Abundance; and in Art had my delight.
Yet now I greatly grieve, who understand
  What precious time in vanity I spent:
  Our frail thoughts flee, as chaff by breezes fanned;
Vain, Benvenuto, is regret, and so, content
  I rise aloft, as erst I made descent
  Upon the flower of this fair Tuscan land.

I began to write this my life with mine own hand, as may be seen from certain appended papers, but thinking that I was losing too much time, and it seemed to me unreasonable waste, I fell in with a son of Michele di Goro of Pieve a Groppine, a little lad of about fourteen years of age, and somewhat delicate, (and) I began to set him to write, and whilst I worked I dictated to him my Life; and since I took some pleasure in it, I worked much more assiduously, and executed much more work, therefore I left to the said (lad) this undertaking which I hope to continue as far as I shall remember.

Book One

ALL men of every sort, who have done anything that is meritorious, or that indeed resembles merit, ought, if they be truthful persons and of good report, to set forth their lives with their own hand: but they should not commence so noble an undertaking before they have passed the age of forty years. Recognizing such a fact, now that I have travelled along my life's span for full fifty-eight years, and am in Florence, my native place, whilst recalling the many afflictions that befall those who live, and being troubled with these same afflictions less than I have ever been before up to this age: even it would seem to me that I am in greater content of mind and health of body than I have ever been in times past: and remembering certain agreeable blessings and certain incalculable calamities; looking back upon these I am struck with astonishment that I should have arrived at this age of 58 years, in which I am, by the grace of God, so happily proceeding onwards.

Although these men, inasmuch as they have labored with the very smallest trace of merit, have made themselves known to the world, the fact alone ought to be sufficient for them, that they see themselves men of mark; but because they must live in the same manner as others live, we experience in this respect a certain amount of worldly curiosity (*boriosità*), which arises upon many different points. The first duty is to make known to others that the hero traces his descent from persons of merit and very ancient lineage. I am called Benvenuto Cellini, the son of M° Giovanni d'Andrea di Christofano Cellini; my mother was M ͣ Elisabetta, daughter of Stefano Granacci: and both of them were Florentine citizens. We find it set out in the chronicles made by our most ancient and reliable Florentines, according to what Giovanni Villani writes, that we may observe how the city of Florence *(Fiorenze)* is constructed in imitation of the beautiful city of Rome, and some traces may be discovered of the Colosseum and of the Baths. These traces are near to Santa Croce; the Capitol was where the Mercato Vecchio stands to-day; the Rotonda is entirely standing, which was made for a temple of Mars, and to-day is dedicated to our patron, San Giovanni. That this was so can be very clearly seen and cannot be denied: but the said edifices are much smaller than those in Rome. They say that the man who caused them to be built was Julius Caesar, together with certain other Roman nobles, who having conquered and taken Fiesole, erected a city on that spot; and each of them undertook one of these remarkable structures. Julius Caesar had a brave chief captain who was called Fiorino da Cellino (which is a fortress about two miles from Monte Fiasconi). This Fiorino having taken up his abode below Fiesole,

on the spot where Florence now is, in order to be near the river
Arno for the convenience of his army, all his soldiers and such other
persons as had dealings with this said captain used to say: "Let us go
to Fiorenze," because the said captain bore the name of Fiorino, and
because in that place where he had his said dwelling, from the
natural features of the place, there grew a vast quantity of flowers.
So in giving a commencement to the city, since this seemed
to Julius Caesar a most beautiful name, and one appropriately
given to it, and because flowers bring good omen, he gave this
name of Fiorenze to the said city; and in order besides to confer
a sort of favor upon his brave captain; since he liked him so much
the more because he had drawn him from a very humble condition,
and because so brave a man had been created by himself. Learned
romancers and investigators of such etymologies say that that name
(was given to the city) because it was built beside the flowing Arno.
It does not seem that this (etymology) can stand, because Rome is
upon the flowing Tiber, Ferrara upon the flowing Po, Lyons upon
the flowing Saone, Paris upon the flowing Seine; they, however,
have different names, and those arising in another way. We find it
thus, and for this reason we believe it to have arisen from this brave
man. Besides, we find that there are some of our Cellini in
Ravenna, the most ancient city in Italy, and there they are great
nobles; they are also in Pisa, and I have found them in many places
throughout Christendom; and in this very State there also remain
some of the stock, addicted, moreover, to the profession of arms;
for it is not so many years back that a youth named Luca Cellini, a
beardless lad, entered into combat with a soldier, a skilled and very
valiant man, who had fought on previous occasions in the lists,
called Francesco da Vicorati. This Luca, by his own valour, sword
in hand, conquered and slew him with so much bravery and skill,

that he made every one marvel, since they had expected the opposite result. So that I boast of having my descent from brave men.

Now as regards such honor as I have acquired for my house, under the known conditions of our life to-day and by means of my profession, which is not a matter of great consequence, I will speak of it in its own place, glorying much more in that having been born in humble circumstances I have added some honorable foundation to my family, than if I had been sprung from high lineage and by base qualities had stained or extinguished it. I will therefore commence with how it pleased God that I should be born.

My ancestors lived in the Val d'Ambra, and there they had great possessions; and like little lords they lived there in retirement, on account of the party strife of the period. They were all men addicted to the pursuit of arms and very brave. At that time one of their sons, the younger one, whom they called Christofano, quarrelled violently with certain of their neighbors and friends; and because the heads of the houses on both sides joined in, and it was seen that a fire had been ignited of such magnitude that it was bringing danger of total destruction to both families, the elder members having pondered upon this point, by agreement, my side removed Christofano; and so the other side took away the other originator of the feud. They sent their man to Siena; ours sent Christofano to Florence, and there they purchased for him a small house in the Via Chiara from the monastery of Sant' Orsola; and they also bought him some very good lands at Ponte a Rifredi. The said Christofano took a wife in Florence, and had sons and daughters, and having provided for all his daughters, his sons divided the rest of his substance, after the death of their father. The house in the Via Chiara with certain other small matters fell to one of the said sons, who bore the name of Andrea. He also took a wife and had four male children. The first had the name of Girolamo, the second Bartolomeo, the third Giovanni (who was afterwards my father), the fourth Francesco. This Andrea Cellini understood thoroughly the method of the architecture of those times, and made his living by it as his profession. Giovanni, who was my father, gave himself more than any of the others to this kind of work. And because as Vitruvius says, among other things, that for any one who wishes to do well in that art it is needful that he know something of music and good drawing; Giovanni, having become a fine draughtsman, began to give his attention to music, and learnt along with it to play exceedingly well upon the viol and the flute; and being a person of studious habits he seldom went out of the house. They had for their next-door neighbor a man named Stefano Granacci, who had several daughters, all very beautiful. As it pleased God, Giovanni saw one of these said damsels, who bore the name of Elisabetta; and so much did she please him that he asked for her as his wife; and since both their fathers, from being such near neighbors, knew each other very well, it was easy to make up this match; and each of them thought that he had arranged his affairs extremely well. First of all these two good old souls agreed to the alliance; then they commenced to discuss the dowry; and there arose between them a certain amount of friendly dispute, for Andrea said to Stefano: "Giovanni my son is the most brilliant youth both in Florence and in all Italy, and if I had desired to find him a wife before this, I could have had one with a larger dowry than they give in Florence in our rank;" and Stefano said: "You have a thousand reasons, but I have my five girls with as many other children, so that when I reckon up my accounts, this is as much as I can afford." Giovanni was standing a little way off listening, hidden from them; and, coming upon them suddenly, he said: "My father, I have desired and loved that girl, and not the money. Woe to those who wish to repair their fortunes out of the dowries of their wives. Truly! how can you boast that I am so clever, if I do not know how to provide the expenses of my wife, and to satisfy her wants with some sum of money less than you desire? Now I want you to understand that the wife is my share, and that I wish the dowry to be yours." At this, though Andrea Cellini, who was somewhat passionate, was rather indignant, within a few days Giovanni took home his wife, and never asked for any other dowry. They enjoyed their youth and their holy love for eighteen years, with, however, a great desire to have children; since in eighteen years his said wife miscarried of two male children, through want of skill on the part of the doctors; then she conceived again, and brought forth a girl, to whom they gave the name of Cosa, after my father's mother. Then two years later she conceived again; and because those desires which come to pregnant women, upon which they set so much faith, were exactly similar to those at her previous confinement; to such an extent, that they were convinced that she would bring forth another girl like the first; they had agreed to give her the name of Reparata to recall my mother's mother. It happened that the birth took place on the night of All Hallows, at the end of All Saints' Day, at half-past four of the clock in the year 1500 precisely. The midwife, who knew that they expected a girl, when she had washed the infant, swathed it in very fine white cloths, and went softly to my father Giovanni, and said: "I bring you a fine gift such as you do not expect." My FATHER, who was a true philosopher, was walking up and down, and he said: "Whatever God gives me that will always be acceptable to me"; and having lifted the cloths he saw with his own eyes the unexpected male child. Clasping his aged hands together, he raised them and his eyes to Heaven, and said: "Lord, I thank Thee with all my heart. This is very acceptable to me, and may he be Welcome (*Benvenuto*)." All those persons who were present joyfully asked him how he would like to name the child. Giovanni never answered them aught but "May he be Welcome (*Benvenuto*)"; and having resolved upon it, such name was given me in Holy Baptism, and so designated I desire by the Grace of God to live.

My grandfather Andrea Cellini was still alive, when I had already reached the age of about three; and he was past one hundred years. One day they had been altering a certain pipe of a cistern, and from the same there issued a great scorpion, which they had not noticed, and it had dropped down from the cistern to the ground, and went away under a bench. I saw it, and running after it laid my hands upon its back. The said (animal) was so large that, holding it in my little hand, from one side there issued the tail and from the other both the mouths. They say that I ran to my grandfather in great glee, crying out: "Look, grandpapa, at my fine little crab." When he realized that it was a scorpion, out of great fear and anxiety on my behalf, he was like to have fallen down dead; and he begged it of me with many endearments. I clung to it so much the more, sobbing out that I would not give it up to any one. My father, who was also at home, ran up at so much noise, and horrified knew not how to find a means that this poisonous animal should not kill me. At that moment he happened to see a pair of small scissors. Caressing me, therefore, he cut off the tail and the mouths. Then, when that danger had been averted, he took it for a good omen.

When I was about five years old, my father being in our small cellar, in the which they had been washing the clothes, and where there was still a good fire of oak boughs, Giovanni, with his viol in his arms, played and sang to himself beside that fire. It was very cold; and as he gazed into the fire, by chance he saw in the midst of the hottest flames a little animal like a lizard, which was sporting about amidst that most scorching blaze. Having immediately perceived what it was he caused my sister and me to be summoned, and pointing it out to us children, he gave me a violent box on the ear, at which I began to cry most excessively. He comforting me kindly, spake to me thus: "My dear little son, I did not give you that blow on account of anything wrong that you have done, but only that you may remember that that lizard which you saw in the fire is a salamander, a creature that has never been seen by any one else of whom we have reliable information." So he kissed me and gave me some coppers.

My father began to teach me to play upon the flute and to sing from note, and although I was of very tender age, when little children are accustomed to take pleasure in a whistle and such-like diversions, I had the greatest dislike to it, and played and sang only to obey him. My father in those days manufactured wonderful organs with wooden pipes, well-tuned cymbals, the best and the most beautiful to be seen at that period: viols, lutes, most beautiful and most excellent harps. He was also an engineer, and labored marvellously in the construction of machinery, such as contrivances for lowering bridges, building mills, and other kinds of engines, and he was the first to excel in ivory carving. But because he was in love with her by whom he became my father and she my mother—thanks perhaps to that little flute—since he paid more attention to it than he ought, he was invited by the Fifers in the service of the State to play along with them. Thus continuing at this employment for a time for his own pleasure, they persuaded him so much that they caused him to become one of their regular company. Lorenzo de Medici and Piero his son, who liked him very much, subsequently perceived that he devoted himself wholly to his fife, and left in desuetude his fine talent and his fine profession. They therefore caused him to be removed from that post. My father took this very ill, and it appeared to him that they had done him a very great injury. Immediately he returned to his profession and made a mirror, about a *brac-*

cio in diameter, of bone and ivory, adorned with figures and foliage, with careful finish and fine design. The mirror was in the form of a wheel; in the midst was the mirror itself; around it were seven circles, in which were carved and inlaid the Seven Virtues in ivory and blackened bone; and the whole mirror, and likewise the said Virtues, were balanced in such a way, that in turning the said wheel all the virtues revolved; and they had each a weight at their feet which kept them upright. And since he had some knowledge of the Latin language he inscribed around the said mirror a Latin inscription which ran: "Through all the turns that the Wheel of Fortune makes, Virtue remains upright."

"Rota sum; semper, quo me verto stat virtus."

A little while after this his post of fifer was restored to him. Although some of these events happened before I was born, I record them because I do not wish to omit anything. At that time all the fifers were most honorable artisans, and some of them belonged to the Greater Arts of Silk and Wool; for the which reason my father did not disdain to practise such a profession. The greatest desire that he had in the world regarding my prospects was that I should become a great musician: the greatest annoyance that I could have in the world was when he argued with me, telling me that, if I liked, he saw so much promise in me in that respect, that I might be the first performer in the world. As I have said, my father was a great adherent and most friendly towards the house of Medici; and when Piero was expelled, he entrusted to my father a great many matters of serious import. Later on, at the coming into power of the magnificent Piero Soderini, my father being still in his post of musician, Soderini, being aware of my father's remarkable genius, began to employ him as engineer in many most important undertakings, and while Soderini remained in Florence his goodwill towards my father was as great as it is possible to imagine in the world. And at this time, because I was of tender age, my father had me carried in arms, and made me play upon the flute, and I executed the soprano part in concert with the palace musicians before the Signoria; and I played from score whilst a tabard held me in his arms. Then the Gonfalonier, who was the said Soderini, took great pleasure in making me prattle, and gave me sweet-meats, and said to my father: "M° Giovanni! Teach him along with music those two other most beautiful arts of yours." To which my father answered: "I do not want him to exercise any other art but that of music and composition; because in this profession I hope to make him the greatest man in the world, if God shall spare his life." At these words one of those old councillors answered, saying to M° Giovanni: "Do what the Gonfalonier tells you. Can he ever be other than a fine musician?" Thus passed a certain period until the Medici returned. Directly the Medici were restored, the cardinal, who was subsequently Pope Leone, showed many favors to my father. From the escutcheon that was on the palace of the Medici, whilst they were in exile, the balls had been removed, and there had been painted thereon a great red cross, which was the arms and insignia of the Commune: so that directly after their return the red cross was erased, and upon the said shield was replaced their red balls, set moreover in a golden field, with very fine adornments. My father, who had a certain amount of genuine natural poetic instinct, together with something of the prophetic (which was certainly a divine attribute in him), beneath the said scutcheon, as soon as it was uncovered, wrote these four lines. They ran as follows:

> These noble arms that, buried out of sight
> Beneath the Holy Cross so long have lain,
> With a new joy and glory shine again,
> Awaiting Peter's sacred mantle bright.

This epigram was read by all Florence. A few days later Pope Julio the Second died. Cardinal de' Medici having gone to Rome, was, contrary to the expectation of everyone, made Pope Leone X, the liberal and magnanimous. My father sent to him his four pro-phetic lines. The Pope then sent to tell him to come thither, for it would be to his advantage. He did not want to go; therefore, in-stead of a reward, his post at the palace was taken from him by Jacopo Salviati, as soon as ever he was appointed Gonfalonier. This was the reason for my setting myself to work at a goldsmith's; and I partly studied that profession and partly continued my music, much against my will. When he (my father) spoke to me upon this point, I besought him to let me draw so many hours a day, and all the rest I would give myself up to music, merely to content him. To this he replied: "Then you take no pleasure in music?" To which I answered, "No," because it seemed to me an art too inferior to that which I had in my soul. My excellent father, in despair at such a circumstance, set me in the workshop of the father of Cava-liere Bandinello, who was named Michelagniolo, a goldsmith from Pinzi di Monte, and who was very skilled in such arts. He had no glory of family origin, but was the son of a charcoal merchant. This remark is not made by way of condemning Bandinello, who has founded his own house—if it were come about from a worthy stock. However that may be, I have no occasion to speak about him here. When I had been there some days, my father took me away from the said Michelagniolo, because he could not live without seeing me constantly. Thus with a bad grace I continued to play until I was fifteen years of age. If I wished to describe the great events that happened to me up to that age, and in what great danger was my very life, it would make whoever read of such things marvel indeed; but in order not to be too lengthy, and because I have much to say, I will leave them out.

When I had reached the age of fifteen years, against the wish of my father, I apprenticed myself as a goldsmith with a man who was called Antonio di Sandro, the goldsmith, nicknamed Marcone the goldsmith. He was a very good artificer, and a man of much worth, high principled and liberal in all his affairs. My father did not wish him to give me a salary, as he was accustomed to do to his other workmen, in order that, since I had taken upon myself to practise that trade of my own free will, I could satisfy my desire to draw as much as I pleased. And I did so very willingly, and that excellent master of mine took mighty pleasure thereat. He had an only (natural) son, to whom he very frequently gave his orders, so as to spare me. So great was my desire, or in truth my inclination, or both combined, that in a few months I overtook some of the able, and even some of the more advanced, young men in the trade, and began to draw some profit from my labors. During this time I did not omit sometimes to give pleasure to my excellent Father, playing now upon the flute, and now upon the cornet; and I always caused his tears to fall, mingled with deep sighs, whenever he heard me.

Cosimo de' Medici, Duke of Florence, the patron for whom Cellini made his famous statue of Perseus, shown here in a portrait by Giorgio Vasari with Cellini and other artists and architects.

Piero, so that in great wrath he said: "I knew well that it was yo[u]
who hindered this my so greatly desired object, and that it was yo[u]
who caused me to be removed from my post at the Palace, paying m[e]
with that great ingratitude with which men are accustomed t[o]
recompense important benefits. I caused them to give you a pos[t],
and you have got mine taken from me; I taught you to play with a[ll]
the skill that you know, and you hinder my son from doing m[y]
will; but bear in mind these prophetic words: there will not pass,[I]
do not say years or months, but a few weeks, before, for this so dis[-]
honorable an ingratitude of yours, you will come to grief." T[o]
these words Pierino replied and said: "Master Giovanni, the greate[r]
part of mankind, when they grow old, along with that sam[e]
advancing age, become crazy, as you have done, and at this I do no[t]
wonder, because you have given away most liberally all your posses[-]
sions, without considering that your children would have need o[f]
them, whereas I contemplate doing exactly the opposite, namely, t[o]
leave so much to my children that they may be able to assist yours.['']
To this my father replied: "No bad tree ever bore good fruit; indeed
the contrary; and I tell you further, that you are a bad man, and that
your children will be insane and poor, and will come for alms to my
virtuous and wealthy offspring." So he departed to his own home,
both of them muttering wild words at one another. Whereupon I,
who took the part of my good father, quitting that house in his company, told him that I would like to go and take my vengeance upon
that rascal for the injuries that he had done him, on condition "that
you let me apply myself to the art of drawing." My father said:
"My dear son, I have also been a fine draughtsman. Both for a relief
from those wonderful labors of yours, and out of love for me, who
am your father, who begot you, brought you up and laid the foundation of so many honorable talents, as a recreation from them, will
you not promise me that you will sometimes take that flute and that

Chapter Two

AT that period I had a very bold and very hot-headed brother of
mine, younger than myself by two years, who became, subsequently, one of those fine soldiers who enjoyed the training of that
glorious lord Giovannino de' Medici, father of Duke Cosimo. This
youth was about fourteen, and I two years older. One Sunday, at
about twenty-two of the clock, he was between the Porta San
Gallo and the Porta Pinti, and there entered into conflict with a
youth of about twenty, with swords in their hands; so stoutly did he
press upon him, that having sorely wounded him, he followed up
his success still more. There were a great many persons present,
among whom were many of the man's relatives; and when they
saw that the matter was faring badly for him, they armed themselves with many slings, and one of them struck that poor youth,
my brother, on the head; immediately he fell to the ground, insensible as one dead. I, for it happened by chance that I was there, both

without friends and unarmed, cried out as loud as I could to my brother that he should retire, for what he had done was sufficient; in the meanwhile the chance occurred that he in that fashion fell down as if dead. I immediately ran to him, and seizing his sword set myself in front of him and in opposition to a number of swords and many stones. I never left my brother, until there came from the Porta di San Gallo some valiant soldiers who delivered me from that violent onset, marveling much that there should be so great valor combined with such youth. So I bore my brother as far as our home as one dead, and when he reached his home he was resuscitated with great difficulty. When he was cured, the Eight, who had already condemned our adversaries, and banished them for a term of years, banished us also for six months to a distance of ten miles from the city. I said to my brother, "come with me"; and so we left our poor father, and he, instead of giving us a sum of money, because he had none to give, gave us his blessing. I went to Siena to find a certain honest man who was called M° Francesco Castoro; since on a previous occasion, when I had run away from my father, I had betaken myself to this excellent man, and stayed with him some days, until my father sent for me back again, working always in the goldsmith's trade. The said Francesco, when I came to him, immediately recognized me, and put me to a job. When I had thus set myself to work, the said Francesco gave me a home as long as I stayed in Siena; and thither I took my brother and myself, and I applied myself to work for many months. My brother had begun Latin literature, but he was so much of a lad that he had not yet acquired a taste for virtue, but went about in dissipation.

At that time Cardinal de' Medici, who was afterwards Pope Clemente, at the prayers of my father enabled us to return to Florence. A certain pupil of my father's, prompted by natural mischievousness, told the said Cardinal that he ought to send me to

Bologna to learn music thoroughly from a master who was there, who was called Antonio, a really brilliant man in that profession of music. The Cardinal told my father that if he would send me thither, he would give me letters of recommendation and of assistance. My father, who was dying of desire for that very thing, sent me: whereupon I, being desirous of seeing the world, went willingly. When I reached Bologna, I set myself to work with one whom they called M° Ercole, the son of the Fifer *(del Piffero),* and I began to earn some money; and meanwhile I went every day for lessons in music, and in a few weeks I made very great progress in that accursed art; but I made much greater profit out of the goldsmith's trade, for, having received no help from the said Cardinal, I put myself in the house of a Bolognese miniature painter who was called Scipione Cavalletti (he lived in the street of our Lady *del Baraccan*), and there I applied myself to designing and working for an individual whom they called Gratia Dio *(Thank God)* the Jew, with whom I earned a great deal. At the end of six months I returned to Florence, whereat that Pierino the fifer, who had formerly been my father's pupil, took it very ill. And I, to oblige my father, went to see him at his home, and I played the cornet and flute in concert with a brother of his, who bore the name of Girolamo, was several years younger than the said Piero, and was a very excellent and good young man, quite the contrary to his brother. Upon on of these occasions my father came to the house of this Piero to he us play; and, taking the greatest satisfaction out of that performan of mine, said: "I shall indeed make a wonderful musician out of against the will of those who have desired to hinder me." To Piero replied (and he spake the truth): "Your Benvenuto will much more profit and honor if he attends to the goldsmit than to this fifing *(epipherata)."* My father took very mu brage at these words, having seen that I too had the same op most tuneful *(lascivissimo)* cornet, and with some pleasurable delight to yourself play upon them with enjoyment?" I said "Yes! and most willingly, for love of him." Then my good father said that these very gifts would provide the greatest revenge that I could inflict for the injuries that he had received from his enemies. A whole month had not passed from these words, when the said Pierino, having caused a vaulted cellar to be made in one of the houses that he owned in Via dello Studio, was one day in the ground-floor chamber of it, above the vault that he had caused to be made, with a large company, and it happened by chance that he was talking about my father, who had been his master. Just as he was repeating the words that he had said regarding his downfall, and had scarcely uttered them, when the chamber where he was, from the vault being insecurely pitched, or indeed through the true power of God, who does not pay on Saturday,—collapsed; and since the stones of the vault and the bricks fell in with him they broke both his legs; whilst those who were with him, remaining above upon the edges of the vault, suffered no injury, but stood dumb-founded and astonished, especially at the remark that he had a short time before repeated in mockery. When he knew of this, my father, arming himself, went to see him, and in the presence of his own father, who was called Niccolaio da Volterra, trumpeter to the Signoria, he said: "Oh! Piero, my dear pupil, I am very much grieved at your misfortune; but if you remember well, it is but a little while ago that I warned you of it; and just as much will happen regarding your children and mine as I have told you." A little time after the ungrateful Piero died of that same ailment. He left a wanton wife and a son, who some years later came to me for alms in Rome. I gave it to him, because it is my nature to give alms; and almost with tears I recalled that happy condition in which Pierino was when my father pronounced to him those words, namely, that the sons of the said

Pierino would hereafter turn for alms to his virtuous children. And enough has perhaps been said upon this point, and let no one ever make jest of the prophecies of a worthy man, whom they have unjustly reviled, because it is not he who speaks, but rather the voice of God Himself.

Attending, however, to the goldsmith's trade, I assisted by means of it my good father. His other son and my brother, by name Cecchino, as I have said above, although he had caused him to commence Latin literature,—because he desired to make me, the elder, a great performer and musician, and him, the younger, a fine learned lawyer,—he was unable to force that which nature had inclined us to: nature, which made me prone to the art of design, and my brother (who was of fine and graceful proportions) entirely devoted to the pursuit of arms; and, although he was still very young, he was on his way from his first lesson in the school of that most glorious lord Giovannino de' Medici. Having reached home when I was not there, he was badly off for clothes; and finding our sisters, they, unknown to my father, gave him my fine new cloak and frock, handsome garments which, over and above the assistance that I gave to my father and to my good and honest sisters, I had had made with the savings from my labors. Finding myself deceived, and the said garments taken from me, and not finding my brother, from whom I wished to recover them, I asked my father why he had permitted me to suffer so great a wrong, since he saw that I labored so willingly to assist him. To this he replied that I was his good son, but that he had regained the other one whom he thought that he had lost; and that it was a necessity, or rather a precept of God Himself, that he who had any good thing should give to him that had not; and that out of love for him I ought to bear this injury: God would give me the increase of every good thing. I, like a youth without common sense, turned upon my poor unhappy father; and having collected the meagre remains of my clothing and money, directed my course toward one of the city gates; and not knowing which of the gates it might be that would lead me to Rome, I found myself at Lucca, and, by way of Lucca, at Pisa. And at the time that I arrived at Pisa I was about the age of sixteen years; and, as I paused beside the central bridge, at a spot which they call the "Fish Stone," beside a goldsmith's shop, I stood watching attentively what the master of the shop was doing, when the said master asked of me who I was and what was my profession; upon which I said that I labored a little at the same trade that he did. This worthy man told me to come into his shop, and immediately set before me the materials for work, and uttered these words: "Your open countenance makes me believe that you are both worthy and good." So he set before me gold, silver, and precious stones; and when that first day's work was completed, he took me in the evening to his own house, where he lived honestly with his handsome wife and children. Recalling the grief that my good father might have on my account, I wrote to him that I was in the house of a very good and worthy man, who was called Master Ulivieri della Chiostra, and that with him I was executing many beautiful and splendid works; and that he must be of good courage, for I was endeavoring to learn, and that I hoped with that same skill to bring to him soon something both of profit and honor. My good father immediately replied to my letter saying thus: "My son, the affection that I bear for you is so great, that were it not for a high sense of honor, which I observe above all other things, I should have at once made arrangements to come to you, because I indeed seem to be without the light of my eyes if I do not see you every day, as I was accustomed to do. I shall devote my attention to finishing (my task) of leading my family in the path of virtue and honor, and do you attend to the study of virtue: and I only desire you to remember these few (*quattro*) simple words, and observe and never to forget them: 'In that house wherein you wish to stay, live in honesty and steal nothing.' "

This letter fell into the hands of my master Ulivieri, and, unknown to me, he read it. Afterwards he told me that he had read the letter, and pronounced these words to me: "Truly, Benvenuto mine, your open countenance did not play me false, as is proved to me by a letter from your father, which has come into my hands; according to which he must be a good and worthy man; therefore consider that you are now in your own home and as in your father's house." Whilst I remained in Pisa I went to see the Campo Santo, and there I found many fine antiquities, that is to say, marble coffers; and in many other spots in Pisa I saw a number of other ancient objects, regarding which, every day that I could spare from my work at the shop, I made a diligent study; and when my master, out of his great affection for me, came to see me in the little chamber that he had allotted to me, and saw that I spent all my time thus honestly, he conceived for me a love as if he had actually been my father. I made a great profit during the one year that I stayed there, and executed some fine and important works in gold and in silver, which gave me the greatest courage to proceed further. My father at this juncture wrote to me most piteously that I should return to him, and in every letter reminded me that I ought not to lose that art of music which with so much labor he had taught to me. Upon this there departed immediately from me all desire ever to return to the place where he was, so much did I hold in abhorrence that accursed art of music; and it seemed to me that I had truly been in Paradise for the whole year that I had passed in Pisa, where I had never practised once. At the end of the year my master Ulivieri had occasion to go to Florence to sell certain gold and silver filings (*spazzature*) that he had; and because in that very bad climate I had been assailed by a slight attack of fever, with it upon me, and in my Master's company, I returned to Florence; where my father showed the greatest courtesies to my master, imploring him civilly, unknown to me, that he would be pleased not to take me back to Pisa. Continuing sick, I remained thus about two months, and my father with great devotion caused me to be doctored and cured, continually saying that it seemed to him a thousand years ere I should be cured, that he might hear me play a little. And whilst he argued with me regarding this music, keeping his finger on my pulse, for he had some knowledge of medicine and of Latin literature, he felt in that same pulse, directly he began to talk about music, so great a change, that he was frequently terrified and departed from my side in tears; in such measure that when I perceived his great unhappiness on this score, I told one of my sisters to bring me a flute; for although I still continued to have fever, since that instrument involved but very little strain, it did me no harm to play with so fine an execution in fingers and tongue, that my father, bursting in upon me unexpectedly, blessed me a thousand times, saying that during the time that I had been away from him I seemed to have made a vast improvement; and he besought me that I would persevere in it so that I should not lose so fine an accomplishment. When I was cured I returned to my worthy friend, Marchone the goldsmith, who provided me with the means of earning something, with which earnings I assisted my father and my family.

At that time there came to Florence a sculptor who was named Piero Torrigiani. He came from England, where he had resided many years, and, since he was a great friend of my master's, he came every day to (see) him. And when he saw my drawings and my work, he said: "I have come to Florence to engage as many young men as I can: for having a great work to execute for my king I want the aid of my Florentine fellow-citizens; and since your style of execution and your designs are more those of a sculptor than of a gold-smith, and as I have vast works in bronze to carry out, I will make you at one and the same time both skilful and wealthy." This man was of the most handsome presence, and most bold-looking; he had more the air of a great soldier than of a sculptor, especially in his magnificent gestures and his sonorous voice, together with a trick of contracting his brows enough to terrify most men. And every day he talked of his bold doings among those beasts of Englishmen. In this connection he chanced to speak of Michelagniolo Buonarroti, which was caused by a drawing that I had made, a copy of a cartoon by that most divine Michelagniolo. This cartoon was the first fine work wherein Michelagniolo displayed his marvellous talents, and he executed it in competition with one made by another artist, namely, Lionardo da Vinci, which were to adorn the Sala del Con-siglio in the Palace of the Signoria. They represented events when Pisa was taken by the Florentines; and the admirable Lionardo da Vinci had chosen to illustrate a battle of cavalry, together with the capture of certain standards, as divinely composed as it is possible to imagine. Michelagniolo Buonarroti in his painting depicted a number of foot soldiers who, since it was summer-time, were in the act of bathing in the Arno; and in that instant he shows that an alarm has been given, and those naked infantry are rushing to arms with such fine gestures that there has never among ancient or other modern artists been seen a work that attained to so high a pitch of greatness; and as I have said, the work of the great Lionardo was most beautiful and wonderful. These two cartoons stood, one in the Palace of the Medici, and the other in the Sala del Papa. Whilst they continued in existence they formed a school of Art for the world. Although the divine Michelagniolo subsequently painted the Great Chapel for Pope Julio, he never by half reached this point; his talents never again arrived at the power of these early efforts.

Chapter Three   *1518-1523*

W E now return to Piero Torrigiani, who with my drawing in
his hand, spake thus: "This Buonaaroti (*sic*) and I from
boyhood used to go to study in Masaccio's chapel in the Church of
the Carmine; and because Buonaaroti was accustomed to make fun
of all those who were drawing there, one day when the said youth
was annoying me among the rest, he aroused in me more anger than
usual, and clenching my fist I gave him so violent a blow upon the
nose, that I felt the bone and the cartilage of the nose break under
the stroke, as if it had been a wafer; and thus marked by me he will
remain as long as he lives." These words begat in me so great a
hatred, since I saw continually the works of the divine Michelagniolo, that, notwithstanding that I had conceived a desire to go with
him to England, I could not bear even to see him.

I applied myself continually in Florence to study after the fine
style of Michelagniolo, and from that I have never deviated. At that
period I commenced an intercourse and a very close friendship with
a charming youth of my own age, who was also working in the goldsmith's trade. He bore the name of Francesco, son of Filippo, the

son of that most excellent painter, Fra Filippo. In our relations with one another there arose so great an affection that we never passed either day or night apart; and, moreover, since his home was full of those beautiful studies that his brilliant father had made, which consisted of a number of books of drawings by his own hand, representations of the fine antiquities of Rome: the which when I saw them enchanted me very much, and for about two years we kept company together. At this time I executed a work in silver in low relief as large as the hand of a small boy. This article served for the clasp of a man's girdle, for they then wore them so big. There was carved upon it a group of leaves, arranged after the ancient manner, together with many small cherubs and other very fine masks. This work I executed in the workshop of a man named Francesco Salinbene. When this work was seen by the Goldsmiths' Guild, I acquired the reputation of being the most promising young man in that trade. And perchance a certain youth, Giovanbatista, surnamed Tasso, a wood-carver, a youth of precisely my own age, began saying that if I would like to go to Rome, he would willingly accompany me (this conversation that we had together took place immediately after dinner); and since I was enraged with my father over the usual subject of music, I said to Tasso, "You are a man of words and not of deeds." Tasso then replied to me: "I also am in a rage with my mother, and if I had money enough to take me to Rome I would not turn back even to close up that wretched little shop that I possess (at present)." To these words I replied that if it was on that account that he remained I was possessed of sufficient funds to take us both to Rome. Conversing thus together, as we walked along we found ourselves at the Gate at Sanpiero Gattolini without noticing it. Upon which I said to him: "Tasso mine, we are at this gate where neither you nor I expected to be; now since I am here it seems to me as though I had completed half the journey." Being thus in agreement, he and I said as we continued our journey, "What will our old folks say this evening?" Having said this we entered into a compact together not to think of them any more until we should have arrived in Rome. So we bound our aprons upon our backs, and proceeded almost in silence as far as Siena. When we were in Siena, Tasso said that he was footsore, so that he did not want to come any further, and he begged me to lend him the money to return home. To which I replied that there would not be enough left for me to go forward: "you should have thought of this ere leaving Florence; and if it be only on account of your feet that you do not want to come further we will find a horse returning to Rome, and then you will have no excuse for not coming." Having therefore hired a horse, when I saw that he did not answer me, I took the road towards the gate that leads to Rome. He, when he saw that I was determined, not ceasing to grumble, limping along to the best of his ability, came slowly at a good distance behind me. When I reached the gate, pitying my poor companion, I waited for him and took him up behind me, saying to him, "What would our friends say of us tomorrow, if when we had set out to go to Rome, we had not sufficient courage to go beyond Siena?" Whereupon the excellent Tasso admitted that I spoke the truth, and being a lively creature he began to laugh and sing; and thus continuing to sing and laugh we took our way to Rome. My age was then exactly nineteen, in correspondence with the century. When we had arrived in Rome I immediately engaged myself with a master-craftsman, whom they called Firenzuola. This man bore the name of Giovanni, and was from Firenzuola in Lombardy; and he was a most skilful workman in the fashioning of plate and articles of large size. When I showed him a small idea of the model of that buckle which I had executed in Florence with Salinbene, he was wondrously pleased and spake these words to me, turning to a youth whom he employed, who was a Florentine, and was called Giannotto Giannotti,—who had, moreover, been with him some years—he spake as follows: "This is one of those Florentines who know their business, but you are one of those who know it not." Thereupon recognizing Giannotto I turned to accost him. For before he went to Rome, we often set to work together to draw, and had been very intimate comrades. But taking great offence at the words which his master had spoken, he said that he did not recognize me, nor did he know who I was. Upon which I being indignant at such statements, said to him: "Oh! Giannotto, once my intimate friend, for we were often to be found in such and such places, and used to draw, eat, drink and sleep at your country-house, I do not need you to go bail for me to this worthy man your master, because I hope that my own hands may suffice to testify without your aid what sort of workman I am." When I had finished these words, Firenzuola, who was very excitable and violent, turned to the said Giannotto and said to him: "Oh! you vile rascal! Are you not ashamed to use such treatment and conduct towards one who has been so intimate a companion of yours?" And turning to me in the same excited manner he said: "Come into the shop and do as you have said; so that your hands may prove of what you are capable;" and he set me to carry out a most beautiful commission in silver for a cardinal. It was a casket copied from that in porphyry which stands before the door of the Rotonda. Besides copying it I enriched it with so many beautiful grotesques that my master went about eulogizing it and exhibiting it throughout the trade, because so well-executed an object should have issued from his workshop. It was about half a *braccio* in size; and was arranged to serve as a salt-cellar, to be kept upon the table. This was the first-fruits of the earnings that I tasted in Rome: and one portion of these same earnings I forwarded to the assistance of my good father. The other portion I reserved to live upon myself: and with it I went about studying the remains of antiquity until my funds came to an end when it suited me to return to the shop to work. My comrade, Batista del Tasso, did not stay long in Rome, but returned to Florence. Having taken up again fresh work, the desire came upon me, when I had completed what I had on hand, to change my employer, being seduced thereto by a certain Milanese, who was called Master Pagholo Arsago. My former master Firenzuola raised a great disturbance with this Arsago, uttering in my presence certain insulting expressions: whereat I took up my parable in defence of my new master. I told him that I had been born a free man, and thus free I meant to live; and that he had no reason to complain of his conduct, still less of me, for there remained in his hands a few *scudi* due upon our contract: and that as a free journeyman I wished to go where I liked: knowing that I did wrong to no man. My new master also made a few remarks, stating that he had not summoned me, and that I should oblige him by returning with Firenzuola. To this I rejoined that I was not aware that I had done wrong in any way, and since I had finished the work that I had begun, I wished to be at my own disposal and not at that of anyone else, and whoever wanted my services might ask me for them. To this Firenzuola replied: "I have no wish to ask anything further of you, and never upon any account do you come into my presence." I reminded him of the money due to me. He began to jeer at me; upon which I replied, that just as I could manipulate my tools upon the jobs that he had seen, was I not less skilful with my sword for the recovery of my dues. At these words there stopped by chance an elderly man, who was called Master Antonio da Sanmarino. This man was by far the most able goldsmith in Rome and had been Firenzuola's master. Having listened to my argument, which I uttered in such a manner that he could very easily understand it, he immediately undertook my cause, and said that Firenzuola should pay me. The disputes were violent, because this Firenzuola was marvellously skilled in arms, very much more indeed than in the art of the goldsmith. But reason turned the situation, and I assisted it with the same spirit, to such purpose that I was paid; and in course of time the said Firenzuola and I were reconciled, and I stood godfather at his request to one of his sons.

Continuing to work with Master Pagholo Arsago I earned a great deal, always sending the greater part to my good father. At the end of two years, at the prayers of my good father, I returned to Florence and set myself to work once more with Francesco Salinbene, with whom I made very good earnings and took great pains to learn. Having renewed my relations with Francesco di Filippo, although I was much given up to certain diversions on account of that accursed music, I never omitted to devote certain hours of the day or of the night to my studies. I made at that time a silver Heart's-Key (*chiavaquore*); for so they were called in those days. It was a girdle the width of three fingers, which they were accustomed to make for newly-wedded brides; and it was made in low relief with some small figures besides upon it in full relief. I made it for a man named Raffaello Lapaccini. Although I was very badly paid for it, I acquired from it such reputation as was of more advantage to me than the price that I ought justly to have received. Having at this period worked for many divers employers in Florence, where I was acquainted with some men of worth among the goldsmiths, such as was Marchone, my first master, there were others who bore the name of very good men, but who, by over-reaching me in my work, robbed me shamefully as far as they were able. Upon seeing this I avoided them, and reckoned them as evil fellows and thieves. One goldsmith amongst the rest, named Giovanbatista Sogliani, courteously accommodated me with a part of his shop, which was in a corner of the Merchato Nuovo, beside the bank kept by the Landi. Here I executed many beautiful little works and earned a good deal: I was able to assist my family very much. I aroused the envy of those evil masters whom I had formerly served, who were called Salvadore and Michele Guasconti (they owned three large shops for the carrying on of the goldsmith's trade, and executed many commissions): to such an extent, that when I saw that they were injuring me, I complained to a certain worthy man, saying that those knaveries ought to have sufficed, which they exhibited towards me under the cloak of the treacherous goodwill displayed by them. When this remark reached their ears they boasted that they would make me greatly repent such a speech; to which I who knew not the color of fear paid little or no attention. One day it chanced that as I was leaning against the shop of one of them, he called out to me, partly rebuking, and partly defying me. To which I replied that if they had done their duty by me I should have spoken those things of them that one says of good and worthy persons: but since they had done the opposite the fault lay with them and not with me. Whilst I stood arguing, one of them, who was called Gherardo Guasconti, their cousin, instigated perhaps by their common consent, spied a beast of burden that was passing. (It was a beast laden with bricks.) When the said load came up to me, Gherardo pushed it on to me in such a way that it hurt me very much. Turning myself round suddenly and seeing him laughing, I struck him such a blow on one of his temples that he fell down insensible as though dead. Then I turned to his cousins and said: "Thus do they treat cowardly thieves like you." And upon their wishing to make some attack upon me, because there were many of them, I being infuriated, drew a little knife that I carried, saying thus: "If any one of you issues from your shop, another had better run for a confessor, for the doctor will have naught to do." My words struck such terror into them that no one ventured to the assistance of their cousin. As soon as I had departed, the fathers and

the sons hurried to the Eight, and there stated that I had with force
of arms assaulted them in their shops; an event that had never occurred in Florence. The Eight (Judges) caused me to be summoned; whereupon I appeared: and administering to me a severe
reprimand they rebuked me because they saw me in my cloak only
whilst the others were in civil dress of mantle and hood; and moreover, because my adversaries had been to speak with all the judges
at home in private, whilst I having no personal acquaintance with
any of those judges, had not spoken with them, trusting to the great
justification that I had; and I told them that on account of the great
injury and insult that Gherardo had shown me, provoked to very
great anger, I had given him nothing more than a *buffet,* which did
not seem to me sufficient to deserve so severe a censure. Scarcely
would Prinzivalle della Stufa, who was one of the Eight, allow me
to finish the word *buffet,* before he said: "You gave him a violent
blow and not a buffet." When the bell had been rung and we all
had been put outside, Prinzivalle spoke to his colleagues in my defence: "Consider, sirs, the simple-mindedness of this poor young
man, who accuses himself of having struck a buffet only, thinking
that to be a minor fault than to give a violent blow: whereas the
penalty for a buffet administered in the Mercato Nuovo is twenty-
five *scudi,* whilst that for a violent blow is little or nothing. He is a
very virtuous youth, and supports his indigent family by his very
strenuous exertions; and would to God our city had an abundance
of his kind, for there is a great need of them. There were among
them some of those twisted-hooded fellows (*arronzinati cappuc-
cetti*), who, influenced by the prayers and false witness of my adversaries (because they were of the faction of Fra Girolamo), would
have had me put in prison and condemned to (a fine of) a measure
of charcoal; but in this matter the excellent Prinzivalle wholly prevailed. So they condemned me to a small fine of four bushels of

flour, to be bestowed in alms upon the convent of the Murate. Calling us back they immediately commanded me not to say another
word under pain of their displeasure and to obey that punishment
to which I had been condemned. So administering to me a severe
reprimand they sent us to the chancellor. But I kept on murmuring: "It was a buffet and not a violent blow": in such a way that the
Eight burst out laughing. The chancellor in the name of the judges
ordered us both to give securities; and they condemned me only to
pay those four bushels of flour. It seemed to me that I had been
shamefully treated, nevertheless I sent for one of my cousins, who
was called Master Anniballe, the surgeon, the father of Messer
Librodoro Librodori, desiring that he would go surety for me. This
man, however, did not choose to come, at which I was very indignant; fuming I became like an adder, and took a desperate resolution. [It is well known how much the planets do not only guide, but
even coerce us.] Recollecting what great obligation this Anniballe
owed to my family, my fury so much the more increased that it
turned everything to evil, and being besides by nature somewhat
hot-tempered, I composed myself to wait in that office until the Eight
had adjourned for dinner. And whilst I remained there alone, observing that none of the attendants of the Eight were watching me
any longer, bursting with rage, I issued from the palace, ran to my
workshop, where, having found a small poniard, I sprang into the
dwelling of my adversaries, who were both in their shop and their
house. I found them at table, and the young Gherardo, who had
been the original cause of the trouble, threw himself upon me; to
whom I struck a blow with my poniard in the breast, so that it
passed right through his frock (*saio*) and jerkin (*colletto*) to his
shirt, without touching his flesh or doing him any sort of harm.
Since it appeared to me from the disappearance of my hand and the
sound made by his clothes that I had wounded him very seriously,

and he fell terrified to the ground, I cried out: "Traitors! To-day is the opportunity for me to kill you all." The father, mother and sisters believing that it was the Day of Judgement, immediately flung themselves on their knees upon the ground, and with a loud voice and in no measured terms begged for mercy. And when I saw that they offered no defence to me, and that he lay extended upon the ground as one dead, it seemed to me too vile a thing to touch them; but I ran madly down the stairs; and when I reached the street, I found all the rest of the tribe, who were more than twelve in number. One of them had an iron shovel, another a big piece of iron piping, some hammers and anvils, and others sticks. When I came among them like a maddened bull, I threw four or five of them to the ground, and I fell with them, always plying my poniard now on this one, now on that. Those who had kept their feet joined in as far as they were able, showering blows upon me with both hands, with hammers, sticks and anvils. But because God sometimes mercifully intervenes they did me not the least injury in the world, nor I them. My cap only was left, which my adversaries secured, and though they kept themselves at a distance from it, every one of them struck at it with his weapon. Then looking round among themselves for the dead and wounded there was no one who had received any hurt. I departed towards Santa Maria Novella, and immediately met Brother Alesso Strozi, with whom I was unacquainted. To this good friar I commended myself for the Love of God, that he would save my life, for I had committed a great fault. The good friar told me that I need fear nothing; for though I had committed all the crimes in the world, I should be most safe in his little cell. In the space of about an hour the Eight, having summoned an extraordinary meeting, directed the publication of one of the most terrifying of bans that was ever heard against me, placing under the severest penalties whoever should harbor or know me, regarding neither the place nor the quality of any one who should protect me. My poor afflicted and excellent father going in to the Eight, threw himself upon his knees on the ground, imploring mercy for his poor young son: whereupon one of those democrats tossing back the crest of his twisted-up hood, and rising to his feet, with some insulting words said to my poor father: "Get up and go away instantly, lest we send you to-morrow to the gallows." My poor father, nevertheless, boldly answered them, saying, "What God shall have ordained such will be done and no more." Upon which the same man replied that for certain God has ordained it thus. And my father said to him: "I take comfort to myself that you certainly don't know that;" and having gone out of their presence, he came to see me in company with a certain youth of my own age, who was called Piero di Giovanni Landi: (we loved each other more than if we had been brothers). This young man carried under his mantle a splendid sword and a very handsome coat of mail. And when they came to me my brave father told me what had occurred and what the Eight Judges had said. Then he kissed me on the forehead and both eyes; blessed me heartily and spake thus: "May the Grace of God assist you." And taking up the sword and the armor, with his own hands he helped me to put them on. Then he said: "My good son! With these in your possession you must either live or die." Pier Landi, who was there present, never ceased weeping; and when he handed me ten gold *scudi,* I asked him to remove for me a few hairs of my beard, which were the first down. Friar Alesso robed me after the fashion of a monk and provided me with a lay-brother to accompany me. Leaving the convent and issuing by the Porta al Prato, I went along the town-wall as far as the Piazza di San Gallo; and mounting the slope of Montui, at one of the first houses I found a man who was called Grassuccio, own brother to Messer Benedetto da Montevarchi. I immediately unfrocked, and becoming a layman again we mounted two horses which were there for us, and under cover of night proceeded to Siena. The said Grassuccio, being sent back to Florence, visited my father and told him that I had reached safety. My father was greatly overjoyed and it seemed a thousand years ere he met again that member of the Eight who had insulted him. And when he found him he spake thus to him: "Do you see, Antonio, that it was God who knew what should happen to my son, and not you?" To which he replied: "Let us but catch him another time." My father said: "I shall give my attention to thanking God that he has escaped this time."

ARRIVING at Siena, I awaited the post to Rome and joined company with him. When we had crossed the Paglia we met the courier who was bringing news of the newly-elected pope, who was Pope Clemente. Having reached Rome I set myself to work in the shop of master Santi the goldsmith. For although he himself was dead, his son still carried on the business. He, however, did no work himself, but committed all the shop orders to a young man who was called Luca Agniolo da Jesi. This man was a peasant, who as a very small boy had come to work with master Santi. He was small of stature but well-proportioned. This youth did his work better than any man that I had ever seen up to that time, with greatest dexterity and much beauty of design; and he labored solely upon large pieces of plate (*grosseria*), that is to say, very handsome vases, bowls, and such-like articles. Setting myself to work in that shop, I undertook to make certain candlesticks for the Spanish Bishop (of) Salamanca. These same candlesticks were richly ornamented, as far as is suitable to such work. A pupil of Raffaello da Urbino, named Gianfran°°, surnamed *il Fattore* (*i.e. the Artisan*), he was a very brilliant painter; and since he was a friend of the said bishop, he set me high in his favor, to such purpose that I received a great many commissions from this bishop, and earned a great deal of money. At that period I went to draw sometimes in the Chapel of Michelagniolo, and sometimes at the house of Agostino Chigi, the Sienese, in which house there were many very beautiful works of painting by the hand of the most excellent

Raffaello da Urbino. But this was on feast-days, because in the said house there was residing Messer Gismondo Chigi, brother of the said Messer Agostino. They (the family of Chigi) took much pride in seeing young men like myself going to study within their walls. The wife of the said Messer Gismondo saw me often in this house of hers; this lady who was as charming as possible and unusually handsome, coming up to me one day and regarding my drawings, asked me if I was a sculptor or a painter. I replied to the lady that I was a goldsmith. Said she, that I drew too well for a goldsmith; and causing one of her maids to bring a lily of most beautiful diamonds set in gold, showing it to me she desired me to value it. I valued it at eight hundred *scudi*. Then she said that I had valued it very excellently. After that she asked me if I had sufficient spirit to reset it handsomely; I replied that I would do so very willingly, and in her presence I made a rough sketch; and I executed it so much the better, inasmuch as I took pleasure in dealing with this so very beautiful and agreeable a gentlewoman. When I had finished the sketch, there joined us another very beautiful Roman gentlewoman who was upstairs and who on coming down asked the said Madonna Portia what she was doing there. She answered smiling: "I take great pleasure in watching this honest youth draw, for he is clever and handsome." I, having acquired a little confidence, mingled nevertheless with a small amount of honest bashfulness, blushed and said: "Whatever I may be, Madonna, I shall always be most ready to serve you." The gentlewoman, also blushing a little, replied: "You know very well that I want you to serve me;" and handing me the lily she told me to take it with me. And she gave me besides twenty gold *scudi* that she had in her pocket and said: "Set it after this fashion that you have designed for me, and preserve for me the old gold in which it is set at present." The Roman gentlewoman then said: "If I were that young man, I would gladly run away (with what I'd got)." Madonna Portia rejoined, that virtues rarely stand alongside vices, and that if I did such a thing, I should very greatly belie that open look of an honest man that I exhibited; and turning away, taking the hand of the Roman gentlewoman, with a most charming smile she said to me: "Adieu, Benvenuto." I stayed on a while longer, engaged upon the drawing that I was making, copying a certain figure of Jove by the hand of the said Raffaello da Urbino. When I had finished I went away and set myself to the fashioning of a little model in wax, whereby to show how the finished work ought subsequently to turn out; and having carried this to the said Madonna Portia to see, that same Roman gentlewoman, of whom I spoke before, being also present, being greatly satisfied both of them with my labors, they paid me so many compliments that, impelled by some small amount of boldness, I promised them that the completed work should be half as good again as the model. So I set to it and in twelve days I finished the said jewel in the form of a lily, as I have said above, adorned with little masks, cupids, animals, etc., and very beautifully enameled, in such a manner that the diamonds of which the lily was composed were improved in appearance by more than half. While I was laboring upon this work, that clever man Lucagniolo, of whom I have spoken above, showed that he was much displeased, saying to me many times over that it would be far more useful and creditable to me to help him in his work on large silver vases, as I had begun to do. To which I replied that I should be able, whensoever I wished, to fashion large silver vases; but that those works upon which I was now engaged did not come my way to do every day; and that in these same commissions there was no less credit to be obtained than in large silver vases, but even much more profit. This Lucagniolo laughed at me saying: "You will see, Benvenuto; for by the time that you have finished that work of yours, I shall hasten to get this vase finished, which I commenced when you (began) your jewel, and by experience I will demonstrate the profit that I shall derive from my vase, and that which you will gain from your jewel." To which I replied that I should willingly enjoy making such a trial with so able a man as he was, because at the completion of such works we should see which of us was in error. So both of us with a slightly scornful smile bent our heads somewhat fiercely, each of us desirous of bringing to a completion the works that we had begun; to such purpose that at the end of about ten days each of us had completed his work with much finish and skill. That of the said Lucagniolo was a very large vase to be used at the table of Pope Clemente, wherein he threw whilst he was at table, meat-bones and the rinds of various fruits; an article made rather more for display than for necessity. This vase was adorned with two fine handles, with many masks, both large and small, with very beautiful foliage, of as fine a grace and design as it is possible to imagine: wherefore I told him that it was the most beautiful vase that I had ever seen. Upon this, Lucagniolo, fancying that he had proved his point, said to me: "Your work appears to me no less beautiful, but we shall soon see the difference between the two." So, taking up his vase, and carrying it to the Pope, the latter expressed himself very greatly satisfied, and immediately caused him to be paid according to the usual custom of the trade for such large works. Meanwhile I carried my work to the said gentlewoman Madonna Portia, who told me with profoundest surprise, that I had far and away exceeded the promise that I had made to her; and then she added, telling me that I must ask for my labors everything that might please me, because it seemed to her that I deserved so much that even in giving me a fortress it would seem scarcely sufficient satisfaction for me; but since she was unable to do this, she smilingly told me to ask whatever she was able to accomplish. To which I replied that the greatest reward desired for my exertions, was that I should have satisfied her ladyship. So smiling also and making a bow, I was withdrawing, saying that I desired no other recompense than that. Then the said Madonna Portia turned to that Roman gentlewoman, and said: "Do you see how great are the company of the virtues that we reckoned to be in him, and that they are not vices?" Whilst both stood surprised, Madonna Portia said: "Benvenuto mine, have you ever heard it said, that when the poor give to the rich, the Devil laughs?" Upon which I replied: "And since he has so many disappointments, this time I would like to see him laugh;" but as I was departing she said that she did not wish on this occasion to do him such a favor. When I returned to my shop Lucagniolo had the money which he had received for his vase in a paper packet; and when I appeared he said: "Let us make here a small comparison between the recompense paid for your jewel beside that given for my vase." To which I replied that he might keep the matter in that state until the following day; because I hoped that, inasmuch as my work in its kind was not less beautiful than his, so I expected to make him see the recompense for it. When the next day arrived Madonna Portia sent one of her stewards to my shop, who called me outside, and having placed in my hand a paper packet full of money on behalf of that lady, said to me, that she did not want the Devil to laugh on any consideration; explaining that what she sent me was not the entire payment that my labors deserved, with many other courteous words, worthy of such a lady. Lucagniolo, to whom it seemed a thousand years ere he could compare his packet with mine, immediately upon my return to his shop, in the presence of his twelve workmen and some other neighbors warned beforehand, who wished to see the result of such a contest, took his packet, and laughing mockingly and saying "Ho, ho" three or four times he emptied the money on to the counter with a great noise. They were twenty-five *scudi di giuli,* whereas he thought that mine might be four or five *scudi di moneta.* Whereupon I,— overpowered by his clamor, and by the glances and smiles of the bystanders,—looking thus a little into my package, and perceiving that it was all gold, from one side of the counter, keeping my eyes lowered, and without the least noise, raised my package high in the air firmly with both hands, which caused the contents to pour out after the fashion of a mill-hopper. My money amounted to half as much again as his; so that all those eyes, which were gazing upon me with some mockery, turning immediately towards him, said: "Lucagniolo, this money of Benvenuto's, inasmuch as it is gold and half as much again, produces a much finer effect than yours." I would certainly have believed that out of envy together with the shame that that Lucagniolo felt, he would have immediately dropped down dead; and that although a third part of that money of mine must come to him, since I was but a workman, for that is the custom: the workman receives two-thirds, and the other third part goes to the masters of the shop—unbridled envy prevailed more than avarice within him, whereas it should have worked in exactly the opposite direction, since this Lucagniolo had been born of a peasant from Jesi. He cursed his trade and those who had taught it to him, declaring that from thenceforward he had no more desire to practise that art of making plate, he only wished to devote his attention to making those little trumperies, since they were so well paid for. Not less indignantly did I retort that every bird sang its own strain; that he was talking after the fashion of the hovels whence he had issued, but that I declared for certain that I could succeed most excellently in fashioning his monstrosities, but that he would never succeed in making that sort of trumperies. So leaving him in a rage, I told him that he would soon be made to see this.

Those who were present vociferously declared him to be in the wrong, reckoning him in the character of the clown that he was, and me in that of a man of worth as I had shown myself to be.

The following day I went to thank Madonna Portia, and I told her that her ladyship had done the opposite of what she had said (she wished to do); for since I had wished to make the Devil laugh, she had made him deny God afresh. We both laughed heartily, and she gave me other fine and important commissions to execute. At this juncture I sought, through the medium of a pupil of the painter Raffaello da Urbino, that the Bishop of Salamanca should employ me to make a large vase for water, called an "ewer," such as they are accustomed to keep upon sideboards for ornament. And the said bishop wishing to order two of equal size, commissioned the said Lucagniolo to make one, and the other of them I had to fashion; and for the decoration of the said vases the said Gioanfrancesco the painter gave us the design. So with extraordinary goodwill I set to work upon the said vase, and I was accommodated with a part of his shop by a Milanese, who was named master Giovanpiero della Tacca. Setting my affairs in order, I reckoned up the money that I should require for certain needs of my own, and all the rest I sent to the assistance of my poor but excellent father, who, while the money was being paid to him in Florence, chanced to meet one of those *"Arrabbiati"* who were members of the Eight at that time when I created that small disturbance, and who with gross abuse had told him that he would certainly send me to the gallows. And since that *arrabbiato* had certain evil scoundrels of sons, my father said with reference to them: "Disasters may fall upon any one, especially upon hot-tempered men when they are in the right, as happened in the case of my son; but you observe from the rest of his life since, that I did know how to bring him up virtuously. May God grant on your behalf that your sons do neither worse nor better for you than that which mine has done for me; for as God has made me such an one as to understand how to bring him up, so where my power was unable to extend He has Himself removed him, contrary to your expectation, out of your violent hands." And departing he wrote the whole circumstance to me, praying me for the love of God to practise my music sometimes, so that I might not lose that fine accomplishment, which he had taught me with so much pains. The letter was full of the most affectionate paternal words that one could ever hear, to such an extent that they moved me to tears of piety, being wishful that ere he died I might content him to a great extent as regards the music, since God grants us all the lawful blessings that we ask of Him faithfully. Whilst I was busying myself over the fine vase for (the Bishop of) Salamanca I had for my assistant one small boy only, who at the very special prayers of my friends, half against my own wish, I had taken as a shop-lad. This boy was about fourteen years of age: he bore the name of Paulino, and was the son of a Roman citizen, who lived on his own private means. This Paulino was the best bred, the most honest, and the handsomest child that I ever saw in my life; and on account of his virtuous behavior and habits, and for his extraordinary beauty, and on account of the great affection that he bore for me, it came about that, for these reasons, I reposed in him as much affection as it is possible for the breast of a man to contain. This excessive love was the reason that, in order to see that exquisite countenance lighten up more often, which, from its natural disposition appeared modest and melancholy; nevertheless when I took up my cornet he immediately broke into a smile so sincere and so beautiful that I do not wonder at all at those fables which the Greeks write concerning their heavenly deities. Perhaps had this lad lived in those days he would perchance have turned their heads yet more. This Paulino had a sister who bore the name of Faustina, than whom I think the Faustina about whom ancient writers rave so much was never so beautiful. When he took me sometimes to their vineyard *(vigna)*, by what I could judge it seemed to me that the worthy man, the father of the said Paulino would have liked to make me his son-in-law. This circumstance caused me to practise my music much more than I had done at first. It happened at this time that a certain Gianiacomo, a fifer from Cesena, who belonged to the Papal household, a very wonderful musician, caused me to be asked by Lorenzo, a trombone-player from Lucca (who is to-day in the service of our Duke), if I were willing to assist them on the occasion of the Pope's *Ferragosto,* by playing on that day upon my cornet the soprano part in several motets, of which they had a very fine selection. Although I had the greatest desire to finish that handsome vase which I had begun—since music is a wondrous thing in itself and partly to give satisfaction to my old father—I was pleased to join such a company; and for eight days previous to the *Ferragosto,* every day for two hours we practised in concert, to such purpose that on that day in August we went to the Belvedere, and whilst Pope Clemente was dining we played those well-composed motets in such a manner that the Pope protested that he had never heard music more charmingly or more harmoniously performed. Calling to him that Gianiacomo he asked from what place and in what manner he managed to secure so good a cornet for the soprano part, and he inquired minutely who I was. The said Gianiacomo told him precisely my name. To this the Pope said: "Then this (fellow) is the son of master Giovanni?" So he replied that I was. The Pope said that he would like to have me in his service among the other musicians. Gianiacomo responded: "Most Blessed Father, regarding this point I do not undertake that you can have him, for his own profession, to which he attends assiduously, is the trade of a goldsmith, and in that trade he works wonderfully, and draws thence far more profit than he would make by music." Upon this the Pope said: "So much the more do I want him, since there is in him a talent the more, which I did not expect. See to arranging for him the same allowance as the rest of you; and tell him on my behalf that he must serve me, and that I will besides give him plenty of daily employment in his other profession;" and extending his hand he gave him in a handkerchief one hundred gold *scudi* of the *Camera,* and said: "Divide these in such a manner that he may have his share." The said Gianiacomo on leaving the Pope came to us and repeated exactly all that the Pope had said, and having divided the money among the eight persons who formed our company, on giving me my share, said to me, "I am going to get you enrolled amongst the number of our company." To which I replied: "Let to-day pass, and to-morrow I will give you an answer." Leaving them I went away thinking whether it was such a thing as I ought to accept, considering how much it might injure me by diverting me from the fine studies appertaining to my own trade. The following night my father appeared to me in a dream, and with tenderest tears besought me, for the love of God and of himself to be willing to take up such an engagement; to whom I seemed to reply, that by no manner of means did I wish to do so. Immediately he appeared to assume so dreadful an aspect as to terrify me, and he said: "If you do not do so you will receive a father's curse, and by doing it may you be blessed by me for ever." On awakening, I ran in terror to get myself enrolled. Then I wrote to my old father, who from excess of joy was seized with a fit, which nearly brought him to his grave; and he immediately wrote to me that he also had dreamed almost the same thing that I had done.

And it seemed to me, when I saw that I had given satisfaction to the honorable desires of my good father, that everything ought to advance for me to an honored and glorious termination. I, therefore, set myself to work with the greatest assiduity to finish the vase that I had commenced for (the Bishop of) Salamanca. This bishop was a very remarkable man, very rich, but difficult to please. He sent every day to see what I was doing: and upon that occasion when his messenger did not find me, the said (Bishop of) Salamanca came in greatest fury, saying that he would take from me the said work and give it to others to finish. This was the result of my employment upon that accursed music. Never the less with the greatest diligence I was at work day and night until having brought it up to such a point that I could exhibit it, I let the said bishop see it: whereby was increased so greatly his desire to see it completed, that I repented myself of having shown it to him. At the end of three months I had finished off the said work with as many beautiful little animals, foliage and masks as it is possible to imagine. I immediately sent it by that shop-boy of mine, Paulino, to be shown to that excellent craftsman Lucagnioli mentioned above. Paulino, with that infinite grace and charm of his, spake thus: "Misser Lucagniolo, Benvenuto says that he herewith sends to demonstrate to you the result of his promises and of your monstrosities, awaiting from you a sight of his trumperies." When he had said these words, Lucagniolo took the vase in his hand, and examined it carefully. Then he said to Paulino: "My pretty boy, tell your master that he is a very brilliant craftsman, and that I beg him to allow me to be his friend, and not permit it to be otherwise." That honest and admirable lad most joyfully brought me the message. Having conveyed the said vase to (the Bishop of) Salamanca, he wished to have it valued. For that said valuation this Lucagniolo was called in, who judged my work so much more highly and praised it at greater length than I myself had expected of him. Taking the said vase (the Bishop of) Salamanca said roughly *(spagnoleschamente)*, "I swear by God that I will make him wait for payment as long as he has loitered in the making of it." Hearing this I remained most discontented, cursing all Spain and those who loved it. There was among the other handsome decorations upon this vase a handle made all in one piece with it; most ingeniously contrived, so that by means of a certain spring it stood straight up over the mouth of the vase. When the said prelate *(monsignor)* was one day proudly displaying this vase of mine to certain of his Spanish nobles, it happened that one of these noblemen, after the said *prelate* had gone away, manipulating too roughly the beautiful handle of the vase, that delicate spring, unable to resist his uncouth violence, broke óff in the hand of the said man. And as it seemed to him that he had done great mischief, he begged the butler, who had charge of it, that he would quickly take it to the master-craftsman who had made it, who would immediately repair it, and he promised to pay him the whole price that he might ask, so long as it was mended quickly. The vase having thus come into my hands, I promised to repair it very quickly, and so I did. The said vase was brought to me before dinner time: at twenty-two of the clock came he who had brought it to me, and he was all of a sweat, for he had run the whole way, since it had happened that my lord had once more asked for it again to show to certain other lords. Wherefore this butler would not permit me to say a single word, crying out: "Quick! quick! bring the vase." Whereupon I anxious to go gently and not to give it up to him, said that I would not act in haste. The said servant flew into such a rage, that with one hand he made as though he would draw his sword, and with the other made an attempt to enter my shop by force; which I immediately prevented his doing with my own weapon, accompanied by many angry words, saying: "I will not give it to you; and go, tell my lord your master, that I want the money for my labors before it goes out of this shop." The man seeing that he would not be able to obtain anything from me by means of threats, set to work to implore me, as one prays to the Rood, saying that if I would but give it to him he would do such and such for me so that I should be paid. These words in no way moved me from my resolution, always telling him the same thing. At last despairing of the matter, he swore that he would come with so many Spaniards, that he would have me cut in pieces; and he departed at a run, upon which I, since I believed to some extent in these assassinations of theirs, determined to defend myself courageously; and having got into order an admirable little fowling-piece of mine, which served me when I went out shooting, I said to myself: "Whoever takes my property along with the results of my labors, let him also take my life." During this debate, which I held with myself, there appeared many Spaniards together with their majordomo, who, after their haughty custom, ordered some of them to enter the shop, take possession of the vase, and beat me. At these words I displayed to them the muzzle of the fowling-piece, all in readiness to fire, and I shouted in a loud voice: "Renegades, traitors, is it in this way that you break into the houses and shops in a (city like) Rome? As many of you thieves as approach this wicket, so many will I strike dead with this gun of mine." And turning the muzzle of the same gun in the direction of their majordomo, and making as though I would fire, I said: "And as for you, you thief, who have set them on, I want you to be the first to die." He immediately set spurs to a jennet, upon which he was mounted, and took to flight at full speed *(a tutta briglia)*. At this great noise out came all the neighbors; and besides some Roman nobles, who were passing by, said: "Kill these renegades, for we will help you." These words carried such force that greatly frightened they departed from me in such case that, compelled by the turn of events, they were obliged to relate the whole story to my lord (the bishop), who was most arrogant, and scolded all his followers and domestics, because they had ventured to commit such an excess, and because having thus begun they had not completed the business. There chanced to come in at this moment that painter who was concerned in this matter; to whom my lord said that he must come and tell me in his name, that if I did not bring the vase immediately the largest piece left of me would be my ears; and that if I brought it he would immediately give me the sum due for it. This threat did not cause me the least fear, and I let him know that I was going at once to tell the Pope. However his wrath passed away from him, and my fear from me, under the guarantee of certain great Roman nobles that the said (bishop) should not injure me; and, with good security for the payment of my labors, having provided myself with a large dagger and my good coat of mail, I went to the house of the said prelate, who had caused his whole household to be drawn up in rank. As I entered I had my Paulino beside me with the silver vase. It was neither more nor less than like passing through the Zodiac, for this one resembled the Lion (*Leo*), that the Scorpion (*Scorpio*), others the Crab (*Cancer*), until we reached the presence of that rascal of a priest (*pretaccio*), who shouted out the most Spanish-priestly (*pretesche spagnolissime*) words that it is possible to imagine. Wherefore I never raised my head to look at him, nor ever answered him a word. At which his anger gave signs of increasing the more; and having directed them to bring me writing materials, he told me to write under my own hand, saying that I was well content and paid by him. At this I raised my head and said that I would very willingly do so, if first of all I had my money. The bishop's anger increased; and his threats and abuse were terrible. In the end I first received my money, then I wrote the receipt, and departed happy and content. Subsequently I heard that Pope Clemente, who had seen the vase at first, though it had not been shown to him as my work, took the greatest pleasure in it, and praised me very much, and stated in public that he took the greatest interest in me; to such an extent that my lord of Salamanca greatly repented having uttered those threats of his to me; and to appease me he sent to me by the same painter to tell me that he desired to give me many fine commissions; to which I replied that I would willingly execute them, but that I wished for the payment for them before I began. These words also reached the ears of Pope Clemente, in whom they provoked the heartiest laughter. There was present Cardinal Cibo, to whom the Pope recounted all the quarrel that I had had with this bishop; then he turned to one of his attendants, and commanded him to give me work to do continually for the palace. The said Cardinal Cibo sent for me, and after much agreeable conversation, told me to make him a large vase, bigger than that of (the Bishop of) Salamanca. So did Cardinal Cornaro, and many others of the then cardinals, especially Ridolfi and Salviati. I received commissions from them all, to such purpose that I earned a great deal. Madonna Portia above mentioned told me that I ought to open a shop that should be entirely my own; and so I did, and I never ceased working for that charming and worthy lady, who gave me very high payments, and it was almost through her means alone that I was shown to the world to be a man of some merit. I entered into a close friendship with the lord Gabbriello Cesarino, who was Gonfalonier of Rome. For this nobleman I executed many commissions. One of these was conspicuous among the rest. This was a large gold medal to wear in a hat. The surface of this medal was sculptured, and the subject was *Leda with her Swan:* and being very much satisfied with the result of my labors, he said that he wanted to have it valued so as to pay me its just price. But since the medal was fashioned with great skill, the valuers in the trade reckoned it at much more than he had expected; wherefore retaining the medal in my own possession, I got nothing for my pains. The same circumstances occurred in the case of this medal as happened in connection with the vase of (the Bishop of) Salamanca. But since these things should not take space in my narrative from the relation of matters of greater importance I will pass them over briefly.

Chapter Five *1524*

ALTHOUGH it entails my departure from the subject of my profession, in my desire to describe my life as a whole I am obliged to detail, not altogether minutely, but at least to allude briefly to, certain events such as the following. Being once upon the morning of (the Feast of) our patron St. John at dinner with many others of our nation, of divers professions: painters, sculptors, goldsmiths, (among other remarkable persons present was one named *Il Rosso* the painter and Gianfrancesco, the pupil of Raffaello da Urbino, and many others). And since I had brought them all to that place informally, they all laughed and jested as is usual when a number of men get together, making merry at so admirable a festivity. By chance there passed by a giddy bullying youth, a soldier (in the service) of the lord Rienzo da Ceri who upon hearing this noise (of merriment), scoffing said many insulting things about the Florentine people. I who was the host of all these excellent and worthy personages, considering that he had offended me, went quietly without anyone noticing me up to this man, who was with a trull of his;—to make whom laugh he was still continuing this ridicule of us. Coming up to him I asked if he was that bold man who was speaking evil of the Florentines.

53

He immediately replied: "I am that man." At which words I
raised my hand and striking him in the face said: "And I am this
man." Instantly we both furiously laid hands on our weapons;
but no sooner had we commenced that affair, than many persons
came between us, more readily taking my part than the other side,
having realized and seen that I was in the right. The day after
there was brought to me a written challenge to fight him, which
I accepted very gladly, saying that it seemed to me this undertaking proceeded much more rapidly than those pertaining to that
other trade of mine; and I immediately went to consult an old
man named Bevilacqua, who had the reputation of having been
the first swordsman in Italy, because he had found himself drawn
more than twenty times into the field of honor (*campo franco*)
and had always come out thence with credit. This worthy man
was a great friend of mine, and knew me through my profession,
and had also been concerned in certain ugly quarrels between me
and others. For the which reason he immediately said cheerfully
to me: "Benvenuto, if you had to do with Mars himself, I am sure
that you would come out of it with honor, because during the
many years that I have known you, I have never seen you take
up any quarrel wrongfully." He therefore took up my affair (as
second), and when we repaired to the appointed spot, sword in
hand, since my adversary settled the matter without bloodshed, I
came out of that business with great honor. I do not relate
further details; for although stories of this kind are very agreeable
to listen to, I want to reserve this relation to the matters which
concern my profession, which is the object that has inspired me
to this particular narrative; and on that head I shall have only too
much to say. Although spurred on by an honest emulation, desirous of making some fresh work that would approach or even
surpass those of that said brilliant craftsman Lucagniolo, I never

departed from my own beautiful art of jewel-fashioning; to such
an extent that in both branches I procured great profit and greater
honor, and in both I continually executed works differing from
those of other people. There was in these days in Rome a most
able craftsman from Perugia, by name Lautizio, who labored in
one trade only, and in that trade was unique in the world. It
happened that since in Rome every cardinal possesses a seal, upon
which is impressed his coat of arms, these seals are made as large
as the entire hand of a small child of about twelve years of age;
and as I have said above, upon them are cut the arms of the cardinal, to which are added very many ornamental decorations; and
for one of these seals well executed they are wont to pay one hundred or more than one hundred *scudi*. For this brilliant executant
I also cherished an honorable rivalry; although this art appeared
very much aloof from the other branches that appertain to the
goldsmith's business; for this Lautizio, in practising this art of
seal-engraving, knew not how to do anything else. Setting myself
to study besides this self-same art, although it is found very difficult,
I was never weary from the labor that it entailed, but I continually
devoted myself to it for the purpose of earning money and learning.
There was besides in Rome another very excellent and brilliant
artist, who was a Milanese, and who was called by the name of
Misser Caradosso. This man worked only on small medallions
engraved with the chisel upon plates of metal, and many other
similar things. He made some "Paxes" in low relief and some
figures of Christ of about a palm in length, executed upon very
thin plates of gold, so beautifully engraved that I judged him to be
the greatest artist that I had ever seen in such things, and for him
I experienced more emulation than for any one else. There were
besides other masters who made medals sculptured in steel, which
are the origin *(madre)* and true guide to those who desire to know

how to make coins properly. In all these different branches I set myself to learn with very great attention. There is besides the most exquisite art of enameling, which I have never seen as well executed by anyone as by one of our Florentines named Amerigho, with whom I had no personal acquaintance, but whose most superb works I knew well; such divine excellence as in no part of the world nor by any man have I ever seen approached even at a great distance. For besides in the carrying out it is most difficult, on account of the fire that is applied at the last upon the work, finished with great labor, which many a time spoils them and plunges them into destruction. Upon this very different branch I also set myself to work with all my power; and although I found it very difficult, so much was the pleasure that I took in it that the said great difficulties seemed to me but a recreation; and this arose from a special gift bestowed upon me by the God of nature of a temperament so good and well-balanced, that I could freely assure myself of accomplishing everything that came into my mind to undertake. These said branches are many and very diverse one from another; so much so that any one who succeeds in one of them, wishing to try the others, hardly ever is as successful as in that branch in which he already excels; wherefore I exerted myself with all my power to practise all these branches equally; and, as I say, I will in its proper place demonstrate how I accomplished such an undertaking.

At this period, when I was still a youth of about twenty-three years of age, a pestilential disease broke out of such unparalleled virulence that there died in Rome many thousands per day. Somewhat terrified by this, I began to take up certain amusements such as my fancy directed, caused moreover by a circumstance that I will relate. For I enjoyed on feast-days visiting the antiquities (of the city), copying them either in wax models or by drawing from them; and since these said antiquities are all in ruins, and amid these same ruins build a great many pigeons, the desire came upon me to employ against them my fowling-piece; and in order to avoid intercourse with anyone, being afraid of the plague, I put my gun upon the shoulder of my boy Pagolino, and he and I went alone to the said ruins. It resulted therefore that very many times I returned laden with very plump pigeons. I did not care to load my gun with more than a single ball, and it was therefore by real skill in that art that I made such large bags. I had a straight fowling-piece made by my own hands; and (so bright was it) both within and without there was never seen a mirror like it. I made besides with my own hands the finest gunpowder, in the composition of which I discovered the finest secrets that have ever up to to-day been discovered by anyone; but with regard to this I will not dilate much, but will give one example to cause surprise to all those who are skilled in such an accomplishment. This was that with powder amounting in weight to a fifth part of the ball, the said ball would carry two hundred paces point blank (*in punto bianco*). Although the great pleasure that I drew from this gun of mine tended to seduce me away from my profession and my studies, this fact is also true, that in another way it gave me back much more than it took from me: for the result was that every time that I went on my hunting expeditions, I greatly improved my health, because the open air did me so much good. Since I was naturally of a melancholy disposition, when I found myself at these amusements, my spirits immediately brightened, and I was able to work better, and with more skill, than when I applied myself to my studies and experiments without intermission; to such purpose that my gun in the long run proved for me more gain than loss. Besides, by means of this diversion of mine, I acquired the friendship of certain curiosity-hunters who watched out for those Lombard peasants, who came to Rome at that season to till the vines. These latter in the course of their tilling the earth often found antique medals, agates, chrysoprases, cornelians, cameos; they found besides precious stones, that is to say, emeralds, sapphires, diamonds, and rubies. These same curio-hunters sometimes got from those peasants for very small sums some of these things; for which I— meeting these curio-hunters occasionally, nay, very often—gave as many gold *scudi* for a thing which they had frequently just bought for scarcely as many pence (*giuli*). This circumstance, exclusive of the great profit that I procured out of it, which was tenfold or more, set me besides in high favor with almost all the Roman cardinals. Of these objects I will only speak of the notable and rarest examples. There fell into my hands, among so many other things, a dolphin's head as large as a big balloting bean. Amongst the other treasures, not only was this the most beautiful, but nature in this case had far surpassed art; for this emerald was of such a fine color that the man who bought it of me for some tens of *scudi* had it set after the fashion of an ordinary stone to wear in a ring; set thus he sold it for some hundreds. I had besides another variety of stone: this was a head made of the most beautiful topaz that the world ever saw. In this object art had equalled nature. It was as big as a large filbert, and the head upon it was as well executed as it is possible to imagine: it represented *Minerva*. There was besides another stone differing from these. This was a cameo; upon it was cut a *Hercules binding the three-jawed Cerberus*. This was of such beauty and fashioned with such fine skill, that our great Michelagniolo protested that he had never seen anything so wonderful. There were besides, among many bronze medals, one that fell into my hands, upon which was the head of *Jove*. This medal was much larger than any that I had ever seen. The head was so beautifully executed that such a medal had never been seen. It had a most beautiful reverse side, with some small figures likewise superbly executed. I could have, beyond these, described many fine things, but I do not wish to dwell upon them lest I become too lengthy. As I have said above, the plague had commenced in Rome. Although I want to turn back a little, I shall not on this account depart from my original object. There arrived in Rome a very famous surgeon who was called master Jacomo da Carpi. This able man, amongst his other cures, undertook certain desperate cases of the French diseases. And since these diseases are very prevalent in Rome amongst the priests,—especially among the richest of them,—when this clever man became aware of this, he showed himself able by the efficacy of certain essences to cure in a marvellous manner these self-same complaints, but he insisted upon a contract before he commenced the cure; and these contracts were reckoned in hundreds, not tens (of *scudi*). This brilliant man had much intelligent knowledge of drawing. Passing my shop one day by chance he saw by accident certain drawings that I had made previously, amongst which were several quaint vases which I had designed for my own amusement. These particular vases were very varied and differed from all those that had ever been seen up to that time. The said master Jacomo wished me to make them for him in silver; which I did particularly willingly, since they were in accordance with my own fancy. Although the said clever man paid me very well for them, the credit that they brought me was worth one hundred times more; for in the Trade of all those excellent goldsmiths they said that they had never seen anything more beautiful or better fashioned. I had scarcely finished them, when this man showed them to the Pope; and the next day afterwards he departed (*s'ando con dio*). He was very well read; he discoursed wonderfully on medicine. The Pope wished him to remain in his service; but this man said that he would not be in the service of any one in the world, and that whoever had need of him might come after him. He was a very astute person, and did wisely in departing from Rome; for not many months after all those persons whom he had doctored fell so ill that they were one hundred times worse than at first; he would have been murdered, if he had stayed. He exhibited my little vases to many nobles, among others to the most excellent Duke of Ferrara; and he said that he had received them from a great lord in Rome, by telling him that if he wished to be cured of his ailment, he wanted those two little vases; and that this very noble had said that they were antiques, and that of his kindness he should ask for something else which it would not seem hard to give him, if he would only leave him these. He said that he had made a feint of being unwilling to cure him, wherefore he got them. This (story) was related to me by Messer Alberto Ben de Dio in Ferrara, and with great pomp he showed me certain clay copies of them, at which I laughed; and since I said nothing further, Messer Alberto Ben de Dio, who was a proud man, angrily said to me: "You are laughing at them, are you? and I tell you that for the last thousand years there has not been born a man who could merely copy them." And so, in order not to rob them of their reputation, remaining silent I admired them with stupefaction. I was told in Rome by many nobles about these works, which appeared to them marvellous and of antique origin; some of these were my personal friends, and emboldened by such a circumstance I confessed that I had made them. They did not want to believe me; whereupon I wishing to be truthful in the matter of such things, had to give proof and make new drawings; for what I said did not suffice, since it chanced that the said master Jacomo cunningly managed to carry off the original drawings with him. Out of this little job I acquired a great deal. The plague having continued many months, I had fought it off, for although many of my comrades were dead, I remained hale and free from illness. It chanced that upon a certain evening among others, that one of my comrades who lodged with me brought home to supper a Bolognese courtesan who was called Faustina. This woman was very beautiful, but was about thirty years of age, and she had with her a little servant maid of between thirteen and fourteen. Since the said Faustina was the property of my friend, for all the gold in the world I would not have touched her. Although she said that she was wildly enamoured of me, I preserved constantly my faith to my friend. But when they were in bed I stole that little serving-maid, who was an absolute virgin, though woe had it been for her had her mistress known of it. I enjoyed myself thus agreeably that night with much more satisfaction than I should have had with her mistress Faustina. When the hour of dinner approached, I was as weary as if I had walked many miles, and desirous of taking food, I felt a violent headache, with many swellings on my left arm, culminating in a carbuncle on the wrist-joint of my left hand on the outer side. In terror, every person in the house, my friend, the big cow and the little one, all fled, whence left alone with a poor little shop-boy of mine, who refused to leave me, I felt stifled at the heart, and realized for sure that I was a dead man. At this juncture there passed along the street the father of this my shop-boy, who was medical attendant to Cardinal Jacoacci, and belonged to his establishment. The said boy called out to his father: "Come here, father, and see Benvenuto, who is in bed with a slight ailment." Without stopping to think what the ailment might be, he immediately came in to me, and feeling my pulse, saw and knew what he would rather not have known. Turning at once upon his son, he said: "You traitor child, you have ruined me: how can I go any more to the Cardinal's?" To which his son replied: "This master of mine, father, is worth much more than all the cardinals

in Rome." Then the doctor turned to me and said: "Since I am
here, I am willing to attend you; there is but one thing that I must
warn you, that if you have had intercourse with a woman, you are
a dead man." To which I replied: "I did so this very last night."
At this the doctor said: "With what sort of person, and how
much?" And I told him: "All last night, and with a very young
maiden." Then perceiving that he had used some foolish expressions, he immediately said to me: "Since they (the sores) are at
present fresh, so that they are not yet putrid, and since the remedy
has been sought in good time, you need not have so much fear, for
I hope in any case to cure you." When he had doctored me and
departed, there immediately appeared one of my dearest friends,
named Giovanni Rigogli, who being deeply grieved for my illness
and for my being thus deserted by my comrade, said: "Do not
doubt, my dear Benvenuto, that I shall ever leave you until I see
you cured." I told this friend not to approach me, for I was
doomed. I besought him only that he would be so kind as to take
a certain fair amount of *scudi,* which were in a box there near my
bed, and that since God had removed me from this world, he
would send them as a gift to my poor father, writing to him kindly
as I had continued to do according as the progress of that disastrous season permitted. My dear friend told me that he did not
want to leave me for any reason whatsoever, and that whatever
from that time might be necessary, in either the one case or in the
other, he knew very well what it behooved one to do for a friend.
And so we went along with the help of God, and beginning to
experience from the wonderful remedies a very vast improvement,
I soon recovered thoroughly from that very serious illness. Whilst
the wound still remained open, with the dressing in it and a
plaster over that, I rode about upon a little wild pony of mine, that
I had. This pony had hair more than four fingers in length; it

was just as big as a good-sized bear, and in truth he resembled a
bear. Upon his back I rode to visit *il Rosso* the painter, who was
living outside Rome towards Civita Vecchia, at a place belonging to
the Count of Anguillara, called Cervetera, and having found my
friend Rosso, he was pleased beyond measure, wherefore I said to
him: "I am come to do for you what you did for me so many
months ago." Bursting out laughing immediately and embracing
and kissing me, he next told me to be silent for the sake of the
Count. Thus happily and pleasantly, with good wine and the best
of food, entertained by the said Count, I stayed there about a month,
and every day I went down alone upon the seashore, and there dismounting, loaded myself with many divers sorts of pebbles, small
snails, and rare and very beautiful shells. The last time (for after
that I went thither no more), I was attacked by a number of men,
who, in disguise, had disembarked from a Moorish galley; and
when they thought that they had confined me into a certain spot,
whence it did not seem possible for me to escape out of their hands,
mounting hastily upon my little nag, being prepared in that perilous
strait to be either roasted or boiled upon the spot (for I saw but little
hope of escaping one or other of those two fates), as it pleased God,
the little nag, which was the one that I have mentioned above,
sprang forward in a way it is impossible to believe; wherefore having saved myself I thanked God. I told the Count about it. He
gave the alarm; the galleys were to be seen at sea. The next day
after, I returned in good health and spirits to Rome.

By this time the plague had almost ceased, to such an extent that
those who remained alive entertained one another with much gaiety.
Out of this circumstance there arose a society of painters, sculptors
and goldsmiths, the best that there were in Rome; and the founder
of this society was a sculptor named Michelagniolo. This Michelagniolo was a Sienese and he was a very brilliant man such as could

rival any other man in this profession; but beyond all other things this man was the most sportive, and the most pleasure-loving that I ever knew in my life. Of this said society he was the oldest member, but at the same time in bodily vigor the youngest. We found ourselves constantly together; at least twice a week. I would not omit that in this our society were the painter Giulio Romano, and Gian Francescho, admirable pupils of the great Raffaello da Urbino. When we had all been meeting more and more often, it seemed good to that excellent leader of ours that on the Sunday following we should assemble at supper in his house, and that each of us should be obliged to bring with him his "crow" (*cornachia*) (for that was the name that the said Michelagniolo had applied to these persons); and that whosoever did not bring one should be obliged to pay for a supper for the whole party. Whoever of us had no acquaintance with such women of the town had to provide themselves at no little expense and inconvenience, so as not to appear disgraced at this noble banquet. I who had thought myself well provided in the person of a very handsome young woman, named Pantassilea, who was deeply enamoured of me, was compelled to give her up to one of my dearest friends called Bachiaccha, who had been and was still madly in love with her. Concerning this matter there had arisen some small amount of amorous irritation, because when she saw that I yielded her up to Bachiaccha at the first request, it seemed to this woman that I took but very little account of the great love that she bore for me; from which in course of time there arose a very serious event, from her desire to revenge herself for the insult she had received from me. This circumstance I will relate presently in its own place. It happened that the hour began to draw near for presenting oneself before this august company, each with his "crow," and I found myself unprovided; and moreover it seemed to me that I should be doing wrong to fail in so mad a sport; and what affected me still more was that I did not want to take under my protection, amid so much brilliance, any draggle-tailed scarecrow (*spennachiata cornachiuccia*). I bethought me of a joke to add a louder laugh to their merriment. With this resolution I summoned a youth of about sixteen years of age, who resided next door to me. He was the son of a Spanish brassfounder. This youth was learning Latin literature, and was very studious; he bore the name of Diego. He was very handsome in appearance, with a marvellous complexion. The outline of his head was much more beautiful than that antique one of Antinous, and I had portrayed it many times; by which I had acquired much credit in my work. This boy had no acquaintance with any one, so that he was not known by sight. He dressed very badly and carelessly; he was entirely wrapped up in his admirable studies. Inviting him into my house I begged him to let me attire him in some women's clothes which I had there ready. He easily consented, and dressed himself up quickly, and I with the finest modes of adornment rapidly enhanced the great beauties of his handsome countenance; I put two rings in his ears in which were set two large and fine pearls; the said rings were split; they only clipped the ears which seemed to be pierced; then I put around his throat most handsome gold necklaces and rich jewels; moreover I adorned his beautiful hands with rings. Then sportively taking him by the ear I drew him before a large mirror of mine. When the youth had seen himself, with some conceit he said: "Bless me! Is that Diego?" Then I said to him: "That is Diego, of whom I have never asked any sort of favor: now I only beg that same Diego that he will oblige me in one honorable satisfaction: and it is this, that I want him to come with me in that particular costume to supper with that brilliant company of whom I have spoken to him so many times." The modest, virtuous and clever lad, putting from him that conceit, casting his eyes to the ground, stood thus for some time without saying a word; then on a sudden raising his face he said: "With Benvenuto I will go. Let us start at once." Having put over his head a large towel, which they call in Rome "a summer-cloth" (*panno di state*), we reached the place where everyone had already arrived and they all came to meet us; the said Michelagniolo was placed beside Julio and Giovanfrancescho in the middle. When the towel was removed from the head of that beauteous creature of mine, Michelagniolo who, as I have said on other occasions, was the most witty and most agreeable man that one can possibly imagine, having laid both his hands, the one on Julio and the other on Gianfrancescho, as far as he was able by that effort, made them bow down, and kneeling upon the ground himself demanded mercy, and called out to all the company saying: "Look, look how the angels of paradise are fashioned; for though they call them angels, observe how there are also female angels"; and shouting aloud he said: "Oh! Beauteous angel! Oh! angel worthy! Save me and give me thy blessing." At these words the charming creature smiling raised his right hand, and gave him a Papal benediction with many charming words. Then Michelagniolo, rising to his feet, said: that in the case of the Pope one kissed his feet, but in that of angels one kissed their cheeks; and when he did so the youth blushed deeply, by reason of which his beauty was very greatly increased. Thus matters proceeded, the room was full of sonnets, which each one had made and handed to Michelagniolo. The lad began to read them and he read them all; this increased his incomparable loveliness to such an extent, as it would be impossible to describe. Much and wonderful conversation followed, upon which I do not wish to dilate, for I am not here for that purpose. Only one remark I recall being said, because that admirable painter Julio made it, who, having cast his eyes critically upon everyone around him, but fixing them more especially upon the women than upon the others, turning to Michel-

agniolo, spake thus: "My dear Michelagniolo, that name of yours
of 'crow' does very well to-day for these ladies, although they are
somewhat less beautiful than crows beside one of the loveliest peacocks that it is possible to imagine." The meal being ready and set
in order, as we were preparing to sit down, Julio asked leave to be
the person to arrange us at table. When this was conceded to him,
having taken the ladies by the hand, he set them all upon the inner
side and my lady in the middle. Then he set all the men upon the
outside and me in the middle, saying that I deserved every sort of
high honor. There was there for a background to the women a trel-
lis of real and very beautiful jasmine, which made such a lovely foil
for those ladies as it would be impossible to describe in words. So we
each pursued with greatest delight that rich supper, which was most
wonderfully abundant. Then when we had supped there followed a
little admirable music of voices accompanied by instruments; and as
they sang and played with the score before them, my beauteous creature asked leave to sing his part; and since he acquitted himself in
that art of music almost better than the others, he caused so much
astonishment, that the remarks made by Julio and Michelagniolo
were no longer in that bantering tone as at first, but were all serious
expressions sobered down and full of astonishment. After the music
a certain Aurelio Ascolano who recited delightfully without preparation (*alla improviso*) began to laud the ladies with heavenly and
beautiful words; and whilst he was chanting, the two girls, who had
that beauty of mine between them, never ceased chattering; for
whilst one of them related in what manner her misfortune came
about, the other asked my beauty how hers had occurred, and who
were her friends, and how long it was since she had arrived in Rome,
and many other similar things. It is true that if I were to describe
merely such trifles, I ought to speak of the many disasters which
occurred also, caused by that Pantassilea, who was wildly enamoured

of me: but because they do not belong to my subject, I pass them by briefly. This conversation of these coarse women now caused annoyance to my beauty, upon whom we had conferred the name of Pomona; the said Pomona wishing to escape from these unpleasant remarks of theirs, began to wriggle first on one side and then on the other. He was asked by the woman whom Julio had brought, if she felt any discomfort. He replied yes, and that he thought that he was some months advanced in pregnancy, and that after the manner of women he was suffering great discomfort in his stomach. Immediately the two women who had him between them, moved with compassion for Pomona, laying their hands upon his stomach, found out that he was a boy. Quickly withdrawing their hands with insulting words, such as they are accustomed to use to handsome youths, they rose from the table, and the cry immediately spreading with great laughter and with great astonishment, the lively Michelagniolo demanded leave of everyone to administer to me a penance of his own contriving. Having gained consent, amid loudest shouts he raised me aloft saying: "Long live the gentleman! Long live the gentleman!" and he said that this was the punishment that I deserved, for having perpetrated so fine a trick. Thus ended that most delightful supper and day; and everyone of us returned to his own home.

Chapter Six 1524

IF I wanted to describe precisely of what sort and how many were the numerous objects that I fashioned for divers kinds of men, my narrative would be too long. It does not concern me to say more at present than that I applied myself with every sort of attention and diligence to make myself acquainted with that diversity and variety of art of which I have spoken above. Thus I continuously labored upon all sorts of things; and because there has not yet come into my mind occasion for detailing some of my most remarkable works, I will wait to insert them in their proper place: for they will come in soon. The said Michelagniolo, the Sienese sculptor at that time, was constructing the tomb of the dead Pope Adriano. Julio, the said Roman painter, went away into the service of the Marquess of Mantua. The other members of our society retired, some here, some there, upon their own affairs: in such a manner that the said brilliant company was almost wholly broken up. At this time there fell into my hands certain little Turkish poniards, and the handle of each weapon was of iron as well as the blade; the sheath was, moreover, of iron likewise. These said objects were engraved, by means of iron tools, with a quantity of very beautiful foliage after the Turkish manner, and very delicately inlaid with gold: the which thing provoked greatly in me a desire to experiment also with a view to laboring myself in that branch, so different from the others; and when I saw that I succeeded very well, I made a number of articles. These same objects were very much handsomer and much more durable than the Turkish ones, for many different reasons. One of these was that, in the case of my steel articles, I cut very deeply beneath the surface, which they are not accustomed to do in Turkish work. Another was that the Turkish foliage (designs) are of no other species but arum leaves with some blossoms of the sunflower; and although they have a certain amount of elegance, they do not continue to satisfy as do our (forms of) foliage. For in Italy there are various methods of designing foliage; for instance, in Lombardy they make very lovely groups of foliage, copying the leaves of ivy and bryony in most beautiful curves, which make them most agreeable to behold; the Tuscans and the Romans in this fashion take a much better choice, for they imitate the leaves of the acanthus, called "bear's paw," with its stalks and flowers curling in different ways; and in among this said foliage there are charmingly introduced some little birds and divers animals, from which may be discovered the good taste of the artist. Some of these ideas they find naturally in wild flowers, such as those that they call "snapdragon"; for thus by means of certain flowers there can be devised, with the addition of the other clever imaginings of those brilliant craftsmen, those things which are called by those who know no better "grotesques." These grotesques have acquired this name from modern people through their being found by students in certain caverns in the ground at Rome, which caverns were in ancient times chambers, baths, studios, saloons, and other similar places. These students found them in these cavernous places, which because since ancient times the ground has risen in those spots, whilst they have remained below, and because the term applied to these low places in Rome is "grottoes"; from this circumstance they acquired the name of "grotesques" (*grottesche*). The which is not their proper name; for indeed, just as the ancients delighted in the composition of monsters, cohabiting with goats, cows and horses, thus producing those abortions which they denominate "monsters"; so these craftsmen fashion with their foliage this kind of "monsters": and "monsters" is their true name and not "grotesques." The foliages of this kind, which I devised, when inlaid after the above-mentioned method, was much more beautiful to look upon than were the Turkish ones. It chanced that at this time in certain vases, which were ancient funeral urns full of ashes, among those same ashes were found certain iron rings of ancient workmanship inlaid with gold, and in each one of these same rings was set a little shell. On applying to those (who were) learned (in such things), they told me those persons wore these rings who desired to remain firm in mind in whatever extraordinary accident might befall them as well in good fortune as in bad. Upon this I was set to work by the request of certain noblemen great friends of mine and I fashioned some of these little rings; but I made them of well-tempered steel: then when handsomely engraved and inlaid with gold they made a most beautiful appearance; and it happened sometimes that for one of these small rings, for my workmanship alone, I received more than forty *scudi*. At this period also were worn certain gold medallions, upon which every lord or noble liked to have sculptured his own fancy or device; and they wore them in their hats. Of these objects I made a great many, and they were very difficult to fashion. And since the very brilliant man of whom I have already spoken, named Caradosso, made some of them, for which, when including more than one figure, he would not take less than one hundred gold *scudi* apiece; wherefore, not so much on account of the price as on account of his dilatoriness, I was preferred before him by certain of the nobles, for whom I made, amongst other things in competition with this very able craftsman, a medal, upon which medal there were four figures, over which I labored very carefully. It chanced that these said nobles and lords, setting it beside that made by the admirable Caradosso, said that mine was far better fashioned and more beautiful, and that I might ask whatever I liked for my pains; because having satisfied them so well they desired to satisfy me correspondingly. To which I replied that the greatest reward for my pains, and the one that I most desired, was to have approached near to the works of so very splendid a master, and that if this seemed to their lordships to be the case I called myself very well-paid. So departing immediately those gentlemen sent after me so very liberal a gift, that I was contented, and my desire to do good work was so much increased that it was the cause of that which will be heard of by-and-by.

Although I shall be departing somewhat from (the subject of) my profession, I want to relate some of those troublesome accidents that occurred in this toilsome life of mine, and since I have already narrated further back about that gay company and of the amusing jests that happened in connection with that woman, of whom I have spoken, Pantassilea, who bore for me that deceitful and tiresome affection, and who had been so very greatly enraged with me on account of that trick, where Diego the Spaniard already mentioned was introduced to that supper party; she having sworn to revenge herself upon me, an opportunity arose, which I will describe, wherein my life was subjected to very great danger. And this was, that there came to Rome a youth named Luigi Pulci, son of one of the Pulci family who had been decapitated for having abused his own daughter. This said youth had a most wonderful poetic genius, and a knowledge of good Latin literature. He wrote well; he had a grace and form of exceptional beauty; he had left the service of some bishop (I do not know who), and was eaten up with the French disease. And since, when this lad was in Florence, on summer nights in certain parts of the city they used to hold meetings in their own streets, where this youth was reckoned among the best of those who sang without preparation (*allo inproviso*). It was so agreeable to listen to him, that the divine Michelagniolo Buonaaroti (*sic*), that most excellent sculptor and painter, invariably, whenever he knew where he was, with greatest delight and pleasure went to hear him; and a certain man named Piloto, a most brilliant man, a goldsmith, and I bore him company. In this way arose the acquaintance between Luigi Pulci and me. Wherefore, many years having passed by, he in that evil plight discovered himself to me, and begged me for the love of God to assist him. I, moved with compassion on account of his great talent, my love for my native place, and since such an act was in accordance with my natural disposition, took him into my house and had him attended to in such a way, that since he was so young he was soon restored to health. Whilst he was regaining his health, he was continually studying, and I had assisted in providing him with many books according to my ability; to such purpose that this Luigi, recognizing the great kindness which he had received from me, thanked me many times with words and tears, saying that if God should ever put in his way any good luck he would render to me the recompense for such benefits as I had shown him. To which I replied that I had not done for him all that I could have wished, but as well as I was able, and that it was the duty of human beings to assist one another. I reminded him only that he should render this kind office that I had shown to him, to any other who had need of it from him, just as he had need of it from me; and that he should love me as a friend, and I would reckon him as such. This young man began to frequent the Court of Rome, in which he soon found a situation, and became attached to the service of a bishop, a man of eighty years of age, who was known as the Bishop of Ghurgensis. This bishop had a nephew, who was called Misser Giovanni: he was a Venetian noble. This said Misser Giovanni showed himself to be greatly enamoured of the merits of this Luigi Pulci, and under the excuse of these talents of his had made him as much his intimate (companion) as if he had been his own self. The said Luigi having mentioned me, and of the great obligation under which he lay to me, to this Misser Giovanni, caused the said Misser Giovanni to desire to make my acquaintance. By this it chanced that having upon one of those evenings arranged a little meal for that before-mentioned Pantassilea, to which supper I had invited a number of my gay friends, just as we were proceeding to table there arrived the said Misser Giovanni with the said Luigi Pulci, and after exchanging some civilities, they remained to supper with the rest of us. That shameless hussy upon seeing the handsome youth, at once commenced designs upon him; for the which reason when that pleasant supper was over, I called the said Luigi Pulci aside, begging him in the name of all the obligations that he boasted of owing me not to seek in any way whatsoever communication with that whore. At which requests he replied to me: "Bless me, my dear Benvenuto, do you then take me for a madman?" Upon which I said: "Not for a madman, but for a youth. And I swear by God that I have no thought in the world on her account, but I should be very grieved on your account if through her you should break your neck." At which remarks he swore that he prayed God that if he ever spoke to her he might immediately break his neck. This poor lad must indeed have taken this oath before God with all his heart, for he did break his neck, as shall presently be here related. The said Misser Giovanni displayed for him a base and unseemly affection; for this said youth was seen every day to vary his garments of velvet and of silk, and it was known that he was wholly given over to wickedness, and had abandoned all his fine and admirable talents, and he made pretence of not seeing me and not recognizing me, because I had rebuked him, telling him that he had given himself a prey to disgusting vices, which would cause him as I said to break his neck. That friend of his, Misser Giovanni, bought him a very fine black horse, upon which he expended one hundred and fifty *scudi*. This horse was most admirably trained; to such purpose that this Luigi went every day to caracole upon this horse before the dwelling of that courtesan Pantassilea. Though I had observed this circumstance, I paid no attention to it, saying that everything fell out according to its own nature; and I attended to my own studies. It happened one Sunday evening that we were invited by that Sienese sculptor Michelagniolo to sup with him; and it was summertime. At this supper was present the before-mentioned Bachiacha, and with him he had brought that said Pantassilea, his former flame. So as we were at table supping, she was seated between me and the said Bachiacha. When we came to the best part of the supper, she rose from the table, saying that she wished to go and relieve herself, because she felt a pain in her stomach, and that she would return directly. Whilst we went on chatting most agreeably and supping, she remained upstairs much longer than she should have done. It chanced that, pricking up my ears, I seemed to hear thus subdued jesting in the street. I held a knife in my hand, which I was employing for my table uses. The window was so close to the table that by raising myself a little, I saw in the street that said Luigi Pulci in company with the said Pantassilea; and I heard one of them,

Luigi, say: "Oh! woe betide us, if that devil of a Benvenuto should see us!" And she replied: "Have no fear. Hark what a noise they are making. They are thinking of everything else but us." At which words I, since I had recognized them, flung myself out of the window (*gettai da terra la finestra*) and seizing Luigi by the cloak, with the knife that I had in my hand would certainly have slain him. But as he was mounted upon a white nag, to which he gave the spur, he left his cloak in my hands, in order to escape with his life. Pantassilea took refuge in a church close at hand. Those who were at the table, immediately rising, all came to me begging me not to upset either myself or them on account of a whore. To them I answered that I should not trouble myself on her account, but rather on account of that wicked youth, who had shown at how small account he valued me. And so I would not allow myself to be swayed by any of the arguments of those brilliant and worthy men. Instead, having seized my sword I went by myself into the Prati; for the house wherein we were supping was near the Porta di Castello which leads to the Prati. Proceeding thus towards the Prati I had not gone far ere the sun set and I at a slow pace returned to Rome. It was already night and dark, but the gates of Rome were not shut. It was nearly two hours (after sunset), when I passed by the house of this Pantassilea, with the determination that if that Luigi Pulci were there I would make them both suffer for it. When I saw and learnt that there was no one in the house but a drudge named Canida, I went to lay aside the cloak and the scabbard of my sword, and came thus to the said house, which stood behind the Banks upon the margin of the river Tiber. Opposite this house there was a garden belonging to an innkeeper who was called Romolo. This garden was enclosed by a thickset hedge of thorns, in which I straightway hid myself, waiting for the said woman to come home in company with Luigi. Some time passed when there came thither that said friend of mine, Bachiacha; whether he had really guessed (where I was) or he had been told. Softly he called me: "Gossip"; (for so we addressed each other in joke); and he besought me for the love of God, saying these words, almost weeping: "Gossip mine, I implore you not to do any harm to this poor woman, for she has committed no fault at all." To which I replied: "If at this first word of mine you do not take yourself out of my sight, I will give you one on the head with this sword." This unlucky "gossip" of mine from sheer terror immediately felt a disturbance in his stomach, and was obliged to go a little way off for he had need to obey (a call of nature). It was a starry night, which caused a very great brightness. On a sudden I heard a noise of many horses and they came up from both sides. These were the said Luigi and the said Pantassilea, accompanied by a certain Misser Benvegnato of Perugia, chamberlain to Pope Clemente, and with them they had four most valorous Perugian captains, with some other very bold young soldiers; there were in all more than twelve swordsmen. When I saw this troop, realizing that I knew not by what road I could escape, I tried to thrust myself into that hedge; and because those prickly thorns hurt me and goaded me as one does a bull, I had almost resolved to make a leap for it and fly. At this moment Luigi had his arm round the neck of the said Pantassilea, saying: "I shall kiss you once again to the confusion of that traitor of a Benvenuto." At this, maddened by the said thorns and urged on by the said words of the youth, leaping out I raised my sword, and with a loud voice I shouted: "You are all dead men." At this the blow of my sword fell upon the shoulder of the said Luigi; and though those bestial friends (*satiracci*) of this poor youth had armour-plated him entirely with coats (of mail) and other similar contrivances, the blow was a very heavy one; and my sword turning caught the said Pantassilea on the nose and in the mouth. As they both fell to the ground, Bachiacha with his breeches halfway down his legs howled and fled. When I furiously turned upon the others with my sword those brave men hearing a great noise which had arisen in the inn, and thinking that there must be therein a troop of one hundred persons, although they bravely drew their weapons, two among their horses taking fright threw them into such confusion, that whilst two of their best riders were thrown, the rest took to flight. And I having seen this satisfactory result by a very hasty departure came off with honor from this affair, not wishing to tempt fortune more than I ought. During that so infinite a confusion some of those soldiers and captains were wounded by their own swords, and the said Misser Benvegnato, the Pope's chamberlain, was dashed down and trampled on by his own mule; and one of his servants having drawn his sword fell down along with him and wounded him severely in the hand. This mishap caused Misser Benvegnato to swear after that Perugian fashion of theirs louder than all the others, saying: "By the . . . of God, I am determined that Benvegnato shall teach Benvenuto how to live;" and he directed one of those captains of his, perhaps a bolder man than the rest, but who on account of his youth lacked sense (that he should come to me). This said youth came to look for me in the place whither I had retired, in the house of an influential Neapolitan noble, who, having heard of and seen some of the examples of my trade, as well as the disposition of my mind and of my body fitted for deeds of arms (which was the reason why this nobleman was well disposed towards me) (had conceived a great affection for me) to such purpose that I, seeing myself made much of, and finding myself moreover in my own element, made such a reply to that captain that I believe he must have much repented that he had come into my presence. A few days afterwards, when the wounds of Luigi and of the whore, and of those others were somewhat healed, this great Neapolitan noble was sought out by

that Misser Benvegnato,—whose anger had subsided,—to get me to
make peace with that said youth Luigi, and (to say also) that as to
those brave soldiers they had had nothing to do with me personally;
they merely wished to make my acquaintance. To this request that
nobleman replied freely that he would bring me to whatever place
they wished, and that I would willingly make peace; with this condition that neither on the one side nor upon the other should there
be bandying of words, for it would be too contrary to the credit of
either side; it would be sufficient only to carry out the form of drinking together and kissing, and that he was willing to do the talking
by which he would gladly save the situation. And thus was it done.
One Thursday evening the said nobleman took me to the house of
the said Misser Benvegnato, where were assembled all those soldiers
who were present at that skirmish, and they were still at table. With
my nobleman were more than thirty strong men, all fully armed; a
circumstance that the said Misser Benvegnato did not expect. When
we came into the chamber, first the said nobleman, and then I after
him, spake these words: "God save you, Sirs. We have come to
you, Benvenuto and I, who love him as my very own brother; and
we are ready to do all that you have the will to do." Misser Benvegnato, seeing that the hall was filled by so many persons, said:
"We only ask for peace, and nothing more." Misser Benvegnato
therefore promised that the Court of the Governor of Rome should
not give me any trouble. We ratified peace: whereupon I immediately returned to my shop, where I was unable to remain one hour
without that Neapolitan nobleman, who either came to look me up
or sent for me. Meantime the said Luigi Pulci, being cured, was out
every day mounted upon that black horse of his, that had been so
well trained. One day among the rest it had been drizzling and he
was curvetting his horse exactly opposite Pantassilea's door, when
slipping down he fell and the horse upon him; having broken his

right leg at the thigh, he died a few days later there in the house of the said Pantassilea, and fulfilled the oath before God that he had made so solemnly (*di quore*). Thus one sees that God takes count of good and evil, and gives to each one his own deserts.

ALL the world was already in arms. Pope Clemente had sent to beg of the lord Giovanni de' Medici (the help of) certain bands of soldiers, who when they arrived made so much disturbance in Rome, that it was unsafe to remain in the public workshops. For this cause I withdrew into a convenient little cottage behind the Banks; and there I labored to the orders of all those friends whom I had acquired. The works of mine at this period were not objects of great importance; it is therefore not necessary to dwell upon them. I delighted much at this time in music and in pleasures of a similar character. Pope Clemente, having, by the advice of Misser Jacopo Salviati, disbanded those five companies that the lord Giovanni (who had lately died in Lombardy) had sent him, Borbone, learning that there were no troops in that city, in greatest haste urged his army towards Rome. In this emergency the whole city took up arms; and because I was a particular friend of Alessandro, son of Piero del Bene, who at the time when the Colonna invaded Rome had desired me to guard his residence: on this more serious occasion therefore he besought me that I would procure a company of fifty men as a guard for the said house, and that I would take the com-

mand of them as I had done in the time of the Colonna; whereupon
I procured fifty most valiant young men and, well paid and lodged,
we took up our abode in his house. When the army of Borbone had
already appeared before the walls of Rome, the said Alessandro del
Bene begged me that I would go with him to keep him company;
so one of the best men in my company and I went with him; and
on the way there joined us a youth named Cecchino della Casa. We
reached the wall of the Campo Santo, and thence we saw that marvellous host, which had already made every sort of effort to gain
an entrance. At that point in the fortifications which we approached
there were many youths killed by the assailants (*quei di fuora*).
The fight therefore was at its hottest. There was as thick a fog as it
is possible to imagine. I turned to Alessandro and said to him: "Let
us return home as quickly as possible for there is no help at all to be
given here; you see those (the enemy) are mounting the walls and
these (the defenders) are falling back." The said Lessandro, terrified, replied: "Would to God that we had not come here"; and so
turned round in great haste to depart. I reproved him, saying:
"Since you have brought me here, we must perform some courageous act" (*atto da huomo*); and turning my arquebuse in the direction where I saw the thickest and most serried crowd in the combat,
I took aim into the midst of it, precisely at a man whom I noticed as
conspicuous above the rest (on account of the fog I was not able to
distinguish whether this man was on horseback or on foot). Turning immediately to Lessandro and Cechino I told them to fire off
their arquebuses; and I showed them the way whereby the fire of
the besiegers should not injure them. When we had each done this
twice, I looked carefully over the wall, and saw an extraordinary
tumult among them, which arose from the fact Borbone himself
had been slain by those shots of ours; for from what I have heard
since, he was that chief whom I saw conspicuous above the rest.

Departing thence, we went by the Campo Santo and entered the City near San Piero; and having passed out thence at the church of Santo Agniolo, we arrived at the principal gate of the Castello with greatest difficulty, because the lord Renzo da Ceri and the lord Horatio Baglioni were wounding and slaying all those who were absenting themselves from the fight at the city walls. When we reached the said great gate part of the enemy had already entered Rome, and we had them upon our heels (*alle spalle*). Those in the Castello wishing to let down the portcullis of the great gate, made way a little, in such wise that we four got inside. As soon as I was within, the Captain, Pallone de' Medici, took possession of me; and because I belonged to the staff of the Castello, he compelled me to leave Lessandro; which I did very much against my will. I therefore climbed to the keep (*mastio*) at the same moment that Pope Clemente was entering the Castello by way of the corridors: for he had not wanted before then to leave the Palazzo di San Piero, being unable to believe that the enemy would force an entrance. As soon as I found myself within on those terms, I attached myself to a certain troop of artillery, under the command of a gunner named Giuliano the Florentine. This Giuliano, spying over the battlement of the Castello, saw the sacking of his own humble home and the torturing of his wife and children: and in such a position was he that, for fear of injuring his own family, he dared not employ his artillery: therefore throwing his blazing fuse upon the ground he tore his cheeks with bitterest wailing; and likewise also did certain of the other gunners. For which cause I laid hold of one of those fuses, directing certain other men who were there, who were not so afflicted, to assist me. I turned certain field-pieces and falconets in such directions as I saw that it was needful, and I slew with them many of the enemy's forces. Had I not done so, that body of them, who had entered Rome that morning would have come straight upon the Castello; and it was possible for them to have easily effected an entrance, because the artillery was doing them no injury. I continued to fire: wherefore some of the Cardinals and lords blessed me and bestowed upon me the greatest encouragement. Wherefore I, emboldened, endeavored to achieve impossible tasks. It is sufficient that I was the means of protecting the Castello that morning, and that those other gunners returned to carry on their own duties. I continued at this all that day: when evening came, whilst the army was entering Rome by the Tresteveri Quarter, Pope Clemente having set at the head of all the gunners a famous Roman nobleman, who was named Misser Antonio Santa Crocie, this great personage came up to me the first thing, and complimented me. He posted me with five splendid pieces of artillery upon the very highest point of the Castello, which is designated "the Angel." This fortification (*luogo*) runs right round the Castello, and looks toward the Prati and towards Rome. Therefore he gave me as many men under me as I could command, to assist me in manœuvring my artillery; and he caused a payment to be made to me in advance, sent me some bread and a small quantity of wine, and then besought me that I would continue (the defence) in that way in which I had begun. I, because I sometimes felt a greater inclination for this profession than for that which I regarded as my own, pursued it so gladly that I succeeded better in it than in my said (true business). When night came, and the foe had entered Rome, we that were in the Castello (especially myself, who am always overjoyed at seeing new sights), stood watching this unutterable portent (*novità*) and the conflagration: events which those who were in any other place but the Castello could neither see nor imagine. Nevertheless I do not wish to set myself to describe such a thing: I will only continue to deal with this my own autobiography which I have begun, and the matters which specially appertain thereto. Continuing unceasingly to employ my guns, by means of them, in the one whole month during which we were besieged in the Castello, there happened to me many very important events, all worthy of being related: but because I do not want to be too prolix, nor do I desire to picture myself too far removed from my rightful profession, I will omit the greater part, recounting only those of which I am compelled to speak, which will be but a few and those the most noteworthy. And here is the first: the said Misser Antonio Santa Crocie having directed me to come down from the "Angel," in order that I might train my guns upon certain houses near the Castello, into which some of our enemies from outside were seen to enter, whilst I was taking aim, a cannon-shot came in my direction, which struck a corner of a battlement, and carried away so much of it, that it escaped injuring me, although the greater quantity struck me all at once on the chest: and since it stopped my breathing, I fell prostrate on the ground like one dead, but I heard all that the bystanders were saying. Among those who greatly mourned was that Misser Antonio Santa Crocie, who said "Alas! we have lost the best aid that we had." There had come up at this noise a certain comrade of mine, who was called Gianfrancesco the fifer (this man was more inclined to medicine than to playing the fife), and bursting into tears immediately ran for a small flagon of the best Greek wine, and having made a tile red-hot, upon which he had laid a good handful of wormwood, he then sprinkled upon it some of that good Greek wine; and as soon as the said wormwood was well saturated he laid it quickly upon my breast, where he could see distinctly the mark of the blow.

Such was the potency of that wormwood that I immediately recovered those scattered wits of mine. But when I wished to begin to talk, I could not do so, because certain fools of young soldiers (*soldatelli*) had filled my mouth with earth; since it seemed to them that they had with it given me the viaticum, but with which they would sooner have excommunicated me, because I could not recover myself, this earth giving me more trouble even than the blow. Having then escaped from this danger, I returned to the turmoil of my guns, continuing to fire them with all my power, and with greater result than I could have imagined. And because Pope Clemente had sent to ask assistance from the Duke of Urbino, who was with the army of the Venetians, telling the ambassador to inform his Excellency that as long as the said Castello held out he would kindle every evening three beacons upon the roof of the said fortress, accompanied by three cannon-shots, repeated thrice; which, as long as this signal continued, showed that the Castello had not surrendered. I had the task of making these fires and of firing these cannon shots. All day I was continually training my guns upon such spots where they could execute some great damage: for the which reason the Pope liked me even better, because he saw that I performed the art (of gunnery) with that amount of skill that such things required. The succor from the said Duke never came: on the which point, since I am not here for this purpose, I will say no more. Whilst I was aloft engaged upon my diabolical task, there came to see me some of those cardinals who were in the fortress; but more often the Cardinal of Ravenna and the Cardinal de' Gaddi, whom I many times told not to come up to me, because those horrid red caps (*berrettuccie*) of theirs were conspicuous from a distance: for they and I ran very great danger from those palaces close by, such as was the Torre de' Bini; to such an extent was this so that at last I had them barred out, and gained from them great ill-will on that account. Also there came often to me the lord Oratio Baglioni, who liked me very much. One of those days when he was conversing with me, he saw a commotion in a certain hostelry, which was outside the gate of the Castello, at a place called Baccanello. This hostelry had for its sign a sun of a red color painted between two windows. The windows being closed, the said lord Horatio opined that within, over-against that sun between those two windows, a soldiers' mess were making merry. Wherefore he said to me: "Benvenuto, if you will give your attention to discharging this small gun (*mezzo cannone*) of yours within an arm's length (*braccio*) of that sun, I believe that you will do a fine job, for I hear a great noise, wherefore there ought to be men of great importance there." I replied to his lordship: "I have quite sufficient courage to hit that sun in the middle; but that a tub full of stones which was there, near the muzzle of the said gun, by the force of the explosion and the blast of wind that the cannon would create would be thrown to the ground." To which the said lord responded: "Don't waste time, Benvenuto; in the first place, it is impossible from the manner in which it stands that the blast from the cannon will cause it to fall; but even if it did fall and the Pope himself were beneath it, it would be less serious than you think; therefore fire away." I, troubling no more about it, fired at the centre of the sun, exactly as I had promised. The tub fell over, as I predicted, and its contents were discharged exactly between Cardinal Farnese and Misser Jacopo Salviati, who might well have both been crushed: the reason of this was that the said Cardinal Farnese was just chiding the said Misser Jacopo because he was the cause of the Sack of Rome; and in pouring insults upon one another, they stood apart to give space for their violent words, which was the reason that my tub did not crush them both. Hearing the great noise that was being made in the court below, the excellent lord Horatio descended thither in great haste; wherefore I looking out (over the place) where the tub had fallen heard some people saying: "It would be a good thing to kill those gunners"; for which cause I trained two falconets upon the stairs that led up to us, resolving in my mind to fire one of those falconets into the first man that mounted them. The servants of Cardinal Farnese must have been ordered by him to come and do me some injury; for which reason I got myself in readiness and held a fuse in my hand. Recognizing some of them I said: "You drones, if you don't clear out from here, and if there is any of you that dares set foot upon those stairs, I have two falconets here ready with which I will pound you to dust; and go and tell the Cardinal that I have done what my superiors ordered me to do, which things are planned and done for the defence of those priests, and not for their injury." When they had taken themselves off, the said lord Horatio Baglioni himself came running, whom I ordered to stand back, lest I slew him, for I knew very well who he was. His lordship, not without trepidation, paused a little, and called out to me: "Benvenuto, I am your friend." To which I replied: "My lord, mount alone, and then you can come in any way that you like." His lordship, who was very haughty, stopped a little, and said to me irritably: "I have a good mind not to come up further and to do exactly the opposite of what I intended to do for you." To which I replied, that, since I had been set in that post to defend others, so also I was prepared to defend myself. He assured me that he was coming alone; but when he had mounted the stair, the fact that his expression was more altered than it should have been, was the reason of my keeping my hand upon my sword and standing with it in an attitude of defence. At this he began to laugh, and as the color returned to his face, said to me very amiably: "My dear Benvenuto, I like you as much as ever I am able, and at such time as God wills I will demonstrate this to you. Would to God that you had killed those two rogues, for one of them is the cause of this great disaster, and the other is likely to be sometime the cause of even worse." He then told me that if I were asked, I should not say that he was there with me when I fired off that volley: and for the rest I was to fear nothing. The disturb-

ances were very great and the affair lasted a long while. Upon this
point I do not wish to dilate further: it is sufficient that I was in the
way of executing vengeance on my father's behalf upon Misser
Jacopo Salviati, who had done him a thousand evil turns. Uninten-
tionally, however, I did give him a great fright. Regarding Farnese I don't want to say anything, because it will be perceived in its
own place what a good thing it would have been if I had slain him.
I set myself to firing my guns, and with them I every day performed
some very notable feat: to such purpose that I acquired unlimited
credit and thanks from the Pope. Not a day passed in which I did
not slay some one of the enemy beyond the walls. It happened one
day among others, that the Pope was promenading upon the round
keep and saw in the Prati a Spanish colonel, whom he recognized by
certain traits, recollecting that he had formerly been in his service:
and whilst he was regarding him, he talked about him. I, who was
above, beside the "Angel," knew nothing of this, but I spied a man,
clad all in rose-color, with a small dart in his hand, who stood
there directing the throwing up of the entrenchments; and planning
what I could do to oppose him, I chose one of my falconets (*geri-
falco*) that I had there, a piece of artillery that is larger and longer
than a *sacro,* almost like a demi-culverin. This piece I emptied, and
then loaded it with a good quantity of fine powder mixed with
coarse: then I aimed it very carefully at the red man, giving it a tremendous *parabola,* because he was so far away, since in the profession it is not customary to employ guns of that kind for such a long
distance. I fired it off, and it struck the red man exactly in the
middle, who out of arrogance had stuck his sword in front of him
after a certain Spanish fashion of his: so that when my cannon ball
reached him, striking upon that sword, we saw the said man cleft
into two pieces. The Pope, who did not expect such a result, was
greatly pleased and astonished; because it seemed to him impossible

that a cannon could reach so distant a mark, and because he could not understand how this event could possibly have happened that that man was divided into two pieces: and having sent to summon me he asked me (about it). Whereupon I told him all the care that I had taken in my method of firing: but as to how the man came to be in two pieces, neither he nor I knew the reason. Going down on my knees I besought him to absolve me from the homicide, and from the other things that I had done in that fortress in the service of the Church. At which request the Pope, raising his hands and making a large distinct cross upon my face, told me that he blessed me; and that he pardoned me all the homicides that I had ever committed, and all those that I ever should commit in the service of the Apostolic Church. Leaving him, I went up again and pressing on never ceased firing: and my shots were hardly ever without result. My draughtsmanship and my studies in the fine arts, and the brilliance of my musical accomplishments, were all (absorbed) into playing (*sonare*) upon those guns, and if I should have to describe in detail the splendid achievements that I accomplished in that cruel hellishness (*infernalità chrudele*), I should make the world wonder: but in order not to be too long drawn-out I pass it over. I will only speak of certain of the most notable things, which are necessary to my purpose. And this is one, that while thinking day and night what I could do to play my part in the defence of the Church, I watched how our enemies changed guard and passed through the principal gate of Santo Spirito, which was within reasonable range; but because my aim had to be sideways, I could not manage to execute that great amount of damage that I desired to do. Nevertheless I every day slew a great many people: to such purpose that the enemy seeing that this passage was interrupted, mounted one night more than thirty barrels upon the top of a roof, which blocked that view for me, I, who gave a little more of my attention to this circumstance than I had previously done, trained all my five pieces of artillery, pointing them in the direction of the said barrels, and waited until 22 of the clock at the exact moment when they changed the guard: and because they, thinking themselves secure passed along more leisurely and in much greater crowds than usual, when I fired off my guns not only did I throw to the ground those barrels that were in my way, but in that volley alone I slew more than thirty men. Whereupon, following it up then twice more, I threw the soldiers into such disorder that inasmuch as they were laden with the spoils of the great Sack, some of them, anxious to enjoy the fruit of their exertions, frequently wanted to mutiny in order to return home. Held in check, however, by that brave captain of theirs, who was called Gian di Urbino, to their very great inconvenience they were compelled to take another road in order to change their guard: which inconvenience involved (a detour) of more than three miles, whereas this former route meant but half a one. When I had completed this exploit all those lords who were in the Castello paid me splendid compliments. This event was such that in reference to its important consequences, I have wished to relate it in order to complete this episode, because I am not dealing with that profession which is the main object of my narrative; for if I wished to embellish my autobiography with such things as these, I should have far too much to say. There is but one other event, which I will relate in its own place. Anticipating (*saltando innanzi*) a little, I will tell how Pope Clemente with a view to saving his tiaras with all the mass of splendid jewels belonging to the Apostolic Treasury, caused me to be summoned, and shut himself up in a chamber with Cavalierino and me alone. This Cavalierino had formerly been stable-boy to Fillippo Strozzi: he was a Frenchman, a person of the humblest origin; and since he was a valued servant, Pope Clemente had made him very rich, and trusted him even as himself: so that when the

said Pope and Cavaliere and I were shut up in the before-mentioned
apartment, they set before me the said tiaras with all that vast quantity of jewels belonging to the Apostolic Treasury: and they commissioned me that I should set them all free from the gold in which
they were set. And so I did. Then I packed each of them in a little
piece of paper and we sewed them into certain garments upon the
persons of the Pope and the said Cavalierino. Then they gave me
all the gold, which amounted to about two hundred pounds, and
told me that I must melt it down with as much secrecy as I could.
I went back to the "Angel," where my room was, which I could lock
up so that no one should disturb me; and I there made for myself a
little blast furnace of bricks; and I fitted into the bottom of the said
furnace a large ash-pan (*ceneracciolo*) in the form of a platter,
throwing the gold from above upon the coals, so that little by little
it fell through into that platter. Whilst I was working at this little
furnace I was continually on the watch how I could injure our
enemies; and since we had the trenches of our enemies at
less than a stone's throw beneath us, I caused them some
loss in the said trenches with certain ancient projectiles, of which
there were several piles, the former ammunition of the fortress.
Having selected a *sacro* and a *falconet,* which were both a little
broken at the muzzle, I filled them up with these projectiles, and
then setting fire to these said guns they volleyed down like mad,
executing in the said trenches much unforeseen damage, in such
measure that, keeping these guns constantly in readiness, whilst I
went on fusing the said gold, a little before the hour of vespers, I saw
some one mounted upon a mule coming along the bank of the entrenchments. The said mule moved very rapidly; and the rider
was speaking to the men in the trenches. I stood ready to fire off
my guns before he came straight opposite me; therefore having fired
with good judgment, when he reached that point one of those pro-

jectiles reached him and struck him full in the face; the rest (of the charge) struck the mule, which fell dead; in the trench we heard a very great tumult. I fired the other piece, not without doing them great injury. It was the Prince of Orange, who from within the trenches was carried to a certain hostelry near at hand, whither there quickly hurried all the flower of the army. When Pope Clemente heard what I had done, he immediately sent to summon me; and when he asked me about the matter, I told him everything; and said besides that the man must be a person of the highest importance, because to that hostelry whither he had been carried there had immediately assembled all the chief men of that army, as far as I could judge. The Pope with very great wisdom sent to summon Misser Antonio Santa Croce, which noble was the head and leader of all the gunners, as I have said. He told him to order all of us gunners that we should aim all our guns, of which there were a vast number, upon that particular house, and that at a signal of an arquebuse-shot, every one should open fire; in such fashion, that by slaying their leaders, that army, which was, as it were, between props, would be altogether put to rout; and because at some time God must have heard the prayers which they made so frequently, by that means he would free them from those impious rogues. Having set our artillery in readiness, according to the direction of Santa Croce, we were awaiting the signal, when Cardinal Orsino heard of it, and began to upbraid the Pope, saying that he ought not to do this thing on any account, because they were on the point of concluding a treaty; and that if they slew those men, the soldiery without a leader would invade the Castello by storm, and their destruction would be complete indeed; therefore they did not wish such an act to be committed. The poor Pope, in desperation, seeing that he was assailed both within and without, said that he would leave the decision to them. So the order being rescinded, I, because I was impatient, when I knew that they were coming to give me the order not to fire, let off a demi-cannon that I had, which struck a pilaster of a courtyard in that house, against which I saw a great many people leaning. This shot did such serious damage to our enemies that they were forced to abandon the house. The said Cardinal Orsino wished to have me hanged, or in any case put to death; from which fate the Pope stoutly defended me. The high words which passed between them, although I know them, since I make no profession of writing history, it is not my business to repeat; I will only attend to my own doings.

Chapter Eight   *1528-1529*

THE gold that I had melted down I carried to the Pope, who thanked me effusively for what I had done, and directed Cavalierino to give me twenty-five *scudi,* excusing himself that he had no more that he could give me. A few days after this the truce was signed. I went with the lord Horatio Baglioni together with a company of three hundred men in the direction of Perugia; and there the lord Horatio wished to put me in command of the company, which at that time I did not wish (to undertake), saying that I desired first to go and see my father, and to purge the Ban that I had out against me in Florence. The said lord told me that he had been made Captain-General of the Florentines: and ser Piero Maria di Lotto sent by the said Florentines was then on the spot, to whom the said lord Horatio commended me greatly as his servitor. Thus I came to Florence with several other comrades. The plague was indescribably great. When I arrived in Florence I found my good father, who thought that I should either have perished in that Sack, or should return to him in a state of destitution. But exactly the contrary event had resulted: I was alive, (laden) with much money, with a servant and well mounted. When I met my old (father), he was in such great joy that I saw that he certainly thought that while embracing and kissing me he would expire on the spot in consequence. I recounted to him all the horrors of the Sack, and having placed in his hand a large sum of *scudi,* which I had earned by my soldiering, after my good father and I had exchanged embraces, he immediately went to the Eight to buy off the Ban. And it happened by chance that there was among the Eight one of those who had laid it upon me, and he was the one who had indiscreetly on that occasion said to my father that he would like to send me to the gallows: upon which account my father addressed some suggestive words to him as an act of retaliation in consequence of the favors that the lord Horatio Baglioni had shown towards me. Matters being so far settled, I told my father that the lord Horatio had chosen me as a captain, and that it behoved me to begin thinking about forming my company. My poor father, greatly distressed at these words, immediately implored me for the love of God that I would not carry out such an enterprise, although he knew that I was fitted for that and even greater undertakings, saying at once that he had another son, my brother, who was exceedingly valiant in war, and that I ought to direct my attention to that wondrous art, in which I had up to that time labored for so many years and with so much application. Although I promised to obey him, like a sensible person he considered that if the lord Horatio came, since I had given him my promise, and for other reasons, I could never fail to follow him in warlike matters. So as a clever ruse he thought of removing me from Florence, saying thus: "My dear son, the plague is indescribably great in this place, and I always seem to see you come home with it on you; I remember when I was young that I went to Mantua, in which district I was very kindly received, and that there I stayed several years. I beg and command you that for love of me— even to-day rather than to-morrow—you remove yourself from here and go thither."

Since I always took pleasure in seeing the world, and I had never been in Mantua, I went willingly, taking some of the money that I had brought with me. The larger portion of it, however, I left with my good father, promising always to assist him, wherever I might be, and leaving my elder sister to take care of our poor parent. This sister bore the name of Cosa, and since she had never wished for a husband, she had been received as a nun at Santa Orsola, and she therefore remained as helper and housekeeper for our old father, and director for my other younger sister, who was married to a certain Bartolomeo, a sculptor. So having departed with my father's blessing I took my excellent horse and with it I went to Mantua. I should have a great deal too much to say, if I wished to describe minutely this small journey. Since the land was darkened by pestilence and war, it was therefore with very great difficulty that I then reached the said Mantua. Upon my arrival there, I sought to commence working. Wherefore I was set to work by a certain master Nicholo, a Milanese, who was goldsmith to the Duke of the said Mantua. When I had set myself to work, about two days later I went to see that most excellent painter, Misser Julio Romano, mentioned above, a very great friend of mine. This Misser Julio showered unbounded caresses upon me, and took it very ill that I had not dismounted at his house; for he lived like a lord and was executing a commission for the Duke outside the gates of Mantua, at a place called Te. This work was vast and wonderful as may be seen perhaps still. The said Misser Julio immediately spoke of me to the Duke with many words of commendation, who commissioned me to make a model to hold a relic of the blood of Christ, which they have and which they say was brought thither by Longinus. He then turned to the said Misser Julio telling him that he must make a design for the said reliquary for me. To this Misser Julio replied: "My lord, Benvenuto is a man who has no need for the drawings of others; and this Your Excellency will be very well able to judge, when you see his model." Setting to work to make this said model, I drew a sketch for the said reliquary such as could easily contain the said phial; then upon the lines thereof I made a small model in wax. This was (in the form of) a seated Christ who in His lifted

left Hand raised aloft His great Cross, against which He was leaning, and with the fingers of His right Hand He made as though to
open the Wound in His Breast. This model when completed
pleased the Duke so much that his compliments were boundless,
and he made me understand that he would keep me in his service
on such terms that I could live there in wealth. At this juncture,
when I had paid my respects to the Cardinal his brother, the said
Cardinal begged the Duke that he would be so kind as to allow me
to make His Most Reverend Lordship's pontifical seal: which I commenced to do. While I was laboring upon this work, I was overcome by quartan fever: the which, when the bouts of fever were
upon me, took away my self-control; whereat I cursed Mantua and
its rulers and all who lived there of their own free-will. These words
of mine were reported to the Duke by that said Milanese goldsmith
of his, who saw very clearly that the Duke was wishing to engage
me. The said Duke on hearing these weak words of mine was
greatly enraged with me; wherefore since I was furious with Mantua, our passion was equal. Having finished my seal,—which was
at the end of about four months,—along with several other small
works made for the Duke under the Cardinal's name, I was well
paid by the said Cardinal; and he begged that I would return to
Rome, to that wondrous land where we had made acquaintance.
Setting out from Mantua with a good round sum of *scudi,* I arrived
at Governo, the place where was killed that most valiant lord Giovanni. Here I had a slight attack of fever, which, however, did not
in any way interrupt my journey; and it ceased at that very place,
for I never had it any more. Then on reaching Florence I had
thought to find my dear father, but on knocking at his door, there
appeared at the window a certain hunchbacked woman in a violent
rage, who drove me away with much abuse, saying that I was
plaguing her. To this hunchback I replied: "Tell me, oh! ill-

mannered deformity! is there no other countenance but yours in this house?" "No, and bad luck (*malanno*) to you." To which I responded in a loud voice: "And may this one (*i.e.* countenance) not last there for two hours." At this juncture a woman neighbor came out who told me that my father and all the rest of my family were dead of the plague: which, since I had partially guessed the truth, was the cause of less grief to me. Next she told me that that younger sister of mine who was called Liperata still remained alive, and that she had been taken in by a pious woman, who was called mona Andrea de' Bellacci. I departed thence to go to an inn. By chance I met a very great friend of mine. This man was called Giovanni Rigogli. Dismounting at his house, we went into the public square, where I received the news that my brother was alive, whom I went to look for in the house of a friend of his, who was called Bertino Aldobrandi. Having found my brother we exchanged an infinite number of embraces and salutations, and they were the more extravagant because to him of me and to me of him had come the news of the death of both of us. Then bursting into a very exceeding great laugh, he took my hand and said to me: "Come along, brother, I will take you into such a place as you would never imagine: that is to say, to where I have re-married our sister Liperata, who most certainly takes you for dead." And as we went to that place we recounted to one another the very fine things that had occurred to us. And when we reached the house where my sister was, so great was the shock to her of the unexpected news that she fell into my arms in a dead faint; and had it not been for the presence of my brother, the act was such that without any explanation her husband (as in fact (he did) at first) would not have thought that I could be her brother. Upon Cechin my brother speaking to and assisting the fainting woman, she soon recovered; and though she wept a very little for her father, her sister, her husband, and her

little son, she made preparations for supper; and in that happy ⟨
union (*nozze*) we talked no more about the dead, but rather t⟨
subjects suited to reunions (*nozze*); thus cheerfully and in gr⟨
content we finished our supper.

Constrained by the entreaties of my brother and sister, they we⟨
the cause of my remaining in Florence, for my desire was to tu⟨
my steps towards Rome. Besides which that dear friend of mi⟨
(for I mentioned above how much in certain straits I had been ⟨
sisted by him), that is, Piero di Giovanni Landi: well! this Piero to⟨
me that I ought to stop for some time in Florence; because t⟨
Medici having been expelled from Florence, that is to say the lo⟨
Ipolito and the lord Alesandro, who were afterwards respectivel⟨
the one Cardinal and the other Duke of Florence, this said Piero to⟨
me that I ought to stay a little while to see what would be done ne⟨
I began therefore to work in the Mercato Nuovo, and I set a gre⟨
quantity of precious stones and made good profits. At that tim⟨
there arrived in Florence a Sienese named Girolamo Marretti. Th⟨
Sienese had resided a long time in Turkey and was a person of
lively intelligence. He came to my shop and directed me to mak⟨
him a gold medallion to wear in a hat. He desired that I shoul⟨
represent upon this medallion *Hercules opening the lion's mout⟨*
So I set to work to make it, and whilst I was working at it Miche⟨
agniolo Buonaaroti often came to see it: and since I labored hard ⟨
it the attitude of the figure and the fierceness of the animal differ⟨
greatly from the work of all those who had up to that time execute⟨
such work. Moreover from the fact that this species of work wa⟨
totally unknown to that divine Michelagniolo, he praised this wor⟨
of mine so much that he aroused in me so great a desire to excel ⟨
was of inestimable value (to me). But since I had nothing else t⟨
do but to set precious stones, although this employment brought m⟨
in the largest earnings that I could make, I was not satisfied; becaus⟨

I wanted to execute works of greater merit than mere stone-setting. At this juncture there chanced (to appear) a certain Federigo Ginori, a youth of very high spirit. This youth had lived at Naples for many years, and since he was very handsome in figure and appearance, he had fallen in love in Naples with a princess. So, wishing to have a medallion made upon which was an *Atlas with the world upon his shoulders,* he desired of the great Michelagniolo that he would make him a slight sketch for it. At which he replied to the said Federigo: "Go and look for a certain young goldsmith who bears the name of Benvenuto; that man will serve you very well, and he certainly has no need of a design from me. But lest you think that I want to shirk the trouble of such a small job, I will very willingly make you a small sketch. Meantime speak to the said Benvenuto, that he also may make you a sketch model; then the better of the two can be put in hand." This Federigo Ginori came to look for me and told me his wishes, after relating how much that glorious Michelagniolo had praised me, and (said) that I must also make a sketch model in wax, whilst that splendid man had promised to make him a sketch drawing. Those words of that great man gave me so much encouragement, that I immediately set to work with very great diligence to make the said model: and when I had completed it a certain painter, a great friend of Michelagniolo, named Giuliano Bugiardini, brought to me the drawing for the *Atlas.* At the same time I showed to the said Giuliano my sketch model in wax. It was so very different from that drawing of Michelagniolo, that the said Federigo and also Bugiardino, agreed that I ought to make (the medallion) in accordance with my own model. So I began to do so, and the most excellent Michelagniolo saw the work and praised me so much (on account of it) that it proved of invaluable (encouragement to me). It was a figure (of Atlas), as I have said, chiselled upon a plate of metal; he bore the Heavens upon his back, made in the form of a crystal ball, its Zodiac being carved upon it in a field of lapis-lazuli. Combined with the said figure it produced such a beautiful effect as to be indescribable. Beneath was a lettered inscription, which ran *Summa tulisse iuvat.* The said Federigo being satisfied paid me most liberally. Misser Aluigi Alamanni, who was at this period in Florence, was a friend of the said Federigo Ginori, who brought him many times to my workshop, and he of his kindness admitted me to a very intimate friendship. Pope Clemente having declared war upon the city of Florence, and in preparation for defence the city having issued orders to her popular militia in every quarter, I was also commandeered in my turn. I prepared myself lavishly; and I joined company with the highest nobility of Florence—who appeared to be greatly united in their desire to fight in such defense—and those sorts of speeches were made in every quarter of the town that are usual on such occasions (*qual si sanno*). Moreover the young men came much more together than was their usual custom, nor did they ever talk of anything else but this. One day at midday, when there were in my workshop a number of rough men (*omaccioni*) and youths of the first families in the city, there was brought to me a letter from Rome, which had come from a certain man, who was called in Rome master Jacopino della Barca. This man was (really) named Jacopo dello Sciorina, but in Rome (he was called) *della Barca,* because he kept a boat that plied upon the Tiber between the Ponte Sisto and the Ponte Santo Agniolo. This master Jacopo was a very clever person, and an agreeable and very clever conversationalist. He had formerly been in Florence as a master of design for the work of the Cloth-weavers. This man was a great friend of Pope Clemente, who took great pleasure in hearing him talk. One day, during one of these chats it chanced that the subject arose of the Sack and of the defence of the

Castello; and in this connection the Pope, remembering me, said the kindest things of me that it is possible to imagine; and he added that if he knew where I was it would give him satisfaction to have me back again. The said master Jacopo said that I was in Florence: wherefore the Pope commissioned him to write to me that I should return to him. The contents of this said letter were to the effect that I ought to return to the service of Clemente, and that it would be to my advantage. Those young men who were there present, wished to know what that letter contained; wherefore to the best of my power I concealed its purport. Then I wrote to the said master Jacopo begging him to take my words neither for good nor for ill, but in no manner whatsoever to write to me again. The said man, however, since his desire so greatly increased, wrote me another letter, which was so extravagant in its expressions that if it had been seen I should have run great risk. This (letter) said on behalf of the Pope that I should come at once, for he wished me to carry out works of very great importance; and that if I wished to prosper I should leave everything immediately, and not remain to act in opposition to a Pope along with those wild madmen. When I saw the letter it put me into such a state of terror that I went to look for that dear friend of mine, who was called Pier Landi; who, as soon as he saw me, immediately asked me what news I had received that I showed myself so disturbed. I told my friend that the news which I had received that gave me that great distress, I could on no account repeat; I only begged him that he would take those keys which I gave him, and would hand over my jewels and gold to such and such (*al terzo e'l quarto*) persons as he would find written down in my account-book, then that he would take the contents of my house and with that customary good nature of his take some small amount of care of it, and that in a few days he should know where I was. This prudent youth, perhaps making a near guess at the facts, said to me: "Brother mine! Be off quickly, and then write to me, and don't give a thought to your affairs." Thus I did. He was the most faithful friend, the most prudent, the most honest, the most discreet, the most lovable that I have ever known. Leaving Florence, I went to Rome; and thence I wrote to him.

Chapter Nine

D IRECTLY I arrived in Rome I sought out some of my former
friends, by whom I was very well received and made much
of; and I immediately set myself to execute all sorts of work for gain;
but none worthy of description. There was a certain old goldsmith,
who was called Raffaello del Moro. This man had a high reputation
in the trade and was besides a very honest man. He begged me that
I would be pleased to go and work in his shop, for he had some commissions of importance to carry out, which were (likely to be) very
profitable. So I went willingly. More than ten days had passed
by, during which I had not endeavored to see that said master
Jacopino della Barca; who, when he saw me by accident, made me
a most effusive welcome; and upon his asking me how long it was
since I had arrived, I told him that it was about fifteen days. This
(good) man took that very ill, and told me that I must hold a Pope
in very little account, who had already with great urgency caused
him to write three times for me: and I, though I had taken it much
more ill of him, answered nothing, but rather swallowed down my
wrath. This good man, who had a vast supply of words, entered
upon a torrent of them, and said so much upon the point, that
presently, when I saw him tired out, I said nothing further to him
except that at his convenience he should take me to the Pope. He
replied that any time would do. Whereupon I answered him: "And
I am always ready." He began to go towards the Palace, and I with
him. It was Holy Thursday. When we arrived at the Pope's apartments, because he was well known and I was expected, we were

immediately admitted. The Pope was in bed, slightly indisposed, and with him were Misser Jacopo Salviati and the Archbishop of Capua. When the Pope saw me he was very extraordinarily delighted: and I, when I had kissed his feet, with such deference as I could muster, approached near to him, showing that I wished to tell him some matters of importance. Immediately upon his making a sign with his hand the said Misser Jacopo and the Archbishop retired to some distance from us. I began at once, saying: "Most Blessed Father, from the time when the Sack took place until now I have been unable to confess or communicate, because they (the priests) will not absolve me. The case is as follows: that when I melted down the gold and spent all that labor in unsetting those jewels (of yours), Your Holiness gave directions to Cavalierino to give me a certain recompense for my work, from whom I received nothing, rather he more readily uttered abuse. When I retired to the place where I had melted down the said gold, on removing the ashes I found about a pound and a half of gold in very many little grains like millet; and since I had not sufficient money to enable me to live decently in my own house, I thought that I would use that and restore it later when an opportunity should come to me. Now I am at Your Holiness' feet, who art the true confessor; may you grant me such favor that I may have leave in order to confess and communicate, and by the means of the pardon of your Holiness, I may regain the Grace of my Lord and God." Then the Pope with a slight gentle sigh (recalling perhaps his own straits) spake these words: "Benvenuto, I have certainly the power that you attribute to me, by which I can absolve you from any improper action that you may have committed, and I am besides willing to do so. Therefore tell me everything most freely and with good courage, for even if you have taken the value of the whole of one of those tiaras, I am most disposed to pardon you." Thereupon I replied: "I have had no more, Most Blessed Father, than the quantity that I have told you; and this did not amount to the value of one hundred and forty ducats, for so much did I receive for it from the mint at Perugia, and with it I went home to comfort my poor old father." The Pope said: "Your father was as virtuous, good and worthy a man as was ever born, and you are not at all degenerate from him; I am very sorry that the sum was so small. Nevertheless such as you say that it was I reckon it as a gift to you, and I entirely pardon you. Make this assurance to your confessor, if there is nothing else that applies to me. Then when you have confessed and communicated, let me see you again and (it shall be) to your advantage." When I had left the Pope's side, and Misser Jacopo and the Archbishop had come to him, his Holiness spoke of me as kindly at it was possible for any other man in the world to have done; and he told them that I had confessed and been absolved. Then he added, telling the Archbishop of Capua, that he should send for me and ask me if I had any needs beyond this particular matter, for he gave him entire authority to absolve me of everything, and to show me besides as many courtesies as ever he could. As I was departing with master Jacopino, he with greatest curiosity asked what were those close and lengthy discussions that I had had with the Pope. When he had asked this question more than twice, I told him that I did not wish to tell him, because they were matters that did not concern him, therefore he must not ask me any more. I went to complete all that remained of my agreement with the Pope. Then when the two feast-days were over I went to see him: who showing me more kindnesses than on the first occasion, said to me: "If you had come a little sooner to Rome I would have commissioned you to re-make those two tiaras of mine that we destroyed in the Castello; but since they are things of but little value without their gems, I will employ you upon a work of the very greatest importance, wherein you will

be able to show what your skill amounts to; and this is a morse
which has to be made round in the fashion of a trencher, and as big
as a little trencher of a third of a *braccio* (in diameter). Upon thi
I want you to fashion a (figure of) God the Father in low relief, and
in the centre of the said (design) I want you to place that large
finely cut diamond (*bella punta del diamante*), together with man
other precious stones of the greatest value. A certain Caradosse
formerly began (to do this for me) and never completed it. I wan
to have this thing finished quickly, because I would like to have
some little pleasure out of it. Be off therefore now and make a fin
sketch model." And he directed me to be shown all the jewels; and
straightway I went away immediately. Whilst Florence wa
still invested, that Federigo Ginori, for whom I had made the me
dallion of Atlas, died of consumption, and the said medallion fel
into the hands of Misser Luigi Alamanni, who a short time after
wards carried it himself as a gift to King Francis, King of France
accompanied by some of his most beautiful writings. The king
being beyond measure pleased with this medallion, the most talented
Misser Luigi Alamanni spoke of me to His Majesty, together with
some details regarding my personality outside my profession, with
so much kindness that the king gave evidence of having conceived
a desire to make my acquaintance. Whilst I was directing all the
care of which I was capable upon that said small model, which
made exactly the same size that the finished work was to be, many
of those goldsmiths in the trade, who thought themselves capable
of executing this very thing heard of it. And since there had com
to Rome a certain Micheletto, a very brilliant craftsman in engraving
gems, who was besides a most intelligent jeweller, and he was an
elderly man and of high reputation, to his skill were entrusted th
Pope's two tiaras. Whilst I was making this said model, he mar
velled much that I did not have recourse to him, for he was an

intelligent man and in high favor with the Pope. At last seeing that I did not go to him, he came to me to ask me what I was doing. "Something that the Pope has committed to me"; replied I to him. Then he said: "The Pope has directed me to inspect all the things that are being made for His Holiness." To which I replied, that I would ask the Pope first, and then I should know what answer I must make to him. He told me that I should repent doing so; and going away from me in a rage he hunted up all the other members of the Trade, and when they had discussed the question, they all committed the matter to the said Michele; who with that fine skill of his caused more than thirty designs, all differing one from another, to be made for this undertaking by certain brilliant draughts-men. And since he had the ear of the Pope at his disposal, making a compact with another jeweler who was named Pompeo, a Milan-ese, who was a great favorite with the Pope and was a relative of Misser Traiano, the Pope's first chamberlain; these two, that is to say, Michele and Pompeo, began telling the Pope that they had seen my model, and that it seemed to them that I was not a fit instru-ment to perform so wondrous an undertaking. To this the Pope replied that he also must see it; then if I were not fit, he would seek out some one who was. They both said that they had several ad-mirable designs for this very thing. To which the Pope replied that he was very glad to hear it, but that he did not wish to see them before I had finished my model; then he would look at everything together. In the course of a few days I had completed the model, and on taking it one morning to the Pope, that Misser Traiano made me wait, and at the same time sent in haste for Micheletto and Pompeo, telling them to bring the drawings. When they had ar-rived we were all admitted; whereupon Michele and Pompeo im-mediately began to spread out their drawings, and the Pope to examine them. And since the draughtsmen were unused to the art of jewellery they did not understand the positions (suitable) for precious stones; still less had they who were jewellers explained to them that it is necessary for a jeweller when figures are to be introduced amid his precious stones to know how to compose, otherwise no good result can follow. For which reason in all these designs they had adjusted that wonderful diamond in the centre of the breast of that (figure of) God the Father. The Pope, since he was (a man) of very excellent taste, when he saw this very thing, was not at all pleased at it. And when he had looked at about ten (of the designs), throwing the rest upon the ground, he said to me, who was standing there apart: "Show me here your model, Benvenuto, in order that I may see if you have fallen into the same mistake that these have done." I came forward and having opened a little round box, it seemed as if a veritable flash (of lightning) shone in the eyes of the Pope, and he said in a loud voice, "If you had actually been in my own body, you would not have carried it out otherwise than as I see it here; these men knew no better way of bringing shame upon themselves." Many great nobles having come up, the Pope showed them the difference that existed between my model and their drawings. When he had praised it very much, whilst they stood terrified and awkward in his presence, he turned to me and said: "I only know of one mischance that is of the greatest importance; my dear Benvenuto, the wax is easy to manipulate; the whole question is to make it in gold." To these words I boldly replied, saying: "Most Blessed Father, if I do not complete it ten times better than this my model, let it be agreed that you pay me nothing for it." At these words there arose a great stir amongst those nobles, who said that I was promising too much. But there was one of the nobles, a very learned philosopher, who spoke up in my favor: "With that handsome physiognomy (*finnusumia*) and symmetry of figure which I observe in this young man, I foretell all that he says and even more." The Pope said: "It is for that reason that I think so also." Calling that chamberlain of his, Misser Traiano, he told him to fetch thither five hundred gold ducats of the Camera. Whilst they were waiting for the money, the Pope again examined more leisurely in what a beautiful manner I had combined the diamond with that (figure of) God the Father. This diamond I had affixed in the very centre of the composition, and above the stone itself I had arranged the (figure of) God the Father seated in a certain fine sideways position, which produced a most beautiful harmony in effect, and in no way interfered with the stone. Raising his right hand He was pronouncing a benediction. Beneath the said diamond I had placed three cherubim, who with arms raised aloft supported the aforesaid precious stone. The one of these cherubim in the middle was in full relief, the other two were only in half. Around were a vast number of different cherubim, grouped amid other fine precious stones. The rest (of the figure) of God the Father was clad in a mantle which floated around Him, and from (within the folds of) which issued many cherubim, together with many other fine decorations, which made a very beautiful effect. This work was executed in a white stucco upon a black stone. When the money arrived the Pope gave it to me with his own hand and begged me with the greatest amiability that I would contrive to let him have it (the Morse) during his lifetime, and that it would be to my advantage (to do so). Carrying away the money and the model, it seemed to me a thousand years before I could put my hand to the work. Having commenced immediately to work with great application, at the end of eight days the Pope sent to me by one of his chamberlains, a very great Bolognese nobleman, to tell me to go to him and take with me as much as I had already done. Whilst I was on the way, this said chamberlain, who was the most charming person that there was in that court, told me that it was

not so much that the Pope desired to see that work, but that he wished
to give me another commission of the highest importance; and this
was the dies for the money coined in the Mint of Rome; and that
must be ready to be able to give an answer to His Holiness; that it
was for this purpose that he had warned me. When I reached the
Pope, and had exhibited to him that plaque of gold, whereon was
only sculptured as yet God the Father, even sketched thus it displayed more talent than that small wax model; to such an extent
that the Pope in astonishment said: "From now onwards I shall be
willing to believe everything that you say": and having paid me
many unlimited compliments, he said: "I want to give you another
commission, which will be as pleasing to me as this and even more,
if you throw your heart into the execution of it." And when he told
me that he was very anxious to make the dies for his coin, and asked
me if I had ever made such things before, and if I had the courage
to undertake it, I replied that I had the very greatest courage, and
that I had seen how they were made; but that I had never actually
made them myself. There was in the presence a certain Misser Tommaso da Prato, who was Datary to His Holiness, and since he was a
great friend of those friends of mine, he said: "Most Blessed Father,
the favors that your Holiness is showering upon this young man,
since he is by nature most ardent, are the reason of his promising a
world of fresh things; but your having given him one great commission, and now giving him another greater one will be the cause of
one of them interfering with the other." The Pope turned angrily
upon him and bade him go to his office; and directed me to make a
model of a large gold doubloon, upon which he wished that there
should be a nude Christ with his hands bound, and an inscription
which should run: *Ecce Homo;* and on the reverse were to be a
Pope and an Emperor who together support a cross that is showing
signs of falling, and an inscription which should run: *Unus spiritus*

et una fides erat in eis. When the Pope had committed to me (the making of) this handsome coin, there came up the sculptor Bandinello (who had not as yet been created *cavaliere*); and with his accustomed presumption clothed in ignorance, he said: "To goldsmiths of this kind, and for such fine work, it is necessary to supply them with designs." At which I immediately turned round and said that I had no need of his designs in my trade; but that I had good hopes that at some time I should with my designs upset his trade. The Pope showed himself as delighted with these words as it is possible to imagine, and turning to me said: "Go now, my dear Benvenuto, and attend with spirit to serve me, and lend no ears to the talk of these madmen." So I departed; and with great haste made two steel dies; and having stamped one coin in gold, one Sunday after dinner I took the coin and the dies to the Pope, who when he saw them remained astounded and pleased not so much at the fine work which pleased him beyond measure, as still more did the promptness that I had exercised cause him to marvel. And in order to increase still further the satisfaction and wonder of the Pope, I had brought with me all the old coins, which had been made in times past by those brilliant craftsmen who had served Pope Julio and Pope Leone; and having seen that mine pleased him much more, I drew from my bosom a petition, in which I asked for the said office of keeper of the dies of the Mint; which office provided six gold *scudi* of salary per month, besides the dies which were paid for by the Master of the Mint, and which were reckoned at three to a ducat. The Pope having taken my petition and turned away, gave it into the hand of his Datary, telling him that he must send it to me immediately. The Datary taking the document, and preparing to put it into his pocket, said: "Most Blessed Father, Your Holiness should not run on so fast; these are things which deserve some consideration." Whereupon the Pope said: "I have quite understood you;

give me here that document;" and taking it he signed it immediately with his own hand. Then he gave it back to him and said: "There can be no further discussion on the matter; send it to him now, for so I desire it: the shoes of Benvenuto are worth more than the eyes of all these other clowns." And so having thanked His Holiness I went away to my work rejoicing beyond measure.

I STILL continued working in the shop of that Raffaello del Moro above-mentioned. This honest man had a pretty little daughter, for whom he had conceived designs upon me; and I having partly divined this, was desirous of it also; but, although I cherished this desire, I showed no sign of it whatsoever; rather I remained so discreet that I aroused his astonishment. It chanced that this poor girl had contracted a disease in her right hand, which had decayed those two small bones which connect the little finger and the other finger next to it. And because the poor child was, through the carelessness of her father, treated by an ignorant quack, who said that this unhappy girl would remain crippled in her entire right arm, even if nothing worse resulted, I, seeing the wretched parent so terrified, told him not to believe all that that ignorant surgeon had said. Whereupon he told me that he had no acquaintance with any doctors, who were surgeons, and besought me that if I knew anyone, I would bring him. I immediately called in a certain master Jacomo from Perugia, a man much skilled in surgery; and when he had seen this poor little girl, who was in terror, for she must have foreboded what that ignorant quack had said; whereat this clever man told her that she would have no evil consequence, and that she would have very good use of her right hand, and although those two last fingers would be a little weaker than the others, they would not on that account give her the least inconvenience in the world. And having set to work to treat her, in the course of a few days, when he wished to extract a small portion of the diseased part of those small bones, her father

summoned me, in order that I might come and see a little wha
suffering this girl had to endure. For the purpose the said maste
Jacopo took certain large steel instruments, and when I saw tha
with these he made little progress and caused very great pain to th
said girl, I told the master to stop and to wait a few minutes (*un*
ottavo d'ora) for me. Hurrying into the workshop I made a littl
tool of steel, very thin and bent: and it cut like a razor. Returnin
to the master, he began to work with so much gentleness that sh
felt no pain at all, and in a short space of time he had finished. Fo
this, besides other things, this honest man reposed so much the mor
affection upon me than he had for his two male children: and thu
he attended to the cure of his pretty little daughter. Whilst I wa
in closest friendship with a certain Misser Giovanni Gaddi, who wa
a clerk of the closet, this Misser Giovanni delighted greatly in th
arts (*virtù*), although he practised none of them himself. Ther
were with him a certain Misser Giovanni, a very cultured Greek;
Misser Lodovico da Fano, like him, a man of culture; Misser An
tonio Allegretti, and then the young Misser Annibal Caro. Fron
other cities were Misser Bastiano, the Venetian, a most excellen
painter, and myself; and at one time we met almost every day at th
said Misser Giovanni's. Wherefore, on account of this friendshij
that worthy man Raffaello, the goldsmith, spake to the said Misse
Giovanni: "My dear Misser Giovanni, you know me well. An
because I want to give that young daughter of mine to Benvenuto
since I find no better go-between than your lordship, I pray you t
assist me and to fix yourself such dowry as may seem to please yo
out of my estate." This hare-brained personage scarcely allowe
that poor worthy man to finish speaking, than without any sort o
reason, he said: "Talk no more, Raffaello, upon this point, becaus
you are farther apart from your object than January is from black
berries." The poor man, much cast down, quickly sought to marr

her; and her mother and all the family remained very cross with me, and I did not know the reason. And since it seemed to me that they were paying me back in bad coin for the many civilities that I had shown them, I sought to open a shop near them. The said Misser Giovanni told me nothing until the said girl was married, which took place within the space of several months. I was applying my-self with great attention to the completion of my work, and to the service of the Mint; for the Pope again commissioned me (to make) a coin of the value of two *carlini,* upon which was a portrait-bust of His Holiness, and on the reverse a *Christ walking upon the sea,* Who was stretching out His Hand to St. Peter, with an inscription round it which said: *"Quare dubitasti?"* This coin gave such exceeding satisfaction that a certain secretary of the Pope, a man of the highest talent, named Sanga, said: "Your Holiness can boast of having a kind of coin, such as was never seen amongst the ancients with all their pomp." To this the Pope replied: "Benvenuto can boast be-sides of serving an Emperor like me, who appreciates him."

Continuing the great work in gold, I showed it frequently to the Pope, for he pressed me to let him see it, and every day he mar-velled at it yet more. A brother of mine was in Rome in the service of Duke Lessandro, for whom at that time the Pope had pro-cured the Dukedom of Penna. There were in the service of this Duke very many soldiers, men of merit, brave fellows, of the school of that very great lord Giovanni de' Medici, and my brother from amongst them was esteemed by the said Duke as much as any of the bravest of them. This brother of mine was one day after dinner in the workshop of a certain Baccino della Crocie, beside the Banks, whither all those brave men were accustomed to repair; and he had laid himself upon a seat and was dozing. At this moment there passed by the picket of the Bargello, who were conducting as pris-oner a certain captain (named) Cisti, a Lombard, himself also of the school of that famous lord Giovannino, but who was not then in the service of the Duke. The captain Cattivanza degli Strozi was within the shop of the said Baccino della Crocie. When the said captain Cisti saw the said captain Cattivanza degli Strozi he called out to him: "I was bringing along the many *scudi* that I owed you: if you want them come for them, before they accompany me to prison." This captain was however willing enough to put others to the test, but did not care to experiment himself; wherefore, finding that there were there present certain very bold youths, more venturesome than strong for so great an enterprise, he bade them approach the captain Cisti, and make him give them that money of his, and that if the picket made any resistance, they were to employ force, if they were brave enough. These youths were but four, and all four were beardless. The first was called Bertino Aldobrandi, another Anguillotto of Lucca; of the others I do not remember the names. This Bertino had been trained and was the actual pupil of my brother, and my brother had for him as unbounded an affection as it is possible to imagine. Behold then these four brave youths approached the Bargello's picket, who were more than fifty police, including pikemen, arquebusiers, and (men with) two-handed swords. To be brief they laid hands upon their weapons, and those four youths pressed the picket so wonderfully, that if the captain Cattivanza had only appeared for an instant, without even drawing his weapon, those youths would have put the picket to flight; but having resisted for a while, that Bertino received certain severe wounds, which struck him to the ground; Anguillotto moreover at the same time received a wound in his right arm, so that being unable to hold his sword any longer he withdrew as best he could. The others did likewise; Bertino Aldobrandi was carried off the ground badly wounded. Whilst these things were happening we were all at table, for that morning we had dined more than an hour later than was our usual custom. Hearing this noise, one of those boys, the eldest, rose from the table to go and see the fray (*mistia*). He was called Giovanni, and I said to him: "For mercy's sake do not go; for in cases like this there is certain loss without any sort of gain." His father said the same thing to him: "My son, you must not go." The lad without hearing any one ran down the stairs. When he reached the Banks, where the great fray was going on, having seen Bertino carried off the ground, turning back at a run he met Cechino, my brother, who asked him what was the matter. Giovanni, though warned by some people that he should not speak of it to the said Cechino, heedlessly related how it was that Bertino Aldobrandi had been slain by the picket. My poor brother gave vent to so great a roar that it might have been heard ten miles away. Then he said to Giovanni: "Woe is me. Could you tell me which of those men has slain him?" The said Giovanni said: "Yes"; and that it was one of those who carried a two-handed sword and a blue feather in his cap. My poor brother having gone forward and having recognized the murderer by this mark, threw himself with that marvellous readiness and pluck of his into the midst of the entire picket, and without being able to restrain himself in the least, running a thrust into the vitals of that said (man), and right through to the other side, with the hilt of the sword he pressed him to the earth; then he turned upon the others with such valour and boldness that he alone was putting them all to flight; were it not that in turning round to strike an arquebusier, the man in his own defence fired off his weapon, and hit the brave but unlucky young man above the knee of the right leg: and when he came to the ground the said picket half in flight hastened to depart, lest another (warrior) similar to this one should follow it up. Hearing that tumult continue, I also rose from the table, and buckling on my sword (for everyone at that period wore one), on reaching the

Ponte Sant' Agnolo I saw a group of many persons. For which rea son going forward, having been recognized by some of them, wa was made for me, and I was shown that which I would have lea desired to see, although I was displaying the greatest curiosity t see it. When first I came up I did not recognize him, for he wa clad in different clothes from those in which I had seen him but short while before; so that he, having recognized me first, said "My dearest brother, do not let my great misfortune disturb you for my trade was one that involved such. Have me removed from here quickly, for I have but a few more hours to live." (The fact of) the case having been related to me whilst he was talking, wit that brevity which such accidents necessitate, I replied to him "Brother, this is the greatest sorrow and the greatest grief that coul occur to me in the whole course of my life; but be of good courag for before you close your eyes, you shall see your revenge wrought b my hands upon the man who has injured you." His words an mine were to this effect but (were) very brief. The picket was fift paces distant, because Maffio, who was their Bargello, had directe some of them to return to take away that corporal whom my broth had slain: so that having very quickly crossed those few paces (be tween us), wrapped and wound up in my cloak, I came right up Maffio, and most certainly I should have killed him, because the were many people there, and I had interposed myself among the with truly as much rapidity as it is possible to imagine. I had ha drawn my sword when Berlinghiero Berlinghieri, a most valia young man and my great friend, flung himself from behind upo my arms, and with him were four other young men like himse who said to Maffio: "Take yourself off, for this man alone wou have slain you." Maffio asked: "Who is he?" They replied: "H is own brother to him you see there." Not wishing to hear mo he withdrew in haste to the Torre di Nona. And they said to m

"Benvenuto! This obstacle that we have placed upon you against your will is done with a good object. Now let us go and assist him who is at the point of death." Turning round therefore we went to my brother, whom I caused to be carried into a house. A consultation of doctors being immediately held, they dressed (his wound) without agreeing to take off his leg entirely, which would perhaps have saved him. Immediately that he had been bound up there came thither Duke Lessandro, who was tending him kindly, when my brother who was still conscious, said to Duke Lessandro: "My lord! Naught grieves me more than that Your Excellency is losing a servant, than whom you may perhaps be able to find others more valiant in this profession, but none who will serve you with as much affection and fidelity as I have done." The Duke said that he must endeavor to live; for the rest he knew him very well for a worthy and brave man. Then he turned to some of his attendants, telling them that this brave young man must want for nothing. When the Duke had departed a rush of blood, which could not be staunched, was the cause of his brain giving way to such an extent that he was raving all the following night, except that when they wished to give him the communion he said: "You would have done well to have confessed me before this; now it is impossible that I can receive this Divine Sacrament in this already broken frame. Be content only that I taste of it through the divine gift of my eyes, by means of which it shall be received by my immortal soul: and that alone implores of Him Mercy and Pardon." When he had finished these words, and the Sacrament had been carried away, he immediately relapsed into the same ravings as before, which were composed of the greatest frenzies and the most horrible words that men could ever imagine: nor did he ever cease all night until day-break. When the sun was above our horizon, he turned to me and said: "Brother mine, I do not wish to stay here any longer, because these fellows

will make me do something big, by which they would have to repent having annoyed me"; and flinging out with both his legs,
which we had enclosed in a very heavy box, he shifted them after
the manner of mounting a horse: then turning his face towards me
he said three times: "Good-bye, Good-bye," and his last word
accompanied that most courageous spirit. When the proper hour
arrived, which was a little later than 22 of the clock, I had him
buried with the greatest ceremony in the Church of the Florentine;
and afterwards I caused to be made a very handsome marble slab
upon which were carved some trophies and banners. I do not wish
to omit, that, when one of his friends asked him who it was that
had fired that arquebuse, whether he would recognize him, he said:
"Yes!" and gave a description of him; and this, although my brother
had kept it from me in order that I should not learn such facts, I
had grasped very well, and I will relate the sequel in its own place.
Returning to the said tablet, certain brilliant scholars, who knew my
brother, gave me an epitaph saying that that admirable youth deserved it; and it ran as follows: *Francisco Cellino Florentino, qui
quod in teneris annis ad Joannem Medicem ducem plures victorias
retulit et signifer fuit, facile documentum dedit quantae fortitudinis
et consilii vir futurus erat, ni crudelis fati archibuso transfossus,
quinto aetatis lustro iaceret, Benvenutus frater posuit. Obiit die
xxvii Maij, MDXXIX.*

He was twenty-five years of age, and because he was called
Cecchino del Piffero (*i.e.* the son of the Fifer) by the soldiers,
whereas his proper name was Giovanfrancesco Cellini, I wished to
inscribe that real name of his, by which he was known, beneath our
coat of arms. This name I caused to be cut in very beautiful antique
characters; which I further directed to be made all broken, except
the first and the last letter. Regarding those broken letters, I was
asked by those scholars who had composed for me that beautiful

epitaph, for what reason I had made them in that way. I told them that those letters were broken because that wondrous instrument of his body was spoiled and dead; and those two complete letters, the first and the last, symbolized, the first, the memory of the great favor of that gift which God has bestowed upon us in this our Soul inspired with His Own Divinity: this could never be broken; the other complete letter, the last, stood for the glorious fame of his brave virtues. This idea pleased them very much, and since then some others have availed themselves after this fashion. Beside (the name) I caused them to carve upon the said stone our arms of Cellini, which I altered from that which is proper to us; because there are to be found in Ravenna, which is a most ancient city, Cellini of our family, most honored gentlefolk, who bear for their arms a lion rampant of a golden color upon an azure field, with a red lily held in his right paw, and the label above with three little golden lilies. This is our true Cellini Coat of Arms. My father showed me one upon which was the paw only with all the rest of the said bearings; but it would please me more to follow that of the Cellini of Ravenna above-mentioned. Returning to that Coat which I placed upon my brother's tomb, it was a lion's arm, and instead of the lily I placed a hatchet in its claw, with the field of the said Arms divided into four quarters; and that hatchet which I put (there) was only that I might not forget to do vengeance on his behalf.

I continued with the closest application to finish that work in gold for Pope Clemente which the said Pope greatly desired, and he had me summoned two or three times a week, desiring to see the said work, and his pleasure in it continually increased. And he reproved me many times, as if rebuking me for the great sadness that I experienced on account of this brother of mine; and once amongst other occasions, seeing me more depressed and pale than I should have been, he said to me: "Oh! Benvenuto, I did not know that you were mad; have you not understood before now that there is no remedy for death? You are trying to follow him." Having left the Pope I continued my work and the dies for the Mint, and for my sweetheart (*inamorata*) I had taken to courting that arquebusier, who had slain my brother. This man had formerly been a cavalry soldier, but was subsequently placed with the arquebusiers among the number of the corporals of the Bargello; and what made my anger increase the more was that he boasted after this fashion, saying: "If it were not I that had slain that brave youth, had ever so little delay occurred, he alone would have put us all to flight with great loss." I, knowing that that great fury at seeing him so often was taking from me my sleep and my appetite, and was bringing me into a bad state, though I did not care about performing so low and far from laudable an action, one evening I made up my mind to put myself out of so great a torment. The man lived in a house near to a place called the Bloody Tower (*Torre sanguigna*), alongside a house wherein was lodging one of the most popular courtezans of Rome, who was called the Lady Antea. A little while after it had rung 24 of the clock, this arquebusier was standing at his own door with his sword in his hand, and he had supped. With great wariness I approached him with a large Pistojan dagger, and as I aimed at him a back-stroke, thinking to cut his head clean off (*levargli il collo di netto*), he also turned round very quickly, so that the blow fell upon the end of the left shoulder and shattered the whole bone. Raising himself up, he dropped his sword and, bewildered with the great pain, took to running. Whereupon I following him, caught him up in four steps, and raising my dagger above his head since he was lowering it very much, the weapon penetrated exactly the bone of the neck and the middle of the nape, and it entered into both parts so deeply that I could not recover the dagger, although I made great efforts to do so; for from the said house of Antea there sprang forth four soldiers with their swords drawn in their hands, to such purpose that I was forced to draw my own sword to defend myself from them. Leaving my dagger I departed from thence, and for fear lest I should be recognized I went to the house of Duke Lessandro, which stood between the Piazza Navona and the Ritonda. When I arrived there, I caused someone to speak to the Duke, who let me know that if I were alone, I must only keep quiet and fear nothing, and that I should go on working upon the Pope's commission, which he desired so much, but that for eight days I must do my work at home: especially since those soldiers who had interfered with me had come up, with that dagger in their possession, and they were relating how the matter had come about, and the great trouble that they had had to withdraw that dagger from the neck-bone and head of the man, who was a person whom they did not know. At this moment Giovan Bandini, having come up, said to them, "This dagger is mine, and I had lent it to Benvenuto, who wished to revenge his brother." These soldiers talked a great deal upon the subject, regretting that they had interrupted me, although the revenge was amply complete. Eight days more passed by: the Pope did not send to summon me as he was accustomed to do. Then when he did send to call me by that Bolognese gentleman, his chamberlain, of whom I have already spoken, this (personage) with great courtesy informed me that the Pope knew everything, and that His Holiness was very well disposed towards me, and that I must attend to my work and remain quiet. When I reached (the presence of) the Pope, he regarded me so grimly, that his glances alone seemed to me a terrifying menace. Then on directing his attention to my work his countenance began to clear, and he praised me beyond measure, saying that I had made great progress in so short a time. Then looking me in the face he said: "Now that you are cured, Benvenuto, take care of your life";

and I, for I understood him, told him that I would do so. I opened directly a most beautiful shop near the Banks opposite to that Raffaello, and there I finished the said work in the course of a few months.

The Pope having sent me all the jewels, except the diamond, which for some necessities of his own he had pledged to certain Genoese bankers, I had all the other stones, but of this diamond I had only a cast. I employed five most excellent workmen, and besides this work I carried out many commissions; to such an extent that the shop was full of many valuables in the way of works (completed) of precious stones, and of gold and silver. I kept in the house a shaggy dog, very large and handsome, which Duke Lessandro had given me; for although this dog was excellent for the chase, because he brought me every sort of bird and other animal that I had killed with my arquebuse, he was besides most splendid as a guardian for the house. It happened at this time, in accordance with the period of life in which I then was (that is to say) at the age of twenty-nine, that I had taken as my servant-maid, a young girl of extremely beauteous form and grace, who served me as a model for the purposes of my trade. She also gratified my youthful desires with carnal pleasures. For the which reason I had my chamber a long way apart from those of my workmen, and at a good distance from the shop, connected with a little hole of a closet (*bugigattolo*) for this young maid-servant; and since I very often enjoyed myself with her, and although I have a much lighter slumber than any other man ever had upon earth, on these occasions of sexual operations it was sometimes most heavy and profound. It so happened that one night amongst others, having been watched by a thief, who, under the pretext of saying that he was a goldsmith, had cast his eyes upon those precious stones, he planned to rob me of them. For this object he broke into the shop, found a great many small works in gold and silver, and whilst proceeding further to break open some drawers to find the precious stones that he had seen, that said dog threw himself upon him, and he with difficulty defended himself from him with a sword; whereupon the dog running many times throughout the house, entered into the chambers of those workmen, which were open, since it was summer-time. Then because they would not hear that loud barking of his, he drew the blankets from off their backs; yet still they paid no attention; then seizing them first one and then another by the arms, he woke them by force, and barking in that furious manner of his showed them the way by going along before them. And when he saw that they did not want to follow him, for these traitors became displeased, volleying at the said dog with stones and sticks (and this they could do to him because it was by my orders that they should keep a light burning all night), and at last shutting their rooms tight, the dog having lost all hope of assistance from these rascals, set himself to the job by himself: and having run downstairs, not finding the thief in the shop, he overtook him; and struggling with him, had already rent his cloak and taken it from him. If it were not that he called to certain tailors for help, begging them for the love of God to assist him to protect himself from a mad dog, they believing that this was the truth, sprang out and with much difficulty drove the dog away. When day came, they (the assistants) descending into the shop, saw it broken into and open, and all the drawers forced. They began to cry out in a loud voice: "Alas! Alas!" Whereupon I hearing them, terrified at the noise, came out myself. They then coming up to me cried out: "Oh! Unhappy beings that we are, for we have been robbed by someone who has broken open and taken away everything." These words were of so great a significance, that they would not permit me to go to my own chest, to see whether the Pope's precious stones were in it: but from so great an anxiety I

entirely lost all control over myself (*ismarrito quasi afatto il lum
degli occhi*), and I told them themselves to open the chest to see how
many of those precious stones of the Pope's were missing. These
young men were all in their shirts; and when then upon opening th
chest, they saw all the stones and the gold work together with them
recovering their spirits they said to me: "There is no harm done
since the work itself and the stones are all here: although this thie
has reduced us all to our shirts; for last night, on account of the
great heat, we all undressed in the shop and left our clothes there."
My courage immediately recovered its balance, and thanking God
I said: "Go and get yourselves all clad afresh and I will pay for
everything, when I hear more at leisure how this event came about."
What grieved me most and was the cause of making me confused
and terrified so much beyond my real nature was that perhaps the
outside world would have thought that I had made up this fiction
of a thief solely in order to steal the stones myself; and because it
had been said to Pope Clemente by one of his most trusted servant
and by others (and these were Francesco del Nero, Zana de' Biliotti
his accountant, and the Bishop of Vaison and many other like per
sonages): "How is it, Most Blessed Father, that you trust so great
a treasure of precious stones to a young man, who is all ablaze, and is
more immersed in the profession of arms than in his trade, and who
is not yet thirty years of age?" Upon which the Pope inquired in
reply, if any of them knew that I had ever done anything to give
them (reason for) such a suspicion. Francescho del Nero, his treas
urer, quickly replied, saying: "No, Most Blessed Father, because he
has never had such an opportunity." To this the Pope replied: "
hold him for an entirely worthy man, and even if I saw some evil
in him, I should not believe it." This was the thing that gave me
the greatest uneasiness, and it suddenly came to my memory. When
I had given the order to the young men that they might be reclad,

took the piece of work together with the precious stones, affixing them as best I could into their places and with it I went immediately to the Pope, who had been told by Francesco Del Nero part of those rumors that he had heard regarding my shop, and had immediately aroused the Pope's suspicions. The Pope having more quickly imagined evil than the opposite, turning upon me a terrible look, said in a haughty voice: "What have you come to do here? What is it?" "Here are all your precious stones and the gold, and nothing is missing." Then the Pope, his countenance clearing, said: "So you are indeed the Welcome One (*benvenuto*)." Having shown him the piece of work, and whilst he was examining it, I recounted to him all the details of the thief and of my anxieties, and that which had been my greatest (cause of) distress. During which recital he turned many times to look me closely in the face, and since that Francesco del Nero was present, for that reason he seemed half annoyed that he had not been more sure. At last the Pope, bursting out laughing at the number of those things that I had told him, said to me: "Go and mind that you are an honest man, such as I know you to be."

WHILE I was applying myself to the said work and laboring continuously for the Mint, there began to appear throughout Rome certain false coins stamped with my own dies. They were immediately taken to the Pope; and, suspicion having fallen upon me, the Pope said to Jacopo Balducci, the Master of the Mint: "Use the greatest diligence to find the malefactor, for we know that Benvenuto is an honest man." This treacherous Master, being my enemy, said: "God grant, Most Blessed Father, that it may result as you say; since we have some doubt." At this the Pope turned to the Governor of Rome, and told him to use some exertion to find this evil-doer. During these days the Pope sent for me; then, by ingenious conversation, he led up to the subject of the money, and when well upon it he said to me: "Benvenuto, should you have the courage to coin false money?" To which I replied, that I believed that I could do it better than all the lot of those men who did occupy themselves upon so vile a business; for those who practise such vilenesses are men who neither know how to earn money, nor are they men of great skill: and if I, with my small amount of skill, have gained so much as to have saved: for when I make my dies for the Mint, every morning before I dine I succeed in earning at least three *scudi;*—for thus it was always the custom to pay for the dies of the coin, and that rascal of a Master hated me, because he would have liked to have made a better bargain;—to me it was amply sufficient that I had earned this by the grace of God and of the world; for in the coining of false money I could not arrive at earning as much. The Pope paid closest attention to my words; and whereas he had given orders that they should take particular care that I did not depart from Rome, he told them to continue their search with diligence, but to pay no attention to my movements, because he had no wish to insult me in such a fashion as to be the cause of his losing me. Those to whom he warmly gave this commission, were certain clerks of the Camera, who having employed those due exertions, because it affected them, immediately found the real culprit. It was a coiner belonging to the Mint itself, who was called by the name of Ceseri Macheroni, a Roman citizen; and along with him was arrested a metal-founder of the Mint. This same day I was passing by the Piazza Navona, having with me that fine setter (*can barbone*) of mine, when as I arrived before the door of the Bargello, my dog sprang with very great violence, barking loudly, into the doorway of the Bargello upon a youth whom a certain Donnino, a goldsmith from Parma, formerly a pupil of Caradosso, had just caused to be so detained because he had a suspicion that the fellow had robbed him. This dog of mine used such force in his desire to rend that youth, that he moved the police-officers to pity, especially since the daring young fellow defended his case with much boldness, and Donnino could not bring forward sufficient evidence, and still more from the fact that one of the corporals of the police who was present was a Genoese, and knew the father of the youth. To such purpose was it that between the dog's assault and these other circumstances, it so fell out that they were willing to let that young man depart in any case. But when I came up, and the dog, who knew no fear either of sword or cudgel, threw himself again upon that youth, they told me that unless I called my dog off, they would kill him for me. Holding back the dog to the best of my ability, as the young man drew back his cloak, there fell from the hood (*capperuccia*) certain paper packages, which Donnino recognized to be his property. I also recognized a little ring: for which reason I at once said: "This is the thief who broke into and robbed my shop, wherefore my dog recognizes him." And loosing the dog, he threw himself upon him once more: whereat the thief implored pardon of me, saying that he would give me back what he had of my property. Recovering control of the dog, he gave me back the gold, silver and rings that he had belonging to me, and twenty-five *scudi* into the bargain; then he begged mercy of me again. In reply to which I told him that he should beg mercy of God, for I would do him neither good nor evil. And having returned to my business, a few days later that Ceseri Macherone of the false money was hung near the Banks, before the door of the Mint; his comrade was sent to the galleys; the Genoese thief was hung in the Campo di Fiore: whilst I remained in higher credit as a man of worth than I was before. When I had nearly finished my piece of work, there occurred that very great inundation which deluged all Rome with water. Whilst I stood watching what was happening, the day being already far spent, it struck twenty-two of the clock, and the waters were still increasing beyond measure. And since the front part of my house and shop were in the Banks, and at the back the ground rose several *braccia*, because it faced towards Monte Giordano, so that thinking first of all of my safety, and next of my honor, I put all those precious stones about my person, and left that work in gold in the charge of those workmen of mine; and thus I descended barefoot from my windows at the back, waded through the water as best I could, until I reached Monte Cavallo, where I found Misser Giovanni Gaddi, clerk of the Camera, and Bastiano, the Venetian painter. Approaching Misser Giovanni, I gave to him all the said precious stones in order that he might keep them in safety for me: he took as great care of me as if I had been his brother. Then after a few days, when the raging of the water had abated, I returned to my shop, and completed the said work with such good luck, thanks to the Grace of God and to my own great exertions, that it was considered the most beautiful piece of workmanship that had ever been seen in Rome; to such an extent, that on carrying it to the Pope, he was unable to exhaust his praises of me; and he said: "If I were a wealthy Emperor I would give to my Benvenuto as much landed estate as his eye could range; but, though we nowadays are but poor bankrupt sovereigns, in any case we will provide him with as much daily bread as shall suffice for his small desires." Allowing the Pope to finish that torrent of words of his, I begged for the post of *bedel,* which was then vacant. To which request the Pope replied that he wished to give me something of far greater importance. I answered His Holiness that he might give me this small thing in the meantime by way of pledge. Bursting out laughing he said that he was happy (to do so), but that he did not wish me to perform the duties of the post, and that I must arrange with my fellow bedels that I should not act, he in return granting them a certain favor, which they had asked of the Pope, which was the power to recover their incomes under his authority. And thus it came about. This bedelship brought me in a little less than two hundred *scudi* per annum in income. Continuing afterwards to serve the Pope, sometimes upon one small job and sometimes upon another, he directed me to make a design for a very magnificent chalice; wherefore I made both the said design and a model. This model was of wood and wax; instead of the knop of the chalice, I had made three small figures of fair size, in full relief, which were Faith, Hope, and Charity. Then upon the foot I had placed to correspond three scenes in low relief in three circles: in one was the *Nativity of Christ,* in another the *Resurrection of Christ,* and in the third was *St. Peter crucified head downwards*: for thus was I commissioned to make it. As I progressed with this said work, the Pope wished very often to see it; so much so that, since I was aware that His Holiness had then remembered no more to give me anything, when there fell vacant (the post of) Friar of the Privy Seal Office, one evening I begged it of him. The excellent Pope, remembering no more that eager longing which he had displayed for the completion of that other work of mine, said to me: "The office of the Privy Seal brings in more than eight hundred *scudi,* so that if I gave it to you, you would spend your time scratching your stomach, and you would lose that beauteous art which you have in your hands, and I should have the blame." I replied at once that "cats of a good breed hunt the better for repletion than for starving; so that sort of honest men who are inclined to be talented set themselves to work much better when they have the means of livelihood most abundantly; wherefore Your Holiness should know that those princes who protect the greatest number of that sort of man water their talent; for by contrast, talents are born meager and scrofulous; and Your Holiness should also know that I never asked for the post with the expectation of getting it. Happy am I that I have that poor bedelship! As for this other this is just what I expected. Your Holiness will do well, since you do not wish to bestow it upon me, to give it to some talented person who deserves it, and not to some great ass who will spend his time scratching his stomach, as Your Holiness says. Take example from the honored memory of Pope

Julio, who gave this post to Bramante, that most excellent architect."
Directly I had made my obeisance I went out in great rage. Bastiano, the Venetian painter, coming forward, said: "Most Blessed
Father, may Your Holiness be willing to bestow it upon some one
who employs himself upon works of genius; and since, as Your
Holiness knows, I also labor with good will in such matters, I pray
that I may become worthy of it." The Pope answered: "This devil
of a Benvenuto will not listen to rebuke. I was disposed to give the
post to him, but it is not right of him to be so haughty with a Pope;
therefore I don't know what I shall do." The Bishop of Vaison,
immediately coming forward, begged on behalf of the said Bastiano,
saying: "Most Blessed Father, Benvenuto is young and is much
better suited to wear the sword than the friar's robe; let Your Holiness be content to give this post to this talented man Bastian; and
to Benvenuto you will perhaps be able to give something good,
which will be more suitable than this thing." Then the Pope, turning to Misser Bartolomeo Valori, said to him: "When you meet
Benvenuto, tell him on my behalf that it was really he who caused
Bastiano the painter to get the (post of) Privy Seal; and that he
remain assured that the first better post that becomes vacant shall be
his; and that in the meantime he attend to well-doing, and finish
my commissions." The next evening after, at two hours after nightfall, meeting Misser Bartolomeo Valori at the corner of the Mint (he
had two torch-bearers before him and was proceeding in haste, having been sent for by the Pope), when I saluted him, he stopped and
called me to him, and repeated to me with greatest kindness what
the Pope had told him to tell me. To which words I replied that
I should complete my work with greater diligence and application
than I had ever shown in previous work; but nevertheless without
any sort of hope of ever receiving anything from the Pope. The
said Misser Bartolomeo rebuked me, saying that I ought not to

respond in that way to the overtures of a Pope. To which I replied that by putting hope into any such words, knowing that I should not have satisfaction in any way whatsoever, I should be an idiot to reply otherwise; and leaving him, I went away to attend to my own business. The said Misser Bartolomeo must have repeated to the Pope my bold words, and perhaps more that I did not say, to such purpose that the Pope passed more than two months before sending for me, and during this time I was never inclined to go to the Palace on any account. The Pope, inasmuch as he longed for that piece of work, commissioned Misser Ruberto Pucci that he should take a little notice of what I was doing. This worthy fellow came to see me every day, and always made some amiable remark to me and I to him. When the time drew near that the Pope wished to start on his way to Bologna, then at length, perceiving that I would not go thither of my own accord, he caused me to learn through the said Misser Ruberto, that I must take my work to him, for he wished to see how far I had got on with it. Wherefore I took it to him, and pointing out that all the important part of the said work was completed, I begged him that he would leave me five hundred *scudi;* partly on account for the work done, and partly because I very greatly needed gold, so that I might be able to complete the said work. The Pope said to me: "Attend, attend to its completion." Taking my leave, I replied that I would finish it if he would let me have the money. With that I went away. The Pope having started for Bologna left Cardinal Salvigna Legate of Rome, and left him directions to hurry me on with this said work; and he said to him: "Benvenuto is a person who esteems his own talents but slightly, and us less; therefore see that you urge him on, so that I may find it finished." This beast of a Cardinal sent for me at the end of eight days, telling me to bring along the work; to whom I went without it. When I arrived, this Cardinal immediately said to

me: "Where is that hotch-potch (*cipollata*) of yours? Have you
finished it?" To which I replied: "Oh! my most reverend lord, I
have not finished my hotch-potch, nor shall I finish it unless you
give me onions to finish it with." At these words the said Cardinal,
who had more the face of an ass than of a man, became half as ugly
again; and coming at once to the point of the matter (*a meza
spada*), said: "I will send you to a galley and then you will have the
grace to finish your job." Dealing with this beast, I became a beast
also, and I said to him: "My lord, when I shall commit crimes
which merit the galley, then you shall put me there; but for these
faults I have no fear of your galley: and I say more, that because of
your lordship, I will never complete the work further: and don't
send for me any more, for I will never come into your presence again
unless indeed you compel me to come with your police." The good
Cardinal kindly made some attempts to make me understand that I
ought to set to work, and that I ought to bring it to show to him;
so much so that I said to those (messengers) of his: "Tell my lord to
send me the onions, if he wishes me to complete the hotch-potch."
Nor did I ever answer in other words, so that he abandoned this lost
cause. The Pope returned from Bologna, and immediately asked
about me, why that Cardinal had previously written the worst account he could of my case. The Pope, being in the greatest fury
that it is possible to imagine, let me know that I must go to him
with the work. I did so. During the time that the Pope stayed in
Bologna I had developed an inflammation in my eyes, with so much
pain that for anguish I could scarcely live, so that this was the principal reason that I had not progressed with the work; and so severe
was the ailment that I thought that I should most certainly become
blind; so much so that I had made up a reckoning how much would
suffice for me to live on when quite blind. Whilst I was on my way
to the Pope, I thought out the method that I could employ to make

my excuses for not having been able to carry forward the work; I thought that whilst the Pope was looking at it and examining it I could relate to him the facts; which opportunity did not occur for me, because when I reached him, he immediately said with coarse expressions: "Give me here that work; is it finished?" I uncovered it; immediately with greater fury he said: "In God's truth I tell you, that you make a boast of not caring for anyone, but if it were not for my honor before the world I would have you, together with your work, cast out of yonder windows." Wherefore I, seeing that the Pope had become so very bad a beast, endeavored to withdraw myself from his presence. Whilst he continued to bully me, having placed my work under my cloak, I mutteringly said: "The whole world would not make a blind man able to execute such works as these." Loudly raising his voice, the Pope shouted: "Come here. What do you say?" I remained in two minds whether to rush hastily down the stairs; then I took a resolution and throwing myself upon my knees, and shouting loudly, because he did not cease to shout,—I said: "And if I am become blind through an infirmity, am I obliged to work?" To this he replied: "You have had sufficient sight to come hither, nor do I believe that any of those things that you say are the truth." To which I, noticing that he had somewhat lowered his voice, replied: "Your Holiness may ask his doctor, and he will find out the truth." He said: "More at leisure we will find out if it be as you say." Then seeing that he was paying attention to me, I said: "I do not believe that there be any other cause of this my great misfortune than Cardinal Salviati, for he sent for me directly after Your Holiness had departed, and when I reached him, applied to my work the name of a 'hotch-potch,' and told me that he would make me finish it in a galley; and such was the power of those ill-natured words, that from extreme passion I immediately felt my face flame up, and there came into my eyes a heat so immeasurable that I could not find the way to return home: a few days later there fell upon my eyes two cataracts: for which reason I saw no light at all, and from that time I have not been able to work at all upon Your Holiness' order." Rising from my knees I went away (*andai con dio*); and it was reported to me that the Pope said: "Even if one gives commissions to people, one cannot supply discretion with them; I did not tell the Cardinal to use so much violence; for if it is true that he has an affection of the eyes, which I will find out through my physician, he would be entitled to some compassion." There was there present a nobleman of high rank, a special friend of the Pope's, and a very honorable man. When he asked the Pope what sort of a man I was, saying: "Most Blessed Father, I am asking you this since it appeared to me that you have been at one and the same time in the greatest rage that I ever saw you in, and in the greatest (state of) compassion: wherefore on this account I ask Your Holiness, who is this man? for if he is a person who deserves to be assisted, I will show him a prescription (*seghreto*) to enable him to cure that ailment;" the Pope replied as follows. "That is the greatest man that was ever born in his profession; and one day when we are together I will let you see some of his wonderful works, and him along with them; and it will be a pleasure to me to see if any cure can be found for him." Three days later the Pope sent for me after dinner, and this nobleman was there present. Directly I arrived, the Pope caused that Morse of mine to be brought. In the meantime I had produced that Chalice of mine; whereat that nobleman said that he had never seen so marvellous a piece of work. When the Morse arrived his astonishment was much more increased. Looking me in the face he said: "He is still young to know so much, and he is also very fitted to acquire more knowledge." Then he asked me my name. To which I replied: "Benvenuto is my name." He answered: "Welcome (*Benvenuto*) shall I be to you this time;

take some corn-flowers (*fioralisi*) with their stems, flowers and roots all together, then proceed to distil them over a slow fire, and with that liquid bathe your eyes several times a day, and you will most certainly be cured of this ailment; but you must previously take a purge, and then continue (to use) the said water." The Pope addressed me some kindly words; so that I went away partially happy. And it was the truth that I had acquired the ailment; but I believe that I caught it from that handsome young servant-girl whom I was keeping at the time that I was robbed. That Gallic disease proceeded to develop itself for more than four whole months, then it covered my entire body at once: it was not after the manner that one sees in other cases, but it seemed that I was covered with certain small red blisters, as large as farthings. The doctors would never style it the *French disease,* though I told them the reasons why I believed it to be such. I continued to doctor myself according to their methods, and gained no advantage thereby. Then however at last having resolved to take *lignum* against the advice of those principal doctors of Rome, I took this *lignum* with all the precaution and abstinence that it is possible to imagine, and in a few days I felt a very vast improvement; to such an extent that at the end of fifty days I was cured and healthy as a fish. Then, in order to give myself some recreation for that great strain that I had endured, as winter came on for my amusement I took to shooting (*la caccia della scoppietto*), which entailed my going through water and wind, and standing in bogs; to such an extent that in a few days my illness returned one hundred times worse than I had it at first. Submitting myself again into the hands of the doctors, and though continually treated, I grew always worse. Fever coming upon me, I was disposed to take *lignum* again: the doctors did not wish it, saying that if I began it with the fever upon me, in eight days I should die. I determined to do so against their wishes; and keeping to the same regulations that I had observed on the previous occasion, when I had drunk for four days of this blessed water of *lignum,* the fever went away entirely. I began to experience a very great improvement (in health), and during this time that I was taking the said *lignum* I was always progressing with the models for that piece of work: and during that period of abstinence I made the most beautiful articles, and those of the rarest invention that I ever made in my life. At the end of fifty days I was thoroughly cured, and thenceforward with the greatest diligence I gave my attention to securing my health for the future.

Then when I had come out from that long fast I found myself as free from my ailments as if I had been reborn. Although I took pleasure in securing that desired health of mine, I did not also cease from working; in so much that to that said work and to the Mint, to each of them I most certainly gave that share of (my attention) which was due to them.

I T chanced that that said Cardinal Salviati who had against me that great hatred above related was made Legate of Parma. There was arrested in Parma a certain Milanese goldsmith, a coiner of false money, who by name was called Tobbia. Being condemned to the gallows and to the stake, the matter was spoken of to the said Legate, and he was represented to him as a very able craftsman. The said Cardinal caused the execution of the penalty to be suspended, and wrote to Pope Clemente, saying that there had fallen into his hands the ablest man in the world in the gold-smiths' trade; and that he had just been condemned to the gallows and to the stake for being a coiner of false money; but that this man was a simple and good fellow, for he said that he had asked the opinion of a confessor of his, who he said had given him permission to enable him to do it (*i.e., to coin the false money*). He added further: "If you make this able man come to Rome, Your Holiness will be able to lower that mighty insolence of your Benvenuto, and I am very sure that the labors of this Tobbia will please you much more than those of Benvenuto." Where-fore the Pope made him come immediately to Rome. And then when he had arrived, summoning us both thither, he directed each of us to make a design for (mounting) an unicorn's horn, the finest that was ever seen; it was sold for seventeen thousand ducats of the Camera. The Pope, desirous of presenting it to King Francis, was inclined in the first place to adorn it richly with gold, and commissioned us both to make the said designs.

When we had done so, we each of us carried our design to the Pope. The design of Tubbia was in the fashion of a candlestick, wherein was imbedded that fine horn after the fashion of a candle; and on the foot of this said candlestick he made four little heads of the unicorns with very common-place taste; so that when I saw the thing I could not restrain myself from laughing discreetly. The Pope observed this and immediately said: "Show me your design;" which was merely the head of the unicorn; in correspondence with that said horn I had fashioned the finest kind of head that it is possible to see; for I had taken it partly from the conformation of the head of the horse, and partly from that of the stag, enriched with the most beautiful sort of mane and other decorations, such that immediately mine was seen every one gave it the palm. But since there were present at this contest certain Milanese personages of very great influence, these people said: "Most Blessed Father, Your Holiness is sending this handsome object as a gift into France; do you know that the French are coarse men, and will not recognize the excellence of this work of Benvenuto; but these pyxes will please them as well, which, moreover, will be made much more quickly; and Benvenuto will attend to the completion of your Chalice, and you will cause two works of art to be made at one and the same time; and this poor man, whom you have made to come hither, will also arrive at some employment." The Pope, anxious to have his Chalice, lent himself very willingly to the advice of those Milanese; so that the next day he commissioned the work on that unicorn's horn to Tubbia, and let me know through his Keeper of the Wardrobe that I must finish his Chalice. To which order I replied that I desired no other thing in the world than to complete that fine work of mine; but that if it had been of any other material than gold I could easily finish it unassisted; but since it was in fact of gold, it was necessary that His Holiness should give me some, if he desired that I should be able to finish it. At these words this low-born courtier said: "Dear me (*Oime*)! Don't ask for gold from the Pope, or you will make him fly into such a rage that it will be woe, woe to you." Upon which I said: "Oh! Sir You (*misser voi*)! your lordship! teach me a little how one can make bread without flour? In the same way without gold one can never finish that work." This Keeper of the Wardrobe said to me, for it seemed to him that I had somewhat made sport of him, that he would repeat all that I had said to the Pope; and so he did. The Pope, flying into the fury of a wild animal, said that he would wait and see whether I was such a madman as not to finish it. Thus two months passed by, and although I had said that I would not do a stroke to it, I had not acted thus, but rather I had continually labored upon it with the greatest devotion. Seeing that I did not bring it to him he began to look upon me with much disfavor, saying that he would punish me anyhow. There was present when he said this a Milanese jeweller of his. This man was named Pompeo, and he was near relative of a certain Misser Traiano, the most highly favored servitor that Pope Clemente had. These two by agreement said to the Pope: "If Your Holiness were to take the Mint from him, perhaps you will make the desire come to him of finishing the Chalice." Then the Pope said: "Rather two evil things would occur, the one that I should be badly served at my Mint, which is of so much importance to me, and the other that I should most certainly never have the Chalice." These two said Milanese, observing that the Pope was badly disposed towards me, at last prevailed so much that he took from me the Mint, and gave it to a certain young Perugian, who for a nickname was called "Fagiuolo." That Pompeo came to me on behalf of the Pope to tell me that His Holiness had taken from me the

A gold and enamel salt-cellar made by Cellini for King Francis I of France, now in the collection of the Vienna Art Museum. The male figure, representing the sea, presides over its product, the salt. The female figure, representing earth, has at her right hand a receptacle for pepper.

Mint, and that if I did not finish the Chalice he would take from me other things. To this I replied: "Tell His Holiness that he has taken the Mint away from himself and not from me, and that the same thing will occur with regard to those other things; and that when His Holiness wishes to give it back to me, I shall on no account be willing to retake it." To this wretched and unlucky fellow it seemed a thousand years ere he reached the Pope to repeat to him all these things and something of his own that he put into my mouth. Eight days later the Pope sent this same man to tell me he no longer wished me to finish that Chalice, and that he wished for it exactly in that state and at that point to which I had brought it. To this Pompeo I answered: "This is not a thing like the Mint which can be taken from me; but it is true that the five hundred *scudi* which I had belong to His Holiness; these I will immediately give up to him; but the work itself is mine, and I will do with it as I please." Pompeo ran off immediately to report this, together with certain other biting words that I had with just cause levelled at himself. About three days after, one Thursday, there came to me two of His Holiness' most favorite chamberlains, one of whom is even now alive, for he is a bishop, who was called Misser Pier Giovanni, and he was Keeper of the Wardrobe to His Holiness; the other man was of even higher lineage than this one, but I do not remember his name. Having come to me they spake thus: "The Pope has sent us, Benvenuto: he says that, since you are not willing to understand him by the more easy method, you must either give up to us his piece of work, or we take you to prison." Then I looked them most cheerfully in the face, saying: "My lords, if I were to give this piece of work to His Holiness, I should be giving up my own work and not his, and as yet I do not wish to give him my work; for having brought it so very forward by my own great labors, I do not wish it to fall into the hands of some ignorant beasts, who with but little effort would spoil it." There was present when I said this that goldsmith called Tobbia above-mentioned, who presumptuously demanded from me even the models for this work;—the expressions worthy of such a rogue which I uttered to him it is not necessary to repeat here.—But since those lords of the Chamber pressed me that I should hasten (to do) whatever I wished to do, I told them that I was ready. Having taken up my cloak, before I left my workshop, I turned myself, with great reverence and with my cap in my hand, towards an image of Christ, and said: "Oh! Benign and Immortal One! Our Just and Holy Lord! All things that Thou doest are according to Thy Justice, which is without equal. Thou knowest that I have just reached in my life the age of thirty years, nor up to now have I ever been threatened with imprisonment for anything. Since now Thou willest that I go to prison, I give Thee thanks with all my heart." Then turning myself to the two chamberlains, I spoke thus with a certain somewhat lowering look: "A personage like me deserved police-officers of no less importance than your lordships. Set me therefore between you and take me as your prisoner wheresoever you like." Those two most courteous men burst out laughing, set me between them, and, continuing to chat agreeably, they conducted me to the Governor of Rome, who was called Maghalotto. When we arrived, there was with him the Procurator Fiscal. They were waiting for me, and those chamberlains still laughing said to the Governor: "We consign to you this prisoner, and do you take good care of him. We are very glad to have taken this duty from your followers, because Benvenuto has told us that since this is his first arrest, he did not deserve police-officers of lesser importance than we are." Departing immediately they went to the Pope, and when they told him everything exactly, at first he showed signs of wishing to fly into a passion, but he afterwards forced himself to laugh because there were present some lords and cardinals, friends of mine, who greatly favored me. Meantime the Governor and the Fiscal partly bullied me, partly exhorted me, partly counselled me, saying that it was reasonable that a person who had ordered another man to do a piece of work could retake it of his own accord, and in any way that might be pleasing to him. To which arguments I replied that justice did not warrant this, nor could a Pope do it; for he (Clement VII) was not a Pope of that nature of which are certain little tyrant lordings (*signoretti tirannelli*), who do the worst they can to their people, observing neither law nor justice; a Vicar of Christ, however, could do none of these things. Then the Governor with some of his police-agent's (*birreschi*) manners and expressions said: "Benvenuto! Benvenuto! You are going about seeking that I should treat you as you deserve." "You will treat me with honor and courtesy if you desire to treat me as I deserve." Again he said: "Send for the piece of work at once, and see that you do not wait for a second command." At this I said: "My lords, grant me the favor that I may yet say four words in my own defense." The Fiscal, who was a much more discreet police-agent than was the Governor, turned to the Governor and said: "My lord, grant him the favor of one hundred words; so long as he gives up the piece of work, that will be quite enough for us." I said: "If there were any sort of man who directed a house or a palace to be built, he could justly say to the master-workman who was building it, 'I do not wish you to work any further upon my house or upon my palace'; and after paying him for his labors justly he could dismiss him. If also it were a nobleman who had ordered the setting of a precious stone worth one thousand *scudi,* when he saw that the jeweller was not serving him according to his wishes he could say, 'Give me back my precious stone, for I do not like your work.' But in this particular case there are none of these arguments; because it is neither a house nor a precious stone; nothing further can be required of me, except that I return the five hundred *scudi* that I have received. Therefore, my lords, do whatever you can, there is nothing to be had from me except the five hundred *scudi*. Tell the Pope so. Your threats cause me no fear at all; for I am an honest man, and have no fear of my own faults." The Governor and the Fiscal rising, told me that they were going to the Pope, and that they would return with his commands, which would be woe to me. So I remained under guard. I walked up and down a hall; and they stayed nearly three hours ere they returned from the Pope. During this time there came to visit me all the aristocracy of our tribe of merchants imploring me earnestly that I would not continue to dispute with a Pope, because it might be my ruin. To whom I replied that I was very thoroughly resolved as to what I wanted to do. Directly the Governor, in company with the Fiscal, returned from the Palace, causing me to be summoned, he spoke to this effect: "Benvenuto, I am certainly not pleased that I have returned from the Pope with a command such as I have received; therefore you must either find the piece of work at once or think about arranging your affairs." Whereupon I replied that "since I had never believed up to that time that a holy Vicar of Christ could perform an act of injustice, I should like to see it before I believed it; do therefore whatever you are able." The Governor then rejoined, saying: "I have to say two other words to you on behalf of the Pope, and then I will proceed with the commission given to me. The Pope says that you are to bring the piece of work here, and that I am to see it placed in a box and to seal it, then I am to carry it to the Pope, who promises on his oath not to break the enclosure under its own seal, but immediately to restore it to you; but this he wishes to have done in this way in order to secure also the question of his own honor." To these words I laughingly replied that I would very willingly give up my work after the manner in which he proposed, because I would like to know how to reckon what was the worth of a Pope's oath. And therefore, having sent for my work, I gave it over to him sealed up after the manner that he proposed. The Governor having returned to the Pope with the said work in the said condition, the Pope took the box, according to what the said Governor reported to me, turned it over several times; then he asked the Governor if he had seen it; who replied that he had seen it, and that in his presence it had been sealed up in that way; then he added that the thing had seemed to him very wonderful. Wherefore the Pope said: "Tell Benvenuto that the Popes have the power of loosing and binding far greater things than this"; and whilst he said these words with some little annoyance he opened the box, removing the strings and the seal wherewith it was bound; then he regarded it very carefully, and from what I gathered showed it to that goldsmith Tubbia, who praised it much. Then the Pope asked him if he had the courage to make a work of that sort; the Pope told him that he must follow that pattern exactly; then he turned to the Governor and said to him: "See if Benvenuto will give it up; for if he will thus relinquish it he shall be paid the entire price at which it is valued by men of knowledge (in these things); or if indeed he is willing to finish it let him fix a term (for its completion); and if you see that he is willing to do so, let those reasonable accommodations that he asks for be given to him." Then the Governor said: "Most Blessed Father, I that know the terrible nature of that young man, grant me authority that I may be able to give him a good scolding after my own fashion." To this the Pope answered that he could do what he pleased as regards words, although he was certain that it would only make (the matter) worse; then when he saw that there was nothing else could be done, he must tell me to take his five hundred *scudi* to that Pompeo his jeweller above-mentioned. The Governor having returned, causing me to be summoned into his chamber, with one of his fierce looks said to me: "Popes have authority to loose and to bind the whole world, and such acts are immediately ratified in Heaven as well done; behold therefore your work unloosed and inspected by His Holiness." Whereupon I immediately raised my voice and said: "I thank God that I now know how to reckon the value of the oath of Popes." At that the Governor spoke to me and used many immoderate blusterings, and then perceiving that they profited him naught, in despair altogether at the business, he recovered a somewhat suaver manner and said to me: "Benvenuto, it distresses me very much that you will not understand your own advantage; go then and take your five hundred *scudi* when you like to the above-mentioned Pompeo." Taking up my work I went away and immediately carried the five hundred *scudi* to that Pompeo. And because perhaps the Pope, thinking that for inconvenience or for some other reason I would not have brought the money so soon, and desirous of reuniting the thread of my servitude, when he saw that Pompeo came into his presence smiling with the money in his hand, the Pope covered him with abuse, and lamented very much that the matter should have turned out in this way; then he said: "Go and find Benvenuto at his workshop and show him as many civilities as your ignorant animal nature (*bestialità*) is capable of, and tell him that if he would like to finish that work to form a reliquary for me to carry therein the Host (*Corpus Domini*) when I go with it in procession, I will give him the accommodation that he desires to finish it; provided that he works." Pompeo coming to me, called me outside the workshop, and paid me the most repulsive asinine compliments, telling me all that the Pope had commissioned him. To which I replied at once, that "the greatest treasure that I could desire in the world was to have recovered the favor of so great a Pope, which had been lost for me, and not through my own fault, but indeed through the misfortune of my own overpowering ailment, and through the wickedness of those envious men who took pleasure in making mischief; and since the Pope has an abundance of servitors, don't let him send you round again, for your safety's sake; for mind well your own business. I shall never fail neither by day nor by night to consider how to do all that I can in the service of the Pope; and remember well that when you have related this of me to the Pope, that you do not interfere in any sort of way in any of my affairs, for I will make you remember your mistakes with the punishment that they deserve." This man related everything to the Pope in much more beastly terms than I had employed to him. Thus the matter rested for a space, and I attended to my workshop and my own business.

THAT goldsmith Tobbia above-mentioned attended to the
completion of the garniture and ornamentation of that unicorn's horn; and the Pope had besides told him to begin the
chalice according to that same fashion that he had seen mine.
And when he began to have exhibited to him by the said Tobbia
what he had done, finding himself ill-satisfied, he grieved very
much that he had broken with me in regard to it, and blamed the
work of that craftsman and those who had introduced him; and
Baccino della Croce came many times to tell me on behalf of the
Pope that I ought to make that reliquary. To whom I replied
that I begged His Holiness that he would let me rest on account
of the severe illness that I had had, from which I was not yet
wholly free; but that I would demonstrate to His Holiness that
of those hours during which I could work I would spend all in
his service. I had set myself to make his portrait, and I was
making a medal in secret; and those steel dies for stamping this
said medal I was making at home; and in my shop I kept a partner who had been my shop-lad, who was named Felice. At that
time, as young men do, I was enamoured of a young Sicilian girl,
who was very beautiful; and when she also showed that she liked

me very much, her mother perceived the circumstance, suspecting
that which could have occurred (this was that I had been planning
for a year to elope with the said girl to Florence, very secretly from
her mother): she having become aware of this fact, departed one
night secretly from Rome and went in the direction of Naples;
and, giving out that she was going by Civita vechia, she went by
Ostia. I went after them to Civita vechia, and committed innumerable follies to find her again. Such matters would be too
long to narrate here precisely; it is sufficient to say that I was on
the point of either going mad or dying. At the end of two months
she wrote to me that she was in Sicily very unhappy. In the meantime I had given myself up to all the pleasures that it is possible to
imagine, and had taken up another love-affair, if only to extin-
guish that one.

It happened to me through certain curious chances (*diverse
stravaganze*) that I formed a friendship with a certain Sicilian
priest, who was of a very lofty genius and very learned in Greek
and Latin literature. It occurred on one occasion in the course of
a conversation, that he chanced to speak of the Art of Necromancy,
regarding which I said that I had had throughout the whole
course of my life a very great desire to see or hear something of
this Art. To which remarks the priest rejoined: "That man who
enters upon such an undertaking has need of brave and firm
courage." I answered that of bravery and firmness of courage I
should excel could I only find the means of carrying the matter
out. Thereupon the priest answered: "If you have sufficient courage for this thing, I will satisfy you in all the rest." Thus we
were in agreement to commence such an enterprise. The said
priest one evening amongst others got everything in order and
told me that I must find a companion or two. I invited Vincentio
Romoli my very great friend, and he (the priest) brought with

him a man from Pistoia, who also studied Necromancy. Proceeding to the Coliseum (*Culiseo*), the priest having robed himself there after the manner of necromancers, set himself to drawing circles on the ground with the most elaborate ceremonial that it is possible to imagine in the world; and he had made us bring precious essences and materials for lighting a fire, and besides some evil-smelling drugs. When all was in readiness, he made the entrance into the circle; and taking us by the hand one by one he set us within the circle; then he allotted our duties; he gave the pentacle into the hand of that other necromancer his companion, to us others the care of the fire for the perfumes; then he betook himself to his incantations. This business lasted more than an hour and a half; there appeared several legions (of spirits), to such an extent that the Coliseum was quite full of them. I was looking after the precious perfumes, when the priest became aware that there were so large a number present, and turning to me said: "Benvenuto, ask them some question." I told them to cause me to be with my Sicilian Angelica. On that night we received no answer; but I took the very greatest satisfaction from it so that I became very keen about such matters. The necromancer said that it would be necessary for us to go another time, and that I should be satisfied in respect of all that I asked, but that he wished me to take with me a little virgin lad. I took one of my shop-boys, who was about twelve years old, and I invited again that said Vincentio Romoli; and a certain Agniolino Gaddi, because he was our intimate companion, we took also to this affair. When we arrived again at the appointed spot, the necromancer having made the same preparations with that same and even more wonderful precision, set us within the circle, which he had again made with more wondrous art and more wondrous ceremonies; then to that friend of mine Vincentio he gave the charge of the perfumes

and of the fire; and he (Vincentio) took with him the said Agniolino Gaddi; then he put the pentacle into my hand, which he told
me I must turn in the direction of those places where he pointed
out to me, and beneath the pentacle I stationed that little lad, my
shop-boy. The necromancer commencing to utter those very terrible invocations, summoned by name a great number of those
demons, heads of those legions (of spirits), and commanded them
by the Virtue and Power of God, the Uncreate, the Ever-Living and
the Eternal, in the Hebrew language, and very frequently besides
in Greek and Latin; to such purpose that in a short space of time
they filled the whole Coliseum one hundred times more than
they had that first time. Vincentio Romoli, together with that
said Agniolino attended to keeping up the fire, and to the vast
quantity of precious perfumes. I, by the advice of the necromancer,
again asked that I might be with Angelica. The necromancer
turning to me said: "Do you hear what they have told you? That
within the space of one month you will be where she is," and he
added again, that he begged me to keep steady, for the legions
were a thousand times more than he had summoned, and that
they were of the most harmful (kind); and since they had carried
out what I had asked for, it was necessary to be civil to them; and
patiently get rid of them. On the other hand the lad who was
beneath the pentacle, in greatest terror said, that there were in
that place a million of the fiercest men who were all threatening
us: he said besides that there had appeared four enormous giants,
and they were armed, and showed signs of wishing to attack us.
Upon this the necromancer, who was trembling with fright, endeavored with suave and gentle manner the best he could to get
rid of them. Vincentio Romoli, who was trembling violently,
looked after the perfumes. I, who had as much fear as the rest
of them, endeavored to show less, and was inspiring them all

with the most marvellous courage; but I was certain that I was a dead man on account of the terror which I saw in the necromancer himself. The lad had placed his head between his knees, saying: "I wish to die like this, for we are all dead men." Again I said to the lad: "These creatures are all inferior to us, and what you see is but smoke and shadow; therefore raise your eyes." When he had raised his eyes, he cried out again: "The whole Coliseum is on fire, and the fire is coming down upon us;" and putting his hands to his face, he said again that he was dead, and that he did not wish to see any more. The necromancer implored me, begging me that I would keep steady, and that I would direct them to make fumes of assafoetida: so turning to Vincentio Romoli I told him to quickly burn some assafoetida. Whilst I was telling him this, I was looking at Agniolino Gaddi, who was so terrified that the pupils of his eyes were starting out for he was more than half dead, so I said to him: "Agniolo, in these situations one should not be afraid, but should give oneself to action and to being of assistance; therefore put on quickly some of that assafoetida." The said Agniolo, in that moment that he wanted to move, made a flatulent trumpeting with so great an abundance of excrement as was much more powerful than the assafoetida. The lad at that horrible stench and that noise raised his face a little, on hearing me laugh a bit, and his fear being a trifle assuaged, he said that they were beginning to depart in great haste. Thus we continued up to the time when they began to ring for matins. Again the lad told us that but few remained, and those at a distance. When the necromancer had completed all the remainder of his cere- monies, having unrobed and repacked a great bundle of books that he had brought, we all together issued with him from the circle, huddling ourselves one beneath another; especially the lad, who was placed in the middle, and had taken hold of the necromancer by his robe and of me by my cloak; and continually whilst we were going towards our homes near the Banks, he kept on telling us that two of those (spirits), whom he had seen in the Coliseum were going skipping along (*saltabeccando*) in front of us, sometimes running above upon the roofs, and sometimes along the ground. The necromancer said that in all the very many times that he had entered the magic circles, so great an adventure had never occurred to him, and he tried to persuade me to consent to join with him in enchanting a book, from which we should derive infinite wealth, because we should demand of the demons that they should show us some of the treasures of which the earth is full, and by that means we should become very rich; and that these love-affairs were vanity and crazinesses which did not amount to anything. I told him that if I knew the Latin language I would very willingly do such a thing. Nevertheless he continued to persuade me, saying that the Latin language would serve me to no purpose, and that if he had desired he could have found many persons well-instructed in Latin; but that he had never found anyone of as sound a courage as I had, and that I ought to listen to his counsel. With these discussions we arrived at our homes, and each one of us dreamed devils the whole of that night. And meeting again the next day, the necromancer pressed me that I should pay attention to that undertaking; wherefore I asked him what time would be required to carry out such a business, and whither we should have to go. To this he replied that in less than one month we should conclude the matter, and that the place most adapted for it was in the mountains of Norcia; although one of his teachers had performed such an enchantment near here at a place called the Badia di Farfa; but that he had had some difficulty, which would not occur in the mountains of Norcia; and that those Norcian peasants are trustworthy persons, and have some practice in this kind of thing, to such purpose that they can in a case of necessity render a wonderful amount of assistance. This priestly necromancer had most certainly persuaded me so much that I was willingly disposed to do this thing, but I said that I wanted first to finish those medals that I was making for the Pope, and I confided about them to this said man and to no one else, begging that he would keep them secret. I continually asked him, however, if he believed that at the time indicated I should find myself with my Sicilian Angelica, and seeing that the time was drawing very near, it seemed to me a very remarkable thing that I did not hear anything of her. The necromancer assured me that I should most certainly find myself where she was, because they (the spirits) never fail, when they make promises in the manner that they had then done; but that I must remain with my eyes open, and guard myself against any misfortune that might happen to me in that connection, and that I must strengthen myself to endure something against my own natural disposition, because he foresaw a very great danger therein; and that it would be a good thing for me if I went with him to enchant the book, for by that means that great danger of mine would pass away, and it would be the cause of making myself and him very lucky. I, although I was beginning to have more desire to do this than he had, said to him that, because there had come to Rome a certain master Giovanni da Castel Bolognese, a very able craftsman in the execution of medals of the same sort that I made in steel, therefor I desired nothing in the world so much as to enter into competition with this brilliant man, and to issue upon the world with such an undertaking; by the which I hoped, through its great merit and not by the sword, to confound those several enemies of mine. This man, however, continued saying to me: "For mercy's sake, Benvenuto mine, come with me and escape a great danger that I discern for you." Whilst I was disposed in all ways and by all means to wish to finish my medal first we were already nigh upon the end of the month; wherefore since I was so wrapped up in my medal I remembered nothing else, neither Angelica, nor any other such thing, but I was wholly intent upon my work. One day amongst the rest, near the hour of vespers I had occasion to repair, outside my regular hours, from my house to my workshop; for I had my workshop at the Banks and I occupied a cottage behind the Banks, and went very rarely to the workshop; for all the regular business I left in the hands of that partner of mine who was named Felice. Whilst I was thus a little while in the workshop I remembered that I had to go and speak to Lessandro del Bene. Rising immediately and reaching the Banks, I met a certain great friend of mine, who was called by name Ser Benedetto. This man was a notary and had been born in Florence, the son of a blind man, who begged alms, and who was a Sienese. This Ser Benedetto had lived many many years in Naples; then he had returned to Rome, and acted for certain merchants of the Chigi family. And since that partner of mine had many and many a time asked for certain sums of money, that he should have had from him for some rings that he had entrusted to him, on this particular day, meeting him at the Banks he demanded his money in a rather rough manner, which was his custom. Now the said Ser Benedetto was in company with his employers; so that they seeing him do that thing in such a way, scolded severely that Ser Benedetto, saying that they would like to be served by some one else, so as not to have to hear any more of such yelpings. This Ser Benedetto tried to defend himself with them as best he could, and asserted that he had paid that goldsmith, and that he was not accustomed to curb the rage of mad people. The said Sienese took that expression in bad part and promptly drove him away. Departing then, he was going in haste to my workshop, perhaps to do some injury to the said Felice. It chanced that just in the middle of the Bank quarter, we met together: whereupon I, for I knew nothing about it, according to my accustomed manner, saluted him most civilly; he replied to me with many insulting words. For the which reason there occurred to me all that the necromancer had said to me; to such purpose that, keeping a bridle as much as I was able upon that which with his words the said man was urging me to do, I said: "Ser Benedetto my brother, do not try to vent your rage upon me, for I have done you no injury, and I know nothing of these affairs of yours; and since in all this you have to do with Felice, kindly go and finish it with him; for he knows very well how to answer you; wherefore, since I know nothing about the matter, you do me wrong in railing at me in this fashion, especially since you know that I am not the man to bear insults." At this the said man said, that I did know everything and that he was a man able to make me bear a greater burden than that, and that Felice and I were two great blackguards. Already there were assembled many persons to watch this contest. Goaded by his ugly words, I quickly stooped down to the ground and took up a lump of mud (*un mozo di fango*) (for it had been raining) and I took it hastily in my hand to give him a volley in the face. He lowered his head, in such a way that with it I struck him upon the crown of his head. Within this mud was embedded a piece of hard stone with many sharp angles, and catching him with one of these angles upon the crown of his head he fell swooning to the ground like one dead; for seeing such an abundance of blood, it was thought by all the bystanders that he was dead. Whilst this said man was still upon the ground, and some people were giving orders to have him carried away, there passed by that jeweller Pompeo already spoken of above. The Pope had sent for this

man to give him some commissions for precious stones. Seeing
that man in bad case, he asked who had given him the blow.
Wherefore it was told to him: "Benvenuto has given it him because the animal sought for it." The said Pompeo hurriedly coming into the Pope's presence said to him: "Most Blessed Father,
Benvenuto has just now (*adesso adesso*) slain Tubbia; for I have
seen it with my own eyes." At this the Pope infuriated gave commission to the Governor, who was there present, that he should
arrest me, and that he should hang me immediately upon the spot
where the homicide had been committed; and that he must use
every diligence to catch me, and not to appear before him until he
had hanged me. When I saw that I had brought this unlucky
man to the ground, I immediately bethought me of my own interests, recalling the power of my enemies, and what could be
brought forth by such an event. Departing thence, I withdrew
myself to the house of Misser Giovanni Gaddi, Clerk of the Camera,
desiring to set my affairs in order with the most expedition, so that
I could be off right away (*con dio*). On this head the said Misser
Giovanni counselled me that I should not be in such haste to get
away, for perhaps it might be that the danger was not so great
as it appeared to me: and directing Misser Anibal Caro, who lodged
with him, to be summoned, he told him to go and learn the upshot.
Whilst he was giving the above-mentioned directions with regard
to this matter, there appeared a Roman nobleman, who lived with
Cardinal de' Medici, and who was sent by him. This nobleman,
having called Misser Giovanni and myself aside, told us that the
Cardinal had related to him those words which he had heard said
by the Pope, and that no one had any means by which they
could help me, and that I must do all in my power to escape this
first outburst of rage, and that I must not trust my safety in any

house in Rome. Immediately upon this nobleman's departure, the said Misser Giovanni, looking me in the face, showed signs of tears, and said: "Alas! Woe is me! That I have no means of being able to help you." Whereupon I replied: "By God's help, I will help myself well enough by my own aid; I will only ask you that you supply me with one of your horses." There was already in readiness a black Turkish horse, the handsomest and best in Rome. I mounted upon it with a wheel-arquebuse before me at the saddle-bow, ready prepared to defend myself with it. When I reached the Ponte Sisto, I found the whole of the Bargello's guard on horseback and on foot; so making a virtue of necessity, having boldly urged the horse to a trot, by the favor of God, hidden from their eyes, I passed freely; and with as much haste as I was able, I betook me to Palonbara, a place belonging to the lord Giovanbatista Savello, and thence I sent back the horse to Misser Giovanni, nor did I in the least wish that he should know where I was. The said lord Gianbatista, when he had entertained me two days, counselled me that I should remove myself from thence and proceed towards Naples until this storm had passed away; and providing me with an escort he caused me to be set upon the road to Naples, upon which I found a sculptor friend of mine, who was going to San Germano to finish the tomb of Pier de' Medici at Monte Casini. This man was called by the name of Solosmeo. He gave me the news that Pope Clemente had that same evening sent one of his chamberlains to enquire how the above-mentioned Thubbia was; and on finding him at work, and that nothing at all had happened to him, nor that he even knew anything, when he reported this to the Pope, the said (pontiff) turned to Pompeo and said to him: "You are a scoundrel, but I declare to you indeed, that you have stirred up a serpent that will bite you and will give you your deserts." Then he turned to Cardinal de' Medici, and commissioned him that he should take a certain amount of care of me, for on no account did he wish to lose me. So Solosmeo and I proceeded singing towards Monte Casini, with the intention of going thence together to Naples.

WHEN Solosmeo had inspected his works at Monte Casini we proceeded together towards Naples. When we had arrived at about half a mile from Naples, there met us an innkeeper, who invited us to his inn, and told us that he had lived many years in Florence with Carlo Ginori, and that if we went to his inn he would have the very best entertainment made for us because we were Florentines. To that innkeeper we replied many times that we did not wish to go with him. This man, however, sometimes passed before and sometimes followed behind us, frequently repeating to us the same things, that he would like to have us at his inn. Wherefore since he became an annoyance to me, I asked him if he knew where to direct me to a certain Sicilian woman, who bore the name of Beatrice, and who had a beautiful young daughter of hers, who was called Angelica: and who were courtesans. This innkeeper, since it seemed to him that I was mocking him, said: "May God give ill-luck to courtesans and those who like them;" and setting spurs to his horse, he made as though determined to leave us. It seemed to me that I had lifted from my back in a fine fashion that animal of an innkeeper, although by that circumstance I had not greatly profited (*estessi in capitale*) because there was recalled to me that great love which I bore for Angelica, and while I was discoursing about it with the said Solosmeo, not without some amorous sighs, we saw the innkeeper returning to us in a great hurry, who, when he got up to us, blurted out: "Two, or rather three, days ago it was that there arrived next door to my inn a woman and a young girl, who bore those names; I do not know whether they are Sicilians or from some other country." Whereupon I replied: "That name of Angelica has so great a power over me that I am willing in any case to come to your inn." We proceeded in agreement along with the innkeeper into the city of Naples and dismounted at his inn, and it seemed to me a thousand years that I was setting my affairs in order, which I did most expeditiously; and entering the said house next door to the inn, I found there my Angelica, who made me the most boundless endearments that it is possible to imagine in the world. So I remained with her from that hour of twenty-two of the clock until the following morning, with such enjoyment as I have never had equalled. And whilst I was revelling in this pleasure, I remembered that upon that day precisely expired the month that was foretold to me by the demons when in the magic circle. Therefore let every man who entangles himself with these (spirits) consider the incalculable perils that I have passed through. I found in my purse by chance a diamond which I commenced showing about among the goldsmiths; and although I was still young I was so well known in Naples for a man of some merit, that very many courtesies were shown me. Among the others a certain most excellent fellow, a jeweller, who had the name of Misser Do (mo)menico Fontana. This honest man left his workshop for three days whilst I was in Naples, nor ever departed from my side, showing me many most beautiful antiquities that were in Naples and outside the city; and he took me besides to make my obeisance to the Viceroy of Naples, who had let him know that he had a wish to see me. When I reached His Excellency he gave me a very honorable reception; and while we were doing this, the above-mentioned diamond caught the eyes of His Excellency: and having made me show it to him, he said that if I should have a desire to part with it that I would kindly not prefer any one to himself.

Upon which, when I had received back the diamond, I offered it again to His Excellency, and I told him that the diamond and I were both at his disposal. Whereupon he said that the diamond pleased him very much but that it would please him still more if I would stay with him; for he would make such terms with me that I should be satisfied with him. We exchanged many civil words one to another; but when we afterwards came to the merits of the diamond, being commanded by His Excellency that I should ask in one single word the price for it that seemed good to me, I replied that two hundred *scudi* was its value exactly. To this His Excellency replied that it seemed to him that I had in no way exceeded its worth; but that since it had been set by my hands, knowing that I was the ablest craftsman in the world, it would not, if set by another hand, reach that excellence of effect that it now displayed. Thereupon I said that the diamond had not been set by me and that it was not well set; and such effect as it made, it made from its own fine quality; and that if I were to reset it, I should improve it very much from what it now was. And inserting my thumb-nail into the claw-setting of the diamond, I withdrew it from the ring, and polishing it somewhat I handed it the Viceroy; he satisfied and astonished drew me an order, so that I should be paid the two hundred *scudi* that I had demanded. Returning to my lodging I found letters which had come from Cardinal de' Medici, which told me that I must return to Rome with great speed, and at once go and dismount at the house of His Most Reverend Lordship. Having read the letter to my Angelica, with lovesick tears she besought me that out of my kindness I would either stay in Naples, or that I would take her with me; to which I replied that if she were willing to come with me I would give into her keeping those two hundred ducats that I had received from the Viceroy. When the mother saw us in this close conversation, she approached us and said to me:

"Benvenuto, if you want to take my Angelica to Rome, leave me a (sum of) fifteen ducats, so that I can lie in, and then I will come also." I told the old rogue that I would gladly leave her thirty, if she were willing to give me my Angelica. Having thus made our compact, Angelica begged me that I would buy her a robe of black velvet, because it was cheap in Naples. I was content with all this; and having sent for the velvet, made the bargain and everything, when the old woman, who thought that I was more cooked than raw, demanded of me a gown of fine cloth for herself, and many other charges for her daughter, and much more money than that which I had offered her. Upon which I turned to her pleasantly and said: "My dear Beatrice, is not that enough which I have offered you?" she answered: "No!" Thereupon I retorted that what did not suffice for her would suffice for me: and having kissed my Angelica, we parted, she with tears and I with laughter, and turned myself immediately towards Rome. Departing from Naples by night with my money upon my person, so that I should not be way-laid nor assassinated, as is the custom of Naples, when I found my-self at Selciata I defended myself with great skill and valor of body against a number of horsemen who had come to assassinate me. Then some days after, having left Solosmeo to his works at Monte Casini, I arrived one morning to dine at the inn at Adanagni. When near the inn I fired at some birds with my arquebuse, and killed them; and a small piece of iron that was in the lock of my gun tore my right hand. Although it was not an injury of importance it seemed bad enough from the great quantity of blood that poured from my hand. Having entered the inn, and put my horse in his stall, mounting upon a large platform, I found many Neapolitan noblemen, who were just sitting down to table; and with them was a young gentlewoman, the most beautiful that I ever saw. When I was come up, there mounted after me a very brave young servant-man of mine with a great halbert in hand: in such a way that we, the weapon and the blood, struck so much terror into those poor noblemen, especially since that place itself was a haunt of assassins, that rising from the table in a great fright they prayed to God to aid them. At which I remarked laughing that God had assisted them and that I was the man to defend them against whoever should wish to injure them; and asking of them some little assistance to bind up my hand, that most beauteous gentlewoman took one of her kerchiefs, richly embroidered in gold, desiring to bind me up with it; I objected: she immediately tore it in half and with greatest tenderness bound me with her own hand. Thus being somewhat reassured we dined very merrily. After the dinner we mounted our horses and proceeded in company. Their fear was not yet quite subsided; wherefore those noblemen cleverly made me entertain that gentlewoman, remaining somewhat in the rear; and I rode alongside of her upon a handsome little horse of mine, warning my servant that he should remain at a little distance from me: in such fashion that we discoursed of those things that the druggist does not sell. Thus I journeyed to Rome with the greatest pleasure that I have ever experienced.

When I was arrived in Rome I proceeded to dismount at the palace of the Cardinal de' Medici; and having found His Most Reverend Lordship I conversed with him, and thanked him much for having contrived my return. Then I begged His Most Reverend Lordship that he would make me secure from imprisonment, and, if that were possible, from the pecuniary penalty also. The said lord paid most willing attention to me; he told me that I need not trouble about anything; then he turned to one of his gentlemen-in-waiting, who was called Misser Pierant° Pecci, a Sienese, directing him that he should tell the Bargello in his name not to dare to touch me. Next he asked him how the man was faring whom I had struck on the head with the stone. The said Misser Pierant° said that he was doing very badly, and would do yet worse; the reason being that having learnt that I was returning to Rome, he said that he wished to die in order to do me a bad turn. At which words, with a loud laugh the Cardinal said: "The man could not have taken any other way than this to let us know that he was born a Sienese." Then turning to me he said to me: "For our credit and your own, have patience four or five days before you visit the Banks; from then onwards go where you wish, and let idiots die in their own way." I went to my own house, and set myself to work to finish the medal, which I had already commenced, of the head of Pope Clemente, which I made with a reverse representing a (figure of) *Peace*. This was a small woman's figure clad in thinnest garments girded up, with a small torch in her hand, with which she was setting fire to a pile of weapons bound together in the form of a trophy; and there was visible part of a temple, in the which was displayed Fury bound with many chains, and around it was a lettered motto, which ran: *Clauduntur Belli Portæ.* While was finishing the said medal the man whom I had struck was cured, and the Pope never left off asking for me: and since I avoided going near the Cardinal de' Medici, because it chanced that on all the occasions that I came into his presence His Lordship gave me some work of importance to carry out, by which means he hindered very much the completion of my medal, it happened that Misser Pier Carnesechi, who was very greatly in favor with the Pope, took the pains to occupy himself about me: so in a diplomatic manner he told me how much the Pope desired that I should serve him. To whom I said that "in a few days I will demonstrate to His Holiness that I have never abandoned his service." A few days after, having completed my medal, I stamped (examples of) it in gold, silver, and copper. Having exhibited it to Misser Pietro, he immediately introduced me to the

Pope. It was after dinner one day in the month of April, and it was fine weather: the Pope was in the Belvedere. When I arrived in the presence of His Holiness, I put into his hand the medals together with the steel dies. Taking them and recognizing immediately the great artistic power that there was in them, he looked Misser Piero in the face, and said: "The ancients were never so well served in the way of medals." Whilst he and the others were examining now the dies and now the medals, I most modestly began to speak, and I said: "If the influence of my perverse planets had not met with a greater power that has hindered that which they were in the act of violently displaying against me, Your Holiness, without your fault or mine, would have lost one of his faithful and loving servants. However, Most Blessed Father, there is no mistake in these cases, where one risks everything (*dove si fa del resto*), to employ that method to which certain poor simple men allude, when they say that one must mark off seven and cut off one. Because a villainous lying tongue of one of my worst adversaries so easily aroused the anger of Your Holiness that you were provoked to so great a fury as to commission the Governor that he should immediately arrest and hang me; and later having seen the untowardness of such an act, doing (thereby) so great a wrong to your own self, by depriving yourself of one of your servants (for Your Holiness yourself says that he is one), I think most certainly that, as regards God and as regards the world, Your Holiness would then have had no small a remorse. However, good and virtuous fathers, likewise masters of the same kind, upon their sons and their servants ought not to let their arm fall so precipitately; for it may chance that their regret may subsequently serve to no purpose. Since that God has hindered this malign course of the stars, and preserved me to Your Holiness, I pray you another time not to be so easily inflamed against me." The Pope stopped in his examination of the medals, and with close attention bent to listen to me; and because there were in the presence many lords of highest rank, the Pope, coloring somewhat, showed signs of being ashamed, and not knowing any other way of getting out of that confusion, said that he did not remember ever having given such an order. Then I perceiving this, entered upon other subjects of conversation, in order that I might divert (attention) from that confusion which he had exhibited. His Holiness having again entered into discussion about the medals, asked me how I had managed to stamp them so wonderfully, seeing that they were so large; that he had never seen any antique medals of so large a size. Upon that point we discussed a bit, and he being afraid lest I should read him another little lecture worse than the previous one, told me that the medals were most beautiful, and that they were most acceptable to him, and that he would like me to make another reverse according to his fancy, if such a medal could be struck with two reverse sides. I said, "Yes!" Thereupon His Holiness commissioned me that I should represent the scene of *Moses when he struck the rock so that water came out,* with a motto above, which said: *"Ut biba(t) populus."* And then he added: "Go! Benvenuto, for you will scarcely have completed it ere I shall have given thought to your prospects." When I was gone away the Pope boasted in the presence of all that he would give me so much that I should be able to live richly without ever laboring any more for other people. I attended with care to the completion of the reverse of *Moses.*

AT this juncture the Pope fell ill; and the physicians being of
opinion that the illness was likely to prove fatal, that adversary of mine being afraid of me, commissioned certain Neapolitan soldiers that they should do to me what he was afraid that I should do to him. Therefore I had much trouble in protecting my poor life. Continuing (my labors) I completed the reverse entirely: when I carried it to the Pope I found him in bed in the very worst state of health. In spite of all this he paid me great compliments, and wished to see the medals and the dies: but though he directed them to give him his spectacles and lights in no way could he distinguish anything. He set himself to fumble them somewhat with his finger; then when he had done so for a little while he heaved a deep sigh, and said to certain people that he was very sorry on my account, but that if God restored him to health he would put everything right. Three days afterwards the Pope died, and though I found that I had lost my labor, I took good heart, and said to myself that by means of those medals I had made myself so well known, that by any Pope that succeeded I should be employed with

perhaps better luck. Thus I put good heart into myself, wiping out entirely (*in tutto e per tutto*) the great injuries that Pompeo had done me; and putting on all my armor, I went to Sanpiero and kissed the feet of the dead Pope, not without tears. Then I returned to the Banks to reflect upon the great confusion that happens on such occasions. And whilst I was sitting at the Banks with many of my friends, Pompeo chanced to pass by in the midst of ten very well-armed men; and when he was directly opposite to where I was, he stopped, somewhat as if he wanted a quarrel with me. Those who were with me, brave and eager young men, were making signals to me that I ought to take it up, upon which I immediately considered that if I drew my sword some very serious injury would follow for those who had no fault at all in the matter; wherefore I judged that it would be better that I alone should put my life in jeopardy. When Pompeo had stood there the length of two Ave Marias he laughed with derision in my direction; and when he had moved on those friends of his also laughed, tossing their heads; and with similar acts they displayed much insolence. Those comrades of mine wanted to take up the quarrel; to whom I angrily said that I was a man who knew how to carry out my own disputes, that I had no need of abler fighters than myself; so that each of them should go about his own business. Those friends of mine in indignation departed from me grumbling. Among them was my dearest friend, who bore the name of Albertaccio del Bene, own brother to Alessandro and Albizo (who is to-day in Lyons extremely wealthy). This Albertaccio was the most admirable youth that I ever knew, and the most spirited, and loved me as much as his own self; and since he knew well that that act of self-restraint was not due to meanness of soul, but to the most daring bravery (for he knew me extremely well), in reply to my words he begged me, that I would do him so great a favor as to call upon him in everything that I had it in my mind to do. I said to him: "Albertaccio mine, dearest to me above all the others, a time will very soon come when you will be able to give me your assistance; but in this case, if you love me, pay no attention to me, and go about your own business, and take yourself off quickly as the others have done, for there is no time to lose." These words were spoken hurriedly. In the meanwhile my enemies of the Banks were gone away at a slow pace towards the *Chiavica* (a place called thus) and had reached a junction of streets which ran in different directions; but that (street) wherein was the house of my enemy Pompeo was the street which leads straight to the Campo di Fiore; and for some purpose the said Pompeo had entered into that druggist's shop which stands at the corner of the Chiavica, and he stayed with that said druggist some little time over some business of his; though I was told that he was boasting of that insult which it seemed to him that he had done me; but in every way that was indeed his ill-luck: because when I arrived at that corner, he was just coming out of the druggist's, and those ruffians of his had separated, and had just received him into their midst. Drawing a little sharp dagger, and forcing the rank of his ruffians, I laid my hands upon his breast with such quickness and coolness of spirit, that none of the said men were able to prevent me. As I aimed to strike him in the face, the fear that he experienced made him turn his countenance away, wherefore I caught him exactly under the ear; and there I struck him two blows only, for at the second he fell dead by my hand, which was never my intention; but as they say, "Blows are not struck according to bargains." Withdrawing the dagger with my left hand, with my right I drew out my sword in defence of my life, whereupon all those ruffians ran to the dead body, and made no attack upon me; so I withdrew myself alone along the Strada Julia, thinking where I could take refuge. When I had gone three hundred paces, there joined me Piloto, the goldsmith, my very great friend, who said to me: "Brother, since the mischief's done, let us see about your safety." To whom I replied: "Let us go to the house of Albertaccio del Bene, for to him a little while ago I said that the time would soon come that I should have need of him." When we reached the house of Albertaccio, his kindnesses were unbounded; and soon there appeared the flower of the youths of the Banks of all nationalities, except the Milanese; and all of them offered to lay down their lives for the safety of mine. Misser Luigi Rucellai besides sent to offer me in a splendid manner the use of his possessions, and many other men of position like him; because they all with one accord blessed my hands, for it seemed to them that that man had put upon me too much, and they marvelled much that I had borne it so long. At that moment Cardinal Cornaro, having learnt the circumstance, sent on his own account thirty soldiers, with as many great halberds, pikes and arquebuses, to escort me to his lodging with all proper respect; and I accepted the offer, went with them, and more than as many of those said young men kept me company. At this juncture that Misser Traiano, his relative, first chamberlain to the Pope, being informed (of the facts), sent to Cardinal de' Medici a Milanese nobleman of rank, to tell the Cardinal of the great crime that I had committed, and that his most reverend lordship was under obligation to punish me. The Cardinal immediately answered and said: "He would have committed a great crime not to have committed this lesser one. Thank Misser Traiano on my behalf, that he has informed me of that which I did not know." And turning suddenly he said, in the presence of the said nobleman, to the Bishop of Frulli, his own gentleman in waiting and personal attendant: "Seek diligently for my Benvenuto and bring him here to me, for I wish to assist and protect him; and whoever does anything against him will do it against me also." The nobleman, coloring deeply, departed, and the Bishop of

Frulli came to look for me at the house of Cardinal Cornaro; and, finding the Cardinal, he told him that Cardinal de' Medici had sent for Benvenuto, and that he wanted to be the person to protect him. This Cardinal Cornaro, who was as touchy as a bear cub, replied very angrily to the Bishop, saying that he was as fitted to protect me as Cardinal de' Medici. Upon this the Bishop said that, as a favor, would he allow him facilities to speak one word (with me) independent of that matter, regarding other concerns of the Cardinal. Cornaro said for that day he must reckon as having already talked with me. Cardinal de' Medici was very indignant, but the very next night, without the knowledge of Cornaro, I went with a very good escort to visit him; I begged him then that he would do me so great a kindness as to leave me in the house of the said Cornaro, and I told him of the great courtesy that Cornaro had shown to me; wherefore that, if His Most Reverend Lordship would let me stay with the said Cornaro, I should have a friend the more in my necessities; or that, however, he might dispose of me in any way that was pleasing to His Lordship; who replied that I might do whatever seemed good to me. Having returned to Cornaro's house, a few days later Cardinal Farnese was made Pope, and directly he had issued his commands on matters of the greatest moment, the Pope afterwards asked for me, saying that he did not want any one else but me to strike his coins. To these remarks there responded to His Holiness a certain nobleman, his most intimate acquaintance, who was called Misser Latino Juvinale: he said that I was a fugitive on account of a homicide committed on the person of a Milanese named Pompeo, and he added all the arguments on my behalf in a very favorable light. At which statements the Pope said: "I did not know of the death of Pompeo, but I know very well the arguments on Benvenuto's side, therefore make out immediately an order of safe-conduct for him, with

A gold and enamel salt-cellar by Cellini, long in the family of Prince
Rosigliosi and now in the collection of the Metropolitan Museum of
Art, New York.

which he may be most secure." There was in the presence a great
friend of that Pompeo, and a man very intimate with the Pope,
who was called Misser Anbruogio, and was a Milanese; and he
said to the Pope: "In these first days of your Papacy it will not be
a good thing for you to confer pardons of this kind." Upon which
the Pope turning upon him, said to him: "You do not know the
case as well as I do. Know then that men like Benvenuto, unique
in their profession, ought not to be bound by the law; but much
more so in his case, for I know how much reason he has." And
directing the safe-conduct to be made for me, I immediately entered upon his service with the greatest attention. That said Misser
Latino Juvinale came to look for me, and commissioned me that
I should make the Pope's coins. By the which circumstance all
those enemies of mine woke up; they began to hinder me so that
I should not carry out this commission. At which the Pope perceiving such an attempt, scolded them all, and desired that I should
execute it. I began to fashion the dies for the *scudi,* upon which
I made a half figure of St. Paul (*sanpagolo*), with a lettered inscription which ran: *Vas electionis.* This coin gave much more
satisfaction than the (coins) made by those who were in competition with me. In such a way that the Pope said that the others
need talk no more about the coins, because he desired that I should
make them and no one else. So I boldly applied myself to work;
and that Misser Latino Juvinale presented me to the Pope, because the Pope had given him this duty. I was desirous of recovering the *motu-proprio* of the office of die-stamper at the Mint.
On this point the Pope allowed himself to take advice, saying that
first it was necessary that I should receive pardon for the homicide,
which I should have during the octave of St. Mary of August
(*per le sante Marie di agosto*) by commission of the *Caporioni* of
Rome; for thus it is customary every year upon this solemn feast

to bestow upon these *Caporioni* twelve outlaws; meantime another safe-conduct would be made out for me, under which I could rest secure up to that said time. When these enemies of mine saw that they could not by any means hinder me at the Mint, they tried another expedient. The dead Pompeo having left three thousand ducats dowry to a young bastard daughter of his, they arranged that a certain favorite of the lord Pier Luigi, the Pope's son, should ask for her as his wife through the medium of the said lord; and thus it came about. This said favorite was a country lad, brought up by the said lord, and, from what they say, but little of that money reached him, for the said lord laid his hands upon it and wanted to use it himself. But since the husband of this girl many times, to please his wife, had besought the said lord that he would have me arrested, which the said lord had promised to do when he should see that the favor which I enjoyed with the Pope had somewhat diminished; and matters remaining in this condition for about two months, when that servitor of his sought to recover his (wife's) dowry, the lord did not respond accordingly, although he let the wife understand that in any event she should have vengeance for the death of her father. Although I knew something of this, I presented myself many times to the said lord, who made a show of conferring upon me the greatest favors. On the other hand he had arranged one of two courses, either to cause me to be murdered, or to have me arrested by the Bargello. He commissioned a certain little devil of a Corsican soldier of his that he should make as neat a job of it as he could; and those other enemies of mine, especially Misser Traiano, had promised to make a present of one hundred *scudi* to this little Corsican, who said that he would do it as easily as sucking a fresh egg. I, when I heard of this matter, went about with my eyes open, and with a good escort, and very well armed with a coat of mail and gauntlets, for I had obtained such permission. This said little Corsican, thinking out of greed to earn all that money without risk, believed that he could carry out such a business by himself alone; insomuch that one day after dinner he caused me to be summoned on behalf of the lord Pier Luigi; whereupon I immediately went, since the lord had spoken to me of his desire for making some large silver vases. Leaving my house in haste with, however, my accustomed armor, I went quickly along the Strada Julia, thinking that I should find no one about at that hour. When I reached the other end of the Strada Julia to turn to the Farnese Palace, since it is my habit to turn the corners widely (*i.e.*, at a wide angle), I saw this little Corsican, already referred to, rise from a seat and come out into the middle of the street: so that I did not disturb myself, but stood in readiness to defend myself; and slackening my pace somewhat, I drew near to the wall to give a wide passage to the said little Corsican. Whereupon, he having drawn himself near to the wall, when we presently came well up to each other, I recognized directly by his gestures that he had a wish to do me some mischief, and that seeing me alone in this way he thought that the matter would result in his favor. Wherefore I began to speak to him and said: "Brave warrior, if it had been night you could say that you had mistaken me, but since it is daylight you know very well who I am, that I am one who has never had anything to do with you, and has never done you any injury, but that I shall be well able to do you a service." At these words, in a bullying fashion, without removing himself out of my way, he told me that he did not know what I was talking about. Whereupon I said: "I know very well what you want, and what you are saying to me; but that business that you have undertaken to do is more difficult and dangerous than you think, and could perhaps lead in the opposite direction; and remember that you have to deal with a man who would defend himself against a hundred men; and that this is not an undertaking to be admired by brave men, such as you are." Meanwhile I still stood in an attitude of defence (*cagniesco*), whilst both of us changed color. Meantime people had appeared, who had already recognized that our words were warlike ones: for he, not having sufficient courage to lay hands upon me, said: "Another time we shall meet again." To which I replied: "I shall always meet again men of worth, together with those who bear a resemblance to such." Departing, I proceeded to the house of the lord Pier Luigi, who had not sent for me at all. Returning to my workshop, the said little Corsican let me know through one of his greatest friends and mine, that I need not be on my guard against him any more, for he wished to be a good brother (in arms) to me; but that I must keep a good look out with regard to the others, for I was in very great danger; for men of great influence had sworn to compass my death. Sending to thank him, I guarded myself in the best way I could. Not many days later I was informed by a great friend of mine that the lord Pier Luigi had issued an express commission that I was to be arrested that evening. This was told to me at twenty of the clock, wherefore I talked it over with some of my friends, who advised me that I should immediately depart. And because the order was given for the first hour of the night, at twenty-three I mounted into the post (waggon) and hied me to Florence; for since that little Corsican had not had the courage to carry out the undertaking that he had promised, the lord Pier Luigi on his own personal authority had given orders that I should be arrested, merely to appease a little that daughter of Pompeo's, who wanted to know where her dowry was. Not being able to satisfy her revenge by either of the two methods that he had planned, he thought of another, of which we will speak in its proper place.

I ARRIVED in Florence, and I had an audience with the Duke Lessandro, who gave me a wonderful reception and sought that I should remain with him. And because there was in Florence a certain sculptor called Tribolino, and he was a gossip of mine, since I had stood god-father to a son of his; whilst talking with him, he told me that one Jacopo del Sansovino, who had once been his first master, had sent to summon him; and because he had never seen Venice (*Vinetia*), and for the profit that he expected (to make out) of it, he was going thither very willingly. And when he asked me if I had ever seen Venice, I replied, "No!" Whereupon he begged me that I go with him for pleasure (*aspasso*); to which I agreed. I therefore replied to Duke Lessandro that I wished first to go as far as Venice; after which I would return willingly to his service; and he desired me to promise this, and commanded me that before I departed I would come and talk to him. The next day after I had got myself in readiness, I went to take my permit from the Duke, whom I found in the Palazzo de' Pazi, in which at the time were lodging the wife and daughters of the lord Lorenzo Cibo. Having let His Excellency know that I wanted, with his kind permission, to go to Venice, there returned with his reply Cosimino de' Medici (to-day Duke of Florence), who told me that I must go and find Nicholò da Monte Aguto, and that he would give me fifty gold *scudi,* which money His Excellency the Duke was presenting to me out of his affection, that I might the better enjoy myself, and afterwards I must return to serve him. I received the money from Nicholò, and I went home for Tribolo, who was all ready; and he asked whether I had packed up my sword. I answered him that whoever went mounted upon a journey ought not to pack up his sword. He said that in Florence it was customary to do so, because there was a certain Ser Mauritio, who for the very slightest thing (*ogni pichola cosa*) would give the rope's-end to San Giovanbatista himself; it was therefore needful to carry our swords packed up until we were outside the city-gate. I laughed at this, and thus we set out. We joined company with the courier to Venice, who was called by the surname of Lamentone. We went on in company with him, and having passed Bologna one evening amongst the rest we arrived at Ferrara; and there when lodged at the inn in the Piazza the said Lamentone went to find some of the exiles, to carry them letters and messages on behalf of their wives; for it was so arranged with the consent of the Duke that the courier alone could speak to them, and no one else, under pain of the same ban that they were under. At this juncture, it being a little after twenty-two of the clock, we went, Tribulo and I, to see the return of the Duke of Ferrara, who had been to Bel Fiore to see the jousting. At (this spectacle of) his return we met many exiles who stared fixedly at us, as if to compel us to speak to them. Tribolo, who was the most timorous man that I ever knew, never left off saying: "Don't look at them, and don't speak to them, if you wish to return to Florence." Thus we waited to see the Duke's return; then we went back to the inn, where we found Lamentone. And when it was nearly one hour of the night, there appeared Nicholò Benintendi, and his brother Piero, and another very old man, who I believe was Jacopo Nardi, along with several other young men; and directly they came in they each asked the courier after their own families in Florence; Tribolo and I kept apart, so as not to speak to them. After they had conversed a bit with Lamentone, that Nicholò Benintendi said: "I know those two very well; why do they make so much bones about not wishing to speak to us?" Tribolo, however, told me to keep quiet. Lamentone told them that that licence which had been given to him was not extended to us. Benintendi rejoined saying that that was donkey-stuff (*asinità*), calling down plagues upon us and a thousand other pretty things. Whereupon I raised my head with as much self-control as I could and knew, and I said: "Good gentlemen, you can harm us very much, and we are able to gain no advantage from you; and although you have uttered certain words that are not becoming, not even on this account do we wish to be angry with you." That old man Nardi said that I had spoken like a young man of worth as I was. Nicholò Benintendi thereupon said: "I despise both them and their Duke." I replied that he wronged us, for we had nothing to do with his affairs. That old man Nardi took our part, telling Benintendi that he was wrong: whereat he continued to utter insulting words. For the which reason I told him that I would both say and do things that he would not like; therefore he should mind his own business and leave us alone. He replied again that he despised both the Duke and us, and that we and he were a pack of donkeys (*un monte di asini*). At which words giving him the lie in his throat (*mentitolo per la gola*), I drew out my sword; and the old man who wished to be downstairs first, fell down a few of the steps and they all one upon another on the top of him. For the which reason I bounding forward laid about my sword along the walls with greatest fury, crying out: "I will slay you all;" and I took the greatest care not to do them any harm, which I could too easily have done. At this noise the landlord cried out: Lamentone shouted: "Don't do that;" some of them screamed: "Oh, my head;" others: "Let me get out of this;" it was an indescribable muddle (*bussa*); they seemed a herd of swine. The landlord came with a light; I withdrew upstairs and put up my sword. Lamentone told Nicholò Benintendi that he had done wrong; the landlord said to Nicholò Benintendi: "It is a question of life and death to draw weapons here, and if the Duke knew of these insolences of yours, he would have you hanged by the neck; so that I do not wish to do to you that which you deserve; but let me never catch you again in this inn, or woe betide you." The landlord came up to me, and when I wished to excuse myself to him would not permit me to say anything, telling me that he knew that I had a thousand reasons, and that I must guard myself well from them during my journey. When we had supped there appeared a boatman to transport us to Venice; I asked him if he were willing to give me the boat to myself (*la barca libera*); he was glad to do this, and in such a way we made our bargain. In the morning at an early hour we took our horses to go to the landing-stage, which was I know not how few miles distant from Ferrara; and when we reached the landing-stage we found the brother of Nicholò Benintendi with three other companions, who were waiting until I came up; amongst them they had two pikes (*dua pezi di arme in asta*), and I had bought a fine big spear in Ferrara. Being also very well armed, I was not at all terrified, as was Tribolo, who said: "God help us! These people are here to murder us." Lamentone turned to me and said: "The best thing that you can do is to return to Ferrara, for I see that the business is a dangerous one. For mercy's sake, Benvenuto, let the anger of these mad beasts pass." Whereupon I said: "Let's go on, for God helps those who are in the right; and you shall see how I will help myself. Is not that boat engaged for us?" "Yes," said Lamentone. "And we shall be in it without them, as far as my valor can accomplish it." I urged forward my horse, and when I was fifty paces off I dismounted and went boldly forward with my spear. Tribolo stayed behind, and was crouched up on his horse, so that he seemed to be the very cold itself; and Lamentone the carrier puffed and blew, so that he seemed to be a gale of wind; for that was his usual way of acting; but he did it more then than usual, whilst he remained considering at what end that devil's business would arrive. When I reached the boat the boatman set himself in front of me, and told me that those several Florentine gentlemen were desirous of joining our party in the boat, if I had no objection. To which I replied: "The boat is engaged for us and not for any one else, and it grieves me to the heart not to be able to be with them." At these words a bold youth of the Magalotti (family) said: "Benvenuto, we will arrange so that you will be able to do so." Whereupon I said: "If God and the right that I have, together with my own strength, have any will or power, you will not make it possible for me to do what you say." And as I said these words I leapt into the boat. Turning the point of my weapon towards them I said: "With this I will show that I cannot do it." When that Magalotti, desiring to make a little show-off, drew his weapon and came forward, I jumped up on the edge of the boat, and gave him such a violent thrust, that if he had not fallen backwards to the ground, I should have run him through and through. His other comrades instead of assisting him retreated backwards, and when I saw that I could kill him, instead of giving him (another blow), I said to him: "Get up, brother, and pick up your arms and begone. You have seen clearly that I cannot do what I do not want to do, and that which I could do I have not wanted to do." Then I summoned into the boat Tribolo and the boatman and Lamentone; thus we proceeded toward Venice. When we were ten miles along the course of the Po, those young men had gone on board a light vessel and caught us up;

and when they came level with us that fool Pier Benintendi said to me: "Come along now, Benvenuto, for we shall see each other again in Venice." "Go forward, for I am coming," said I, "and I permit you to see me again anywhere you like." Thus we reached Venice. I took advice from a brother of Cardinal Cornaro, asking him that he would procure me the favor that I might be able to wear my arms; he told me that I might carry them freely, for the worst thing that could occur to me was to lose my sword. So wearing our weapons, we went to visit Jacopo del Sansovino, the sculptor, who had sent for Tribolo; and to me he displayed great courtesies and wished to give us some dinner, and we remained with him. On speaking with Tribolo he told him that he had no wish for his services at that moment, and that he must come again another time. At these words I burst out laughing, and jokingly said to Sansovino: "Your home is too distant from his if he is to come again another time." Poor Tribolo, in dismay, said: "I have here the letter in which you wrote to me that I was to come." To this Sansovino replied, "that men like himself, of worth and talent, might do that and even greater things." Tribolo shrugged his shoulders and said "Patience" several times. Upon this, paying no attention to the abundant dinner that Sansovino had given to me, I took the part of my comrade Tribolo, who had right on his side. And while at that board Sansovino had never ceased chattering about his great exploits, speaking ill of Michelagniolo, and of all those who practised that same art, praising himself alone exceedingly; this circumstance caused me so much annoyance, that I had not eaten a mouthful that I enjoyed, and I merely uttered these two words: "Oh, Misser Jacopo, men of worth perform the acts of men of worth, and those talented beings who execute beautiful and brilliant works are recognized much better when they are praised by others than when they are praised so confidently by themselves." At these words he and we rose from the table murmuring. That same day when I was about in Venice, near the Rialto I met Piero Benintendi, who was with a number of people; and when I saw that they were seeking to do me some harm, I retired into a druggist's shop, so that I might let that danger pass by. Subsequently I heard that that young man of the Magalotti family, to whom I had shown courtesy, had scolded them severely; and so that matter passed.

A few days after that we returned towards Florence, and when we were seeking accommodation at a certain place which is on this side of Chioggia on the left-hand side coming towards Ferrara, the inn-keeper wanted to be paid according to his mode (of reckoning) before we went to sleep; and when we told him that in other places it was customary to pay in the morning, he said to us: "I want to be paid in the evening and in my own way." At these words I said that men who wanted to act in their own way must needs make a world after their own way, for in this world it was not customary (to do) so. The inn-keeper retorted that I need not go bothering his brains, for he wished to act in that particular way. Tribolo was trembling with fright and nudging me that I should keep quiet, lest things should be worse for us; so we paid him according to his way; then we went to bed. We certainly had very fine beds, entirely new, and truly clean. For all this I did not sleep at all, meditating all that night how I must act to revenge myself. Once it came into my thoughts to set fire to the house; at another to cut the throats of four fine horses that he had in his stable: I saw clearly that it would be easy enough for me to do this, but I did not see that it would be easy to secure the safety of myself and my comrade. I took a last expedient of putting my property and my party on board the boat, and so I did; and having attached the horses which drew the boat to the tow-rope I told them not to start the boat until I returned because I had left a pair of my slippers in the place where I had slept. So returning to the inn, I called to the inn-keeper; who replied that he had nothing to do with us, and that we might go to blazes. There was there a youngster stable-lad of his who told me very drowsily: "The landlord would not move for the Pope himself, for there is sleeping with him a certain little slut whom he has much coveted;" and he asked me for a tip (*la bene andata*); whereupon I gave him several of those small Venetian coins, and told him to delay awhile the man who drew the tow-rope, until I should hunt for my slippers and return thither. Going upstairs I took out a small knife that cut like a razor; and the four beds that were there I cut all to bits with that knife, in such a way that I knew that I had done a damage of more than fifty *scudi*. And returning to the boat with certain pieces of that bed-furniture in my pocket I hastily said to the guide of the tow-rope that he must quickly get ready to start. When we had got some way from the inn my gossip Tribolo said that he had left certain small straps (*coreggine*) which bound up his travelling-bag, and that he wanted to return for them at any cost. Upon which I told him not to worry about two small straps, for I would make him as many big ones as he would want. He told me that I was always on the joke, but that he wanted to turn back for his straps at any cost, and he was for compelling the tow-rope man to stop; and I said that he must go forward, the while I related the great havoc that I had wrought upon the landlord; and when I showed him a sample of certain pieces of the bed-furniture and the rest, there fell upon him so great a trembling, that he did not leave off saying to the tow-rope man: "Move along, move along quickly," and he never reckoned himself safe from this danger until we were returned within the gates of Florence. When these were reached, Tribolo said: "Let us pack up our swords for the love of God, and don't you do anything more; for it has seemed to me that I have had my entrails always in a basin." I answered him: "My gossip Tribolo, you need not pack up your sword, for you have never loosened it"; and I said this to him by accident, for I had never seen him show a sign of manhood during that journey. At which remark, looking down at his sword, he said: "Before God, you speak the truth, for it remains packed up in that very manner that I arranged it before I came out of my home." To this gossip of mine it seemed that I had been unfortunate company, because I resented and defended myself against those who had desired to do us injury; and to me it seemed that he had done much worse by me in not setting himself to aid me in such needs. Let anyone who stands outside judge this without prejudice. When I was dismounted, I immediately went to find Duke Lessandro, and I thanked him warmly for the present of the fifty *scudi*, telling His Excellency that I was most ready in all that I was good for to serve His Excellency. He immediately commanded me that I should make the dies for his coins; and the first that I made was a coin of forty *soldi*, with the head of His Excellency upon one side, and on the other a San Cosimo and a San Damiano. These were silver coins, and they pleased him so much that the Duke ventured to say that they were the most beautiful coins in Christendom. So said all Florence, and every one who saw them. For the which reason I asked of His Excellency that he would confirm to me a pension, and cause the rooms of the Mint to be allotted to me. He told me that I must attend to serving him, and that he would give me much more than that which I was asking for; and in the meantime he told me that he had given directions to the Master of the Mint, who was a certain Carlo Acciaiuoli, and that I must go to him for all the money that I wanted; and this I found to be true; but I drew out the cash so thriftily, that there always remained something due to me, according to my own account. I made, besides, the dies for the *julius,* which was a San Giovanni in profile, sitting with a book in his hand, such that it seemed to me that I had never made a work as beautiful; and upon the other side were the arms of the said Duke Lexandro. After that I made the die for *half-juliuses,* upon which I fashioned a head in full face of a youthful San Giovanni. This was the first coin with the head in full face on so thin a piece of silver (*in tanta sottiglieza di argento*) that was ever made, and this particular difficulty does not appear except to the eyes of those who are skilled in such a profession. After this I made the dies for the gold *scudi,* upon which was a cross on one side, together with certain little cherubim, and on the other side were the arms of His Excellency. When I had made these four kinds of coins, I begged His Excellency that he would determine upon my pension and allot to me the above-mentioned rooms, if my service was pleasing to him; to which petition His Excellency replied kindly that he was very satisfied, and that he would give orders to that effect. Whilst I was speaking to him, His Excellency was in his wardrobe (*guardaroba*), and was examining a wonderful fowling-piece that had been sent to him from Germany, which beautiful weapon, when he saw that I was looking at it with close attention, he put into my hands, saying that he knew very well how much I delighted in such things, and that in earnest of that which he had promised to do for me, I might take from his wardrobe any arquebuse to my taste except this one; for he knew very well that there were many handsomer and as good. This offer I accepted and thanked him for; and when he saw me commencing to search around with my eyes, he directed the wardrobe keeper, who was a certain Pretino da Lucca, to allow me to take exactly what I liked; and when he had with most kindly words departed, I remained and chose the handsomest and best arquebuse that I had

ever seen and that I ever possessed, and this I took home with me.
Two days later I took to him certain small designs, for His Excellency had asked me to fashion some articles in gold, that he
wished to send as a gift to his wife, who was still in Naples. Again
I asked him regarding my self-same affairs, that he would hasten
them on. Whereupon His Excellency told me that he wished first
that I would make the dies for a fine portrait of himself, such as I
had made for Pope Clemente. I commenced the said portrait in
wax, for the which reason His Excellency gave orders that at whatever hour I went to portray him, I was always to be admitted.
I, for I saw that this business of mine was going to be a long one,
summoned a certain Pietro Pagolo of Monte Ritondo, in the district
of Rome, who had been with me in Rome from early boyhood; and
finding that he was with a certain Bernardonaccio, a goldsmith,
who did not treat him very well, I therefore took him away from
him and trained him very carefully to stamp those dies for the
coins; and meanwhile I made the Duke's portrait: and many times
I found him dozing after dinner along with that Lorenzino of
his, who subsequently slew him and no one else; and I marvelled
much that a Duke of that kind was so confiding. It chanced that
Ottaviano de' Medici, who seemed to have the control of everything,
desirous of favoring, against the Duke's will, the old Master of the
Mint, who was named Bastiano Cennini, a man of antiquated type
(*all' anti caccia*) and of limited knowledge, had mixed his clumsy
iron tools together with mine among the dies for the *scudi;* wherefore I complained to the Duke, who, recognizing the truth of the
matter, took it very ill, and said to me: "Go tell Ottaviano de'
Medici this, and show it all to him." Whereupon I went immediately; and when I showed to him the harm that had been done
to my beautiful coins, he said to me in an asinine way: "It pleases
us to do so." I answered him that it ought not to be so, and that

it did not please me. He said: "And what if it should please the
Duke to have it so?" I answered him: "It would not be pleasing
to me; for such a thing is neither just nor reasonable." He said
that I had better take myself off, and that I must swallow (*man-
gerei*) it in that way even if I burst." Returning to the Duke I
narrated to him all that we, Ottaviano de' Medici and I, had argued
so disagreeably: for the which reason I besought His Excellency not
to let them harm the fine coins that I had made, and that he would
give me leave to go away (*buona licentia*). Thereupon he said:
"Ottaviano wants too much, and you shall have what you want,
for this is an insult that he pays to me." This same day, which was
a Thursday, there came to me from Rome an ample safe-conduct
from the Pope, telling me that I must go quickly to obtain the pardon at the Feast of St. Mary of Mid-August, so that I could free
myself from that charge of homicide that I had committed. Going
to the Duke, I found him in bed, for they told me that he had
been dissipating; and having finished in a little over two hours
what I needed to his wax medal, on showing it to him completed,
it pleased him very much. Whereupon I showed to His Excellency
the safe-conduct that I had received by the Pope's directions, and
that the Pope had summoned me back that I might do certain work
for him; on this account I was going to regain that beautiful city
of Rome, and in the meantime I would serve him in the matter of
his medal. At this the Duke said half in anger: "Benvenuto, do as
I wish you, do not go away, for I will pay you the pension, and will
give you the rooms in the Mint, with much more of that which
you do not know how to ask of me, for you ask what is just and
reasonable; and who would you like to use the beautiful dies that
you have made for me?" Whereupon I said: "My lord, everything
has been thought out, for I have here a pupil of mine, who is a
young Roman, and whom I have trained; he will serve Your

Excellency very well, until I return with your medal finished, to stay with you then for always. For I have in Rome my shop still open, with workmen and other business; when I have received the pardon I will leave all the devotion of Rome to one of my pupils, who is there, and then with the kind favor of Your Excellency I will return to you." At this conversation there was present that Lorenzino de' Medici above mentioned, and no one else; the Duke several times signed to him that he also should combine in making me stay; upon the which subject the said Lorenzino never said anything else except: "Benvenuto, you will do the best for yourself by staying." .To which I replied that I wished to regain Rome at any cost. He said nothing more, and stood regarding the Duke continuously with a most evil expression. I having completed the medal to my satisfaction, and having locked it up in its small casket, said to the Duke: "My lord, be of good cheer, for I will make you a much finer medal than I made for Pope Clemente, for it is reasonable that I should do better, since that was the first that I ever made; and Misser Lorenzo here, as a person of learning and of very great ingenuity, shall provide me with some very beautiful reverse for it. To these words the said Lorenzo immediately replied, saying: "I have been thinking of nothing else, but how I could supply a reverse that might be worthy of His Excellency." The Duke smiled evilly, and, looking at Lorenzo, said: "Lorenzo, you shall supply him with a reverse, and he will make it here, and will not go away." Lorenzo answered quickly, saying: "I will make it as rapidly as I can, and I hope to create something that will make the world marvel." The Duke, who sometimes looked upon him as a crazy creature and sometimes as a coward, turned himself in his bed and laughed at the words that he had said. I departed without any other ceremonies of leave-taking, and left them alone together. The Duke, who did not think that I should go, said nothing further to me. When he learnt subsequently that I had left, he sent after me one of his servants, who caught me up in Siena, and gave me fifty gold ducats on behalf of the Duke, telling me to enjoy them out of affection for him, and to return as quickly as I could; and, "on behalf of Misser Lorenzo I tell you that he is devising a wonderful reverse for that medal which you want to make." I had left all the directions with Pietro-pagolo, the Roman above-mentioned, as to the way in which he was to apply the dies; but since the operation was a very difficult one, he never succeeded too well. I remained a creditor of the Mint for labor and tools to the amount of more than seventy *scudi*.

I PROCEEDED to Rome, and I carried with me that most beautiful wheel-arquebuse that the Duke had given me, and made
use of it many times upon the way with very great satisfaction
to myself, deriving remarkable results from it. I arrived in Rome;
and though I owned a cottage in the Strada Julia, since it had not
been set in order, I dismounted at the house of Misser Giovanni
Gaddi, Prelate of the Camera, with whom at my departure from
Rome I had left in charge my many fine arms and many other
things that I greatly valued; moreover I did not wish to dismount
at my own workshop; and I sent for that Felice, my partner, and
made him immediately set in most excellent order that cottage
of mine. The next day afterwards I went to sleep therein, in
order to prepare very carefully my clothes and all that was necessary for me, wishing the following morning to go and visit the
Pope to thank him. I had two little serving-boys, and below my
house there was a laundress who cooked for me in a most cleanly

manner. Having that evening given a supper to several of my friends, and that supper having passed off with greatest enjoyment, I retired to sleep; and the night had perhaps barely passed, for the morning was still more than an hour before daybreak, when I heard a knocking with greatest violence at the door of my house, so that the blows were in quick succession. Wherefore I called to the elder of my servants, who bore the name of Cencio; (he it was whom I took into the magic circle). I told him to go and see who that madman was who at that hour was knocking so savagely. Whilst Cencio was going I, having lit another lamp, for I always kept one (burning) continuously at night, immediately put on, over my shirt, a fine shirt of mail, and over that, a few clothes at random. Cencio returning, said: "Alas! alas! my master, it is the Bargello with all his guard, and he says that if you do not open quickly he will break down the door; and they have torches and a thousand things with them." Upon which I replied: "Tell them that I am putting on a few clothes, and I will come thus in my shirt." Imagining that this was an attack, such as had already been made upon me by the lord Pierluigi, in my right hand I took a wonderful poniard that I had, and in my left the safe-conduct. Then I ran to the window at the back, which looked over certain gardens, and there I saw more than thirty police officers; wherefore I realized that I could not escape upon that side. Having set those two young lads in front of me, I told them that they must open the door exactly when I should tell them. Getting myself ready, the poniard in my right hand, and the safe-conduct in my left, in regular attitude of defence, I said to those two young lads: "Don't be afraid, open." Vittorio, the Bargello, with two others, immediately sprang inside, thinking that they could easily lay hands upon me; but when they saw me thus prepared, they drew back, and said: "Something else besides barking is needful here." Whereupon I said, throwing to them the safe-conduct, "Read that; and since you cannot arrest me, still less will I allow you to touch me." The Bargello thereupon told several of them that they were to arrest me, and that he would see to the safe-conduct later. At this I boldly brandished my weapons and said: "Let God be for the right; either I escape alive, or am taken a corpse." The space was narrow: they showed signs of coming upon me with force, and I was well prepared for defence; for the which reason the Bargello recognized that he could not secure me in any other way than that which I had said. Summoning his clerk (*cancielliere*), whilst he was making him peruse the safe-conduct, he two or three times made as though he would make them lay hands upon me; wherefore I never stirred from the resolution that I had made. Giving up the undertaking, they threw the safe-conduct upon the ground before me, and went away without me. Returning to rest, I felt extremely worn out, nor could I recover my sleep; I had made up my mind that when it was day I would have myself blooded; wherefore I took counsel with Misser Giovanni Gaddi, and he provided me with a leech (*mediconzolo*) of his own, who asked me if I had had a fright. Now you know what sort of medical tact this was when I had related a case of such magnitude, for him to ask such a question? He was a kind of fop (*civettino*) who laughed almost unceasingly, and about nothing; and laughing after that fashion, he told me that I should take a good glass of Greek wine, and that I should strive to be merry and not be afraid. Misser Giovanni, however, said: "Master, a man who was of bronze or marble would under such circumstances be afraid; much more an ordinary man." To this that little leech (*mediconzolino*) replied: "My lord, we are not all made after one pattern: this is not a man of either bronze or marble, but he is of pure iron;" and laying his hand upon my

pulse, with those meaningless giggles of his, he said to Misser Giovanni: "Feel now here. This is not the pulse of a man, but it
is that of a lion or of a dragon." Whereat I, who had a strong pulse,
irritated, perhaps, beyond that point which that stupid doctor had
learnt from neither Hippocrates nor Galen, felt very ill, but in
order not to cause myself more fear, nor more injury than that
which I had experienced already, showed myself to be of good
courage. Meanwhile the said Misser Giovanni was causing them
to make preparations for dinner, and we all ate together. We
were, in company with the said Misser Giovanni, a certain Misser
Lodovico da Fano, Misser Antonio Alleghretti, Misser Giovanni
Ghreco, all persons most skilled in letters, Misser Anibal Caro, who
was very young, nor did they talk of anything else during that
dinner but of this bold performance. And besides, they made that
Cencio, my small servant, who was exceptionally clever, bold, and
very handsome in appearance, recount it; for every time that he
related this mad performance of mine, assuming the attitude that
I had taken, and repeating very excellently also the words that I
had used, he always recalled to me something new; and they often
asked him if he had been afraid; to which questions he replied
that they must ask me if I had been afraid, because he had had
exactly the same (amount of fear) that I had had. This nonsense
became annoying to me, and because I felt very upset, I rose from
the table, saying that I wanted to go to dress myself and him afresh
in blue cloth and silk, for I wanted to walk in the procession there
in four days' time, when the Feast of St. Mary (*le Sante Marie*)
arrived, and I wanted the said Cencio to carry for me the white
lighted torch. Departing, therefore, I went to cut out the blue
clothes, together with a handsome little gown of sarcenet, also blue,
and a little jerkin of the same; and I made for him (Cencio) a
jerkin and a gown of taffetas, also blue. When I had cut out the

said articles, I went to the Pope, who told me that I must speak to his Misser Ambruogio; for he had given orders that I should carry out an important work in gold. So I went to find Misser Ambruogio:—who had been fully informed of the affair of the Bargello, and had himself been in accord with my enemies to make me return to Rome, and had scolded the Bargello because he had not arrested me:—who made excuses, for in the face of a safe-conduct of that kind he could not do it. The said Misser Ambruogio began to talk to me about the business that the Pope had committed to him; then he told me that I must make the designs for it, and that in any event everything would be put right. Meanwhile the day of the Feast of St. Mary arrived; and because it is the custom for those who acquire such pardons as these to surrender themselves to prison, for this reason I repaired to the Pope and told His Holiness that I did not wish to put myself in prison, and that I besought him that he would grant me such a favor that I might not go to prison. The Pope replied that such was the custom, and such I must conform to. At this I knelt down again, and thanked him for the safe-conduct that His Holiness had executed for me; and that with it I would return to serve my Duke of Florence, who was awaiting me with so much longing. At these words the Pope turned to one of his confidential servants and said: "Let the pardon be granted to Benvenuto without the imprisonment. Prepare thus his *motu-proprio* that all may be right." When they had prepared the *motu-proprio,* the Pope counter-signed it: they had it registered at the Capitol; then, on that appointed day, between two noblemen, I walked with much honor in the procession, and received the complete pardon.

Then four days after a very violent fever overtook me with extreme chill; and taking to my bed, I immediately thought the attack mortal. I had the first doctors in Rome summoned, among whom was a certain Master Fran^{co} da Norcia, a very aged doctor, and bearing the highest reputation of those they had in Rome. I recounted to the said doctors what I thought might be the cause of my severe illness, and that I had wished to be blooded, but that I had been advised not; and that if I was in time I begged them to bleed me now. Master Francesco replied that it would not be wise to draw blood now, but that had it been done at the time I should not have been at all ill; now it would be necessary to treat me in another way. So they set to work to doctor me with as much diligence as they were able and knew of; and every day I grew rapidly worse, to such an extent that at the end of eight days the illness had so greatly increased that the doctors, despairing of the case, gave orders that I must be humored, and that everything that I asked for must be given to me. Master Francesco said: "As long as there is breath in him summon me at any hour, for one cannot tell what Nature is able to do in a young man of this kind; moreover, should it happen that he swoon, employ these five remedies one after the other, and send for me, for I will come at any hour of the night; for it would be more pleasing to me to save this man than whichever you please of the cardinals of Rome." There came to visit me two or three times every day Misser Giovanni Gaddi, and every time he kept picking up (some one) of those handsome fowling-pieces of mine and my coats of mail and my swords, and kept continually saying: "This is a beautiful thing and this other thing is more beautiful": likewise my other sketch-models and nick-nacks, in such a way that he became a nuisance to me. And with him used to come a certain Mattio Franzesi, who seemed to think that it was for him also a thousand years ere I died; not because he would chance to derive anything from me, but it seemed as if he desired that whatever Misser Giovanni showed he had a great wish for (should come to pass). I had that Filice, already spoken of as my partner, who afforded me the greatest assistance that one man could ever in this world give to another. My constitution was entirely weakened and brought down, and there did not remain in me sufficient strength, that when once my breath had issued from me I could recover it again; but nevertheless the soundness of my brain stood firm, just as it did when I was not ill. Therefore, while thus conscious, there came to see me in bed a terrible old man who wanted to drag me by force into a very large boat of his; wherefore I called to that Felice of mine, that he should come near me and drive away that old scoundrel. That Felice, who was most affectionate to me, ran up weeping, and said: "Go away, you old traitor! who wants to rob me of every good thing that I possess." Misser Giovanni Gaddi, who was there present, then said: "The poor fellow raves, and there are but a few hours left for him." That other, Mattio Franzesi, said: "He has read Dante, and from this great weakness there has come upon him this rambling." And so he said laughing: "Go away, you old scoundrel, don't annoy our Benvenuto." Perceiving that they were scoffing at me, I turned to Misser Giovanni Gaddi, and said to him: "My dear master, you know that I do not rave, and that it is true about this old man, who is giving me this great annoyance; but you will do me the greatest kindness in taking away from my presence this wretched creature of a Mattio, who laughs at my misfortune; and then when your lordship deigns that I see him again, would you come with Misser Antonio Allegretti or with Misser Annibal Caro, or with some of those others of your talented friends, who are persons of a different discretion, and different talent from this animal." Thereupon Misser Giovanni said in jest to that Mattio, that he must take himself off forever; but since Mattio laughed, the jest became in earnest, for Misser Giovanni never wanted to see him again, and caused them to summon Misser Ant° Alleghretti and Misser Lodovico and Misser Annibal Caro. When these worthy men had arrived I took greatest comfort thereat, and talked with them sensibly for a while, nevertheless urging Felice to drive away the old man. Misser Lodovico asked what it was that I seemed to see and what was the appearance of the man. Whilst I was drawing him accurately in words, this old man took me by an arm, and forcibly drew me towards himself, wherefore I cried out that they should help me because he wanted to throw me beneath the decks of that terrifying boat of his. When I had uttered this last word, there came upon me a very great swoon, and it seemed to me that he threw me into that boat. They say that then during this swoon I tossed myself about and uttered evil words to Misser Giovanni Gaddi, that he had come to rob me, and not out of any sort of charity, and many other most ugly expressions, which caused shame to the said Misser Giovanni. Then they said that I stayed still as one dead; and having stayed beside me more than one hour, when it seemed to them that I was growing cold, they left me for dead. And when they returned to their homes, that Mattio Franzesi got to know it, who wrote to Florence to Misser Benedetto Varchi, my very dear friend, that at such and such an hour of the night they had seen me expire. For the which reason that very talented man and my very great friend, Misser Benedetto, composed an admirable sonnet upon the not true but so generally believed (report of my) death, which I will insert in its proper place. More than three full hours passed before I came to myself again, and having tried all the remedies of the above-mentioned Master Fran^{co}, when he saw that I did not revive, my very dear Felice hastily ran to Master Fran^{co} da Norcia's house, and knocked so much that he awoke him and made him get up, and, weeping, besought him to come home with him, for he thought that I was dead. At which Master Fran^{co}, who was very irritable, said: "My son, what do you think that I can do by coming thither? If he is dead it grieves me more than it does you; do you think that by coming thither with my medical skill I can pump breath into him with an enema, and restore him to life?" When he saw that the poor youth was going away weeping, he called him back, and gave him a certain oil wherewith to anoint my pulses and my heart, and (told him) that he should pinch very sharply my little toes and fingers (*le dita migniole de' piedi e delle mane*); and that, if I revived, he must immediately send to summon him. Felice departing, did as Master Fran^{co} had told him; and when it was almost full daylight, and they seemed to be deprived of hope, they gave orders for the making of my shroud, and for washing me. All of a sudden I revived, and summoned Felice that he should very quickly drive away that old man who was annoying me so. Felice wanted to send for Master Fran^{co}, but I told him not to send for him, and that he must come close to me, for that old man was going away directly, and was afraid of him. When Felice came near me, I took hold of him, and it seemed to me that that old man, infuriated, departed; however I besought him that he would stay always beside me. When Master Fran^{co} appeared, he said that he wished to cure me at any cost, and that he had never in his life seen in a young man greater strength than mine; and setting himself to write, he prescribed for me fomentations, lotions, unguents, plasters, and many innumerable things. Meantime I revived, with more than twenty leeches on my backside, bored, bound up and ground to powder (*forato, legato e tutto macinato*). Many of my friends having come to see the miracle of the dead restored to life, there appeared men of great eminence, and many of them too; in their presence I said that that small quantity of gold and of money (which might amount to about

eight hundred *scudi* in gold, silver, precious stones and cash), these
I wished to be for my poor sister who was in Florence, who bore
the name of Mona Liperata: all the remainder of my goods, as
much my weapons as everything else, I wished to be for my very
dear Filice, and fifty ducats of gold besides, so that he might be
able to clothe himself. At these words Filice flung himself upon
my neck, saying that he did not want anything, except that he
wished me to live. Whereupon I said: "If you wish me to live,
hold on to me after this manner, and rebuke that old man who
is afraid of you." At these words some of them were terrified,
recognizing that I was not raving, but that I was speaking on purpose, and rationally. So my serious illness went steadily on, and
I got but little better. That most excellent Master Francesco came
four or five times a day; Misser Giovanni Gaddi, for he was
ashamed, came into my presence no more. There appeared my
brother-in-law, the husband of my said sister: he came from Florence for the inheritance; and since he was a very worthy man,
he was very pleased to have found me alive; it gave me unbounded
comfort to see him, and he immediately showed me attentions,
saying that he had come with the sole object of taking care of
me with his own hands; and so he did for several days. Afterwards I sent him away, having almost certain hope of health. Then
he left me the Sonnet of Misser Benedetto Varchi, which ran as
follows:

On the Supposed but Falsely-reported Death of Benvenuto Cellini.

Mattio, who shall all our grief console,
And bid our tears and lamentation cease?
Alas! 'tis true, our friend hath found release;
Leaving us here, to heav'n hath soar'd his soul.
His gentle, kindly spirit could not stay;
In art had he no rival here below,
Nor shall this world a greater craftsman know,
This world, from which the best pass first away.
Sweet spirit, if beyond our mortal veil
Love yet is thine, look down from realms above
On him that upon earth thou once didst love;
My loss, not all thy bliss, do I bewail.
Th' august Creator dost thou now behold
Whom here with cunning hands 'twas thine to mould.

The ailment had been so severe that it did not seem possible that it could come to an end; and that excellent man Master Fran^{co} da Norcia, made greater efforts than ever, and every day kept bringing me fresh remedies, seeking to strengthen the poor broken-down machine, and with all those endless efforts it did not seem that it would be possible to bring this spite (*indegnatione*) to an end; in such measure that all the doctors were well-nigh in despair, and did not know what more to do. For I had a raging thirst, but I was restrained (from drinking) according to their orders for many days; and that Felice, to whom it appeared that he had done a fine work in saving me, never left me; and that old man no more gave me so much annoyance, though he visited me some-times in my dreams. One day Felice had gone out, and there remained on duty one of my shop-boys and a servant maid, who was called Beatrice. I asked that shop-boy what had become of that lad of mine, Cencio, and what was the explanation that I had never seen him in my need. This shop-boy told me that Cencio had had a much more severe illness than I had had, and that he was at the point of death. Felice had commanded them that they should not tell me this. When he had told me this circumstance I was very greatly distressed by it; then I summoned that said servant maid Beatrice (a native of Pistoia), and begged her to bring me a great wine-cooler of crystal that was there near me, full of clear and fresh water. This woman ran immediately and brought it to me full. I told her to put it to my mouth, and that if she would let me drink a draught according to my own desire, I would give her a gown. This servant maid, who had robbed me of certain small articles of some importance, for fear lest I should discover the theft, would have been very pleased that I should die; wherefore she let me drink of that water in two draughts, as much as I could, so much that in good sooth I drank more than a flask of it; then I covered myself up and began to perspire and to doze. When Felice returned, after I must have slept about an hour, he asked the boy how I did. The boy replied: "I don't know; Beatrice brought him that wine-cooler full of water, and he drank almost all of it; I do not know now whether he be alive or dead." They say that this poor youth was ready to fall to the ground from the great distress that he felt; then he took an ugly stick, and with it he madly thrashed that servant maid, saying: "Oh! you traitress! You have killed him for me." While Felice was thrashing her, and she was crying out, I was dreaming, and it seemed to me that that old man had cords in his hands; and as he was wishing to give directions for binding me, Felice had come upon him, and struck him with a hatchet, in such a way that this old man fled, crying out: "Let me go, for I will not come to him for a long time." Meanwhile Beatrice, screaming loudly, had rushed into my chamber; whereat, I awaking, said: "Let her alone, for perhaps in order to do me harm she has done me as much good; for you have never been able with all your efforts to do anything of that which she has done. Attend to helping me for I am covered with perspiration, and do it quickly." Filice recovering his courage, dried me and made me comfortable; and I, since I felt the greatest improvement, promised myself restored health. When Master Francesco appeared, seeing this great improvement, and the servant maid in tears, and the shop-boy running in and out, and Filice smiling, this confusion made the doctor think that some extraordinary event had taken place, which had been the cause of this my great improvement. Meanwhile there appeared that other (physician), Master Bernardino, who at the outset had objected to blooding me. Master Francesco, that most clever man, said: "Oh, power of nature! She knows her own needs, and doctors know nothing at all." Immediately that idiot (*cervellino*) of a Master Bernardino answered and said: "If he had drunk a flask more he would immediately have been cured." Master Fran^co da Norcia, an old man and a person of great weight, said: "That were a misfortune that may God bestow upon you." And then he turned to me and asked me if I could have drunk any more; at which I replied: "No, for I had entirely quenched my thirst." Then he turned to the said Master Bernardino, and said: "Do you see that nature has taken precisely what was necessary, and neither more nor less? Thus was she asking what she needed, when the poor young man begged you to bleed him; if you knew that his health depended now upon the drinking of two flasks of water, why did you not say so before? and you would then have had something to boast of." At these words the leech angrily departed, and never came there anymore. Then Master Francesco said that I must be removed from that chamber, and that I must have myself conveyed towards one of the Roman hills. Cardinal Cornaro, having heard of my improvement (in health), had me taken to a place of his that he possessed upon

Monte Cavallo; the same evening I was borne with great car
upon a chair well covered up and closed in. When I arrived ther
I began to vomit; during that vomiting there issued from m
stomach a hairy worm, a quarter of a *braccio* in length; and th
hairs (upon it) were long, and the worm was most hideous, marke
in divers colors, green, black and red. They kept it for the docto
who said that he had never seen such a thing; and then he sai
to Felice: "Take great care now of your Benvenuto, for he is cure
and do not allow him to commit any indiscretions; for thoug
he has escaped this one, another indiscretion now would kill hir
for you; you see, the disease has been so severe, that we shoul
not even have been in time to bring to him the Holy Oil. No
I know that with a little patience and time he will yet execut
other works of art." Then he turned to me and said: "My Ben
venuto, be prudent and do not commit any indiscretions: and whe
you are cured, I want you to make me an *Our Lady* with you
own hands, for I wish to adore her always out of affection fo
you." Wherefore I promised him that thing. Then I aske
him whether I might transport myself as far as Florence. Wherea
he told me that I must get myself a little stronger, and then w
would see what nature would do.

WHEN we (had) passed eight days, the improvement was so slight that I became as it were a weariness even to myself; for I had been more than fifty days in that great suffering; and having made a resolution I got myself ready; and in a pair of panniers, my dear Felice and I proceeded towards Florence; and since I had not written anything I arrived in Florence at my sister's house, where I was wept and laughed over at one and the same moment by that same sister. Upon that day there came to see me many of my friends; among the others Pier Landi, who was the greatest and dearest friend that I ever had in the world; the next day there came a certain Nicholò da Monte Aguto, who was my very great friend, and since he had heard the Duke say: "Benvenuto would have done much better to have died, for he is come here to put his head in a noose, and I will never pardon him for it," Nicholò coming to me said to me despairingly: "Ah me! my dear Benvenuto, what have you come here for? Don't you know what you have done against the Duke? For I have heard him swear, saying that you were come to thrust your head into a noose at all costs." Thereupon I said: "Nicholò, remind His Excellency that already Pope Clemente wished to do the same thing to me, and as wrongfully; and if I am taken care of and allowed to get well, I will show His Excellency that I have been the most faithful servant that he will ever have during the course of his life, and since some enemy of mine has out of envy done me this ill turn, let him wait my recovery of health, for as far as I can I will render such an account of myself as I will make him wonder." Giorgetto Vassellario, an Aretine and a painter, had done me this ill turn, perhaps as a recompense for so many great benefits bestowed upon him; for having entertained him in Rome and paid his expenses, he had thrown my household into confusion. For he had a kind of dry leprosy, which his hands were always scratching, and while sleeping with an excellent shop-lad that I had, who was called Manno, thinking that he was scratching himself, he had scraped one of the legs of the said Manno with some of his dirty claws, of which the nails were never cut. The said Manno gave me notice, and wanted to kill him at any cost. I made peace between them; then I placed the said Giorgio with Cardinal de' Medici, and constantly helped him. This is his return (*merito*), that he told Duke Lessandro that I had spoken ill of His Excellency, and that I had boasted of wishing to be the first to leap on to the walls of Florence in alliance with the exiled enemies of His Excellency. These words, according to what I subsequently heard, that fine gentleman (*galant 'uomo*) Ottaviano de' Medici had caused him to repeat, being desirous of taking revenge for the vexation that the Duke had shown towards him with reference to the coins, and at my departure from Florence; but since I was innocent of this falsehood laid to my charge, I had no fear in the world; and the clever master Fran.co da Montevarchi doctored me with the greatest skill, and it was my very dear friend Luca Martini,—who remained with me the greater part of the day,—who had brought him to me. Meanwhile I had sent back to Rome my most faithful Felice to take charge of my affairs there. When I could raise my head somewhat from the bolster, which was at the end of fifteen days, although I could not walk upon my feet, I had myself carried into the Palazzo de' Medici up to where there is a small upper terrace: thus I had myself set down (*mettere a sedere*) to wait until the Duke should pass by. And many of my court friends coming to talk with me marveled much that I had taken that trouble to have myself carried in that fashion, being in so weak a condition from illness; telling me that I ought to have waited to be cured, and then visited the Duke. There being a number of them assembled together, they all looked upon me as a miracle; not only from their having heard that I was dead, but still more did I appear to them a miracle, because I (yet) seemed to them like a dead man. Thereupon I related in the presence of them all, how it had been told to my lord the Duke by some wicked scoundrel that I had boasted of wishing to be the first to leap on to the walls of His Excellency, and that I had spoken ill of him besides; for the which cause there was in me no courage to live nor to die until I had purged myself of that infamy, and knew who was that rash scoundrel who had spread that false report. To hearken to these words there were assembled a vast number of those nobles, and when they showed that they had very great compassion for me, and some said one thing and some another, I said that I never more wished to depart from that place until I knew who he was that had accused me. At these words there came from among all those noblemen, Master Agostino, the Duke's tailor, and said: "If that is all you want to know, now, even now, you will know." At that moment there passed by the above-mentioned Giorgio, the painter. Thereupon Master Agustino said: "There is the man who has accused you. Now you know yourself if it be true or not." I fiercely, being thus unable to move, asked Giorgio if such a statement were true. The said Giorgio said: "No, that it was not true, and that he had never said such a thing." Master Austino (*sic*) said: "Oh, gallows bird! do you not know that I know it for absolute certainty?" Giorgio immediately departed, saying:

"No, that it was not he." A short time elapsed, and the Duke passed by; upon which I immediately had myself held up before His Excellency, and he stopped. Thereupon I said that I had come thither in that fashion merely to justify myself. The Duke gazed at me and marveled that I was alive. Then he said that I must attend to being an honest man and getting well. Returning home, Niccolò da Monte Aguto came to see me, and told me that I had escaped one of the greatest dangers in the world, a thing which he had never believed possible, for he saw my downfall written in unchangeable ink; and that I must see to getting well quickly and then depart at once, for it (the danger) came from a direction and from a man who would do me evil. Then, having said: "Take care of yourself," he added: "What annoyance have you given to that big scoundrel of an Ottaviano de' Medici?" I replied that I had never caused him any annoyance, but that he had done so to me; and when I recounted the whole story of the Mint, he said to me: "Go away as quickly as you can, and be of good courage, for sooner than you think you will see your revenge." I attended to curing myself: I gave advice to Pietro Pagolo in the matter of the dies for the coin; then I took my departure, returning to Rome, without speaking with the Duke or any one else.

When I had arrived in Rome and had diverted myself sufficiently with my friends, I commenced the Duke's medal; and in a few days I had already completed the head in steel, the finest work that I had ever fashioned of that kind, and there came to see me once at least every day a certain big fool, named Misser Fran.co Soderini; and when he saw what I was doing he said to me many times over: "Oh! cruel wretch! Do you want to immortalize for us that raging tyrant? and since you never made so fine a work, by this we know that you are our cordial enemy, and very much their friend, although the Pope and he have twice wrongfully wished to hang you; that was the father and the son; beware now of the holy spirit." It was held as a certain fact that the Duke Lessandro was the son of Pope Clemente. The said Misser Fran^{co} used to say besides and to swear positively that if he were able he would have robbed me of the dies for that medal. To which I replied that he had done well to tell me so, for I would keep them in such a way that he should never see them again. I caused it to be known in Florence that they should tell Lorenzino to send me the reverse for the medal. Niccolò da Monte Aguto, to whom I had written, wrote to me thus, saying that he had asked that mad melancholy philosopher, Lorenzino, who had told him that day and night he thought of nothing else, and that he would make it as soon as he was able; nevertheless he told me not to set hope upon his reverse, and that I must make one for myself from my own original invention; and that when I had finished it, I must bring it freely to the Duke, for it would be to my advantage. Having made a design for a reverse which seemed to me suitable, with as much care as I could I proceeded with it; but since I was not yet recovered from that inordinate illness, I took great pleasure in going to the chase with my fowling-piece in company with that dear Filice of mine, who knew nothing whatever about the practice of my trade, but since we were together continually day and night, every one imagined that he was most skilled in the business. For the which reason, he being excessively amusing, we laughed together a thousand times over this great credit that he had acquired; and since he was called Filice *Guadagni* (Profits), he used to say, in conversation with me: "I should call myself Filice *Guadagnipoco* (Small-Profits); but you have caused me to acquire so great a renown that I can call myself *De' Guadagni assai* (*i.e.*, of the noble family of Great-Profits)." And I used to say to him that there were two methods of making profits; the first is, that which one earns for oneself, and the second, that which one earns for others; wherefore I praised in him much more that second method, than the first, since he had gained for me my life. These talks we had many and many a time, but among other occasions one day at Epiphany-tide we were together near the Magliana, and it was already almost at the close of day; a day upon which I had slain with my fowling-piece a large number of ducks and geese; and having almost decided not to shoot any more, while daylight lasted we were steadily moving towards Rome. Calling up my dog, who bore the name of Barucco, not seeing him ahead of me, I turned round and saw that the said dog,—as he was trained to do,—was watching certain geese that had settled in a ditch. I therefore immediately dismounted; and getting ready my good fowling-piece, I fired at them from a long distance, and brought down two with a single shot; for I never cared to fire with more than one single bullet, with which I used to fire two hundred *braccia*, and the majority of times struck (my object); [for one cannot do thus by any other methods]; wherefore having brought down both geese, one almost dead and the other wounded, and though thus badly wounded it flew clumsily away until my dog following it brought it to me; when I, observing that the other was plunging down into the ditch, sprang upon it. Trusting myself to my boots, which were very high ones, thrusting forward my foot, I sank beneath the soil; and though I secured the goose, I got the boot of my right leg entirely filled with water. Raising my foot in the air, I emptied out the water, and, mounting my horse, we hurried along upon our return to Rome; but since it was very cold, I felt my leg in a state of freeze, so that I said to Filice: "I must relieve this leg here, for I do not know how to endure it." The excellent Filice, without saying anything further, dismounted from his horse, and having collected thistles and twigs, got ready to make preparations for a fire, and while I waited, having placed my hands among the breast feathers of those geese, I felt them very warm; for the which reason I would not let him make a fire after all, but I filled that boot of mine with the feathers of that goose, and I immediately felt so much relief that it gave me life. Remounting our horses we came steadily towards Rome. When we had arrived at a certain small eminence, it was already night. Gazing in the direction of Florence, we both with one accord uttered a loud cry of astonishment, saying: "Oh, God of Heaven! what great thing is that which we see above Florence?" It was like a great beam of fire that shone and emitted very great radiance. I said to Filice: "We shall certainly hear to-morrow that some great event has taken place in Florence." So we reached Rome; it was very dark; and when we got into the neighborhood of the Banks and near our own home, I was mounted upon my nag, which was proceeding at a most rapid amble, to such purpose that, there having been that day made in the middle of the road a mound of rubbish and broken tiles, that horse of mine, not seeing the mound, nor I either, climbed it at that furious pace, and then went headlong in the descent, in such fashion as to cause a tumble. He put his head between his legs; whereat I, by the special mercy of God, suffered no hurt in the world. When lights had been brought out by the neighbors at that great noise, I had sprung to my feet; therefore, without mounting again, I ran home, laughing at having escaped the misfortune of breaking my neck. When I reached my house, I found certain of my friends, to whom, while we supped together, I recounted the disasters of my sport and that devilish affair of the beam of fire which we had seen; and they said: "What will this signify to-morrow?" I replied: "It must be some new event that has occurred in Florence!" Thus the supper passed pleasantly for us; the next day at a late hour the news came to Rome of the death of Duke Lessandro. Wherefore many of my acquaintances came to me, saying: "You said well, that upon Florence must have chanced some great event." At this there came bouncing along, mounted upon a wretched mule of his, that Misser Fran.^{co} Soderini. Laughing loudly on the way like a madman, he kept saying: "This is the reverse of the medal of that wicked tyrant, which your Lorenzino de' Medici promised you;" and he added further: "You wanted to immortalize the Dukes for us; we want no more Dukes;" and then he mocked at me as if I had been the leader of those factions that set up the Dukes. At this juncture there came up a certain Baccio Bettini, who had a thick skull like a basket, and he also began to mock at me about these Dukes, saying to me: "We have unDuked them (*isducati*), and will have no more Dukes; and you wanted to make them immortal;" with many of this sort of ugly words. These men becoming too much of a nuisance to me, I said to them: "Oh! silly fools! I am a poor goldsmith, who serves whoever pays me, and you are mocking me as if I were the head of a faction; but I do not want on that account to tax you with the insatiability, madnesses, and inability of your predecessors; but I tell you plainly in reply to those many silly jeers in which you are indulging, that before two or three days are passed at the longest you will have another Duke perhaps much worse than this last one." The next day following there came to my shop that Bettini, and said to me: "It would be useless to spend money in couriers, for you know things before they take place. What spirit is it that tells you?" And he told me that Cosimo de' Medici, son of the Lord Giovanni, had been made Duke; but that he was made so under certain conditions, which would have to be kept by him, so that he should not be able to fly about in his own way. Thereupon it was my turn to laugh at them, and I said: "These men of Florence have set a youth upon a wonderful horse; then they have put spurs upon him, given the bridle with his freedom into his hand, and set him in a most beautiful meadow, where are flowers and fruits and very many delights. Then they have told him that he must not pass certain prescribed boundaries. Now tell me, you! who can hold him back when the wish to pass them comes to him? One cannot enforce laws upon the man who is the master of those laws." So they left me alone and gave me no more annoyance.

Having attended to my shop, I continued some of my orders that were not indeed of great moment, because I was attending to the restoration of my health, and besides, I did not seem to be recovered from the great sickness through which I had passed. Meanwhile, the Emperor was returning victorious from the Tunis expedition, and the Pope sent for me, and took counsel with me what sort of honorable gift I advised him to present to the Emperor. To which I replied that it seemed to me that a cross of gold with a (figure of) Christ upon it would be the most appropriate thing to give to His Majesty, an ornamental piece of work which I had almost completed, the which would be very appropriate, and would do very great honor to His Holiness and to me. Having already fashioned three little figures of gold, in full relief, of about one palm in size (these said figures were those which I had begun for the chalice of Pope Clemente), they were fashioned for Faith, Hope, and Charity, whereto I added in wax all the rest of the foot of the said cross; and having carried it to the Pope with the Christ in wax and with many most beautiful ornaments, it greatly satisfied the Pope; and before I parted from His Holiness we remained in agreement with regard to all that I had to do, and afterwards we valued the workmanship of the said work of art. This occurred one evening at the fourth hour of the night: the Pope had given commission to Misser Latino Juvinale that he should cause the money to be given to me the following morning. It seemed to the said Misser Latino, who had a great streak in him of the madman, that he would like to suggest a new idea to the Pope, which came simply out of his own head; for he upset all that had been arranged; and in the morning, when I thought of going for the money, he said with that beastly presumption of his: "It is our business to be the designers, and yours the workmen. Before I left the Pope last evening, we thought of something much better." To these first words, without allowing him to proceed further, I said to him: "Neither you nor the Pope can ever think of anything better than those things wherein the (figure of) Christ is introduced. Therefore tell me now how much courtier nonsense you know." Without saying anything further he departed from me in anger, and sought to hand over the said work of art to another goldsmith; but the Pope would not, and immediately sent for me, and said to me that I had spoken well, but that they wanted to make use of a Book of Offices of the Madonna which was wonderfully illuminated, and which had cost Cardinal de' Medici more than two thousand *scudi* to have illuminated; and this would be appropriate for employment as a gift to the Empress, and that they would subsequently make for the Emperor that thing which I had prepared, for it was truly a present worthy of him; but this was caused by their having so little time, for the Emperor was expected in Rome within a month and a half. For the said book he wanted a cover made of solid gold, richly worked, and adorned with many precious stones. The precious stones were valued at about six thousand *scudi;* so that when the precious stones and the gold were given to me, I set myself to the said work, and applying myself to it, in a few days I made it appear of such beauty that the Pope marveled and showed me the greatest favors, with an agreement that that beast of a Juvinale should not come near me. When the said work was near to completion, the Emperor appeared, for whom there were made many wondrous triumphal arches, and he arrived in Rome with a marvelous pomp, such as it behoves others to write about, because I do not want to dwell except upon such matters as concern myself. Immediately upon his arrival he presented to the Pope a diamond, which he had bought for twelve thousand *scudi*. The Pope sent for me and gave me this diamond in order that I might fashion with it a ring, to the measure of His Holiness' finger; but he desired that I would first of all bring him the Book at the point at which it then was. When I brought the Book to the Pope he was greatly satisfied; then he consulted me as to what excuse he could find with the Emperor, which might be a valid one, because that said work of art was incomplete. Whereupon I said that the valid excuse was that I had told him about my illness, which His Majesty would very easily believe when he saw how wasted and pale I was. Upon this the Pope said that he was much pleased (at the idea), but that I must add on behalf of His Holiness, when presenting the Book, that he was making a gift of me myself; and he told me exactly the manner that I was to assume, the words that I had to say, which words I repeated to the Pope, asking him, that if they pleased him, he would say so. He said to me: "You will speak too well if you have the courage to speak to the Emperor in the way that you are speaking to me." Whereupon I said that I had the courage to speak with much greater confidence to the Emperor; for it happened that the Emperor went about clad just as I went about myself, and that to me it would seem that I was speaking to a man who was made like myself; a fact which did not so happen to me when speaking with His Holiness, in whom I perceived a much greater divinity, as much on account of his ecclesiastical adornments, which displayed a certain royalty (*diadema*) to me, as on account of His Holiness' handsome old age; all these attributes caused me more awe than those of the Emperor. At these words the Pope said: "Go, Benvenuto mine, for you are a clever man. Do us credit, for it will be to your advantage." The Pope ordered two Turkish horses, which had belonged to Pope Clemente, and they were the most beautiful that had ever come into Christendom. These two horses the Pope committed to Misser Durante, his chamberlain, that he should take them down into the corridors of the Palace, and there present them to the Emperor, employing certain expressions that he enjoined upon him. We went down together; and when we reached the presence of the Emperor these two horses entered those halls with so much dignity and with such nobility (of appearance), that the Emperor and everyone marveled. Upon this the said Misser Durante came forward in so awkward a manner and with some of his Brescian dialect, tying up (*annodandosigli*) his tongue in his mouth in such a way that one never saw or heard anything worse; the Emperor was moved somewhat to laughter. At this moment I had already uncovered my said work of art; and when the Emperor, perceiving me, with a most gracious gesture turned his glances in my direction, I came forward immediately and said: "Sacred Majesty, Our Most Holy Father Pope Paulo sends this Book of the Madonna to be presented to Your Majesty, which is engrossed and illuminated by the hand of the greatest man who ever practiced such a profession; and this rich cover of gold and precious stones is thus imperfect on account of my illness; for the which reason His Holiness presents me also, along with the said Book, that I may come after your Majesty in order to finish his Book; and beyond that, in everything that you have a mind to have done as long as I live, I will serve you." To this the Emperor replied: "The Book is acceptable to me and you also; but I want you to finish it for me in Rome; and when it is finished and you cured, bring it along and come and see me." Then in discoursing with me he called me by name, at which circumstance I marveled, because no words had passed wherein my name had occurred; and he told me that he had seen that Morse belonging to Pope Clemente, whereon I had made so many wonderful figures. Thus we extended our conversation for an entire half-hour, speaking of many divers things all clever and agreeable: and so it seemed to me that matters had turned out for me with much greater credit than that which I had promised for myself. When a little pause occurred in the conversation, I made a bow and departed. The Emperor was heard to say: "Give Benvenuto five hundred gold *scudi* immediately," in such a way that he who brought them up asked which was the Pope's man who had spoken to the Emperor. Misser Durante came forward, who robbed me of my five hundred *scudi*. I complained to the Pope, who told me that I must not trouble, for he knew all about it, how I had conducted myself excellently in my conversation with the Emperor, and that of that money I should in any case get my share.

RETURNING to my shop, I set to work with great assiduity to finish the diamond ring; regarding which there were sent to me (four persons), the principal jewelers in Rome; because it had been told to the Pope that that diamond had been set in Venice by the handiwork of the first jeweler in the world, who was called Master Miliano Targhetta, and since that diamond was somewhat thin, it was an undertaking too difficult to execute without great consideration. I was very pleased to see these four jewelers, among whom was a Milanese, named Gaio. This man was the most presumptuous beast in the world, and the one who knew the least; and it seemed to him that he knew the most; the others were most modest and most able men. This Gaio in the presence of us all began to talk, and said: "You must keep Miliano's coloring material (*tinta*) and to that, Benvenuto, you must just take off your hat; for as the coloring of a diamond is the most beautiful and the most difficult process that there is in the art of jewelry, Miliano is the greatest jeweler that there ever was in the world, and this is the most difficult diamond." Thereupon I said that so much was it the greater glory for me to compete with so able a man in such a profession. Then I turned to the other jewelers and said: "Observe that I have preserved Miliano's coloring material, and I will try if in my work I can improve upon it; if not we will recolor it with the same as before." That animal Gaio said that if I did succeeded by that means, he would gladly take off his cap to it. To which I replied: "Then if it is better done it will deserve two liftings of your cap." "Yes," said he, and so I began to compose my colorings. I applied myself with greatest diligence to the composition of my colors, the details of which I will describe in their own place. Most certainly the said diamond was the most difficult that ever before or since had come before me, and that coloring of Miliano was cleverly made; however, I was not yet dismayed. Having sharpened the tools of my brain (*mia ferruzi dello ingegnio*) I did it so well that I not merely came up to it, but I very much surpassed him. Then, having realized that I had surpassed him, I started trying to surpass myself, and with new methods I composed a coloring material that was by a long way better than that which I had (previously) made. Then I sent to summon the jewelers, and I colored the diamond with Miliano's color; afterwards, when thoroughly cleaned, I retinted it with my own. When I showed it to the jewelers, the leading brilliant man among them, who was named Raffael del Moro, having taken the diamond in his hand, said to Gaio: "Benvenuto has surpassed Miliano's color." Gaio, who did not want to credit it, took the diamond into his hand and said: "Benvenuto! this diamond is two thousand ducats better than with Miliano's coloring." Thereupon I said: "Then I have surpassed Miliano, let us see if I cannot surpass even my own self;" and begging them to wait a little while

I went up into my closet, and outside their presence I recolored the diamond, and when I brought it to the jewelers, Gaio immediately said: "This is the most wondrous thing that I ever saw in all my life, for this diamond is worth more than eighteen thousand *scudi,* whereas we valued it at barely twelve." The other jewelers turning to Gaio said: "Benvenuto is the glory of our profession, and deservedly both to his colors and to himself we ought to take off our caps." Gaio then said: "I want to go and tell the Pope, and I want him to have a thousand *scudi* in gold for the setting of this diamond." And hurrying to the Pope he told him everything; for the which reason the Pope sent three times that day to see if the ring were finished. Then at twenty-three of the clock I took up the ring; and since the door was not closed to me, as I was discreetly raising the curtain, I saw the Pope together with the Marchese del Guasto, who must have been urging upon him things that he did not want to do, and I heard him say to the Marchese: "I tell you No, for it behooves me to be neutral and nothing else." When I hastily drew back a little, the Pope himself called to me; whereupon I quickly entered, and carrying that fine diamond in my hand, the Pope drew me thus aside, whereat the Marchese retired. The Pope, while he examined the diamond, said to me, "Benvenuto, keep up a conversation with me that may seem to be of some importance, and don't ever leave off as long as the Marchese remains here in this room." And beginning to walk up and down—since the matter was to my advantage it pleased me—and I began to talk with the Pope regarding the method that I had employed in coloring the diamond. The Marchese stood upright apart leaning against a tapestry hanging, and twisted himself about now upon one foot and now upon another. The subject of this discussion was of such importance that if one wished to discuss it fully, it might have been carried on for three whole hours. The Pope derived such great pleasure out of it that he forgot the annoyance that he had received from the Marchese, who stood there. I had intermingled in the discussion that part of philosophy which belongs to that profession (of ours), in such a way that, when we had conversed thus for nearly an hour, it became an annoyance to the Marchese, and he departed half in a rage; thereupon the Pope showed me the most friendly courtesies that it is possible to imagine in the world, and he said: "Wait, Benvenuto mine, for I will give you another reward for your skill than the thousand *scudi* that Gaio has told me your labor deserves." When I had thus departed the Pope praised me in the presence of those servants of his, among whom was that Latino Juvenale, whom I have spoken of before. This man, since he had become my enemy, sought with every effort to do me harm; and when he saw that the Pope spoke of me with so much affection and praise, he said: "There is no doubt that Benvenuto is a person of wondrous skill: but although every man is naturally supposed to like better those of his own country than outsiders, one ought still to consider in what way one should speak regarding a Pope. He has been heard to say that Pope Clemente was the finest ruler that ever was, and equally talented, but indeed cursed with ill luck; and he says that Your Holiness is exactly the opposite, and that that *tiara* weeps on your head, and that you appear like a dressed-up bundle of straw, but that for you there is nothing but good luck." These words were of such weight, spoken by one who knew exceedingly well how to express them, that the Pope believed them. I had not only not said them, but such a thing had never come into my mind. If the Pope could have done so with credit to himself, he would have done me very great injury; but since he was a person of very great tact, he made pretense to laugh at it; none the less he preserved in himself a dislike towards me so great as to be boundless, and I began to perceive it, for I did not obtain access to his apartments with the facility of heretofore, but rather with very great difficulty. And since I had been for many years a frequenter of those courts, I fancied that some one had done a bad turn against me; and after dexterous inquiry I was told the whole story, but I was not told who the mischief-maker was; and I could not imagine who would have said such a thing, for had I known I would have taken my revenge to a measure of charcoal. I set myself to the completion of my little Book; and when I had completed it I carried it to the Pope, who truly could not refrain himself from praising me greatly. Upon which I told him that he must send me to carry it (to the Emperor) as he had promised me. The Pope answered me, that he would do whatever might seem good to him to do, and that I had done what appertained to me. So he gave directions that I should be well paid. For these works in little more than two months I gained five hundred *scudi;* for the diamond I was paid at the rate of one hundred and fifty *scudi* and no more; all the remainder was given me for the fashioning of that little Book, the making of which was worth more than a *thousand,* since it was a work rich in many figures and foliages, and enamels and precious stones. I took what I could get and made a plan to depart altogether from Rome. In the meantime the Pope sent the said little Book to the Emperor by the hand of one of his nephews, called the lord Sforza, to whom, on his presenting the book, the Emperor was most grateful, and immediately asked after me. The youthful lord Sforza, being instructed, said, that on account of my being ill I had not come. All this was reported to me. Meantime I got myself in readiness to go towards France, and I wanted to go alone; but I could not do so, because of a lad who lived with me, who was called Ascanio. This youth was of very tender age, and he was the most admirable servant that there ever was in the world; and when I took him he had left his former master, who was called Francesco, and who was a Spaniard and a goldsmith. I, for I had not wanted to take this lad, so as not to come into collision with the said Spaniard, said to Ascanio: "I don't want you, lest I cause annoyance to your master." And he did so much that his master wrote me a note that I might freely take him. Thus he had been with me many months; and since he had come away thin and pale, we called him "the little old man" (*il vechino*); and I thought that he was (really) a little old man, because he served me so well and was so skillful that it did not seem reasonable that at his age of thirteen years, which he said that he was, there should be in him so much ability. Now to return, he in those few months put on flesh, and being removed from want became the handsomest youth in Rome; and since he was so excellent a servant as I have said, and because he learned the business marvelously, I set upon him a very great affection as a son, and I kept him clad as if he had been my son. When the youth saw himself restored, it seemed to him that he had had a great piece of good luck to fall into my hands. He often went to thank his former master, who had been the cause of his great luck; and since this master of his had a handsome young woman for his wife, she said to him: "Surgetto, what have you done to yourself that you have become so handsome?" (For so they called him when he lived with them.) Ascanio answered her: "Madonna Fran^ca, it is my master who has made me so handsome and much more good." She in petty spite took it very ill that Ascanio should speak thus; and since she bore the reputation of being an immodest woman, she knew how to employ to this lad some caresses perhaps beyond the customs of honesty; for the which reason I observed that this lad went many times more often than was his custom to see his (late) master's wife. It happened that one day, he having cruelly beaten a little shop-boy, when

I arrived (for I came in from out-of-doors) the said lad, weeping, complained, telling me that Ascanio had beaten him without any reason. At these words I said to Ascanio: "Whether with reason or without reason, never do you come to beating any one of my household, for you shall feel in what manner I know how to beat." He answered me back; whereupon I immediately threw myself upon him, and with my fists and my feet I gave him the heaviest blows that he ever felt. As soon as he could escape from my hands, without his cloak and without his cap he fled from the house, and for two days I did not know where he was, nor still less did I hunt for him; but at the end of two days, there came to speak with me a Spanish nobleman, who was called Don Diego. He was the most liberal man that I ever knew in the world. I had made for him and was making certain works of art, in such measure that he was very much my friend. He told me that Ascanio had returned to his old master, and that if it seemed good to me, would I give him his cap and the cloak that I had presented to him. To these words I replied that Fran^{co} had behaved ill, and that he had acted like a low-born fellow; for if he had told me directly that Ascanio had gone to him (since he was in his house), I would very willingly have let him go; but since he had kept him two days without informing me of it, I did not wish him to stay with him; and that he must manage that I should not in any way see him in his house. So much Don Diego reported; whereupon the said Fran^{co} jested at the matter. The next morning following I saw Ascanio, who was working upon certain rubbishing articles (*pappolate*) in wire beside his said master. As I passed by, the said Ascanio made me a bow and his master a gesture of derision. He sent to me by that nobleman, Don Diego, to ask me if I would be pleased to send back the clothes to Ascanio that I had given him; if not, he did not mind, and that Ascanio should not want for clothes. At these words I turned to Don Diego and said: "My lord Don Diego, in all your undertakings I never saw any one more liberal nor more worthy than you are; but this Fran^{co} is exactly the opposite of what you are, for he is a dishonest renegade. Tell him thus from me, that if before they ring vespers he has not himself brought Ascanio back here to my shop I will kill him at any cost; and tell Ascanio that if he does not leave that house at that hour fixed for his master I will do but little less for him." To these words that lord Don Diego answered me nothing, rather he went and set in operation that threat against the said Francesco, who did not know what to do. Meantime Ascanio had gone to look for his father, who had come to Rome from Tagliacozzi, of which place he was; and he hearing of this disturbance, also counseled Fran^{co} that he should bring Ascanio back to me. Fran^{co} said to Ascanio: "Do you go of your own accord, and your father will go with you." Don Diego said: "Fran^{co}, I foresee some great trouble: you know better than I do what Benvenuto is like; take him back without fail, and I will come with you." I, when I had put myself in readiness, walked up and down the shop, awaiting the stroke of vespers, having prepared myself to carry out one of the most destructive proceedings that I had ever committed during the course of my life. At this juncture there came up Don Diego, Fran^{co} and Ascanio and his father, whom I did not know. As Ascanio entered, I regarded them all with an eye of fury. Fran^{co}, his face the color of death said: "See, I have brought back Ascanio, whom I kept, unaware that I was causing you displeasure." Ascanio humbly said: "Master mine, pardon me, I am here to do all that you command me." Thereupon I said: "Are you come to complete the period for which you are bound to me?" He replied, "Yes;" and never more to depart from me. I then turned and told that shop-lad whom he had beaten to bring out that bundle of clothes; and I said to him, "Here are all the clothes that I have given you, and with them take your freedom, and go wherever you will." Don Diego remained astonished at this, for he expected almost anything else. Upon this Ascanio together with his father besought me that I would pardon him and take him back. When I asked who it was that was speaking on his behalf, he told me that it was his father; to whom after many entreaties, I said: "And since you are his father, out of respect for you I will take him back."

HAVING resolved, as I said a short time since, to go towards France, because I perceived that the Pope did not hold me in the same estimation as before, since by means of evil tongues my great service had been befouled; and for fear lest those who could would do me worse injury, I therefore was disposed to seek another country, in order to see if I could find better fortune; and I would willingly have gone away alone. Having resolved one evening to depart next morning, I told that faithful Felice that he was to enjoy all my substance until my return; and if it chanced that I did not return, I wished that everything should be his. And since I had a Perugian apprentice, who had assisted me in the completion of those commissions for the Pope, I gave to this fellow his liberty, having paid him for his labor. He said to me that he begged me to let him come with me, and that he would come at his own expense; for if it should chance that I stayed to work with the King of France, it would be far better that I should have with me my Italian workmen, and especially some of those persons whom I knew to be capable of assisting me. This man understood so well how to entreat me that I was glad to take him with me after the manner that he had proposed. Ascanio being also present at this discussion, said half crying: "When you took me back, I said that I wanted to stay with you for life, and such it is my intention to do!" I told the said (lad) that I did not want him on any account. The poor lad got himself ready to come after me on foot. When I saw that he had formed such a resolution, I engaged a horse for him also, and putting a small trunk of mine on the crupper, I burdened myself with much more useless lumber (*hornamenti*) than I should have done; and setting out from Rome I came to Florence, and from Florence to Bologna and from Bologna to Venice, and from Venice I went to Padua; where I was removed from the inn by that very dear friend of mine, who was called Albertaccio del Bene. The next day after I went to kiss the hands of Misser Pietro Bembo, who was not yet a cardinal. The said Misser Pietro showed me the most unbounded courtesies that could ever be displayed towards any human being; then he turned to Albertaccio and said: "I want Benvenuto to stay here with all his followers, even if he have a full hundred of them; therefore make up your mind that, if you also want Benvenuto, to stay here with me (yourself) for otherwise I will not give him up to you": and thus I remained to enjoy myself with this most brilliant nobleman. He had a room set in readiness for me, which would have been too magnificent even for a cardinal, and continually desired me to eat at his lordship's side. Then he began with most modest proposals, pointing out that he had had a desire that I should make his portrait; and since I desired nothing else in the world, having prepared for myself certain very white stucco in a small box, I began my task; and the first day I worked for two hours continuously, and I sketched out that clever head with so much charm that his lordship remained in stupefaction at it; and though that man was very great in his scholarship and in poetry to a superlative degree, of this profession of mine his lordship understood nothing in the world; wherefore it seemed to him that I should have finished in that time when I had scarcely begun: so much so that I could not make him understand that I wanted much time in which to fashion it thoroughly. At last I resolved to do the best I knew with the time that it deserved; and since he wore his beard short after the Venetian fashion (*alla venitiana*), I put myself to great trouble to make a head that should satisfy me. However, I finished it, and it seemed to me that I fashioned the most beautiful work that I had ever made as far as appertained to my art. At which I saw him amazed, for he thought that since I had completed the wax model in two hours I ought to make the steel one in ten. When he saw then that I was not able to make the wax one in two hundred hours, and that I was asking for leave to proceed towards France, at this he was much upset, and asked me that I would at least make a reverse for his medal, and this was the horse *Pegasus* (*un caval Pegaseo*) in the midst of a wreath of myrtle. This I did in about three hours' time, imparting to it very excellent style; and he being very well satisfied said: "This horse seems to me a ten times greater matter than is the fashioning of a little head, whereon you have expended so much labor; I do not comprehend this difficulty." Nevertheless he told me and besought me that I should make it in steel, saying to me: "Of your kindness make it for me, for you will make it very quickly if you want to do so." I promised him that though I did not wish to execute it there, wherever I did settle down to work I would carry it out without fail. While we were keeping up this discussion I had been to bargain for three horses to proceed on our way towards France; and he (Bembo) caused me to be secretly watched, for he had very great influence in Padua; in such a way that when I went to pay for the horses, which I had bargained for at fifty ducats, the owner of those same horses said to me: "Oh, illustrious man, I make you a present of the three horses." To which I replied: "It is not you who are presenting them to me; and from that man who is presenting them to me I do not wish (to receive) them, because I have not been able to give him any example of my labors." The good man told me that if I did not take those horses, I should not be able to find any other horses in Padua, and should be compelled to go thence on foot. Upon this I went to the illustrious Misser Pietro, who pretended that he knew nothing about it, and merely flattered me, saying that I must remain on in Padua. I, since I did not wish to do anything of the sort, and was ready to go at any cost, was forced to accept the three horses; and with them I started. I took the road through the country of Grigioni, because the other road was not safe on account of the wars. We passed the peaks of the Alba and the Berlina; it was the 8th day of May and the snow was very deep. With very great danger to our lives we passed (across) these two mountains. When we had passed them we paused in a country, which, if I remember right, they call Valdistà: there we lodged. That night there arrived a Florentine courier, who was named Busbacca. I had heard mention of this courier as a man of credit and able in his profession, and I did not know that he had fallen (from this repute) through his rogueries. When he saw me at the inn, he appealed to me by name, and told me that he was going to Lyons on matters of importance, and that would I of my kindness lend him money for the journey. To this I replied that I had no money that I could lend him, but that if he liked to come along in company with me I would pay his expenses as far as Lyons. The rascal wept and made me fine excuses, telling me that when in matters of importance for the nation a poor courier was in want of money "a person of your standing (*un par vostro*) is bound to assist him"; and besides that, he told me that he was carrying articles of the very greatest moment belonging to Misser Filippo Strozzi; and as he had a case for a beaker, covered with leather, he whispered in my ear, that in that case there was a silver beaker, and that in that beaker were precious stones of the value of many thousands of ducats, and there were also letters of the very highest importance, which Misser Philippo (*sic*) Strozzi was sending. At this I told him that he ought to let me conceal the precious stones about his own person, where they would run less risk than when carried in that beaker; and that he might leave that beaker— which might be worth about ten *scudi*—with me, and I would supply him with twenty-five. At these words the courier said, that he would come with me, being unable to do otherwise, for to leave that beaker would not be honorable to him. Thus we cut off the discussion; and starting next morning, we arrived at a lake, which lies between Valdistate and Vassa: this lake is fifteen miles long at the point where it reaches Vassa. When I saw the boats on this lake, I was terrified; because the said boats are of fir wood, not very large and not very substantial, and are not closely fitted together, nor even pitched; and if I had not seen four German noblemen with their four horses embarking in a similar one I would never have embarked in mine; rather would I much sooner have turned back again; but I thought to myself according to the folly (*bestialità*) that I saw them committing that these German waters would not drown folks as do ours in Italy. Those two young men of mine, however, said to me, "Benvenuto! It is a dangerous thing to embark along with four horses." And I replied to them: "Don't you notice, cowards, that those four noblemen have embarked before us, and are going on their way laughing? If this were wine as it actually is water, I would say that they were going cheerfully to drown therein; but since it is water I know well that they have no desire to be drowned any more than we have." This lake was fifteen miles in length and about three in width; on the one hand was a very high and cavernous mountain, on the other it was flat and grassy. When we had gone about four miles upon it the said lake began to become stormy (*a far fortuna*) to such an extent that those men who were rowing begged us that we would help them to row; so we did for a while. I made signs to them, and told them that they should run us to that shore opposite; they said that it was not possible, for there was not sufficient water there to float the boat and that there are certain shallows upon which the boat would immediately go to pieces and we should all drown; but they begged us, however, that we would help them. And the boatmen shouted to one another, asking for help. When I saw them thus dismayed, having an intelligent horse I arranged the bridle upon his neck and took one end of the halter in my left hand. The horse which was, as they often are (gifted) with some instinct, seemed to have perceived what I wanted to do, for, turning his head towards the fresh grass, I wanted him swimming to draw me also with him. At this moment there arose so great a wave from the lake that it broke over the boat. Ascanio, crying out: "Mercy, my father, help me," turned to throw himself upon me; wherefore I clapped my hand to my dagger, and told them to do as I would show them, for the horses would save their own lives so surely that I hoped that I should also escape by that means; but that if he threw himself upon me I would kill him. Thus we went forward several miles in this mortal danger. When we had gone midway down the lake we found a little tract of level ground where we could rest, and upon this level spot I saw disembarked those four German noblemen. When we wanted to disembark, the boatman would not allow it upon any account. Thereupon I said to my young men: "Now is the time to make some proof of our quality; therefore draw your swords and compel him by force to set us on shore." Thus we did with great difficulty, for they made very great resistance. However, when we were on shore it was necessary to climb two miles up that mountain, which was more difficult to climb than a ladder (*scala a piuoli*). I was fully armed in a coat of mail with big boots and with a fowling-piece in my hand, and it was raining as God alone knows how to send it. Those devils of German noblemen, with those little nags of theirs led by hand, performed miracles, for our horses were not up to this business, and we were bursting with the labor of making them climb that difficult mountain. When we were some way up, Ascanio's horse, which was a most admirable Hungarian beast, was a little ahead of the courier Busbacca, and the said Ascanio had given him his lance that he might help him carry it; it chanced that through false steps the horse stumbled and staggered so much (*ando tanto barchellone*), that being unable to help itself, it impaled itself upon the point of the lance of that rascal of a courier, who had not known how to get out of the way. When it passed right through the throat of the horse, that other shop-lad of mine being anxious to help, his horse also, which was a black horse, stumbled in the direction of the lake, and was held up by a shrub (*respo*), which was very slight. Upon this horse there was a pair of saddle-bags (*bisaccie*), in which were packed all my money together with everything that I had of value; I told the lad to save his own life and to let the horse go to destruction; the fall was more than a mile, and it went sheer down and fell into the lake. Exactly beneath this spot were stationed those boatmen of ours; in such a way that if the horse had fallen, it would have come straight down upon them. I was in front of everybody, and we stopped to see the horse fall, for it seemed certain that he would go to destruction. At this juncture I said to my young men: "Don't think about anything: let us save ourselves, and thank God in all things; for my part I am only distressed on account of this poor man Busbacca, who has bound his beaker and his precious stones, which are to the value of several thousands of ducats, to the saddle-bow of that horse, thinking that to be the safest place; of mine there

are but a few hundred *scudi,* and I have no fear of anything in the
world so long as I have the favor of God." Busbacca thereupon
said: "I am not sorry for my own loss, but I am very sorry for
yours." I said to him: "Why do you grieve for my small loss, and
not for your very great one?" Busbacca thereupon said: "I will
tell you in the name of God; in these chances and in these straits
in which we are, it is needful to tell the truth. I know that your
(losses) are *scudi,* and that they are so in very truth; but that case
of mine for a beaker, wherein I said there were so many precious
stones and so many (other) lies, is entirely filled with *caviare."*
On hearing this I could not do otherwise than laugh; those young
men of mine laughed also; he wept. The horse recovered himself,
when we had entirely given it up. So laughing thus we regained our spirits, and set ourselves to continuing the ascent. Those
four German noblemen, who had arrived before us at the summit
of that steep mountain, sent some persons to us who assisted us; so
that we reached that most wild lodging; where we being wet
through, worn out and famished, were most kindly received, and
there dried ourselves, rested ourselves, satisfied our hunger; and
with certain herbs the injured horse was doctored; and the species
of plant (employed thus), of which the hedges were full, was
pointed out to us. And we were told that by keeping the wound
continually filled with those herbs, the horse would not only be
cured, but would serve us as though it had never had any ailment
in the world: such (therefore) we did. Having thanked the nobleman, and being very much refreshed, we departed thence, and we
went forward thanking God who had saved us from that great
danger. We arrived at a district beyond Vassa; here we rested for
the night, where we heard at every hour of the night a watchman,
who sang in a very pleasing manner; and since all the houses of
those towns are made of fir wood, the watchman said nothing else

but that they should beware of fire. Busbacca, who had been terrified during the day, at every hour that this man sang out, cried
out in his sleep, saying: "Ah, my God, I am drowning;" and this
was due to the fright of the past day; and besides that he was
drunk that evening, because he wanted to vie in drinking that
evening with all the Germans who were there; and he sometimes
said "I am burning"; and sometimes "I am drowning"; at other
times it seemed to him that he was being tortured in the infernal
regions with that *caviare* hung to his neck. This night was so
agreeable that all our misfortunes were converted into laughter.
Rising in the morning with most beautiful weather we proceeded
to dine at a most charming spot called Lacca. There we were
wonderfully entertained; then we took guides, who were on their
return journey to a country called Surich. The guide who led us
went up along the dyked bank of the lake, and there was no other
road; and this dyke also was covered with water, in such a way
that the foolish (*bestial*) guide stumbled, and his horse and himself
went under the water. I who was just behind the guide, stopping
my horse, waited to see the idiot come out of the water; and as if
nothing had happened, he recommenced to sing, and beckoned to
me that I should come along. I threw myself on the right hand
side, and broke through certain hedges: thus I guided my young
men and Busbacca. The guide grumbled, saying to me however,
in German, that if the people of the place had seen me, they would
have slaughtered me. We pressed forward and escaped that further disaster (*quell' altra furia*). We arrived at Surich, a wonderful city, polished up like a jewel. Here we rested one entire day:
then one morning we left in good time, and we reached another
fine city called Soluturno; from there we reached Usanna, from
Usanna to Ginevra, from Ginevra to Lyons, always singing and
laughing. At Lyons I rested four days; I enjoyed myself much

with certain friends of mine; I was paid for the expense that I had incurred on behalf of Busbacca. Then at the end of four days I took the road towards Paris. This was a pleasant journey, except that when we reached Palissa a band of adventurers wanted to assassinate us, and with no little courage we saved ourselves. Then we went as far as Paris without any disturbances in the world: (and) always singing and laughing we reached safety.

Chapter Twenty-one   *1537-1538*

H AVING rested myself awhile in Paris I went to look up
the painter, il Rosso, who was in the King's service. This
Rosso I thought to be the greatest friend that I had in the world, because I had done for him in Rome the greatest kindnesses that one
man can possibly do for another; and since these particular kindnesses can be told in a few words I do not wish to omit mention
of them to show how shameless is ingratitude. With his evil tongue,
when he was in Rome, he had spoken so ill of the works of
Raffaello da Urbino, that his (*i.e.*, Raffaello's) pupils wanted to
kill him at any cost: from this (danger) I rescued him, guarding
him day and night, with the greatest pains. Moreover, by having
spoken evil of that very excellent architect Maestro Antonio de
San Gallo, he caused a commission to be taken from him that
he had succeeded in getting for him from Misser Agniol de Cesi:
then he (San Gallo) began to do so much against him (Rosso)
that he brought him to the verge of dying from starvation; for
the which reason I lent him many tens of *scudi* to live upon. And

not having yet been repaid, knowing that he was in the service of
the King, I went, as I have said, to visit him: I did not think
so much that he would pay me back my money, but I did think
that he would give me help and countenance in order to get me
into the service of that great King. When he saw me, he was
immediately confused, and said to me: "Benvenuto! you have come
at too great an expense on so long a journey, especially at this
time, when men are attending to war, and not to such trifles
(*baiuccole*) as we make." Thereupon I said that I had brought
enough money to enable me to return to Rome in that same manner
that I had come to Paris, and that this (reception) was not a return
for the troubles that I had endured on his account; and I began
to believe what Maestro Antonio da Sangallo had said of him.
Desiring to turn the matter into a joke, since he had perceived
his own vileness, I showed him a Letter of Exchange for five hundred *scudi* on Ricciardo del Bene. This wicked fellow was then
ashamed, and though he wanted to keep me almost by force I
laughed at him and went away along with a painter who was there
present. This man was called Sguazzella: he also was a Florentine;
I went to lodge in his house with three horses and three servants
at so much a week. He treated me very well and I paid him even
better. Then I sought to speak to the King, to whom a certain
Misser Giuliano Buonaccorsi, his treasurer, presented me. In this
matter I was much delayed; for I did not know that Rosso employed every sort of effort that I should not speak to the King.
When the said Misser Giovanni became aware of this, he immediately took me to Fontana Bilio, and set me straight in the presence
of the King, with whom I had a whole hour's most agreeable
audience: and since the King was in readiness to go to Lyons
he told the said Misser Giovanni that he would take me with
him, and that on the road we would discuss some fine works that

His Majesty had it in his mind to order. So I went along after him in the train of the Court, and upon the road I paid very great service to the Cardinal of Ferrara (who had not yet received the Hat). And since every evening I had very long discussions with the said Cardinal, his lordship told me that I must stop in Lyons at an Abbey of his, and that there I could enjoy myself until such time as the King should return from the war, for he was going in the direction of Granopoli, and at his Abbey in Lyons I should have every comfort. When we arrived at Lyons I fell ill, and that youth of mine Ascanio contracted the quartan fever; to such an extent that I took a dislike to the French and their Court, and it seemed to me a thousand years ere I should return to Rome. When the Cardinal saw that I was anxious to return to Rome, he gave me sufficient money that I might make for him in Rome a basin and an ewer of silver. Thus we returned towards Rome (mounted) upon very excellent horses, and coming by the mountains of the Sanpione, and being accompanied by certain Frenchmen, with whom we came some distance, Ascanio with his quartan fever and I with an obstinate feverishness (*febbretta sorda*), which seemed never to leave me, I got my stomach into so irritated a condition, that I had passed four months during which I believe that I had not succeeded in digesting one whole loaf a week, and I greatly desired to reach Italy, anxious to die in Italy and not in France. When we had passed the mountains of the said Sanpione, we found a river near to a place called Indevedro. This river was very wide, and very deep, and across it there was a little bridge long and narrow, without rails. Since there was that morning a very deep white frost, when I reached the bridge,—for I found myself in front of every one—and recognizing that it was very dangerous, I ordered my young men and my servants to dismount, and lead their horses by hand. Thus I crossed the said bridge very comfortably, and

I went along talking about it with one of those Frenchmen, who was a nobleman; the other was a notary, who had remained somewhat behind, and he laughed at that French nobleman and me, who out of fear of nothing at all had been willing to suffer the inconvenience of going on foot. To whom I turned on seeing that he was in the middle of the bridge, and begged him to go cautiously for he was in a very dangerous place. This man, who could not be false to his French nature, said to me in French, that I was a man of little courage, and that here there was no danger at all. While he was saying these words he wanted to urge on his horse a little, whereat the horse immediately stumbled off the bridge, and with his legs towards heaven fell beside a very large rock. And since God many times is merciful to mad folks, this animal (the man) together with the other animal (his horse) fell into a very great whirlpool, wherein both he and his horse sank. Directly I saw this, with a very great speed I set myself to gallop, and with great difficulty leaped upon that stone and, hanging over from it, seized a fold of a gown that this man wore; and by that fold I drew him up, so that though he was still under water, and therefore had swallowed a great deal of water and had been within a little of being drowned, I saw that he was out of danger, and rejoiced with him that I had saved his life. Whereat he replied to me in French, and told me that I had done nothing; for the importance lay in his documents, which were worth many tens of *scudi*: and it seemed that he said these words to me in anger, all dripping and stuttering. Upon this I turned to certain guides that we had, and directed them to assist that animal, and that I would pay them. One of those guides, cleverly and with great labor, set to work to help him, and fished out his documents, so that he lost none of them; that other guide never turned to take any pains to assist him. When then we had arrived at that above-mentioned place, we had made up a purse, which it was my business to disburse, and when we had dined I gave certain monies out of this purse belonging to the party to that guide who had helped to drag him (the notary) from the water; upon which he told me that I must give that money out of my own pocket, for he did not intend to give him anything else but what we had agreed upon for performing the duty of guide. At this I uttered to him many opprobrious remarks. Then the other guide put himself in my way, who had taken no trouble, and wanted me to pay him also; and I therefore said: "He only deserves the reward who has borne the cross": he answered me that he would soon show me a cross at which I should weep. I said to him that I would light a taper to that cross, for the which I hoped that it would fall to him first to weep. And since this place is on the frontier between the Venetians and the Germans, this man ran off to fetch the populace, and came with them with a great spear in front of him. I, for I was mounted upon my excellent horse, lowered the barrel of my arquebuse; and turning to my companions I said: "At the first (shot) I shall kill him; and you others do your duty, for they are highway robbers and have taken this slight occasion merely (as a pretext) for assassinating us." The landlord, where we had eaten, called to one of those leaders (*caporali*), who was an elderly man, and begged him to moderate so much disturbance, saying to him: "This is a most brave young man, and even though you cut him in pieces, he will slaughter a great many of you, and will perhaps manage to escape from your hands after having done all the harm that he is able to do." The affair quieted down, and that old leader of theirs said to me: "Go in peace, for you won't make much of a success (*non faresti una insalata*) if you had a full hundred men with you."

I, who recognized that he was telling the truth and was already prepared and fancied myself dead, when I heard no more insulting

words, tossing my head said: "I would certainly have done everything in my power to show that I was a living animal and a man";
and having recommenced our journey, that evening at the first
halting-place, we made up an account of that common purse, and
I separated myself from that odious Frenchman, remaining great
friends with the other one, who was a nobleman; and with my
three horses only we came to Ferrara. When I had dismounted
I went to the Court of the Duke to make my salutations to His
Excellency, so that I might be able to depart in the morning on
my way to Santa Maria dal (*sic*) Loreto. I had to wait until two
hours of the night, and then the Duke appeared: I kissed his hands;
he gave me a warm welcome, and directed that I should be given
water for my hands. For the which reason I said to him cheerfully: "Most excellent lord! it is more than four months that I
have not eaten, in so much that it is (difficult) to believe that any
one could be alive upon so little; wherefore having realized that I
could take no pleasure out of the royal fare upon your table, I will
stop thus and talk with you while Your Excellency sups, and you
and I will at the same time have more pleasure than if I supped
with you." Thus we commenced a conversation and we continued
it until the fifth hour (of the night). At the fifth hour then I
took my leave, and on going to my inn I found a most wonderfully
prepared banquet, for the Duke had sent to present me with the
perquisites of his own meal with much excellent wine; and by
reason of my having in that way gone more than two hours beyond
my hour for eating, I ate with very great appetite, for it was the
first time after four months that I had been able to eat. Setting
out the next morning, I went to Santa Maria dal Loreto, and from
thence, having made my devotions, I went on to Rome; where I
found my most faithful Filice, to whom I had entrusted the shop
with all its furnishings and belongings, and I opened another much

larger and more spacious, beside that of Sugherello the perfumer; and I thought that that great King Fran⁰⁰ had no more recollection of me. For the which reason I took up many commissions from different lords, and especially I labored at that ewer and basin that I had undertaken to make for the Cardinal of Ferrara. I employed many workmen and did very great business in gold and silver (ware). I had entered into an agreement with that workman of mine from Perugia, who had on his own account written down all the money that had been expended upon his behalf, which money was spent upon his clothes and on many other things; together with the expenses of the journey it amounted to about seventy *scudi,* of which we were agreed that he should pay it off at the rate of three *scudi* per month; for I enabled him to earn more than eight *scudi*. At the close of two months this rascal disappeared from my workshop, and left me laden with many commissions, and said that he did not intend to give me any more money. For this reason I was advised to get the better of him by legal methods (*per la via della iustitia*), for I had it in my mind to cut off his arm; and I should most certainly have done so, but that my friends told me that it was not well that I should do such a thing, for it might chance that I would lose my money and perhaps Rome a second time—for blows cannot be bound by conditions (*i colpi non si danno a patti*); and that I could with that writing that I had under his signature immediately have him arrested. I attended to their advice, but I wanted to carry out the matter with more freedom. I did in fact sue him before the Auditor of the Camera, and won the case; and by virtue of that (verdict), for which I waited several months, I then had him put in prison. I found my workshop crowded with very important commissions, and among others all the ornaments in gold and precious stones of the wife of the lord Gierolimo Orsino, father of the lord Paulo, son-in-law to-day of our Duke Cosimo. These jobs were very nearly at an end, and all the time (the number) of very important commissions was increasing. I employed eight workmen, and together with them, both for honor and convenience I labored day and night. While I so vigorously continued my undertakings there came a letter sent to me in haste by the Cardinal of Ferrara, which read to this purpose: "Benvenuto! our dear friend. In these past days this great and most Christian King recalled you to mind, saying that he desired to have you in his service. To whom I replied that you had promised me that at any time that I sent for you for His Majesty's service you would come immediately. At these words His Majesty said: 'I desire that there be sent to him the provision to enable him to come, according to what one of his like deserves': and he immediately commanded his admiral that he should cause one thousand gold *scudi* to be paid to me by the Treasurer of the Exchequer. Cardinal de' Gaddi was present at this conversation, who immediately advanced and said to His Majesty that there was no occasion for His Majesty to give this order, because he said that he had sent you sufficient money, and that you were already on the way. Now if by chance the matter is, as I believe, quite the opposite of what Cardinal de' Gaddi has said, when you have received this letter of mine, answer immediately, for I will pick up the thread, and will cause you to be given the money promised by this magnanimous King."

Now let the world and whosoever lives in it, take notice how much malign stars with adverse fortune can do to us human beings! I had not spoken twice in my life to this little fool (*pazzerellino*) of a Cardinal-wretch (*cardinaluccio*) de' Gaddi; and this malapertness of his he did not do in order to do me any harm in the world, but he only did it for a whim and from his ignorance, in order to show that he also had some interest in the doings of the men of talent whom the King desired to employ, just as the Cardinal of Ferrara had. But he was afterwards so silly that he never informed me of anything; for I would certainly —so as not to vituperate a foolish puppet out of love for my country—have found some excuse to cover up that silly presumption. Directly I received the letter of the Most Reverend the Cardinal of Ferrara, I answered that I knew nothing in the world of Cardinal de' Gaddi, and that if he had made any proposal of such a kind, I should not have stirred from Italy without the knowledge of His Most Reverend Lordship, and more especially because I had in Rome a greater quantity of business than I had ever had before; but that at a word from His Most Christian Majesty, given to me by so great a lord as was His Most Reverend Lordship, I would remove myself immediately, throwing aside (*a traverso*) every other matter. When I had sent my letters, that traitor of a workman of mine from Perugia thought of an act of malice, which succeeded immediately, owing to the avarice of Pope Pagolo da Farnese, and still more that of his bastard son, then called Duke of Castro. This said workman caused one of the secretaries of the said lord Pierluigi to hear that, since he had been with me as a workman for several years, he knew all my business; wherefore he gave his word to the said lord Pier Luigi, that I was a man worth more than eighty thousand ducats, and that of this sum I had the greater part in precious stones, which stones belonged to the Church, and that I had stolen them in Castel Sant' Agniolo at the time of the Sack of Rome, and that they must see to having me arrested immediately and secretly. I had one morning among others been working more than three hours before daybreak on the commissions of the above-mentioned bride, and while they were opening and sweeping my shop, I had put on my cloak to take a little walk; and having taken my way along the Strada

Julia, I emerged at the corner of the Chiavica; where Chrespino, the Bargello, with all his force (*con tutta la sua sbirreria*) met me, and said to me: "You are the Pope's prisoner." To which I replied: "Chrespino! you have arrested me by mistake." "No," said Chrespino, "you are the talented Benvenuto, and I know you very well, and I have to take you to the Castel Sant' Agniolo, whither go lords and persons of talent like yourself." And because four of those corporals of his threw themselves upon me and wanted to remove with force a dagger that I wore, and certain rings that I had on my finger, the said Chrespino said to them, "Let none of you touch him: it is quite enough for you to do your duty, that he does not escape me." Then coming up to me, with civil expressions he demanded my weapons. While I gave up my arms to him, I remembered that on that very spot I had slain Pompeo. From there they took me into the fortress, and in a room up in the keep they enclosed me in prison. This was the first time that I ever tasted imprisonment up to that age of mine of thirty-seven years.

THE lord Pierluigi, the Pope's son, having observed what a great sum of money value it was, of which I was accused, immediately demanded as a favor of that father of his, that this amount of money might be made a present to himself. Wherefore the Pope willingly granted it to him, and moreover told him that he would also help him to recover it; so that after I had been kept in prison eight whole days, at the end of the eight days, in order to arrive at some termination of this business, they sent to examine me. For which purpose I was summoned into one of those halls that there are in the Pope's castle, a very imposing place; and the examiners were the Governor of Rome, who was called Misser Benedetto Conversini of Pistoia (who was afterwards Bishop of Jesi); the other was the Procurator-Fiscal, of whose name I have no recollection; another, who was the third, was the judge for malefactors, who was called Misser Benedetto da Cagli. These three men began to examine me at first with amiable expressions, and afterwards with most bitter and terrifying threats, originated by my saying to them: "My lords, for more than half an hour you have not ceased asking me about fables and other matters, regarding which it can truly be said that you are babbling, or that you are merely talking (wildly): by babbling I mean that your words have no meaning, or merely talking in order that you may say nothing; therefore I beg that you will tell me what it is that you want of me, and that I may hear your real arguments issue from your mouths, and not fables and babblings." At these words of mine the Governor, who was a native of Pistoia, no longer able to disguise his irritable temperament, said to me: "You are talking very confidently, rather indeed too haughtily: in such measure that I will make this pride of yours become more humble than a dog before the arguments that you shall hear me utter to you, and which shall be neither babblings nor fables, as you call them, but shall be a set of arguments, to which it will be very necessary that you put forth of your best to give us the explanation." And thus he began. "We know for very certain that you were in Rome at the time of the Sack, which was made upon this unhappy City of Rome; and at this period you happened to be in this very Castel Sant' Agniolo, and that you were employed as a gunner; and since your profession is that of a goldsmith and a jeweler, Pope Clemente, because he had known you previously, and because there were no other persons of that trade (at hand), took you into his confidence and made you unset all the precious stones from his tiaras, miters and rings, and then having trust in you, desired you to sew them into his clothing (*adosso*); during which operation you reserved for yourself unknown to His Holiness (stones) to the value of eighty thousand *scudi*. This fact was related to us by one of your workmen to whom you confided it and boasted of it. Now we tell you plainly that you must find the stones or the value of the same; then we will let you go in liberty." When I heard these words, I could not keep from being moved to loudest laughter. After I had laughed a while, I said: "I greatly thank God, that on this first occasion when it has pleased His (Divine) Majesty that I should be imprisoned, I am so fortunate as not to be imprisoned for some weakness, as it would seem most often happens to young men. If this that you say were the truth, there is now no danger for me of being chastised with corporal punishment; for the laws at that period lost all their authority; whereby I could excuse myself by saying, that as an administrator, I might have kept this treasure on behalf of the Sacred and Holy Church Apostolic, waiting to return it to a good Pope, or indeed to any one who might demand it of me, such as you now might, if the fact really was thus." At these words that angry Pistoiese Governor would not allow me to finish my arguments, for he said furiously: "Put it in the way you like, Benvenuto! For us it is sufficient that we have found again our property; and act quickly if you do not want us to act in another way than with words." And as they were preparing to rise and depart I said to them: "My lords, my examination is not finished, therefore finish examining me and then go wherever it pleases you." They immediately resumed their seats, in very great wrath, half showing that they did not want to hear any word that I should say to them, and half relieved, since it seemed to them that they had found out all that they wanted to know. Wherefore I began to this purport: "Know, my lords, that for about twenty years I have dwelt in Rome, and was never in prison either here or elsewhere." At these words that constable (*birro*) of a Governor said: "You have certainly committed some homicides." Thereupon I said: " 'Tis you say so and not I; but if any one came for the purpose of killing you, priest though you be (*cosi prete*), you would defend yourself, and in killing him the holy laws support you; therefore allow me to give my explanations, if you wish to be able to repeat them to the Pope, and if you wish to be able to judge me fairly. I say once more, that for nigh twenty years I have dwelt in this wondrous Rome, and in it I have executed very great undertakings in my profession; and since I know this to be the seat of Christ, I should have been assuredly confident that if a temporal prince had desired to do me some wrong, I should have recourse to this Holy Throne (*cattedra*) and to this Vicar of Christ, who would defend my rights. Alas! where must I go now? and

to what prince, who will defend me from so wicked a wrong?
Ought you not, before arresting me, to find out where I had disposed of these eighty thousand ducats? Besides ought you not to
examine the record of the precious stones which this Apostolic
Camera has written up diligently for five hundred years past until
now? Then when you have found a deficiency you ought thereupon to have impounded all my account-books, together with me
myself. I would have you know that the books wherein are
inscribed all the precious stones belonging to the Pope and the
tiaras, are all in order, and you will not find anything missing of
what Pope Clemente possessed, that is not carefully inscribed
therein. It can only have happened that when that poor man Pope
Clemente wanted to make terms with those thieves of Imperialists,
who had robbed Rome and insulted the Church, there came to
negotiate this contract one who was called Cesare Iscatinaro, (if
I remember rightly), who, when he had almost concluded his
truce with that ill-treated Pope, in order to do him a small courtesy, he (the Pope) let fall from his finger a diamond, which was
worth about four thousand *scudi;* and when the said Iscatinaro
stooped to recover it, the Pope told him that he might keep it out
of affection for him. I indeed was present at these events, and if
this said diamond be missing, I tell you where it is gone to; but I
think that you will most assuredly find this fact also written down.
Then in your turn you ought to feel shame for having injured
one like me, who has carried out so many splendid commissions
for this Apostolic See. Do you know that if it had not been for me
that morning when the Imperialists entered the Borgo, they would
have invaded the Castello without any hindrance; and that I without being rewarded upon that head, threw myself vigorously upon
the guns, which the gunners and the soldiers of the garrison had
abandoned, and inspired courage into one of my good friends

(*compagniuzo*), who was called Raffaello da Montelupo, a sculptor, who also having himself given up had put himself in a corner overcome with terror, and doing nothing. I aroused him; and he and I alone slew so many of the enemy, that the soldiers took another route. It was I who fired a shot at Scatinaro when I saw him talking to Pope Clemente without any sort of respect, but with most brutal ridicule, like the Lutheran and impious man that he was. Pope Clemente upon this made a search through the Castello, who it was, in order that he might hang him. It was I who wounded the Prince of Orange with a shot in the head here beneath the intrenchments of the Castello. Besides that I have made for the Holy Church so many ornaments in silver, gold, and precious stones, so many medals, and such fine and noble coins. Is this then the proud priestlike remuneration that you employ towards a man who has served you and loved you with so much fidelity and with so much ability? Oh! go and relate all that I have said to the Pope, telling him that he has all his jewels; and that I have never had from the Church anything but certain wounds and stonings during that period of the Sack; and that I have never reckoned on anything, except a small remuneration from Pope Pagolo, which he had promised me. Now I am clear both before His Holiness and before you his ministers." While I was speaking these words they remained listening in astonishment; and looking one another in the face, they left me with signs of surprise. They all three went together to relate to the Pope all that I had said. The Pope being ashamed, directed them that they should look over again with very great care all the accounts of the precious stones. Then when they had seen that nothing was missing, they let me remain in the Castello without saying anything further; the lord Pier Luigi, since it seemed even to him that he had been wrong, sought with diligence to procure my death.

During the small disturbances of this period King Francis had already heard in detail how the Pope had kept me prisoner, and so very wrongfully: having sent as an Ambassador to the Pope a certain nobleman of his, who was called Monsignior di Morluc, he wrote to this man that he should demand me from the Pope, as one of His Majesty's servants. The Pope, who was a most able and wonderful man, but who in this affair of mine acted like a person of little worth and a simpleton, answered the said messenger of the King, that His Majesty should not trouble about me, for I was a man who was very troublesome with my weapons, and for this reason he would have His Majesty warned that he should let me alone, for he was keeping me in prison for murders and others of my similar devilries. The King again answered that in his kingdom there reigned the most excellent justice; and just as His Majesty rewarded and favored wondrously men of merit, so on the contrary he punished the troublesome; and since His Holiness had let me depart, not caring for the services of the said Benvenuto, when he saw him in his kingdom, he had gladly taken him into his service; and he demanded him as his servant. These events were of the greatest annoyance and injury to me, for all that they were the most splendid favors that could possibly be desired by one like me. The Pope was roused to so great a fury through the jealousy that he felt lest I should go and tell of that wicked rascality which had been employed against me, that he thought of all the means whereby he could with honor to himself compass my death. The Castellan of Castel Sant' Agniolo was one of our Florentines, who was called Misser Giorgio, a knight of the Ugolini (family). This worthy man displayed the greatest courtesies towards me that one could possibly display in the world, allowing me to go freely about the Castello upon my word of honor alone; and since he understood the great wrong that was done to me, when I wanted to give security to go walking about the Castello, he told me that he could not take it, for it happened that the Pope set too much importance upon this affair of mine, but that he would freely put confidence in my word of honor, for he understood from every one how honest a man I was; and I gave him my word, and so he gave me convenience that I might be able to continue my trade. Upon this, thinking that this wrath of the Pope, as well on account of my innocence, as also on account of the favors of the King, must come to an end, keeping my shop still open, my apprentice Ascanio used to come to me in the Castello and bring me some materials for working. Although I could work but little, seeing myself imprisoned in that way so wrongfully, I nevertheless made a virtue of necessity: I cheerfully bore this perverse fortune of mine the best way I could. I had made very great friends with all those guards and many soldiers of the Castello. And since the Pope came sometimes to supper in the Castello, and during such time as the Pope was there the Castello was not guarded, but stood open freely like an ordinary palace; and since during this time that the Pope remained thus, all the prisoners were accustomed to be shut up with greater care: and whereas to me none of these sorts of things were done: but on all these occasions I walked freely about the Castello; many times some of those soldiers counseled me that I should escape, and that they would assist me (*fatto spalle*), since they knew the great wrong that was done me. To them I replied that I had given my word to the Castellan, who was so honest a man, and one who had done me such great kindnesses. One very brave and very able soldier there was; and he said to me: "My Benvenuto! you know that one who is in prison is not bound nor can be bound to keep his word, any more than any other thing: do what I tell you, escape from this rascal of a Pope and from this bastard son of his, who will take away your life at any cost." I, for I had determined to myself that I would more gladly lose my life than be wanting in my pledged word to that honest man the Castellan, bore this extreme discomfort together with a friar, a very great preacher, of the Palavisina family. This man had been arrested as a Lutheran: he was a most excellent intimate companion, but as a friar he was the biggest scoundrel that ever was in the world, and indulged in all sorts of vicious habits. His fine talents I admired, and his ugly vices I greatly abhorred, and freely rebuked him for them. This friar never did anything else but remind me that I was not obliged to keep faith with the Castellan, because I was in prison. To which argument I replied that although as a friar he was speaking the truth, as a man he was not speaking the truth; for one who was a man and not a friar was obliged to keep his word in every sort of chance, in which he might find himself: therefore, since I was a man and not a friar, I was never going to be false to that simple and honorable word of mine. When the said friar saw that he was unable to obtain the corruption of me by means of the very subtle and clever arguments so wonderfully set forth by him, he thought to try me by another method; and so he let many days pass by, while he read to me the sermons of Fra Jerolimo Savonarola, and gave me so admirable a commentary upon them, that it was finer than the sermons themselves; at which I remained enchanted, and there was not a thing in the world that I would not have done for him, except to break my word, as I have said. When the friar saw me overcome with astonishment at his talents, he thought of another way; for after an ingenious fashion he began to ask me what method I should have employed if the desire had come to me, when they had locked me in, to open those prison doors to escape. I likewise wishing to display some of the subtilty of my genius to this clever friar, told him that I could assuredly open every most difficult lock, and especially those of the prison doors, which would be to me like eating a little fresh cheese. The said friar, in order to make me reveal my secret, sneered at me, saying that there are many things which men say in order that they may obtain some credit with clever persons, whereas if they had afterwards to put in operation the things of which they boasted, they would lose so much credit that it would be disastrous to them; thus he had heard me relate things so far removed from the truth, that if I were put to the proof regarding them, he thought that I should come out of it with but little credit. Upon this, feeling myself tormented by this devil of a friar, I told him that I was always accustomed to promise for myself in words much less than I knew how to perform; and that this thing that I had promised about the keys was the easiest; and with a few words I would make it most clear to him that it was as I had said: and, as I said this, I thoughtlessly demonstrated to him with ease all that I had told him. The friar, pretending that he was paying no attention, immediately with greatest ingenuity understood it all most excellently. And, as I have said above, that excellent man, the Castellan, let me go freely all over the Castello; and not even at night did he lock me in, as he did all the others; he let me also work at every thing that I wished, whether in gold, silver, or wax; and although I had labored several weeks upon a certain basin that I was making for the Cardinal of Ferrara, finding myself inconvenienced by my imprisonment, it became a weariness to me to carry out that sort of work; and, for less discomfort, I only worked upon certain little figures of mine in wax; of which wax the said friar endeavored to get hold of a piece, and with the said piece he set in operation that experiment with the keys that I had so unwisely shown him. He had taken as a companion and assistant a clerk (*cancelliere*) who was in the service of the said Castellan. This clerk was called Luigi, and he was a native of Padua. When they were desirous of having the said keys made, the locksmith betrayed them; and since the Castellan came several times to see me in my chamber, and perceived that I was working with that kind of wax, he immediately recognized the said wax, and said: "Although to this poor man Benvenuto there has been done one of the greatest wrongs that was ever committed, he ought not to do such acts as these towards me, for I have done for him such kindness as I ought not to do: now I shall keep him most straitly locked up, and will never do him another kindness in the world." Thus he caused me to be locked up with considerable unpleasantness, especially as regards the words spoken to me by certain of his devoted servants, who also liked me extremely well, and who now and again kept on reminding me of all the good offices that this lord the Castellan had done on my behalf; in such measure that in this case they styled me an ungrateful man, untrustworthy and without faith. And when one of those servants more rashly than was suitable, uttered these insults to me, I, feeling conscious of my innocence, responded angrily, saying that I was never false to my word, and that I would hold to sustaining such statements with the value of my life, and that further if either he or any one other person should make such unjust statements, I would affirm that every one who said such a thing lied in his throat. Unable to endure this insult, he ran to the Castellan's chamber and brought me the wax together with that model made of the keys. Directly I saw the wax I said that he and I were both right; and that he must arrange for me to speak with the lord Castellan, for I would tell him plainly how the thing had happened, which was a matter of much greater importance than they thought. The Castellan immediately had me summoned, and I told him all the circumstances; for which reason he imprisoned the friar, who betrayed that clerk, so that he was about to be hung. The said Castellan hushed up the matter, which had already reached the ears of the Pope; he saved his clerk from the gallows, and he gave me liberty in the same way that I had had it previously. When I saw this matter carried through with so much severity, I began to think of my own affairs, saying to myself: "If there came upon me another time one of these storms, and this man should have no confidence in me, I should come to be no longer under obligation to him, and should want to employ some little portion of my wits, which I am sure would result otherwise for me than those of that rascal of a friar; and I began to direct them to bring me new and coarse sheets, and I did not send the dirty ones back. When my servants asked me for them, I told them to be silent, for I had given them to certain of those poor soldiers; for if they had known of such a business, those poor fellows would have run the risk of the galleys; to such purpose that my young men and my domestics most faithfully, especially Felice, kept such a matter of the said sheets most carefully secret. I set myself to emptying a palliasse, and I burned the straw, for in my prison there was a chimney to enable one to make a fire. Of these sheets I began to make strips, a third of a *braccio* in width; when I had made that quantity which it seemed to me would be sufficient to descend from the great height of that keep of Castel Sant' Agniolo, I said to my servants, that I had given away what I had wanted to do, and that they must see to bringing me finer ones, and that I would always restore to them the dirty ones. This matter was forgotten. Cardinals Santiquattro and Cornaro made those workmen and servants of mine close up the shop, stating openly that the Pope would hear nothing about letting me go, and that those great favors shown me by the King had injured much more than helped me; for the last words that Monsignior di Morluc had said on behalf of the King were these: Monsigno' di Morluc told the Pope that he ought to hand me over to the ordinary judges of the Court; and that if I had done wrong I could be punished, but if I had not done wrong, reason willed it that he should let me go. These words had given so much offense to the Pope that he had a desire never to let me go again. The Castellan most assuredly helped me as much as he could. When during these days those enemies of mine saw that my shop was shut up, they kept scornfully uttering every day some insulting remark to those servants and friends of mine, who came to visit me in prison. It chanced one day among the others that Ascanio, who every day came twice to me, asked me that I would have made for him a certain little garment out of a blue satin gown of my own, which I never wore; I had only used it that time when I went in it in procession; nevertheless I told him that these were not the times, nor I in the place, for the wearing of such garments. The youth took it so ill because I did not give him this wretched gown, that he told me he wanted to go to Tagliacozze, to his home. In a great rage I told him that he would do me a kindness by taking himself out of my presence; and he swore with very great heat that he would never come into my presence again. When we were talking like this, we were walking around the keep of the Castello. It chanced that the Castellan was also taking a walk; and exactly as we were meeting his lordship, Ascanio said: "I am going, and good-bye forever." To this I replied: "And forever I wish that it may be, and thus in truth let it be: I will give directions to the guards that they are never more to let you pass in:" and turning to the Castellan I begged him with all my heart, that he would tell the guards that they were never more to let Ascanio pass, saying to his lordship: "This little country-bumpkin comes to me to add trouble to my already great trouble; therefore I beg you, my lord, that you will never more let him pass in." The Castellan was very sorry, for he knew him to be of wondrous talent; added to this he was of so handsome a person that it seemed that every one, on seeing him a single time, was specially taken with him. The said youth went away crying, and he was wearing a small scimitar (*stortetta*) of his, that he sometimes wore secretly beneath (his clothes). Issuing from the Castello, and with his face so woe-begone, he met two of those special enemies of mine, one of whom was that Jeronimo of Perugia above-mentioned, and the other was a certain Michele, both goldsmiths. This Michele, since he was a friend of that scoundrel of a Perugian, and an enemy of Ascanio, said: "What is the meaning of Ascanio's weeping? Perhaps his father is dead? I speak of that father in the Castello." Ascanio replied to this: "He is alive, but you shall even now be dead;" and raising his hand, with that scimitar of his he struck him two blows, both upon the head, so that with the first he laid him upon the ground, and with the second he then cut off three fingers of his right hand, though actually aimed at his head. He remained there as one dead. The matter was immediately reported to the Pope, and the Pope in a great rage, uttered these words: "Since the King wishes him to be tried, go and give him three days time, in which to defend his cause." They immediately came and performed the said office, which the Pope had committed to them. That worthy man the Castellan immediately went to the Pope, and explained to him that I was not to blame in this matter, and that I had (actually) driven him (the boy) away. So admirably did he defend me that he saved my life from that great wrath. Ascanio fled to his home at Tagliacozze, and thence he wrote to me, begging my pardon a thousand times, for he knew that he had done wrong to add annoyances to my great troubles; but if God should grant me grace that I might issue from that prison, he would never more wish to leave me. I let him know that he must pay attention to his studies, and that if God gave me my liberty I would by all means summon him.

THIS Castellan had every year certain attacks of illness that entirely turned his brain; and when this attack began to come on he talked a great deal in a sort of babbling fashion; and these delusions were different every year: for upon one occasion it seemed to him that he was a jar of oil; another time it seemed to him that he was a frog and he jumped like a frog; another time it seemed to him that he was dead, and they must needs bury him: thus every year there came upon him some one of these different delusions. This time he began by imagining that he was a bat, and while he was out walking he sometimes used to scream just as softly as bats do. He also made a kind of movement with his hands and his body as if he desired to fly. His doctors when they perceived it, as well as his old servants, afforded him all the pleasures that they could think of; and since it seemed to them that he took great pleasure in hearing me talk, they came constantly for me and took me to him. Wherefore this poor man sometimes kept me four or five whole hours, wherein I never ceased from talking with him. He kept me opposite him at his table to eat, and he never left off talking or making me talk; but during these conversations I used to eat very excellently. The poor man neither ate nor slept, in such a way that he tired me out, so that I could do no more; and looking him sometimes in the face, I saw that the balls of his eyes were full of terror, for one looked in one direction and the other in another. He began by asking me if I had ever had the fancy to fly; to which I replied, that all those things that were most difficult for men I had most gladly sought to do and had done; and as to this subject of flying, since the god of nature had given me a body very fitted and strong for running and leaping, much more than the common run, with that small amount of skill beyond, which I should employ with my hands, I felt assured of the courage to fly. This man began to question me as to the means that I would adopt: to which I replied that having observed the animals which fly, and being desirous of imitating by art that which they had by nature, there was none that I could imitate except the bat. When this poor man heard that name of "bat," which was the delusion under which he was laboring that year he gave a very loud shout, saying: "He speaks the truth; he speaks the truth. This is the thing; this is the thing:" and then he turned to me and said: "Benvenuto! if any one gave you the conveniences, would you also have the courage to fly?" To which I replied that if he was willing to give me my freedom afterwards, I had sufficient courage to fly as far as Prati making myself a pair of wings of waxed Rheims linen (*tela di rensa*). Thereupon he said: "And I too would have enough courage; but the Pope has commanded me to keep guard over you as if over his own eyes, and I know that you are an ingenious devil who would escape: however I will have you shut in with a hundred keys, so that you do not escape me." I set myself to beseeching him, reminding him that I was able to fly, but that out of respect for the pledge that I had given him I had never failed (him); moreover I begged him for the love of God, and on account of the many kindnesses which he had shown me that he would not added a greater misfortune to that great trouble which I was already enduring. While I was saying these words, he gave express orders that they should bind me, and take me to a well-secured prison. When I saw that there was no other remedy, I said to him, in the presence of all his attendants: "Secure me well and guard me well, for I shall certainly escape." So they took me away and shut me up with wonderful precautions. Thereupon I began to think out the plan that I must adopt to escape. Directly I saw myself shut in, I set to work to examine how the prison (cell) in which I was confined was situated; and when it appeared to me that I had assuredly discovered the means of getting out, I began to consider by what method I could descend from the great height of that keep (*mastio*), for so they denominated that great high tower: and having taken those new sheets of mine, which, as I have already said, I had made into strips, and firmly stitched together, I set to work to examine what amount would suffice to enable me to descend. Having reckoned up such amount as would serve me, and got everything into order, I secured a pair of pincers, which I took from a Savoyard, who was one of the watchmen of the Castello. This man had charge of the tubs and cisterns; he also took an interest in carpentry; and since he had several pairs of pincers, among which was a very heavy and large pair, I, thinking that they would be to my purpose, abstracted them, and hid them inside that palliasse of mine. When later the time came when I wanted to make use of them, I began to test with them those nails which held together the iron bands (of my cell-door); and since the door was a double one, it was not possible to see the riveting of the said nails; in such fashion, that in trying to extract one of them I endured very great labor; however I subsequently succeeded at last. When I had extracted this first nail, I proceeded to think out what method I could adopt that they (the jailers) might not perceive it. I immediately prepared a little wax with a few scrapings of rusty iron, which was of the same color exactly as those nail-heads (*cappelli d'aguti*) which I had extracted; and with this same wax I began diligently to imitate those nail-heads in their iron bands: and hand over hand (*di mano in mano*) as many as I extracted, so many did I counterfeit in wax. I left the iron bands, attached each at the top and bottom by some of the same nails that I had extracted; I had afterwards put them back, but they were cut short, and then lightly replaced, so that they held the iron bands in position for me. This business I accomplished with the greatest difficulty, because the Castellan dreamed every night that I had escaped, and therefore sent to inspect my cell from hour to hour; and the man who came had both the name and manners of a constable. He was called *Bozza,* and he always brought with him another man who was named Giovanni, but nicknamed *Pedigniome;* this man was a soldier, and Bozza was a servant. This Giovanni never came to that cell of mine, that he did not utter some insult to me. He was from the neighborhood of Prato, and had been in a druggist's shop in Prato: he examined carefully every evening those iron bands and the entire cell, and I said to him: "Watch me well, for I want by all means to escape." These words caused the greatest enmity to arise between him and me; in such measure that I replaced with very great care all those tools of mine; that is to say the pincers, and a very large dagger, and other things of the same nature: I carefully replaced them all in my palliasse: so too those strips that I had made, these also I kept in this palliasse; and as soon as it was daylight I used immediately to sweep up for myself; and although by nature I delight in cleanliness, I was at that time most (particularly) cleanly. When I had swept up, I remade my bed so nicely, and with some flowers upon it that almost every morning I had brought to me by a certain Savoyard. This Savoyard had the charge of the cisterns and of the tubs; and he also delighted to work at carpentry; and from him I stole the pincers with which I removed the nails from these iron bands. To return then to my bed; when Bozza and Pedignione came, I never said anything to them except that they should keep away from my bed, lest they should stain and spoil it for me; telling them upon such occasions when merely out of mockery they sometimes touched the bed ever so lightly, I used to say to them: "You dirty cowards! I will draw one of those swords of yours, and do you such an injury as will make you marvel. Do you think that you are worthy to touch the bed of a man like me? On this point I shall have no respect for my own life, for I am sure that I shall take yours; therefore leave me alone with my discomforts and with my sorrow; and don't give me any more trouble than that which I have already; if not I will make you see what a desperate man can do." These words they repeated to the Castellan, who commanded them expressly that they should never approach that bed of mine, and that when they came to me they must come without their swords, and they must keep closest watch over me in other respects. Having thus secured the question of my bed, it seemed to me that I had done everything: for herein lay the important part of my whole business. One feast-day evening among the others, the Castellan was feeling very unwell, and since those delusions of his had increased, for he never said anything else but that he was a bat, and that if they should hear that Benvenuto had flown away, they must let him go, that he might catch me up, for he could certainly also fly by night much better than I could, adding: "Benvenuto is a counterfeit bat, and I am a real bat; and since he has been given into my charge, leave it to me to act, for I shall certainly catch him." When he had been for many nights in this delusion, he tired out all his servants, and I by different channels kept hearing everything especially from that Savoyard, who had a liking for me. Having resolved upon this feast-day evening to escape at all hazards, I first most devoutly made a prayer to God, imploring His Divine Majesty that He would defend and assist me in that so perilous an undertaking; then I drew out all the things that I wished to use, and labored with them all that night. When I had come to two hours before day-break I removed those iron bands with very great effort, because the wooden panel of the door, and also the bolt, offered a resistance, so that I could not open it: I had to cut away the wood: finally, however, I opened it, and shouldering those strips which I had wound up after the fashion of reels of thread upon two small pieces of wood, I emerged and went in the direction of the privies of the keep; and having discovered from within two tiles of the roof, I immediately easily leaped on to them. I was clad in a white doublet, and a pair of white stockings, and likewise a pair of white buskins (*borzachini*), in which I had placed that dagger of mine already spoken of. Then I took one end of those strips of mine and attached it to a piece of ancient tile that was built into the said keep: by chance this (tile) jutted out the distance of barely four fingers. The strip was arranged after the fashion of a stirrup. When I had made it fast to the piece of tile, turning myself toward God, I said: "Lord God! Aid my right, for I have one right, as Thou knowest, and because I am helping myself." Letting myself go by degrees, holding myself up by the strength of my arms, I reached as far as the ground. There was no moonlight, but there was a fine brightness (in the atmosphere). When I was on the ground, I looked up at the great height that I had descended so courageously, and went joyfully away thinking that I was free. The which, however, was not the case, for the Castellan had on that side caused to be built two very high walls, and they served him for a stable and a fowl-house; this place was shut in with two heavy bolts outside. When I saw that I could not escape from thence, it gave me very great distress. While I was pacing backwards and forwards, thinking over my affairs, I struck my feet against a long pole, which was hidden under straw. This I raised with great difficulty to that wall; then by the strength of my arms I climbed up to the ridge of the wall. And because that wall had a sharp edge, I was unable to summon strength enough to draw up the said pole; I therefore resolved to make fast a piece of those strips, which were upon the other reel; for the one of the two reels I had left attached to the keep of Castello: so I took a piece of this other strip, as I have said, and having bound it to that joist, I descended this wall, which caused me very great labor, and tired me very much, and I had besides taken the skin off my hands inside, which were bleeding; for which reason I was obliged to rest; and I bathed my hands in my own urine. Staying thus, when it seemed to me that my strength had returned, I leaped on to the last rampart of the (outer) walls, which looks towards Prati: and when I had arranged my reel of strips with which I wanted to encircle a battlement, and after the same method that I had employed for the greater height, to act as regards this lesser one; when I had, as I say, arranged my strip, I discovered behind me one of those sentinels who kept watch. When I saw that my design was hin-

dered, and perceived myself in peril of my life, I prepared to face
that guard; who when he saw my determined spirit, and that I
was coming towards him with my weapon in my hand, quickened
his step, showing his intention of avoiding me. As I had removed
myself some distance from my strips I very quickly turned back
again; and although I perceived another guard, he perchance did
not want to see me. When I reached my strips, having bound
them to the battlement, I let myself go; whereby, whether in very
truth fancying that I was near the ground I had released my hands
to jump, or whether my hands were really tired out, being unable
to resist that strain, I fell, and in this fall I struck my head and
remained unconscious for more than an hour and a half, as far as
I could judge. Then, as day showed signs of breaking, that slight
freshness that comes an hour before sunrise caused me to revive,
but all the same I still remained out of my senses, for it seemed to
me that my head had been cut off, and I appeared to be in Purgatory. Remaining thus, little by little, my powers returned to themselves, and I perceived that I was outside the Castello, and immediately I remembered all that I had done. And because I felt
the shock to my head before I perceived the breaking of my leg,
putting my hands to my head I took them away all covered with
blood; then having made a careful examination I knew and judged
that I had received no injury of importance; nevertheless, when
I wished to rise from the ground I found that I had broken my
right leg three fingers distance above the heel. Nor also did this dismay me: I dragged out my dagger together with its sheath; for
this latter had an end with a very heavy hard ball upon the ex-
tremity of the end, and this had been the cause of my having
broken my leg; for, by striking the bone with the heavy weight of
that hard ball, since the bone could not give way, it was the reason
why it broke in that place. Wherefore I threw away the sheath

of the dagger, and with the dagger I cut off a piece of that strip which I had left over, and as best I could bound the leg together. Then I crawled along with the said dagger in my hand towards the city gate: when, however, I reached the gate, I found it closed; and seeing a certain stone exactly beneath the gate, which, reckoning that it was not very firm, I tried to pull away; then laying hold of it and feeling it shift, it easily yielded to me, and I drew it out; and by this means I entered. It had been more than five hundred paces in a direct line of transit, from the place where I fell to the gate whereby I entered. When I had entered within (the walls of) Rome certain mastiff dogs threw themselves upon me and bit me severely; upon whom, when they returned many times to plague me, I drew that dagger of mine and wounded one of them so sharply, that he howled loudly, to such purpose that the other dogs, as is their nature, ran to that dog: and I set myself to crawling thus towards the Church of the Trespontina. When I had arrived at the mouth of the street which turns towards Santagniolo, from thence I took the road to go towards Sanpiero, for the reason that, as it was growing light, I considered that I was running some danger; and meeting a water-carrier who had his donkey laden up with his buckets of water, calling him to me I besought him that he would take me up (*levassi di peso*), and carry me to the summit of the steps of Sanpiero, telling him: "I am a poor young man, who through the chances of a love affair was desirous of descending from a window; thus I fell and broke a leg. And since the spot whence I came out is one of great note, and I should run the risk of being cut in pieces, I therefore beg you to carry me off quickly, and I will give you a *scudo* of gold;" and I drew out my purse wherein I chanced to have a good quantity. He immediately took me up, and willingly put me upon his back, and carried me to the said summit of the steps of Sanpiero; and there

I made him leave me, and told him that he must return at full speed to his donkey. Crawling thus I immediately took my way, and went towards the house of the Duchess, wife of the Duke Ottavio, and daughter (natural, not legitimate daughter) of the Emperor, who had been the wife of Duke Lessandro, Duke of Florence, for I knew most certainly that in the house of this great princess there were many of my friends, who had come with her from Florence; for besides I had through the medium of the Castellan done her a service; for desiring to help me he had told the Pope that when the Duchess made her entry into Rome I was the cause of saving (the city) from more than a thousand *scudi* of damage, which a heavy rain was doing them; on which account he said that he was in despair, and that I put heart into him; and he said that I had aimed several heavy pieces of artillery in that direction where the clouds were thickest, and already a very heavy rain had begun to fall; whereupon when I began to fire off this artillery, the rain ceased, and at the fourth discharge the sun showed itself, wherefore I was the sole cause that that festivity had passed off so very well. Therefore when the Duchess heard it, she had said: "That Benvenuto is one of those brilliant men, who stood in high favor (*buona memoria*) with the Duke Lessandro, my (late) husband, and I shall always take care of such men should the occasion occur of doing them a kindness;" and she had besides spoken of me to the Duke Ottavio her (present) husband. For these reasons I was going straight to the house of Her Excellency, which was in the Borgovechio in a very fine palace which is there; and there I should have been very sure that the Pope would not have touched me; but since the thing that I had done up to that point had been too wonderful for a human body, God not being willing that I should arrive at so much vainglory, for my own betterment desired to give me a still greater correction, than that which had been passed through; and the cause of this was that while I was crawling along thus up upon those stairs, a servant who belonged to Cardinal Cornaro suddenly recognized me; which Cardinal was lodging in the Palace. This servant ran to the Cardinal's chamber, and waking him up said: "My most reverend lord, your Benvenuto is below, who has escaped from the Castello, and is crawling along all covered with blood: from what it appears he has broken a leg, and we don't know whither he is going." The Cardinal said directly: "Run and carry him hither to me into my chamber." When I reached him he told me that I was not to be disturbed at anything; and he immediately sent for the principal doctors of Rome; and I was attended to by them; and there was one, a certain master Jacomo of Perugia, a very excellent surgeon. This man set the bone for me wonderfully, then he bound me up and with his own hand he bled me; as my veins were swollen much more than ordinarily, and because he desired besides to make the wound a somewhat open one, so great a rush of blood issued that it flew into his face and covered him in such abundance that he could not continue his dressing of me; and taking this circumstance for a very bad omen he dressed me with great difficulty; and many times he wished to leave me, remembering that he also ran no little risk of punishment for having attended me or rather having completed the cure. The Cardinal caused me to be placed in a secret chamber, and went off immediately with the intention of begging for my release from the Pope.

AT this juncture there arose a very great disturbance in Rome; for the strips attached to the great tower of the keep of the Castello had been observed, and all Rome ran to see this remarkable thing. Meanwhile the Castellan had reached the worst delusions of his madness and wanted in spite of all his servants to fly also from that keep himself, saying that no one could retake me except himself by flying after me. Upon this Misser Ruberto Pucci, father of Misser Pandolfo, having heard of this great event, went in person to see it; then he came on to the Palace, where he met Cardinal Cornaro, who told him all the circumstances, and how I was already in one of his rooms being nursed. These two worthy men went together to throw themselves on their knees before the Pope; who, before he would allow them to say anything, himself observed: "I know all that you want of me." Misser Ruberto Pucci said: "Most blessed Father, we are asking for pardon for that poor man, who for his talents deserves to have some consideration, and in addition to them has shown so great a spirit together with so much ingenuity, as does not seem human. We do not know for what crimes Your Holiness has kept him so long in prison; nevertheless, if those crimes were ever so monstrous, Your Holiness is holy and wise, and raises or abases according to your will; but if they are matters in your power to grant, we pray that you will do us this favor." The Pope, feeling ashamed at this, said that he had kept me in prison at the desire of certain friends of his, for being a trifle too bold; but "since We recognize his talents, and desire to keep him near Ourselves, We have given orders that he be treated very well, so that he should have no reason to return to France. We are very much grieved at his great injury; tell him to attend to getting cured; and from his troubles, when he shall be cured, We will relieve him." These two great men came to me, and gave me this good news on behalf of the Pope. At this juncture there came to visit me the nobility of Rome, both young and old, and of every sort. The Castellan, thus out of his mind, had himself carried to the Pope; and when he was in His Holiness' presence, he began to complain saying, that if he did not give me back to him as prisoner, he would be doing him a great wrong, for he said: "He has escaped from me under the pledge that he had given me. Alas! He has flown away, and he promised me not to fly away." The Pope laughing said: "Go! go! for I will by all means give him back to you." The Castellan rejoined, saying to the Pope: "Send the Governor to him, to find out who has helped him to escape, for if it is one of my men, I will hang him by the neck to that battlement whence Benvenuto escaped." When the Castellan had departed, the Pope smiling summoned the Governor, and said: "He is a brave man, and it is a wondrous thing; although when I was young I also descended from that very spot." In this the Pope was speaking the truth, for he had been imprisoned in the Castello for having forged a Brief, since he was the abbreviator of the *Parco maioris*. Pope Lessandro had kept him a long time in prison; then because the matter was too scandalous a one, he had resolved to cut off his head, but, desirous of letting the feast days of Corpus Domini pass over, when Farnese got to know it all, he made Pietro Chiavelluzzi come with several horses, and he corrupted certain of those guards in the Castello with money; to such purpose that on the day of Corpus Domini, while the Pope was in procession, Farnese was put into a basket, and with a rope was dropped to the ground. The rampart of (outer) walls had not then been added to the Castello, but there was only the great tower, so that he had not those great difficulties in escaping that I had: besides he had been justly arrested and I wrongfully. It is enough that he wished to boast to the Governor that he had also in his youth been courageous and brave, and he did not perceive that he was betraying his own great rogueries. He said: "Go, and tell him to speak out freely who has assisted him: be it who it may, it is sufficient that I have pardoned him, and I promise that to you freely." This Governor, who had two days before been appointed Bishop of Jesi came to me; and when he arrived, he said to me: "Benvenuto mine, although my duty is one that terrifies men, I am come to reassure you, and so I have authority to promise you by the express commission of His Holiness, who has told me that he also escaped, but that he had many helpers and many companions, for otherwise he would not have been able to do it. I swear to you by the sacraments, which I am carrying upon me, for I was consecrated Bishop but two days ago, that the Pope has freed and pardoned you, and he is very grieved at your serious injury; but attend to your cure and take everything for the best, for this imprisonment, which you have certainly endured in entire innocence, will be always to your advantage; for you will stamp

down poverty, and there will be no need for you to return to
France, going thither to wear out your life in this place and in
that. Therefore tell me freely the circumstance as it took place,
and who has given you assistance; then take comfort and repose
yourself and get well." I began at the beginning and related all
the whole matter, exactly as it had taken place, and gave him the
most particular details, down to that of the water-carrier who had
carried me upon his back. When the Governor had heard it all, he
said: "These are indeed too great things for one man to have done
alone; they are not credible of any other man but you." So having
made me stretch out my hand, he said: "Be of good cheer and take
comfort to yourself, for by this hand that I am holding you are
free, and, if you live, you shall be happy." When he departed from
me, for he had been inconveniencing (*tenuto a disagio*) a crowd
of important nobles and lords who had come to visit me, saying
among themselves: "Let us go and see that man who works miracles;" these people remained with me; and some of them made
me offers of help and others presents. Meantime the Governor
having reached the Pope, began to relate to him the story that I
had told him; and it exactly chanced that the lord Pier Luigi, his
son, was present; and every one expressed very great astonishment.
The Pope said: "Surely this is too great a thing." The lord Pier
Luigi thereupon rejoined, saying: "Most blessed Father, if you
set him free, he will do much greater things, for this is the spirit
of a man who is over-bold. I want to tell you another (story)
about him, which you do not know. This Benvenuto of yours,
before he was imprisoned, was having some words with a nobleman (in the service) of the Cardinal Santafiore, which words arose
from a trifling expression that this nobleman had uttered to Benvenuto; to such an extent that he replied most bullyingly and with
so much heat, even to the point that he began to show signs of

quarreling. The said nobleman reported (the matter) to the Cardinal Santa Fiore, who said that if he could lay hands upon him, he would relieve the madman of his head. Benvenuto hearing of this kept a fowling-piece of his in readiness, with which he used to fire continually at a farthing (*quattrino*); and one day when the Cardinal was looking out of the window—for the shop of the said Benvenuto was beneath the Cardinal's palace—he, seizing his fowling-piece, got himself in readiness to fire upon the Cardinal. And since the Cardinal was warned of it he withdrew immediately. Benvenuto in order that such a (murderous) intention should not transpire, fired at a wood-pigeon (*colombo terraiuolo*) that was brooding in a nook high up on the palace, and struck the said pigeon in the head; a thing impossible of belief. Now Your Holiness may do all that you wish with him; I do not want to omit having told you of it. And the desire could also come to him, since he considers that he has been wrongfully imprisoned, to fire one day upon Your Holiness. His is a spirit too fierce and too assured. When he slew Pompeo, he gave him two stabs in the throat in the midst of ten men who were protecting him, and then escaped, to their no little shame, for they were worthy men and of ability." There was present at these statements that nobleman (in the suite) of Santa Fiore with whom I had had words, and he confirmed to the Pope all that his son had told him. The Pope became swollen (with passion), and said nothing. I do not wish to omit giving my explanation justly and straightforwardly (*santamente*). This nobleman (in the service) of Santa Fiore came to me one day, and brought me a small gold ring, which was all discolored by quicksilver, saying: "Polish up this old ring for me and do it quickly." I since I had in hand many very important commissions in gold and precious stones, and moreover hearing myself commanded so confidently by one to whom I had never spoken, nor had even seen, told him that I had not a polisher by me at that moment and that he must go to some one else. He without any sort of provocation told me that I was an ass. To which words I replied, that he was not saying the truth, and that I was a man in every respect better than himself; but that if he roused me I would give him heavier kicks than an ass. He reported this to the Cardinal and depicted (my conduct as worthy of) a Hell. Two days later, I was behind the palace shooting into a very high-up nook at a wild pigeon which was brooding in that nook; and I had many times seen firing at that same pigeon a goldsmith, who was called Giovanfran⁰ della Tacca, a Milanese, and he had never hit it. This (particular) day that I was shooting, the pigeon was just showing its head, being suspicious on account of the other times upon which it had been fired at; and since this Giovanfran⁰ and I were rivals in the matter of shooting with fowling-pieces, while certain noblemen and friends of mine were in my shop, they pointed it (the pigeon) out to me, saying: "Look up there at Giovanfrancesco della Tacca's pigeon, at which he has fired so many times; now, see how the poor creature remains on the watch so that it scarcely shows its head." Raising my eyes, I said: "That little bit of head would be quite sufficient for me to kill it, if it will only wait till I can sight my fowling-piece." Those noblemen said that even the man who invented the fowling-piece could not do that. At which I replied: "I wager a jug of that good Greek wine of mine host Palonbo, that if it waits for me to sight my wondrous 'Broccardo' (for so I called my fowling-piece), I will knock it over in that small portion of its noddle (*capolino*) that it is showing." Taking aim immediately, at arm's length, without any other rest, I did what I had promised, not thinking of the Cardinal nor of any one else; rather I reckoned the Cardinal as very much my patron. Let the world therefore take notice, when fortune wishes to deprive a man for the purpose of destroying him, how many different ways she employs. The Pope, swelling and growling (with passion), remained thinking over what his son had told him. Two days afterwards, Cardinal Cornaro went to ask the Pope for a bishopric for one of his nobles, who was called Misser Andrea Centano. The Pope, it is true, had promised him a bishopric: it being thus vacant, when the Cardinal reminded the Pope how he had promised him such a thing, the Pope agreed that it was the truth, and was therefore willing to give it to him; but he wished for a favor from his most reverend lordship, and this was, that he would be willing to give Benvenuto into his hands. Thereupon the Cardinal said: "Oh, if Your Holiness has pardoned him and given me his freedom, what will the world say both of Your Holiness and of me?" The Pope retorted: "I want Benvenuto, and let any one say what they like, since you want the bishopric." The good Cardinal replied, that His Holiness might give him the bishopric, and that he should think over the rest for himself, and then do all that His Holiness both liked and was able to do. The Pope, though somewhat ashamed of the wicked (breach) of his already pledged word, said: "I will send for Benvenuto and, as a small satisfaction to myself, I will put him down in those rooms in my private garden, where he can attend to getting well, and it shall not be forbidden for all his friends to go and see him; and I will also arrange to provide his expenses, until this little whim of mine passes." The Cardinal returned home, and sent immediately by the man who was expecting the bishopric to tell me that the Pope wished to get me back into his hands, but that he would keep me in a lower room in the private garden, where I might be visited by everyone, just as if I were in his house. Thereupon I besought this Misser Andrea that he would be so good as to tell the Cardinal, that he must not give me up to the Pope and must let me act for myself; for I would get myself rolled up in a mattress, and make them carry me out of Rome to a safe spot; for if he gave me up to the Pope, he was most certainly giving me up to death. The Cardinal, when he heard this, it is believed would have liked to do it; but that Misser Andrea, who was concerned for his bishopric, betrayed the matter. So that the Pope sent for me immediately, and had me placed, as he said, in a lower chamber in his private garden. The Cardinal sent to say that I must not eat any of those victuals which the Pope sent me, and that he would send me food; and that he had not been able to act otherwise than he had done, and that I must keep of good courage, for he would assist me so much that I should be set free. Matters standing thus, I was visited every day, and offered many fine things by many great nobles. From the Pope came the victuals, which I did not touch, rather I ate what came from Cardinal Cornaro, and thus I remained. I had among my other friends a young Greek of the age of twenty-five years. This man was most exceedingly vigorous, and wielded the sword better than any man that was in Rome; he was small of spirit, but was a most faithful honest fellow and very ready to believe (what he was told). He had heard it said that the Pope had stated that he wished to recompense me for my misfortunes. This was the truth, for the Pope had said such things at the beginning, but latterly he afterwards spoke otherwise. Wherefore I confided in this young Greek, and I said to him: "Dearest brother! these people want to slay me, so that now is the time to help me: for they think that I do not perceive, through their showing me these extraordinary favors, that they are all done for treachery." This worthy young man said: "Benvenuto mine! Throughout Rome it is said that the Pope has bestowed upon you an appointment worth five hundred *scudi* of revenue, therefore I beseech you of your kindness not to let this suspicion of yours rob you of so great a benefit." And although I besought him with my arms crossed (upon my breast) that he would remove me from thence, for I knew well that a Pope like that one could do me great benefit, but that I knew for very certain that he was studying, secretly for his own credit's sake, to do me great injury; therefore he must act quickly and try to save my life from him; for if he would take me from thence, in the manner that I would tell him, I should always owe my life to him; and when need arose would spend it (in his behalf). This poor young man weeping said to me: "Oh! my dear brother. You want indeed to ruin yourself, but I cannot fail you in whatsoever you command me; therefore tell me the way and I will do all that you tell me, although it be contrary to my wishes." We were therefore agreed, and I had given him all my instructions, which would most easily have succeeded. When I thought that he would come to put in operation all that I had directed, he came to me to say that for my welfare he wished to disobey me, and that he understood thoroughly that which he had heard from men who were near the Pope, and that they knew all the truth regarding my affairs. I, since I was unable to help myself in any other way, remained unhappy and despairing. This occurred on the day of Corpus Domini in (the year) one thousand five hundred and thirty-nine. The time having passed for me after this dispute all that day until nightfall, there came from the Pope's kitchen an abundant supply of viands: also from the kitchen of Cardinal Cornaro there came most excellent provision; and several friends of mine chancing to be present at this (moment) I made them remain to supper with me: whereat I, keeping my leg in splints, in bed, feasted merrily (*feci lieta cera*) with them: so they remained with me. Then when it had passed one hour of the night they departed; and my two servants settled me for sleep, and then lay down in the antechamber. I had a dog, black as a mulberry, (one) of those hairy ones, and he served me admirably out shooting (*alla caccia dello stioppo*), and never stayed more than a step away from me. That night, being under my bed, three times I summoned my servant that he should take him away from under the bed, because he was howling fearfully. When the servants came this dog threw himself upon them to bite them. They were terrified and were afraid that the dog was mad, because he kept barking continually. So we passed on until the fourth hour of the night. On the stroke of the fourth hour of the night the Bargello with a strong guard entered into my chamber. Thereupon the dog issued forth, and sprang upon these men with so much fury, tearing at their cloaks and their hose, and put them into such terror that they thought that he was mad. Wherefore the Bargello, like a practical person, said: "The natural instinct of good dogs is this, that they always divine and foretell the evil that is about to come upon their masters: let two of you take sticks and beat off the dog, and let the others bind Benvenuto upon this chair and take him to the place you know of." As I have said the day just passed was that of Corpus Domini, and it was about the fourth hour of the night. These men carried me shut up and covered over, and four of them went before me, pushing aside those few men who were still about in the streets. Thus they bore me to the Torre di Nona (a place so-called), and put me into prison for life, setting me down upon a little piece of mattress, and giving me one of those guards, who condoled with me all night upon my evil fortune, saying to me: "Alas! poor Benvenuto! What have you done to these people?" Whereat I could very well gather what was going to happen to me, from my being in such a place, and also from what he had informed me. I remained a part of that night tormenting myself with the thought of what could be the reason that God was pleased to give me such a penance; and since I could not find it I was greatly discouraged. That guard afterwards set himself the best he knew to comfort me; whereat I conjured him for the love of God that he would say nothing to me, and would not talk to me, because of my own self I should quicker and better arrive at some resolution. So he promised me. Thereupon I turned all my heart toward God, and I prayed to him most devoutly, that he would be pleased to receive me into his kingdom; and that although I had lamented (my fate), since it seemed to me that as far as the commands of the laws went, my departure (*i.e.* death) in this way was most undeserved; and that although I had committed homicides, His Own Vicar had summoned me from my native land, and had pardoned me by the authority of the (human) laws and of His Own; and that whatever I had done had all been done in defense of this body that His (Divine) Majesty had lent to me; so that I did not understand, according to the rules under which one lives in the world, how I merited that death; but that it seemed to me that that would happen to me which happens to certain unlucky people upon whom when walking along the street a stone falls from some great height upon their heads, and kills them; an event which is seen clearly to be the influence of the stars; not indeed that those stars conspire against us to do us good or evil, but the event takes place during their conjunction, beneath which we are placed; although I know that I have a free will; and that if my faith were exercised in a saint-like manner, I am very certain that the angels of heaven would bear me out of this prison, and would assuredly save me from every one of my afflictions; but because it does not seem to me that I have been made worthy by God of such a thing, it is therefore of necessity that these celestial influences should pour their malignity upon me. Somewhat cast down by this thought, I presently calmed myself, and immediately applied myself to sleep.

When dawn came, my guard awoke me and said: "Oh unfortunate but worthy man! there is no more time now for sleep, for a man has come who has bad news to give you." Thereupon I said: "The sooner I pass out of this earthly prison, the more pleased shall I be, especially since I am secure that my soul is safe, and that I am dying wrongfully. Christ the Glorious and Divine makes me the companion of His Disciples and Friends, who, both He and they, were wrongfully put to death. In the same way am I wrongfully put to death, and I devoutly (*santamente*) thank God for it. Why does not the man come forward who has to pronounce sentence upon me?" Thereupon the guard said: "He is too sorrowful on your account, and he weeps." Then I called to him by name, and he bore the name of Misser Benedetto da Cagli; I said; "Come forward, Misser Benedetto mine! for I am now most excellently prepared and calmed; my glory is far greater in that I die wrongfully, than if I were to die rightfully. Come forward, I beg of you, and provide me with a priest, so that I can speak a few words (*quattro parole*) with him; although there is no real necessity, for my devout confession I have made to my Lord God (Himself); but merely to observe what Our Holy Mother Church has commanded us; for although She is doing me this wicked wrong, I freely pardon it. Come therefore, Misser Benedetto mine! and hasten matters for me ere bodily feeling begin to make me offend." When I had said these words, this worthy man told the guard to lock the door, for without him that duty could not be performed. Going to the house of the lord Pierluigi's wife, who happened to be in the company of the Duchess above-mentioned: and coming into their presence this man said: "My most illustrious mistress, I pray you for the love of God, be so kind as to send to tell the Pope that he send some one else to pronounce that sentence upon Benvenuto, and to perform my duty, for I renounce

it, and never more will I perform it;" and he departed sighing
with deepest grief of heart. The Duchess, who was present, frowning said: "This is fine justice that the Vicar of God administers in
Rome! The Duke, my late husband, liked this man very. much on
account of his goodness, and for his talents, and did not want him
to come back to Rome, keeping him with much affection near to
himself:" and she went away muttering many words of displeasure.
The wife of the lord Pierluigi, who was called the lady Jerolima,
went to the Pope and throwing herself upon her knees—it was in
the presence of several cardinals—this woman said so many strong
things that she made the Pope blush, and he said: "For love of
you We will let him be, although We Ourselves have never had
hostility towards him." These words the Pope uttered on account of the presence of those cardinals, who had heard the words
that that admirable and intrepid woman had said. I remained in
greatest uneasiness, with my heart beating continuously. All those
men who were appointed to the execution of so unpleasant an
office also remained in uneasiness until the hour for dining was
passed; at which hour every man went upon his own business, so
that there was brought to me (the wherewithal) to dine; whereat
I said in astonishment: "Truth has here prevailed more than the
malignity of the celestial influences; I therefore pray God that if it
be according to His pleasure, He will save me from this storm."
I began to eat, and just as I had at first prepared my resolution for
my great misfortune, so I also formed hopes for my great good
luck. I dined with good courage; thus I remained without seeing
or hearing anything else until the first hour of the night. At that
hour came the Bargello with a good portion of his guard, who
set me again upon that seat upon which they had the evening
before brought me into that place, and (removed me) from thence
with many kind words, that I was not to be afraid; and he ordered

his constables to have a care as if it were their own eyes, not to jar that leg of mine that I had broken. They did so; they bore me into the Castello, whence I had escaped; and when we were high up inside the keep, where there is a small courtyard, there they shut me up for a little while.

A T this juncture, the Castellan above-mentioned had himself carried into that place where I was, and sick and ailing as he was, addressed me: "You see that I have caught you again?" "Yes," said I; "but you see that I did escape, as I told you? And if I had not been sold under Papal pledge by a Venetian cardinal for a bishopric, and (that Pope) a Roman of the family of Farnese, both of whom have scratched in the face the holy consecrated laws, you would never have retaken me; but since that this evil act has now been committed by them, do the worst you can, you also, for I have no further care in this world." This poor man began to shout very loudly, saying: "Ah, me! Ah, me! This man cares neither to live nor to die, and he is more fiery than when he was well; put him down there below the garden, and speak no more to me of him, for he is the cause of my death." I was carried into a dark chamber below a garden, where there was much water, full of tarantulas and many noxious worms. There was flung on the

ground for me a wretched pallet of coarse hemp, and for that
evening no supper was given to me; and I was locked in by four
doors. Thus I remained until the nineteenth hour of the next day.
Then food was brought to me; I asked them (my jailers) that
they would give me some of those books of mine to read: by none
of these men was I spoken to, but they reported (my request) to
that poor man the Castellan, who had asked what I was saying.
The next morning there was brought to me a volume of mine of
the Bible in the vernacular, and a certain other book wherein were
the Chronicles of Giovan Villani. When I asked for certain others
of my books, I was told that I should not have any more, and
that I had too many with those. Thus miserably I existed upon
that mattress, for in three days everything was wet; whereon I
remained continuously without being able to move, since I had
a broken leg; and when I desired to get out of my bed for the
necessities of relieving myself, I used to crawl with the greatest
difficulty, so as not to accumulate filth in that spot where I slept.
For one hour and a half of the day I had a little reflection of light,
which entered that miserable cavern by a very tiny aperture; and
during that short space of time only could I read, and the rest of
the day and of the night I remained patiently always in the dark,
never without thoughts of God and of this human frailty of ours;
and it seemed to me certain that in a few days I should end there
and in that manner my unfortunate existence. Nevertheless, the
best way that I could I comforted myself by considering how much
greater distress it would have given me in passing from this life
of mine to feel that unspeakable torture of the (executioner's)
knife; whereas, being in that condition, I should pass away with
a sleeping-draught which would be much more agreeable to me
than that former means of death; and little by little I felt myself sinking to such a point that my excellent constitution became

used to that purgatory. When I felt that it (*i.e.* my constitution) was adapted and accustomed to it, I took courage to endure that indescribable discomfort as long as it lasted for me. I began the Bible from the beginning, and read and pondered over it devoutly, and was so enchanted with it, that if I had been able, I would never have read anything else; but when my light failed me, there immediately sprang upon me all my troubles, and they afforded me so much suffering, that many times I resolved in some way to make away (*spegnermi*) with myself; but since they did not allow me a knife, I had difficulty in the way of being able to accomplish such a thing. Nevertheless, upon one occasion among the others I had fixed a great log of wood that was there and propped it up after the manner of a trap; and I wanted to make it dash down upon my head; the which would have crushed me at once, in such fashion, that when I had arranged all this erection, and was approaching it, resolved to dash it down, when I wanted to pull it down with my hands, I was seized by something invisible and thrown four *braccia* away from that spot, and so terrified that I remained lifeless: and thus I stayed from the dawn of the day until the nineteenth hour, when they brought me my dinner. They must have come many times, when I had not heard them; for when I did hear them, there entered in Captain Sandrino Monaldi, and I heard him say: "Oh, unhappy man! See to what an end has come so rare a genius." Hearing these words, I opened my eyes: whereupon I saw priests wearing long gowns, who said: "Oh, you! You told us that he was dead." Bozza said: "I found him dead, and therefore I said so." They immediately raised me from the spot whereon I was, and having lifted the mattress, which had become wet like macaroni, they threw it outside that room; and having reported these circumstances to the Castellan, he made them give me another mattress.

And so recalling to myself what thing it could have been that
had diverted me from such an act, I thought that it must be something Divine and my Defender. The following night there appeared to me in a dream a wondrous Being in the form of a very
handsome youth, and in a tone of rebuke he said: "Do you know
Who it is that has lent you that body that you wanted to destroy
before His appointed time?" I seemed to answer that I recognized everything as coming from the God of Nature. Then he
said to me: "Do you despise His Works, in desiring to injure
them? Allow yourself to be guided by Him and lose not the hope
of His Power;" with many other similar admirable words, of
which I do not recall the thousandth part. I began to consider
that this angel shape had told me the truth; and casting my eyes
around the prison, I saw a little piece of rotten brick; I therefore
rubbed one (fragment) against another, and made it into the form
of a little paste; then crawling thus I approached one of the edges
of that door of my prison, and I managed with my teeth so that
I broke off a small splinter: and when I had done this, I waited
for that hour of daylight that came into my prison, which was
from twenty and a half to twenty-one and a half of the clock. Then
I began to write in the best way that I could upon certain scraps
of paper that were left over in the volume of my Bible, and I
rebuked the despicable spirits of my intellect for not desiring to
remain any longer in life; who replied to my body, excusing
themselves on account of their misfortunes; and the body gave
them hope of well-being: thus I wrote it in dialogue form:

AFFLITTI SPIRITI MIEI

> *The Body.* Afflicted soul of me,
>   How cruel, thus to hate this life!
> *The Soul.* If against Heav'n you be,
>   Who shall protect us in the strife?
>   Nay, let us go to find a better life.

> *The Body.* Ah! stay yet, do not go!
>   For Heav'n doth promise greater joys
>   Than ever ye did know.
> *The Soul.* Yet stay we for a space,
>   Since the Great God doth grant you grace,
>   Lest greater be your woe.

Having recovered once more my vigor, after I had by my own exertions comforted myself, I continued to read my Bible, and I had in a way accustomed my eyes to that obscurity, so that whereas at first I was wont to read but one hour and a half, I now read for three whole ones. And I pondered in so great wonder over the strength of God's power over those very simple-hearted men, who would have me believe with so much fervor that God satisfied them in all that they dreamed of; I promising myself likewise the help of God, both on account of His Divine Power and Mercy, and also on account of my own innocence; and turning continually towards God, sometimes in prayer and sometimes in meditation (*ragionamenti*), I remained always in these high thoughts of Him; in such measure that there began to come upon me so great a delight in these thoughts of God that I remembered no more any misfortune that I had ever had in the past, but rather I kept singing all day psalms and many other compositions of my own all addressed to God. My nails only which had grown gave me great distress; for I could not touch myself without wounding myself with them: I could not dress myself because they turned either inwards or outwards giving me much pain. My teeth also died in my mouth; and of this I became aware, because the dead teeth being expelled by those which were alive, little by little perforated the gums from below, and the ends of the roots came to piercing the bottom of their sockets. When I perceived this I drew them out, as one draws (a sword) from a scabbard without any more pain or bleeding; thus they were got out very easily for me. Nevertheless I accustomed myself also to these other fresh troubles, sometimes I sang, sometimes I prayed; and sometimes I wrote with that pounded brick above-mentioned; and I began a poem (*capitolo*) in praise of the prison, and in it I related all those chances that had befallen me in it; which poem I will write down presently in its own place. The good Castellan sent often secretly to find out what I was doing; and because on the last day of July I was rejoicing greatly by myself, recalling the great festival that they are accustomed to celebrate in Rome on that first day of August, I was saying to myself: "In all these past years I have celebrated this pleasant feast along with the other frailties of the World; this year I will now celebrate it in company with the Divine Things of God": and I was saying to myself: "Oh! how much more joyful am I on this occasion than on those." Those persons who heard me utter these words, carried them all back to the Castellan; who in angry wonder said: "Oh God! He triumphs and lives in so great affliction. While I in so much comfort am in want, and am dying solely upon his account! Go quickly and put him in that more subterranean cavern, wherein was done to death of hunger the preacher Foiano. Perhaps when he sees himself in so evil a plight, it may be possible to take the nonsense out of him" (*uscire il ruzzo del capo*). Captain Sandrino Monaldi came at once to my prison with about twenty of those servants of the Castellan; and they found that I was upon my knees, and that I did not turn towards them, rather I was adoring a *God the Father surrounded by angels* and a *Christ rising again victorious,* which I had drawn upon the wall with a little charcoal that I had found covered with earth, after the four months that I had lain upon my bed with my broken leg; and so many times had I dreamed that angels came to attend me that after four months I had become strong as if it had never been broken. Nevertheless they (the jailers) came to me as much armed as if they were afraid that I was a noxious dragon. The said captain said to me: "You observe that there are a great many of us, and that we are come to you with great noise, and (yet) you do not turn toward us." At these words, having imagined very well that greater woe which could befall me, and having become accustomed to and firm in misfortune, I said to them: "Unto this God who supports me, to Him (the Ruler) of the heavens have I turned my soul and my contemplation and all my vital powers, and to you I have turned just that which belongs to you; for you are not worthy to behold that which is good in me nor can you touch it; therefore do to that which belongs to you all that you can do." This said captain, in fear, not knowing what I wanted to do to myself, said to four of the strongest of those men: "Lay all your arms aside." When they had set them down, he said: "Leap very quickly upon him and take him. Even were he the devil, should so many of us be afraid of him? Hold him now firmly, so that he does not escape." I, seized by force and roughly handled by them, imagining much worse things than that which eventually happened to me, raising my eyes to Christ said: "Oh Just God! Thou hast paid upon that lofty Tree all our debts; why then must my innocence pay the debts of some one whom I do not know? Nevertheless Thy will be done." Meanwhile they were carrying me away by the light of a great torch. I thought that they wanted to throw me into the trap of Sammalò; for thus was named a dreadful place, which has swallowed up many persons while still alive, for they happen to fall down into a well in the foundations of the Castello. This did not happen to me: wherefore it seemed to me that I had made a very good bargain; for they put me in that very horrid cavern above-mentioned, wherein Foiano died of hunger, and there they let me stay, doing me no other ill. When they had left me, I began to sing a *De Profundis clamavit* (*sic*), a *Miserere* and an *In Te Domine speravi*. All that first day of August I was holding festival with God, and my heart was always rejoicing in Hope and Faith. The second day they drew me out of that hole, and bore me back to where there were my first drawings of those representations of God. To which when I came, I wept before them much for very delight (*dolcezza*) and joy. After that the Castellan wanted every day to know what I did and what I said. The Pope, who had heard the whole circumstances (for the doctors had already given over the said Castellan to death), said: "Before my Castellan dies, I would like him to cause the death of that Benvenuto after his own fashion, for he is the cause of his death, so that he may not die unavenged." The Castellan on hearing these words by the mouth of the Duke Pierluigi said to the said (duke): "Then the Pope gives Benvenuto to me, and wishes me to wreak my revenge upon him? Think no further about him, and leave him to me." If then the heart of the Pope was cruel towards me, worse and grievous was that of the Castellan in its first appearance; and at this juncture that invisible being, who had diverted me from the desire to kill myself, came to me still invisibly, but with distinct words, and shook me, and raised me from my recumbent position, and said: "Ah me! my Benvenuto! Quickly, quickly betake yourself to God with your accustomed prayers, and cry loudly loudly [*sic*] upon Him." Immediately in terror I fell upon my knees, and repeated many of my prayers in a loud voice: after them all, a *Qui habitat in aiutorium;* after this I discoursed with God awhile; and in an instant the same voice said to me plainly and clearly: "Go to your rest, and have no more fear." And this was so, for the Castellan, having given most cruel orders regarding my death, suddenly recalled them, and said: "Is not he Benvenuto whom I have defended so much, and who I know for very certainty to be innocent, and that all this evil has been done to him wrongfully? Oh! How will God ever have mercy upon me and my sins if I do not pardon those who have done me the greatest injuries? Oh! why must I injure an honest and innocent man, who has done me service and honor. Go to! For instead of causing his death, I will give him life and liberty; and I bequeath by my Will that no one demand of him any of that debt for the heavy expense that he would have to pay here." This the Pope heard and he took it very ill. I remained meanwhile at my accustomed orisons and I wrote out my poem; and I began to enjoy every night the pleasantest and most agreeable dreams that one can possibly ever imagine; and it seemed to me that I was always visibly in company with that being whom, while invisible, I had heard and still heard so very often; and of whom I asked no other favor, except that I besought him, and that fervently, that he would take me where I could see the sun, telling him how great was the desire that I had therefor; and that if I could see it but one single time, then I should die happy. Of all the disagreeable things that I had experienced in this prison all had become to me friendly and companionable, and naught disturbed me. Although those devoted adherents of the Castellan, who were expecting that the Castellan would hang me from that battlement whence I had descended, as he had said, when they saw afterwards that the said Castellan had come to another resolution quite the opposite of that, they, because they could not endure it, always caused me some variety of fright, whereby I might derive the fear of losing my life. Although as I say, to all these things I had become so accustomed, that I had no more fear of anything, and nothing more disturbed me, this single desire (remained), that I might dream of seeing the sphere of the sun. Wherefore time passed on, with my fervent prayers at all times (directed) with passion toward Christ, always saying: "Oh True

Son of God! I implore Thee by Thy Birth, by Thy Death upon the Cross, and by Thy Glorious Resurrection, that Thou wilt make me worthy that I may see the sun, if not otherwise, at least in a dream; but if Thou shouldst make me worthy that I should see it with these mortal eyes of mine, I promise to come to visit Thee at Thy Holy Sepulcher." This vow and these fervent prayers of mine to God were uttered upon the second day of October in the year one thousand five hundred and thirty-nine. Then when the following morning came, which was the third day of the said October I awoke at daybreak, about an hour before sunrise; and rising from that wretched lair of mine, I put upon me a little rough clothing that I had, for it had begun to be chilly: and being thus risen I made more devout prayers than I had ever made in the past; for in the said prayers I spake with special supplications to Christ, that He would grant me at the least so much grace that I might know by divine inspiration for what sin of mine I was undergoing so great a penance; and since that His Divine Majesty had not been willing to make me worthy of the sight of the sun even in a dream, I implored Him by all His Power and Merit that he would make me worthy that I might know the reason of that penance. When I had uttered these words, after the manner of a whirlwind, I was seized by that invisible being and carried away, and was taken into a chamber, where that invisible (friend) of mine then visibly showed himself to me in human form, after the fashion of a youth with the down upon his cheek (*giovane di prima barba*); with a most marvelous countenance, handsome, but austere, and not wanton; and he directed me into that chamber, saying: "This so great a concourse of men that you see are all those who up to this time have been born, and since have died." Wherefore I asked him for what reason he had brought me thither: he said to me: "Come forward with me and you shall soon see." I found in my hand a poniard and upon me a coat of mail; and thus he led me through that great chamber pointing out to me how in infinite thousands they were walking, now in one direction, and now in another. Leading me forward, he went out before me through a little postern into a place resembling a narrow street; and when he drew me after him into the said street, upon my issuing from that chamber I found myself unarmed, and I was in a white shirt with nothing upon my head, and I was upon the right hand of my said companion. When I saw myself after this fashion, I marveled, because I did not recognize that street; and having raised my eyes I saw that the brightness of the sun was striking upon a portion of the wall, as if upon the façade of a house, above my head. Thereupon I said: "Oh my friend! What must I do, that I may be able to mount up so that I may see the very sphere of the sun?" He showed me some great stairs that were there upon my right hand, and he said to me: "Go up there by yourself." Going a short distance from him, I mounted backwards (*con le calcagnia allo dietro*) up several of those stairs, and I began little by little to discover the proximity of the sun. I hastened to climb on; and so I went on according to that said manner, until I discovered the whole sphere of the sun. And since the strength of his rays, according to their wont, made me close my eyes, when I saw my mistake, I opened my eyes and, gazing fixedly at the sun, I said: "Oh! my sun! That I have longed for so much. I do not want ever to see anything else, even if your rays blind me." Thus I remained with eyes firmly fixed upon him; and as I stayed a little while in this way, I saw of a sudden all that force of those great rays cast itself upon the left side of the said sun: and the sun remaining clear without his rays, I gazed upon him with greatest pleasure; and it seemed to me a marvelous thing that those rays should be taken away in that fashion. I stood considering what a Divine Grace this had been, which I had received that morning from God; and I said in a loud voice: "Oh! wonderful is Thy Power! Oh! glorious Thy Virtue! How much greater favor art Thou showing to me than that which I looked for!" This sun without his rays seemed to me neither more nor less than a bath of purest molten gold. While I was considering this great thing I saw the center of the said sun begin to swell, and the shape of this swelling to increase, and on a sudden there appeared a *Christ upon the Cross* of the same matter as was the sun; and He was of such fair grace in His most benign aspect, as the human mind could not imagine a thousandth part; and, while I was gazing upon such a thing, I cried loudly: "Miracles! Miracles! Oh! God! Oh! Thy clemency! Oh! Thine infinite Virtue! Of what hast Thou made me worthy this morning!" And while I was gazing and was saying these words, this *Christ* moved towards that part (of the sun) whither his rays were gone, and in the midst of the sun there was again a swelling such as occurred before; and the swelling having increased, it immediately converted itself into the form of a most beautiful *Madonna,* who was displayed as it were seated in a very lofty fashion, with her said Son in her arms in a most charming attitude, as though smiling; she was set between two angels, one on either side, more beautiful than the imagination can attain to. I saw besides within the same sun, on the right hand, a figure clad after the fashion of a priest; this (figure) turned its back to me, and kept its countenance turned towards that *Madonna* and that *Christ.* All these things I saw truly, clearly and distinctly, and I continually gave thanks to the glory of God with a very loud voice. When this marvelous sight had been before my eyes for a little more than an eighth of an hour, it departed from me; and I was borne back into that den of mine. I immediately began to cry out loudly, saying in a loud voice: "The Power of God has made me worthy to be shown all

His Glory, which has perhaps never been seen by any other mortal eye; whereat by this I know that I am free and happy and in favor with God; and you scoundrels shall remain scoundrels, unhappy and in God's displeasure. Know that I am very sure that the Day of All Saints which was that day upon which I came into the world in the year one thousand five hundred precisely,—the first day of November, the night following at four of the clock,—on that day which is approaching you will be compelled to take me out of this gloomy prison; and you will not be able to do any less thing, for I have seen it with my own eyes, and upon that Throne of God (Himself). That priest who was turned toward God and who showed his back to me, was Saint Peter (himself), who was pleading for me; ashamed that in his house they should inflict upon Christians such cruel wrongs. Therefore tell it to whom you like, that no one has the power to do me any more harm; and tell that lord who keeps me here, that if he give me either wax or paper, and the means whereby I can express this Glory of God which He has displayed to me, I will most assuredly make clear to him that thing of which perhaps he stands in doubt."

The Castellan, although the doctors had no hope of his recovery, yet remained with a firm courage in himself, and those delusions of his madness, which were accustomed to distress him every year, left him; and having given himself in all things and through all things to (the care of) his soul, his conscience smote him, and it seemed to him that I had indeed received, and was receiving, a very great wrong; and when he caused the Pope to hear of those wondrous things that I used to relate, the Pope sent to say,—like one who believed nothing, neither in God nor in any other thing,—that I was crazed, and that he must attend as much as ever he was able to his own health. When the Castellan heard these replies he sent to comfort me, and supplied me with writing-materials and

wax and certain small instruments (*fuscelletti*) made for manipulating the wax, with many kindly words which were repeated to
me by a certain man among those servants of his who liked me
very much. This particular man was altogether different from that
body of other wretches, who would have liked to see me dead.
I took those papers and that wax, and began to work: and while
I worked I wrote this Sonnet, addressed to the Castellan.

> If I, my Lord, the truth to you could show
>   Of light eternal, that by God's own Grace
>   To me is granted in this life so base,
> Such trust as kings enjoy were mine to know.
> If the great Pastor of our Church divined
>   All that God in His Glory hath revealed
>   To me alone, from other soul concealed,
> Until this world of woe it left behind,
> The gates of Holy Justice then unbarr'd
>   Would ye behold; vile Fury, fetter'd, cow'd,
>   Falling thro' space, to Heav'n should cry aloud.
> Ah! had I light, alas! more light, that so
>   My art the grief of Heaven might plainly show,
>   And present sorrow vanish as a cloud.

When the next day there came to bring me my food that
servant of the Castellan who liked me, I gave him this Sonnet
written out; who, concealing it from those other ill-disposed servants who wished me evil, gave it to the Castellan; who would
gladly have allowed me to depart, for it appeared to him that
that great wrong which had been done to me was the chief cause
of his own death. He took the Sonnet and having read it through
more than once, he said: "These are neither the words nor the
ideas of a madman, but rather of a good and worthy person";
and he immediately ordered one of his secretaries to carry it to the
Pope, and to give it into his own hand, beseeching him that he
would let me go. While the said secretary was bearing the Sonnet
to the Pope, the Castellan sent me lights for the day and for the

night, with all the conveniences that in that place could be desired; wherefore I began to improve from the weakness of my health, which had become very great. The Pope read the Sonnet many times; then he sent to tell the Castellan that he would very soon do the thing that would be pleasing to him. And certainly the Pope would then have willingly let me go; but the said lord Pierluigi, his son, as it were in opposition to the will of the Pope, kept me there by force. The Castellan's death drawing near, I meanwhile had designed and engraved that wondrous miracle: on the morning of All Saints he sent Piero Ugolini, his nephew, to show me certain precious stones; the which, when I saw them, I immediately said: "This is the countersign of my liberty." Thereupon this youth, who was a person of very few words, said: "Do not ever think of that, Benvenuto." Thereupon I replied: "Take away your precious stones, for I am housed in such a way that I see no light except in this dark cavern, in which it is impossible to discern the quality of the stones; but, as for issuing from this prison, this day will not end entirely before you will come to fetch me out: and it is bound to be so, and you can not do otherwise." He departed and had me locked in again; and, having gone away, he stayed away more than two hours by the clock. After that he came to me without armed (attendants), accompanied by two lads, who helped to hold me up, and thus he transported me into those large chambers that I had at first (this was in 1538), supplying me with all the conveniences that I asked for. A few days later the Castellan (who thought that I was outside and free) through stress of his severe illness, passed out of this present life, and there remained in his stead Misser Antonio Ugolini, his brother, who had given the deceased Castellan, his brother, to understand that he had let me go. This Misser Antonio, from what I heard, had orders from the Pope to allow me to lodge in that spacious prison accommodation, until such time as he should tell him what to do with me. That Misser Durante, from Brescia, already mentioned above, plotted with that soldier, the Prato druggist, to give me some liquor to consume in my food which was deadly, though not immediate; it would act at the end of four or five months. They set about planning to put some pounded diamond into my food; the which is not in itself poisonous in any sort of way, but through its extreme hardness remains with very sharp angles, and does not act like other stones: for in the case of all other stones that very delicate sharpness does not remain when pounded, rather they become as though rounded; and the diamond alone remains with that sharpness (of edge): in such a way that, when entering the stomach along with the other nourishment, during that revolution which food makes in the process of digestion, this diamond clings to the cartilages of the stomach and of the guts, and as the fresh food gradually (*di mano in mano*) pushes it further forward, the diamond (dust) clinging to them in no long space of time perforates them; and from that cause one dies; whereas no other kind of stones or glass mixed in the food has the power to cling, and so disappears with the (digested) food. However, this Misser Durante above-mentioned gave a diamond of some small value to one of these guards. It was said that this duty (of pounding the diamond) had been performed by a certain Lione, a goldsmith of Arezzo, a great enemy of mine. This Lione had the diamond to pound: and since Lione was very poor, and the diamond must have been worth several tens of *scudi,* he gave the guard to understand that the powder which he handed to him was that pounded diamond which he had been ordered to administer to me; and that morning when I had it, they put it into all the viands;—that was on a Friday; and I had it in the salad, and in the ragout, and in the soup. I approached my food with good appetite, for the

Cellini wrote that his Nymph of Fontainebleau "was as fine a specimen of foundry as had ever been seen." Sculpted for the palace at Fontainebleau while he was under the patronage of Francis I, King of France, it was transferred by Henry II to Diane de Poitier's country seat at Anet from where it was moved to its present location in the Louvre.

evening before I had fasted. This day was feast-day. It is very true that I felt the viands scrunch beneath my teeth, but I never thought of such rascality. When I had finished dining there was left a little salad upon the plate, and my eyes chanced to fall upon certain very fine splinters, which were left there. Taking them up immediately and approaching them to the light from the window, where it was very bright, while I examined them I remembered that my food that morning had made that scrunching noise more than usual; and having thought the matter well over, for, as much as my eyes could judge, I firmly believed that it must be pounded diamond, immediately I reckoned myself most certainly a dead man; and so I sorrowfully addressed myself devoutly to holy prayers; and, thus resolved, it seemed to me certain that I was un-done and dead; and for one whole hour I offered the most fervent prayer to God, thanking Him for so easy a death. Since my stars had so destined it for me, I seemed to have gained a fine bargain in passing out by so easy a way; and I was content and had blessed the world, and that time which I had spent upon it. Now I was turning towards a better kingdom by the Grace of God, which I seemed to have most assuredly acquired. And while I was thus (immersed) in these thoughts I held in my hand some of the finest particles of that supposed diamond, which I most certainly judged to be such. Now since Hope never dies, I seemed to be lured by a little vain Hope, which was the reason for my taking a small knife; and picking up those said small grains, I put them on to an iron bar of the prison; then pressing upon them gently the knife's point, increasing it greatly, I felt the said stone crumble; and ex-amining it carefully with my eyes I saw that such was the fact. Immediately I clothed myself with new hope, and said: "This is not my enemy, Misser Durante, but it is a poor kind of stone, which cannot do me any harm in the world." And although I had resolved to stay quiet and to die in peace in that condition, I made a new plan; but in the first place I thanked God and blessed poverty, which, although it is very often the cause of the death of men, that time had become the very cause of my living; since that Misser Durante, my enemy, or whoever it was, having confided to Lione a diamond of the value of more than one hundred *scudi*, that he should pound it for my (destruction), he on account of his poverty had taken it for himself, and had pounded for me a greenish beryl of the value of two *carlini*, thinking, perhaps, because it also was a stone, that it would produce the same effect as the diamond. At this time the Bishop of Pavia, brother of the Count of Sansicondo, named Monsignior de' Rossi of Parma, this Bishop was a prisoner in the Castello on account of certain disturbances that had previously taken place at Pavia; and since he was a great friend of mine I thrust myself out of the hole of my prison, and called to him in a loud voice, telling him that, in order to slay me, those thieves had administered to me a pounded diamond; and I caused that he should be shown by one of his own servants some of that powder which was left over: but I did not tell him that I had recognized that it was not a diamond. I told him that they had most assuredly poisoned me after the death of that worthy man, the Castellan; and for the short period that I should live, I besought him that he would give me one of his loaves per day, since I did not want ever to eat anything more that came from them; so he promised to send me of his own viands. That Misser Antonio, who was certainly not cognizant of that business, made a very great disturbance and wanted to see that pounded stone, thinking himself also that it was a diamond; but thinking that such a matter emanated from the Pope, he passed it over lightly, after having considered what the matter was. I carefully ate of the viands that the Bishop sent to me, and continuously wrote that poem of mine about the prison, setting down day by day all those events that from time to time happened to me, point by point. The said Misser Antonio also sent me food by a certain Giovanni above-mentioned (a druggist), him of Prato, who was a soldier there (*i.e.,* of the Castello garrison). This man was most hostile to me, and, since he had been the man that had brought me the powdered diamond, I told him that I never wanted to eat any of that food which he brought me, unless he first made proof of it for me. Whereat he replied to me, that they made proofs for Popes. Upon which I rejoined that as noblemen are obliged to make proof for the Pope; so he, a soldier and a country druggist from Prato, was obliged to make proof for a Florentine like myself. The man uttered big words and I to him (the same). That Misser Antonio, somewhat ashamed, and also planning to make me pay those expenses that the poor dead Castellan had granted to me, found another of those servants of his, who was a friend of mine, and sent me my viands by him; at which the above-mentioned (servant) made me proof (of the food) without further dispute. This servant told me that the Pope was every day pestered by that Monsignior di Morluc, who was continually demanding me on behalf of the King, and that the Pope had little fancy for giving me up; and that Cardinal Farnese, formerly very much my patron and friend, had been obliged to say that I must not count upon issuing from that prison for some time. To which I replied that I would come out in spite of them all. This worthy young man begged me to stay quiet, and that I should not be heard to say such a thing, for it would injure me very much; and that with that confidence which I had in God, I ought to wait for His Grace, keeping myself quiet. I said to him that the Powers of God have no occasion to fear the malignities of injustice.

WHEN a few days had thus passed by, the Cardinal of Ferrara appeared in Rome; and upon his going to pay his respects to the Pope, the Pope entertained him so long that the hour of supper arrived. And since the Pope was very much a man of the world, he wished to have plenty of leisure to chat with the Cardinal on French affairs. And because while eating men chance to speak of those things which, apart from such an occasion, they perhaps would not speak of; wherefore since that great King Fran^{co} was in all his affairs most liberal, and the Cardinal, who well knew the taste of the King, was besides far more agreeable to the Pope than the Pope imagined: in such measure that the Pope arrived at such a pitch of merriment, both on this account, and also because the Pope was accustomed to make a very lusty debauch once a week, so that he afterwards vomited. When the Cardinal saw the excellent disposition of the Pope, attuned to granting favors, he demanded me on behalf of the King with great earnestness, pointing out that the King had a great desire for such a thing. Thereupon the Pope, feeling that the time for his vomiting was drawing near, and since too great an abundance of wine was also doing its work, said to the Cardinal with a loud laugh: "Now this instant I wish you to take him to your house;" and having given express orders, he rose from the table; and the Cardinal immediately sent for me, before the lord Pierluigi should know about it, for he would not have let me on any account whatsoever come out of prison. The Pope's messenger came in company with two important noblemen (of the suite) of the said Cardinal of Ferrara, and when the fourth hour of the night was passed they took me out of the said prison, and brought me into the presence of the Cardinal, who showed me boundless courtesies; and well housed I remained there to enjoy myself. Misser Antonio, brother of the Castellan, and now in his office, wanted me to pay all the expenses, together with all those perquisites that *Bargelli* and similar people are accustomed to want, nor did he wish to observe anything of that which the deceased Castellan had devised should be done for me. This matter cost me many tens of *scudi,* and moreover the Cardinal afterwards told me that I must keep a good look out if I had any regard for my life, and that if he had not extracted me from that prison that evening I should never have come out: for he had already heard it said that the Pope was much regretting having let me go. It is necessary to turn a step backwards, because into my Poem all these things of which I speak are introduced. When I was staying those several days in the Cardinal's apartment, and afterwards in the Pope's private garden, among my other dear friends there came to see me a treasurer of Misser Bindo Altoviti, who was called by the name of Bernardo Galluzzi, to whom I had entrusted (sums to) the value of several hundreds of *scudi,* and this young man came to see me in the Pope's private garden, and wished to restore it all to me, whereat I told him that I did not know a friend more dear to whom I could entrust my property, nor a place wherein I could have thought of its being safer: this friend of mine seemed to writhe with unwillingness, and I, as it were by force, made him keep it. When at last I came out of the Castello I found that this poor youth, the said Bernardo Galluzzi, was ruined: by which circumstance I lost my property. Besides, during the time that I was in prison a terrible dream was sent to me, as if with a reed there was written upon my forehead words of very great moment: and he who did this to me repeated clearly three times that I should be silent and not reveal them to anyone else. When I awoke I found that my forehead had been marked. However, in my Poem about my imprisonment there are introduced very many similar things. There was also foretold to me (not knowing then what I was relating) all that subsequently happened to the lord Pierluigi, so clearly and so exactly, that I myself have thought that a very angel from heaven had dictated it to me. I do not want also to omit one thing, the greatest that could ever happen to any man, a circumstance which is for the justification of the Divine Power of God and of His Secrets, of which He deigned to make me worthy; for from that time when I beheld such visions onwards, there rested upon me a splendor, a wondrous thing above my head, which is visible to every kind of man to whom I have been willing to point it out, who have been very few. This may be seen above my shadow in the morning from sunrise until two hours after sunrise, and can be seen much better when the herbage is soaked in the soft dew; it may be seen also in the evening at sunset. I became aware of it in France in Paris, for the air in that part of the world is so much freer from fogs, that one may perceive it much more clearly than in Italy, because our fogs are much more frequent; but in any case there are no occasions when I do not see it; and I can show it to others, but not so well as in that said part of the world. I want to set forth my Poem (*Capitolo*) made in prison, and in praise of that said prison; afterwards I will continue the fortunes good and ill that befell me from time to time, and those also that will happen to me during my life still to come.

This Poem I address to Luca Martini, calling upon him to listen to it.

HE who would know the measure of God's might
  And in how far doth man resemble Him,
  Should, as I deem, a while in prison dwell,
Harassed with thoughts of family and home,
  And suffering pain himself unceasingly,
  Shut in a jail, a thousand miles away.
Or would you seek to show yourself of worth,
  Then be arrested guiltless, lying there
  With none to comfort, none to give you aid.
The little that is yours then let them steal;
  Ill-treated, go in peril of your life,
  Nor ever hope for health or freedom more.
Goaded to frenzy, do a desperate deed;
  Break prison-bars; leap from the dungeon-wall;
  And in a fouler place be shut once more.
Now listen, Luca; this is best of all:
  To have a broken leg; to be deceived;
  In a damp cell to lie without a cloak,
And not a soul that ever speaks to you,
  Save when the jailer food brings, and bad news:
  (Native of Prato, soldier, chemist, lout).
Hear, then, how glory puts you to the proof;
  For never seat is there, save on the stool
  Set ready for new work to be achieved;
Express instructions to th' attendant given
  Neither to heed, nor give you aught; the door
  Just opened wide enough to let him through.
Ah! this is fine diversion for the brain!
  No paper, ink, nor pen; no tools, nor fire,
  Tho' all a life's thoughts for expression yearn.
Great pity 'tis, I can so little say:
  Of ev'ry woe conceive an hundred more,
  And yet of each could I discourse at length.
Now, to return to our first purpose: praise
  Unto the prison let me give, where due;
  An angel, to do that, would scarce suffice!
No honest folk are put there, lest it be
  Thro' evil ministers, or state intrigue,
  Envy and malice, scorn, or bitter hate.
The truth to tell, as now discerned by me,
  Here one knows God, and to Him cries aloud,
  Tortured forever by the pains of hell.
However bad a man's repute may be,
  Two years in prison let him but endure,
  He comes out saintly, wise, by all beloved.

Here spirit, body, garb, are all refined;
    Here, the gross man becomes acute of wit,
    So that he spies afar the seats of Heav'n.
List, while I tell to you a wondrous thing.
    I, being minded on a day to write,
    Resort to this strange way to court the Muse.
I pace the room, with furrow'd brow, and bent,
    And when a dent within the door I spy,
    I bite a splinter off to serve as pen.
A bit of brick is lying on the floor,
    And this I quickly crumble into dust,
    And mix the same with water as my ink.
Then, then the flame of Poesy is lit,
    And burns within me, entering, belike
    Where bread goes out; what other way in sooth?
Let me go back to my first fantasy:
    To know what good awaits him, mortal man
    Must first learn all the ill God gave to him.
In jail, all arts of deed and trust
    Are taught; if you would learn the surgeon's skill
    'Twill sweat the very life-blood from your veins.
And then there is a certain natural force
    That makes you eloquent and bold of speech,
    Teeming with lofty thoughts for good and ill.
Blest is the man who for a long while lies
    In a dark dungeon, and at length comes forth,
    For he can speak of battles, truces, peace.
All things must needs for him successful prove,
    And jail has filled his brains with wit so rare
    That they will never lead him now a dance.
Yet you may say: Those years are lost for you;
    Nor is it true that dungeons teach you wit,
    And with real wisdom fill your heart and brain.
Yet, as regards myself, I praise it much.
    But I would gladly see one law enforced.
    He who deserves to pay the penalty
Should not go free. He who doth rule the poor,
    'Tis he should learn these lessons of the jail,
    And so become a sapient governor,
Acting with reason, daring not to swerve
    From the true path of rectitude, that so
    Confusion and distrust might ne'er prevail.
While in this gloomy prison I abode,
    Friars I saw, and priests, and soldiers, too,
    Yet those who most deserved it were not there.

Ah! had you known how mighty was my grief
   When prison-bars let out such rogues once more,
   It makes one weep that one was ever born.
I'll say no more. I am become as gold,
   Such gold as one not recklessly doth spend
   But treasures up to serve for splendid work.
Another thing has come into my mind:
   Of this I spake not, Luca, where I wrote
   Was in a book our kinsman lent to me.
And in the margins there did I record
   The tortures that my maimed body racked:
   For this my muddy ink ran all too slow.
To make an O three times the stick I dipped
   In the brick-paste; could greater woe than this
   Vex the unhappy Spirits in Hell below?
I being not the first unjustly kept
   In jail, I hold my peace and praise once more
   My prison-cell, where heart and brain are racked.
More than the others be my eulogy:
   And let me counsel those who know it not:
   Prison is best, I vow, for workers true.
Yet oh! if He of whom I read would come
   And say to me as once beside the pool:
   "Take thine apparel, Benvenuto, go!"
Salve regina! Credo! should I sing,
   And *Paternoster!* To the poor give alms,
   And to the blind and lame each morn, as well.
How oft when lying in this dungeon deep
   These beauteous lilies made my cheek grow pale,
   So that not France nor Florence should I see again.
If I should view by chance i' the hospital
   The *Annunciation* pictured on the wall,
   Then must I flee as were I brutish beast.
Not of her noble Sacred Self I speak,
   Nor of her glorious holy lilies white
   That gave a luster unto heaven and earth;
At all times now, and eke in every place
   On which I look I ever seem to see
   Those petals curved—too many as I fear!
Ah! what a host of comrades in my grief!
   Bright, gallant spirits, lofty and divine,
   Yet of this crest, the servants and the slaves.
Yea, I have seen this deadly blazon fall
   Like bolt from Heav'n upon the people vain.
   Then shone upon the stone a wondrous light;

Yet shattered first must be the castle bell
   Ere I go free. He told me this, Who all
   In Earth and Heav'n doth order, and make plain.
A gloomy bier beside this I beheld,
   Deck'd with dead lilies; and all mourning shows
   Were there, and folk lamenting by the bed;
Yea, I saw her who wounds and tortures souls,
   Dealing out horror here or there; quoth she:
   "Behold, I slay whoe'er would do thee harm!"
Then on my brow the noble seraph traced
   With Peter's pen the words that thrice concealed
   Within my heart he bade me ever keep;
And him I saw who drives the flaming Sun,
   Rob'd in its splendor, circled by his court.
   What mortal eye ne'er saw, did I behold.
A solitary sparrow chirruped loud
   Upon the castle-wall; whereat I cried:
   "That predicts life for me, and death for you."
Of all my troubles dire I sang and wrote,
   Pleading to God for pardon and for aid,
   Since now I felt mine eyes grow dim in death.
Never was wolf nor lion, tiger, bear
   With such a thirst for human blood as he,
   Nor viper with more venomous a sting.
'Twas he the cruel captain of the thieves,
   The greatest villain of a robber-crew.
   Yet softly let me speak, lest all should know.
If ever famished bailiffs ye have seen
   Storm a poor fellow's house and seize his goods,
   Hurling to earth the Holy Images,
So on a day in August did they come
   To lead me to a tomb more hideous still;
   Yet in November cursed, scatter'd shall ye be!
Then in mine ears a trumpet did resound
   That told me all, as all I told to them,
   Mindful of nought save to assuage my woe.
And, with intent to kill me, they at last
   Pounded a diamond to dust that this,
   Mixed with my food should surely work my death.
Yet when the villain brought the food to me
   I made him taste the victuals first. Quoth I:
   "My foe, Durante, ne'er intended this."
But first to God above my thoughts I turned,
   Praying to Him for pardon for my sin,
   And *"Miserere!"* as I wept, exclaimed.

When my great anguish had been somewhat soothed,
  Unto God's care I freely gave my soul,
  Content to know a better realm, another state.
An angel out of Heav'n I saw descend,
  With glorious palm in hand, who joyously
  Promised that longer life should yet be mine.
And said: "First God shall rid thee of all foes
  By waging on them grievous war, yet thou
  Being set free, shalt be most glad of heart,
Bless'd by our Holy Father in Heav'n and Earth."

Book Two

Chapter One 1539-1540

WHILE I resided in the palace of the above-mentioned Cardinal of Ferrara, I was very universally well-regarded by everyone, and much more visited than I had ever been previously, for every one marveled much that I should have come out and should have lived through so many boundless afflictions; while I was recovering my breath, endeavoring to remember my profession, I took the greatest pleasure in re-writing the Poem recorded above. Then, in order that I might the better regain my strength, I took a resolution to go out into the air for some days, with the permission and the horses of my good (friend the) Cardinal, in company with two young Romans, of whom one was a worker in my own profession; the other his comrade was not of the trade but came to keep me company. Having left Rome, I went in the direction of Tagliacozze, thinking to find Ascanio my

pupil above-mentioned; and when I reached Tagliacozze I found
the said Ascanio, together with his father and brothers and sisters
and step-mother. By them for two days I was made much of (in
a way) that it would be impossible to relate; I departed towards
Rome and I took Ascanio with me. On the way we began to discourse about our art, in such measure that I was pining to return
to Rome in order to recommence my work. When we arrived in
Rome, I immediately prepared myself to work, and retrieved a
silver basin, that I had begun for the Cardinal before I was imprisoned. Together with the said basin was begun a most beautiful
little ewer. This had been stolen from me with a great quantity
of other things of much value. Upon the said basin I made the
above-mentioned Pagolo labor. I also recommenced the ewer, which
was composed of small figures in high and low relief; and the said
basin likewise was composed of figures in full relief and fishes in
low relief, so rich and so well arranged, that every one who saw
it remained astounded, as much on account of the force of the
design, and (the originality) of the invention, as on account of the
finish which those young men employed upon the said works.
The Cardinal came at least twice every day to be with me, along
with Misser Luigi Alamanni and Misser Gabbriel Cesano, and
there for some hours we passed time pleasantly. Notwithstanding
that I had a great deal to do, he kept loading me besides with new
commissions; and he employed me to make his pontifical seal. It
was in size as large as the hand of a lad of twelve years of age;
and on the same seal I cut out (*intagliai . . . in cavo*) two small
scenes, of which one was when St. John was preaching in the
desert, the other when Sant' Ambruogio was discomfiting those
Arians, represented mounted upon a horse with a whip in his
hand, with so much fire and fine drawing, and so cleanly finished,
that every one said that I had surpassed the great Lautizio,

who made this trade his sole one; and the Cardinal out of personal pride used to compare it with the other seals of the Cardinals of Rome, which were nearly all the workmanship of the above-mentioned Lautizio.

The Cardinal also ordered of me in addition, along with those two works above-mentioned, that I should make a model for a salt-cellar; but he would have liked me to exceed the ordinary run of those who had made salt-cellars. Misser Luigi made many admirable observations regarding this salt-cellar; Misser Gabbriello Cesano also said many very fine things upon this subject. The Cardinal, a most courteous listener and satisfied beyond measure with the designs, which these two great critics had devised in words, turning to me said: "Benvenuto mine, the design of Misser Luigi and that of Misser Gabbriello please me so much, that I do not know which one of the two to select. I therefore refer it to you, for it is you who have to put it into execution." Thereupon I said: "See, my lords, of what importance are the sons of Kings and of Emperors, and what a marvelous splendor and divinity it is that appears in them. Nevertheless if you ask a poor humble shepherd for whom he has the most love and the most affection, for those said sons or for his own children, of a certainty he will tell you that he has the most love for his own children. Therefore I also have great love for my own offspring which I bring forth in this my profession; therefore that which I will exhibit first to you, Monsignior my Most Reverend Patron, will be my own work and my own invention; for many things are beautiful to describe, which when afterwards in execution do not correspond well in the result." And turning myself to those two great critics, I said: "You have spoken and I will act." Misser Luigi Alamanni thereupon laughing, with greatest amiability added many clever remarks in my favor: and they became him, for he was handsome in appearance and proportion of

figure, and possessed a pleasant voice; Misser Gabbriello Cesano
was quite the reverse, so ugly and so unpleasant (was he); and so
in accordance with his appearance did he speak. Misser Luigi had
designed in words that I should make a *Venus with a Cupid* together with many emblems all in keeping; Misser Gabbriello had
designed that I should make an *Amphitrite,* wife of Neptune, along
with those Tritons of Neptune and many other things, very beautiful in description but not in execution. I made an oval shape of
the size of well over half a *braccio*—almost two-thirds—and upon
the said shape, as though to display the Sea embracing the Earth,
I made two figures considerably more than a palm in height, which
were seated with their legs entwined one with another, just as one
sees certain long arms of the sea which run into the land; and in
the hand of the male figure, the sea, I placed a very richly decorated
ship: in this same ship much salt could be well and conveniently
placed; beneath the said (figure) I had arranged those four sea-
horses; in the right hand of the said Sea I had placed his trident.
The Earth I had made a woman of such beauteous form as I could
and knew how, handsome and graceful; and in the hand of the
said figure I had placed a temple rich and decorated, placed upon
the ground; and she leaned upon it with the said hand; this
(temple) I had made to hold the pepper. In the other hand I
placed a Horn of Plenty, adorned with all the beauties that I
possibly knew. Beneath this goddess and in that portion that I
showed to be (intended for) the earth, I had arranged all the most
beautiful animals that the earth produces. Beneath the portion of
the sea I had represented all the handsome kinds of fishes and little
snails; that could be included within that small space: in the width
of the remainder of the oval I devised many very rich ornaments. Then having waited for the Cardinal, who came with
those two critics, I produced this work of mine (executed) in wax;

upon which with much noise Misser Gabbriello Cesano was the first (to speak), and he said: "This is a work which could not be completed in the lifetime of ten men; and you, Most Reverend Monsignior, who would desire it, will never have it in your lifetime; therefore Benvenuto has wished to show us his children, but not to give them to us, as we did, for we described those things that can be accomplished, and he has shown to us things that cannot be accomplished." Upon this Misser Luigi Alamanni took my part, though he also did not wish to enter upon so great an undertaking. Thereupon I turned to them and said: "Most Reverend Monsignior, and to you two so full of talent, I say that I hope to complete this work for whosoever should have it, and each of you shall see it completed one hundred times more richly than the model; and I hope that there may be time enough left besides to make much greater things of that kind than this." The Cardinal said angrily: "Unless you make it for the King, to whom I am taking you, I do not believe that it can be made for anyone else;" and having shown me the letters, wherein the King in one passage wrote that he must return quickly bringing Benvenuto with him I raised my hands to heaven, saying: "Oh! that this may quickly come!" The Cardinal replied that I must give my orders and hasten the commissions that I had to do in Rome, within ten days. When the time came for the departure, he gave me a fine and excellent horse; and it was called *Tornon* because Cardinal Tornon had given it to him. Also Pagolo and Ascanio, my pupils, were provided with the means of riding. The Cardinal divided his train, which was very large: one portion, the most noble, he took along with himself; with it he took the road through the Romagna, in order to visit the Madonna del Loreto, and from thence afterwards to Ferrara his home; the other part he turned in the direction of Florence. This was the larger portion, and it was a vast number of persons, to-

gether with the flower of his knights (*la bellezza della sua caval-
leria*). He told me that if I wanted to travel in safety, I might
go along with himself; if not that I ran in peril of my life. I expressed the intention to His Most Reverend Lordship of traveling
with him; but since that which is ordered by Heaven happens as it
must do, it pleased God that there should return to my memory
my own poor sister, who had suffered so much severe distresses at
my great misfortunes. There also returned to my memory my
first cousins (*sorelle cugine*), who were nuns at Viterbo, one an
abbess and the other stewardess, (in such fashion that they were
comptrollers of that rich convent) and since they had endured
upon my account so much grievous distress, and had offered so
many prayers upon my behalf, I reckoned it as most certain that
the prayers of these poor virgins had obtained the Grace of God for
my safety. Therefore, when all these things came into my memory, I turned towards Florence; and whereas I should have traveled
free of expense along with the Cardinal and the rest of his train,
I wanted to travel on my own account; and I was accompanied by
a most excellent master clock-maker who was called master Cherubino, a great friend of mine. Meeting each other by chance, we
made that journey very agreeably together. Having left Rome on
Monday in Holy Week, we three proceeded alone, and at Monteruosi found the said company, and since I had expressed my intention of traveling with the Cardinal, I did not think that any of
those enemies of mine would otherwise have gone to watch for
me. It is a fact (however) that I came off badly at Monteruosi,
for a troop of well-armed men had been sent on ahead of us, to
do me mischief; and God willed it that while we were at dinner,
they,—for they had received notice that I was coming without the
Cardinal's train,—had got themselves ready to injure me. At this
juncture there arrived the said train of the Cardinal and with it I

gladly traveled in safety as far as Biterbo; for from thence onwards
I did not then know of any further danger, and especially since
I traveled always several miles ahead; and the best of those men
who were in that train showed great attention to me. I arrived by
God's Grace sound and safe at Viterbo, and there the greatest kindnesses were shown me by those cousins (*sorelle*) of mine and by
all the convent. Leaving Viterbo, with the above-mentioned (persons), we proceeded upon our way on horseback, sometimes ahead
of and sometimes behind the said train of the Cardinal, in such
a way that on Holy Thursday, at twenty-two of the clock, we
found ourselves one post from Siena; and seeing that there were
several return-mares (*alcune cavalle di ritorno*) there, and that
those people belonging to the posts were waiting to give them to
such passengers as for some small reduction would take them back
to the post at Siena—seeing this, I dismounted from my horse
Tornon, and having set my pillion and stirrups upon that mare,
I gave a *julius* to one of those grooms (*garzoni*) of the postal service.
Leaving my own horse to my young men that they might bring it
after me, I immediately went ahead in order to reach Siena half-
an-hour earlier, so as to visit a certain friend of mine, and to do
certain other of my business. Although I went quickly, however,
I did not race the said mare. When I reached Siena, I engaged
good rooms at the inn which would serve the needs of five persons, and by the landlord's groom I sent the said mare to the (office
of the) post, which was situated outside the Porta Cammollia, but
I had forgotten that my stirrups and my pillion were still upon the
said mare. We passed the evening of Holy Thursday very pleasantly; the morning after, which was Good Friday, I remembered
my stirrups and my pillion. When I sent for them, that postmaster
said that he would not give them up to me, because I had raced his
mare. I sent many times backwards and forwards, and the said

man always kept saying with many insulting and insupportable words that he would not give them up to me; and the landlord where I was lodging said to me: "You will fare well if he does not do something else besides not giving up to you the pillion and the stirrups:" and he added besides: "Know that that man is the most brutal fellow that we have ever had in this city, and that he has there two sons, very brave soldiers, more brutal than himself; therefore purchase again what you need and pass along without saying anything." I bought a pair of stirrups, thinking however with kindly words to recover my excellent pillion: and since I was very well mounted, and well armed with coat (of mail) and gauntlets, and had an admirable arquebuse at my saddlebow, the great brutality, which he (the landlord) told me that that mad beast had, caused me no terror. I had besides accustomed those young men of mine to wear coats (of mail) and gauntlets, and I placed great confidence in that Roman youth, for it seemed to me while we were in Rome, that he would never take them off. Ascanio also, though he was but a lad, also wore them; and since it was Good Friday, I thought that even the ravings of the mad ought really to have some little pause (*feria*). We arrived at the said Porta Camollia; whereupon I saw and recognized this postmaster from the indications that had been given me, as being blind of the left eye. Going to meet him, and leaving apart those young men and those companions of mine, I said pleasantly: "Postmaster, if I give you security that I did not race your mare, why will you not be willing to give me up my pillion and my stirrups?" To this he replied truly after the fashion of a madman, a brutal one, as I had been told: wherefore I said to him: "What? Are you not a Christian? Do you want on Good Friday to cause scandal to both yourself and me?" He said that Good Friday or Devil's Friday did not trouble him, and that if I did not take myself off, with a halberd (*spuntone*) that he had caught up he would throw me to the ground along with the arquebuse that I had in my hand. At these fierce words there drew near an old nobleman, a Sienese, dressed in civilian attire, who was returning from the performance of those devotions which are customary upon such a day; and, having heard from a distance very clearly all my arguments, he boldly approached to reprove the said postmaster, taking my side; and he rebuked his two sons, because they did not do their duty by the strangers who passed by, and (he told them) that in that way they were acting in opposition to God, and bringing blame upon the City of Siena. Those two young men, his sons, shook their heads without saying anything, and went away inside their house. The enraged father, incensed by the remarks of that honorable nobleman, immediately, with shameful blasphemies, lowered the halberd, swearing that he would slay me with it anyhow. When I saw this villainous intention, in order to keep him somewhat back, I made as though to show him the muzzle of my arquebuse: and when he, more furious still, threw himself upon me, the arquebuse, which I had in my hand—for, although in readiness for my own defense, I had not lowered it so as to be directed at him, but had it with its muzzle (pointed) upwards—of its own accord went off. The ball struck the arch of the gateway, and driven backwards struck into the windpipe of the said man, who fell to the earth dead. His two sons ran up quickly, and while one of them seized his arms from a rack, the other caught up his father's halberd. Throwing themselves upon those young men of mine, that son who had the halberd wounded first the Roman Pagolo above the left nipple; the other rushed upon a Milanese who was of our company, who had the appearance of a crazy creature; and it did not avail him that he commended himself by saying that he had nothing to do with me, and defended himself from the point of a partisan with a little cane that he had in his hand. With this he could not ward him off much; so that he was slightly wounded in the mouth. Misser Cherubino was clad like a priest, for although he was a most excellent master clockmaker, as I have said, he held benefices from the Pope with handsome emoluments. Ascanio, since he was very well armed, made no sign of taking to flight, as had that Milanese. Wherefore these two were not injured. I, for I had set spurs to my horse, and, while he was galloping, had hastily got in readiness and loaded my arquebuse, was turning furiously back again; for since it seemed to me that whereas I had acted as in jest I now wished to act in real earnest, and I thought that those young men of mine had been slain, I was resolved to die myself also. The horse had not raced many paces back, when I met them coming towards me, and I asked them if they had suffered any hurt. Ascanio answered that Pagolo was wounded to death by a halberd. Thereupon I said: "Oh, Pagolo, my son, then the halberd has pierced your coat of mail?" "No," said he; "for I had put my coat of mail into my saddle-bag this morning." "Then" (said I) "they wear coats of mail about Rome in order to appear handsome before the ladies? and in dangerous situations, where it is one's business to have them, they keep them in the saddle-bag? You well deserve all the misfortunes that have fallen upon you, and you are the reason that I want also to go and die there also"; and while I was saying these words I continued to turn bravely back again. Ascanio and he besought me for the love of God to be content to save myself and save them, for it was certain that I was going to my death. At this moment I met Misser Cherubino, along with that wounded Milanese: he immediately reproved me, saying that he had received no harm, that Pagolo's wound had gone so much to the right that it had not gone in deep, that the old postmaster lay dead upon the ground, and that his sons with many other persons were getting themselves ready, and for certain they would have us all cut to pieces: "Therefore, Benvenuto, since fortune has protected us from that first onslaught of theirs, do not let us tempt her further, lest she should not protect us (again)." Thereupon I said: "Then if you are satisfied, I also am content;" and turning to Pagolo and Ascanio, I said to them: "Give spurs to your horses and let us gallop as far as Staggia without ever stopping, and there we shall be safe." The wounded Milanese said: "May a canker fall upon our sins! For this misfortune that has befallen me is solely the punishment of the sin of a little meat soup that I ate yesterday, not having anything else to dine upon." In spite of all the great disasters that we were enduring, we were compelled to make some small show of laughter at that fool (*bestia*), and at those silly words that he had uttered. We set spurs to our horses, and left Misser Cherubino and the Milanese, who came along at their leisure. Meanwhile the dead man's sons hurried to the Duke of Melfi that he might give them some light cavalry to catch us up and arrest us. The said Duke, when he knew that we were men (in the service) of the Cardinal of Ferrara, would give them neither the cavalry nor permission (to go after us). Meantime we arrived at Staggia, where we were in safety. When we reached Istaggia, we sought out a doctor, the best that that place could provide; and having caused him to examine the said Pagolo, the wound had only entered the skin (*andava pelle pelle*), and I knew that it would have no evil consequence. We got ourselves ready to dine. Meantime there appeared Misser Cherubino and that mad Milanese fellow, who was continually calling down plagues upon quarrels, and saying that he was excommunicated because he had not been able to say a single Paternoster upon that holy morning. This man was hideous of feature, and had naturally a huge mouth; subsequently in consequence of the wound which he had received in it, the mouth was increased by more than three fingers; and with his comic Milanese accent, and that same silly tongue of his those remarks that he made gave us so much occasion for laughter, that instead of lamenting our misfortunes, we could do nothing but laugh at every word that the man said. When the doctor was desirous of sewing up the wound in his mouth, and had already set in three stitches, he told the doctor that he must pause a bit, for he would not have him out of some feeling of enmity stitch it all up: and laying hold of a spoon, he said that he wanted it left sufficiently open, that that spoon might enter so that he might return alive to his own family. These words which he uttered with certain head-shakings, gave us so great occasion for laughter, that instead of lamenting our own evil fortune, we could never leave off laughing; and laughing continually in this fashion we proceeded to Florence. We dismounted at the house of my poor sister, where we were very wonderfully welcomed by my brother-in-law and by her. Misser Cherubino and the Milanese went about their own business. We stayed in Florence for four days, during which Pagolo was cured; but it was a very great thing that continually when we talked of that fool of a Milanese, it moved us to as much laughter as our other troubles had disposed us to weep; to such purpose that we continually at the same moment both laughed and wept. Pagolo was easily cured; we then departed towards Ferrara; and we found that our Cardinal had not yet arrived in Ferrara. And he had heard of our adventures; and condoling with us he said: "I pray God that He will grant me sufficient grace that I may conduct you alive to that King to whom I have promised you." The said Cardinal assigned to me one of his own palaces in Ferrara, a very beautiful place, called Bel Fiore, adjoining the city walls; there he caused me to prepare myself for working. Then he made arrangements to set out himself towards France without

me; and when he saw that I was very ill-content at remaining, he
said to me: "Benvenuto, all that I do is for your advantage; for
before I take you out of Italy I want you to know very thoroughly
first what you are going to do in France; at this juncture, push on
the most you can this basin and small ewer of mine; and I will
leave orders with one of my stewards that he give you all that you
have need of." And when he had departed I remained very ill-
content, and many times had the desire of going away altogether;
but I was only kept back by the fact that he had procured my freedom from Pope Pagolo; so that, for the rest, I remained ill-content
and at considerable personal loss. Nevertheless having clad myself in
that gratitude that the benefit received deserved, I disposed myself to
have patience and to see what end might come to this business;
and setting myself to work along with those two young men of
mine I made very wonderful progress with that ewer and that
basin. The air where we were lodged was unwholesome, and as
we came towards summer we were all rather ill. During this in-
disposition of ours we went about to see over the estate upon which
we were living, which was very large, and allowed to run wild for
about a (square) mile of open ground, in which were so many
indigenous peacocks that they nested there like wild birds. When
I saw this, I prepared my fowling piece with a certain noiseless
(*senza far rumore*) powder. Then I stalked those young peacocks,
and every two days I slew one, which fed us very plentifully, and
were of such excellence that all our ailments left us. And we continued working for several months most pleasantly, and brought
forward that ewer and basin, which were works that involved great
(expenditure of) time. At this time the Duke of Ferrara adjusted
with Pope Pagolo, the Roman, certain of their ancient differences,
which they had regarding Modena and certain other cities; and
since the Church had a claim to them, the Duke made this peace

with the said Pope by the power of money. The amount of this was great; I believe that it exceeded more than three hundred thousand ducats of the Camera. The Duke had at this time an aged treasurer of his, a pupil of the Duke Alfonso his father, who was called Misser Girolamo Giliolo. This old man could not endure the injury of so great a sum going to the Pope, and he went about the streets crying out, and saying, "Duke Alfonso, his father, with this money would much sooner have taken possession of Rome than have shown it to her;" and no orders would make him pay it. Then at last when the Duke obliged him to cause it to be paid, there came upon this old man so violent an attack of dysentery that it brought him almost to his death. At this juncture, when he was ill the said Duke summoned me, and wanted me to make his portrait, which I did upon a round tablet of black stone, as large as a small table trencher. Those labors of mine pleased the Duke together with my many agreeable discourses; which two things were frequently the reason that for four or five hours at least he remained still, so as to allow me to draw his portrait, and sometimes made me sup at his own table. In the space of eight days I completed this portrait of his head. Then he commanded that I should make the reverse: whereon was figured a woman as Peace with a torch in her hand, with which she was setting light to a trophy of arms. I made this said woman of most beauteous grace in an attitude of joy, and clad in very thin garments; and beneath her feet I represented Fury in despair and mourning, bound with many chains. This work I executed with much care, and the same did me very much credit. The Duke could not cease from expressing his satisfaction, and provided me with the inscriptions for the Head of His Excellency and for the reverse. That upon the reverse ran: *Pretiosa in conspectu domini* ("Right dear in the sight of the Lord"). It symbolized that that Peace had been sold for a (large) sum of money.

DURING the time that I set myself to the fashioning of this said reverse, the Cardinal had written to me, telling me to get myself in readiness, for the King had asked for me; and that in his next letters there would be directions for all that he had promised me. I had my basin put into a case and my ewer carefully packed up; for I had already shown them to the Duke. A Ferrarese nobleman transacted the Cardinal's business, who was called by the name of Misser Alberto Ben de Dio. This man had been confined to his house twelve years, without ever going out, on account of an ailment from which he suffered. One day he sent for me in greatest haste, to tell me that I must take the post at once to go to join the King, who had asked for me with great importunity, thinking that I was (already) in France. The Cardinal as an excuse had stated that I was stopping at one of his abbeys in Lyons because I was rather unwell, but that he would arrange that I should be quickly with His Majesty; whence he was making this speed in order that I should hurry by the post. This Misser Alberto was a very worthy man, but he was a proud one, and by reason of his ailment insupportably haughty; and, as I said, he told me to get myself ready quickly, so that I might hasten by the post. To which I replied that my profession was not practiced by the post, and that if I had to go, I wished to go by agreeable stages and to take with me my workmen Ascanio and Pagolo, whom I had brought from Rome; and I wanted besides a servant on horseback with us, for my service, and as much money as would suffice to convey me thither. This sick old man replied to me with very haughty words, that in the fashion that I described, and not otherwise, traveled the Duke's own sons. I immediately replied to him that the sons of my profession traveled after that fashion which I had described, and since I had never been the son of a duke I did not know how such persons traveled; but that if he employed such extraordinary expressions within my hearing I would not go on any account; for since the Cardinal had broken his pledge to me, and then these disgraceful words had been sharpened upon me, I would assuredly make up my mind not to be willing to worry myself with the people of Ferrara. And turning my back upon him, I grumbling and he threatening, I went away. I went to see the Duke abovementioned with his medal completed; who showed me the most honorable courtesies that were ever performed by any man in the world; and he had directed that Misser Girolamo Giliolo of his that for those labors of mine he should find a ring containing a diamond of the value of two hundred *scudi,* and that he should give it to Fiaschino his chamberlain, who would pass it on to me. So was it done. The said Fiaschino on the evening of the day when I had presented the medal, at the first hour of the night offered me a ring, in which was a diamond which made a great display, and uttered these words on behalf of his Duke: "That that unique talented hand, which had labored so brilliantly, should in memory of His Excellency adorn that said hand with that diamond." When day came I examined the said ring, which was a poor thin diamond, of the value of about ten *scudi;* and since I did not like (to think) that such magnificent words, as the Duke had directed to be conveyed to me, clothed so small a reward, for the Duke thought he had well satisfied me; and since I imagined that it came about through that knave of a treasurer of his, I gave the ring to a friend of mine that he might restore it to the chamberlain Fiaschino in any way that he could. This man was Bernardo Saliti, who carried out this commission admirably. The said Fiaschino immediately came to see me, with very loud exclamations informing me that if the Duke knew that I had sent back a present which he had so graciously bestowed upon me after that fashion, he would take it very ill, and perhaps I should have to repent of it. I replied to the said man, that the ring which His Excellency had bestowed upon me was of the value of about ten *scudi,* and that the work that I had done for His Excellency was worth more than two hundred. But in order to demonstrate to His Excellency that I esteemed his act of courtesy, and that if he would but send me a ring for the cramp—one of those that come from England which are worth about one carlino—I would preserve it in memory of His Excellency as long as I lived, together with those honorable words that His Excellency had directed to be addressed to me; for I reckoned that the munificence of His Excellency had largely paid me for my labors, where that base trinket had insulted me. These words caused so much annoyance to the Duke, that he summoned to him that said treasurer of his; and administered to him the severest scolding that he had ever given him in the past; and he directed that I should be commanded under pain of his displeasure, not to leave Ferrara without causing him to be informed; and he commanded his treasurer to give me a diamond which amounted in value to three hundred *scudi.* The miserly treasurer found one that came to a little over sixty *scudi,* and gave it to be understood that the said diamond was worth more than two hundred. Meanwhile the above-mentioned Misser Alberto had recovered a sensible course, and had provided me with everything that I had asked for. I was prepared to leave Ferrara at all costs that very day; but that busy chamberlain of the Duke's had combined with the said Misser Alberto that for that day I should have no horses. I had loaded a mule with a great deal of my baggage, and with it I had packed up that basin and that ewer which I had made for the Cardinal. At this juncture there came in a Ferrarese nobleman, who was called by the name of Misser Alfonso de Trotti. This nobleman was very old, and was a very affected person, and he greatly loved the Arts; but he was one of those persons who are most difficult to content; and if by chance they ever happen to see anything that pleases them they picture it in their brain as so excellent, that they never more expect to see any other thing that may please them. This Misser Alfonso arrived: whereupon Misser Alberto said to him: "I am sorry that you are come too late: for that ewer and that basin which we are sending to the Cardinal in France is already packed and closed up." This Misser Alfonso said that he did not mind that; and beckoning to one of his servants sent him to his house: who brought him a ewer of white clay, of the pottery of Faenza, very delicately decorated. While the servant was going and returning Misser Alfonso said to the said Misser Alberto: "I want to tell you why I never wish to see any more vases: the reason is, that once I saw one of silver, an antique, so beautiful and so marvelous, that human imagination would not reach the conception of such excellence; and therefore I do not care to see any other such things, lest I spoil the wonderful memory of that one. It was to an important and accomplished nobleman, who went to Rome on certain business of his own, that this antique vase was shown and that privately; who by the power of a great quantity of *scudi* corrupted the man who owned it, and brought it with him into our district, but he keeps the matter so well concealed that the Duke does not know of it, because he would be afraid of losing it entirely." This Misser Alfonso, while he was telling these long tales of his, paid no attention to me, although I was present, because he

Cellini's famous bronze statue of Perseus stands in the Loggia dei Lanzi in Florence for which it was commissioned by Cosimo de' Medici.

was not acquainted with me. Meanwhile this blessed earthenware model, having appeared, was uncovered with so much vainglory, officiousness and pomp, that when I had looked at it I turned to Misser Alberto and said: "I am indeed fortunate to have seen it." Misser Alfonso enraged said, with some insolent words: "Oh! Who are you, who do not know what you are talking about?" To this I replied: "Now listen to me, and then you will see which of us knows best what he is talking about?" Turning myself to Misser Alberto, a very grave and talented personage, I said: "This is a little silver drinking-vessel, weighing so much, that I made at such and such a period for that quack of a Maestro Jacopo, the surgeon from Carpi, who came to Rome and stayed there six months, and with an ointment of his, smeared many tens of unfortunate lords and nobles, from whom he extracted many thousands of ducats. At that period I made this vase, and another differing from it; and he paid me very shabbily for both of them, and now all those unhappy beings in Rome whom he anointed are crippled and in evil case. It is a very great glory for me that my works should be held in so much honor by you wealthy lords; but I tell you plainly, that during those many years since that time I have applied myself as much as ever I could to learning; in such measure that I think that that vase which I am carrying into France is much more worthy of the Cardinal and of the King than was that belonging to that bit of a doctor of yours." When I had uttered these words of mine, Misser Alfonso appeared to be really consumed with desire to see that basin and ewer, which I continually denied him. When we had been some little time at this pass, he said that he would go to the Duke and he would see them by means of His Excellency's authority. Thereupon Misser Alberto Ben di Dio, who was, as I have said, very proud, said: "Before you leave here, Misser Alfonso, you shall see them, without invoking favors from the Duke." At

these words I departed, and I left Ascanio and Pagolo, to exhibit
them; who told me subsequently that they had said the finest things
in my praise. Misser Alfonso afterwards wished that I would be
more intimate with him, whereat it seemed to me a thousand years
ere I could get away from Ferrara, and take myself away from
them. The most that I had in the way of advantage had been the
acquaintance of the Cardinal Salviati and that of the Cardinal of
Ravenna, and of some of those clever musicians, and no one else;
for the Ferrarese are a very miserly race, and covet the goods of
others in every fashion that they can possibly acquire them; thus
are they all. At twenty-two of the clock there appeared the above-
mentioned Fiaschino, and he offered me the said diamond of the
value of about sixty *scudi;* saying with a melancholy expression
and in a few words, that I must take that out of affection for His
Excellency. To whom I replied—"and I will do so." Setting my
feet in the stirrups in his presence, I began my journey of departure; he noted the act and the words; and when he reported
them to the Duke, he in a rage conceived a very great desire to make
me turn back again. That evening I proceeded more than ten
miles, trotting continuously; and when next day I was outside the
Ferrarese territory I was very greatly pleased; for except those
young peacocks that I had eaten for the sake of my health, I knew
of no other good thing in it. We took our way by Monsanese, not
touching the city of Milan on account of the above-mentioned suspicion, in such a way that we arrived sound and safe at Lyons.
Together with Pagolo and Ascanio and a servant we were four,
with four very good horses. When we reached Lyons we stopped
several days to await the muleteer who had that silver basin and
ewer, together with our other baggage; we were lodged in an
abbey which belonged to the Cardinal. When the muleteer arrived
we put all our belongings into a cart, and proceeded towards Paris.

Thus we journeyed towards Paris, and we had some trouble upon the way, but it was not very remarkable. We found the King's Court at Fontana Beleo; we managed to see the Cardinal, who immediately caused us to be provided with lodgings, and for that evening we did very well. The next day the cart appeared; and having got possession of our property, when the Cardinal heard of it he told the King, who immediately desired to me. I went to His Majesty with the said basin and ewer, and when I arrived in his presence, I kissed his knee, and he received me most graciously. While I thanked His Majesty for having procured my freedom from prison, telling him that every good and unique prince in the world, as was His Majesty, was bound to procure the freedom of men who were talented in any way, and especially those who were innocent as I was, that those benefits were inscribed first upon the Books of God, rather than anything else that could be done in the world, this good King waited to listen to me until I had spoken with so much gratitude and a few words suitable to him alone. When I had finished he took the vase and the basin, and then said: "Truly I do not believe that by the craftsman of antiquity was ever seen so fine a method of work; for I well remember to have seen all the finest works, and those made by the greatest masters in all Italy, but I never saw anything that moved my admiration more forcibly that this." These words the said King remarked to the Cardinal of Ferrara in French, with many others more flattering than they. Then turning to me he spoke in Italian, and said: "Benvenuto! Pass your time pleasantly for some days, and comfort your heart, and attend to making good cheer, and meantime we will think about giving you excellent conveniences to enable you to execute some fine work." The Cardinal of Ferrara above-mentioned saw that the King had derived very great pleasure from my arrival; and he said besides that from that small specimen of my

work the King had promised himself to be able to accomplish his
desire of making certain very fine works of art that he had in his
mind. Nevertheless at this period we were following in the train
of the Court: it can be said with discomfort, the reason being that
the King's train drags along continually behind it twelve thousand
horsemen; and this is the least number; for when the Court in time
of peace is complete, they are eighteen thousand; in such fashion
that they always come to be more than twelve thousand. Wherefore
we went following the said Court into such places where there were
sometimes scarcely two houses (available); and, as gypsies do, they
made tents of linen, and many times suffered great discomfort. I
therefore urged the Cardinal that he would induce the King to send
me (away) to work. The Cardinal told me that it was better in
this case to wait until the King remembered it of himself, and that
I must let myself be seen by His Majesty sometimes while he was
eating. When I was doing this one morning at his dinner the King
summoned me: he began to talk to me in Italian, and told me
that he had a mind to execute many fine works, and that he would
soon give me directions (as to the place) where I should have to
work, with provision of all that might be needful for me; together
with many other speeches regarding divers pleasant things. The
Cardinal of Ferrara was present, for he almost continuously ate in
the morning at the King's board; and having heard all these
speeches, when the King rose from the table, the Cardinal of Ferrara spoke on my behalf, as I was afterwards informed: "Sacred
Majesty, this Benvenuto has a very great desire (to get) to work;
for it might almost be said to be a sin for a genius like him to
lose time." The King rejoined that he had well spoken and that
he would arrange with me for my allowance all that I wished for.
The Cardinal upon the evening following the morning wherein he
had received this commission, had me sent for after supper and

told me on behalf of His Majesty that His Majesty was resolved
that I should set my hand to work again; but first he wished me to
know what was to be my allowance. Upon this head the Cardinal
said: "It seems to me that if His Majesty gives you three hundred
scudi per annum of allowance, you can keep yourself very well;
I tell you in addition that you must leave the care of yourself in
my hands, for any day there may arise an occasion of being able
to do you some good office in this great kingdom, and I will always
assist you vigorously." Thereupon I said: "Without my asking
Your Most Reverend Lordship, when Your Lordship left me in
Ferrara, you promised me never to take me out of Italy, until I
knew first the whole position in which I should stand with His
Majesty. Your Most Reverend Lordship, instead of sending to tell
me the position in which I should stand, sent an express direction
that I should come post haste, as if such an art as mine could be
performed post haste. But if you had sent to tell me of the three
hundred *scudi,* as you tell me now, I would not have moved for
six. All the same I thank God and Your Most Reverend Lordship also; for God has employed you as an instrument for so great
a benefit as was my release from prison. Wherefore I tell Your
Lordship that all the great evils that I now experience at Your
Lordship's hands, cannot approach to the thousandth part of the
great benefit that I have received from you; and with all my heart
I thank you, and I take my good leave, and wherever I may be,
I shall always as long as I live pray to God for you." The Cardinal,
enraged, said wrathfully: "Go where you like, for one cannot do
good to people by force." Certain of those worthless courtiers of
his said: "This man appears to himself to be some great personage,
since he refuses three hundred ducats of income." Others of those
men of talent said: "The King will never find a man equal to this
man; and this Cardinal of ours wants to beat him down as if he

were a load of wood." It was Misser Luigi Alamanni, for so I
was informed, who said this. This occurred in Dauphiné, in a
fortress, the name of which I do not remember; and it was the
last day of October. When I left the Cardinal I went to my lodging, three miles distant thence, in company with a secretary of the
Cardinal's, who also came to the same lodging. During the whole
of that journey that secretary never left off asking me what I
wanted done for me, and what it had been my fancy to wish for
in the way of allowance. I never answered him but one word,
saying: "I knew all about it." Then when I reached the lodging
I found Pagolo and Ascanio, who were stopping there; and when
they saw me very upset, they constrained me to tell them what
had happened to me; and when I saw the poor young men dismayed, I said to them: "To-morrow morning I will give you sufficient money for you to return comfortably to your homes; and I
will go without you on a most important piece of business of my
own that for a long time I have had in my mind to carry out."
Our room was wall to wall next to that of the said Secretary, and
it is perhaps possible that he wrote to the Cardinal all that I had in
my mind to do, although I never knew anything about it. The
night passed without my ever sleeping: to me it seemed a thousand
years ere day broke, so that I might carry out the resolution that I
had made. When the dawn came, I gave orders for my horses,
and having quickly got myself in readiness, I presented those two
young men with all that I had brought with me, and fifty gold
ducats besides; and I kept as much for myself, besides that diamond which the Duke had bestowed upon me; I carried only two
shirts, and certain not-too-good riding garments, which I had upon
my back. I could not get away from the two young men, who
wanted to come with me at any cost; wherefore I abused them
severely, saying to them: "One of you has his first beard, and the

other is hand over hand beginning to acquire one, and you have learned from me as much of this poor talent of mine as I have been able to teach you, so that you are to-day the foremost youths (in this trade) in Italy; and are you not ashamed that you have not sufficient courage to get out of your daddy's go-cart which has carried you continually so far? This is indeed a disgraceful thing. If I were to let you go without money, what would you say? Now get you out of my sight. May God bless you a thousand times.— Good-bye!" I turned my horse and left them weeping. I followed a most beautiful road through a wood in order to cover that day forty miles at least through the least known country that I could think of; and I had already covered about two miles. And in that little bit of journey I had resolved never more to visit any part of the world where I was known; nor did I ever wish to execute any other work except a Christ three *braccia* in height, approaching as far as I was able to that infinite loveliness that had been shown to me by Himself. Being already thoroughly resolved about this, I went my way towards the (Holy) Sepulcher. When I was just thinking that I had got so far that no one could find me any more, at this (very moment) I heard horses galloping behind me. And they caused me some suspicion, because in those parts there is a certain kind of bands of men, whom they call "adventurers," who cheerfully assassinate folks upon the highway. And although they every day hang many of them, it seems as if they did not care for that. When these (riders) came up to me, I recognized that it was a messenger from the King, along with that youth of mine, Ascanio. And when he came up to me he said: "On behalf of the King I tell you that you must quickly come to him." To that man I replied: "You come on behalf of the Cardinal; wherefore I will not come." The man replied that, since I would not come by kindly treatment, he had authority to command the populace, that they should put me in bonds like a prisoner. Ascanio also implored me as much as he could, reminding me that when the King put anyone in prison, it was five years at least ere he resolved to take him out again. This mention of prison, recalling to my mind that of Rome, produced in me so much terror, that I quickly turned my horse in the direction wherein the King's messenger told me. He, murmuring continually in French, never stopped all through that journey, until he brought me to the court: sometimes he bullied me, and sometimes he said one thing and sometimes another, (sufficient) to make me deny the world.

WHEN we reached the King's apartments, we passed before those of the Cardinal of Ferrara. The Cardinal, chancing to be at the door, called me to him and said: "Our most Christian King has of his own accord ordered you the same allowance that His Majesty gave to Leonardo da Vinci, the painter, which amounts to seven hundred *scudi* per annum; and besides that he pays for all the works of art that you shall execute for him: for your journey hither he also bestows upon you five hundred gold *scudi,* which he wishes paid to you before you leave this place." When the Cardinal had finished speaking I replied that these were indeed the gifts of such a King as he was. That King's messenger, not being aware who I was, when he saw those great offerings on the part of the King, demanded my pardon many times. Pagolo and Ascanio remarked: "God has helped us to return into so honorable a go-cart." Then the next day I went to thank the King, who directed me to make the models for twelve silver statues, which he wanted to serve as twelve candlesticks about his table; and he desired them to represent six gods and six goddesses, of exactly the same size as His Majesty himself, which was a little less than four *braccia* in height. When he had given me this commission he turned to his comptroller (*tesauriere de risparmi*) and asked him if he had paid me the five hundred *scudi*. He said that he had not been told anything about it. The King took it very ill, for he had commissioned the Cardinal to tell him of it. He also told me that I must go to Paris, and look out for an apartment that might be suitable to carry out such work, for he would cause it to be allotted to me. I took the five hundred gold *scudi,* and went to Paris into an apartment belonging to the Cardinal of Ferrara; and there I began, in the Name of God, to work, and I made four small models in wax two-thirds of a *braccio* apiece—*Jove, Juno, Apollo, Vulcan.* At this juncture the King came to Paris; wherefore I immediately went to see him, and I carried the said models with me, along with those two youths of mine, that is to say, Ascanio and Pagolo. When I saw that the King was satisfied with the said models, and he directed me to make *Jove* as the first in silver of the stated height, I presented to His Majesty those two said young men whom I had brought with me from Italy for His Majesty's service, and (I said) that since I had trained them myself, I should derive much greater assistance from them on account of this early training, than from those (assistants to be found in) the city of Paris. Upon this the King said, that I must arrange for the said two youths a salary such as it might seem to me that by receiving it they would be able to keep themselves. I said that one hundred gold *scudi* for each of them would do well, and that I would take very good care that they earned such a salary. Thus we concluded the agreement. I also told him that I had found a place that appeared to me very suitable for the execution of such works of art; the said place was His Majesty's own particular property, called Le Petit Nesle (*il piccol Nello*), and that it was at that time held by the Provost of Paris, upon whom His Majesty had bestowed it; but since this Provost made no use of it, His Majesty could bestow it upon me, so that I might use it in his service. The King immediately said: "That place is a house of my own; and I know well that he to whom I gave it neither lives there nor uses it: do you therefore employ it for our business;" and he immediately commanded his lieutenant that he should lodge me in the said Nesle. He made some (show) of resistance, telling the King that he could not do it. To this the King replied angrily, that he wished to give his own property to whomsoever he pleased, and to a man who would serve him, for this other was not serving him at all; therefore he must say no more upon the matter. The lieutenant added, besides that it would be necessary to use some small amount of force. Upon which the King said: "Go now, and if small force is not sufficient, try great." He immediately took me to the place; and he had to use force to put me in possession; then he told me that I must take very great care of myself that I were not murdered. I entered into (the place), and I immediately engaged servants and purchased several big pikes (*pezzi d'arme in aste*), and for several days I lived in greatest discomfort: for this man (the Provost) was an important nobleman of Paris, and the other nobility were all my enemies, in such measure that they showed me many insults such as I was unable to resist. I do not wish to leave unrecorded that this period in which I entered into agreement with His Majesty was exactly in the year of Grace 1540, which was exactly the fortieth year of my own age. On account of these great insults I had recourse to the King, begging His Majesty that he would accommodate me elsewhere: to which request the King said to me: "Who are you and what is your name?" I remained greatly taken aback, and did not know what it was that the King meant; and as I stood thus silent, the King repeated a second time the same words as if in a rage. Thereupon I replied that I bore the name of Benvenuto. The King said: "Then if you are that Benvenuto whom I understand, act according to your wont, for I give you full license." I told His Majesty that it sufficed for me only to keep myself in his favor, and for the rest I knew nothing that could injure me. The King, smiling a little, said: "Go, then, and my favor will never be wanting to you." He immediately ordered one of his first secretaries, who was called Monsignior di Villurois, to give instructions to provide for me and to arrange for all my necessities. This Villurois was a very great friend of that nobleman called the Provost, to whom the said property of the Nesle belonged. The place was of triangular form, and adjoined the city walls, and it was an ancient fortress, but did not contain a garrison; it was of considerable size. This said Monsignior di Villurois advised me that I should look for something else, and that at all hazards I should leave the place; for he to whom it belonged was a man of very great power, and he would most certainly have me slain. I answered him that I had come out of Italy into France merely to serve that glorious King, and that as for dying, I knew for certain that I had to die (some day); that a little earlier or a little later gave me no anxiety in the world. This Villurois was a man of very great spirit, and admirable in every way, (a man of) very great wealth: there is nothing in the world that he would not have done to cause me trouble, but he exhibited nothing of this: he was a grave personage, of handsome appearance, and he spoke slowly. He committed (my affairs) to another nobleman, who was called Monsignior di Marmagnia, and who was treasurer of Languedoc (*Lingua d'ocha*). The first thing that this man did, having selected the best apartments in that place was to have them arranged for his own use; whom I informed that the King had bestowed the place upon me, in order that I might work for him, and that I would not let any one else reside there except myself and my servants. This man was haughty, bold, and spirited; and he told me that he wished to do exactly as he liked, and that I was running my head against a wall in wishing to contend against him, and that for everything that he did he had had a commission from Villurois to enable him to do it. Thereupon I told him that I had had my commission from the King, and that neither he nor Villurois could do such things. When I uttered this remark this haughty man retorted with many ugly words in his own French language, to which I replied in my own tongue that he lied. Moved to fury he made as though he would draw one of his small daggers (*daghetta*); wherefore I clapped my hand upon a large dagger of my own, that I constantly wore at my side for purposes of defense, and I said to him: "If you are so foolhardy as to unsheathe that weapon, I will slay you upon the spot." He had two servants with him and I had my two young men; and while the said Marmagnia stood thus beside himself, not knowing what to do—more nearly inclined to the evil course—he said, mutteringly: "I will never put up with such a thing." I saw that the matter was taking a bad turn, and I immediately took a resolution, and I said to Pagolo and Ascanio: "When you see me unsheathe my dagger, throw yourselves upon the two servants and kill them, if you can; for I shall kill him with my first blow. Then we will hasten away together immediately." When Marmagnia heard this resolution of mine it seemed to him that he had done well enough to get out of that place alive. All these things I wrote a trifle more modestly to the Cardinal of Ferrara, who immediately told the King. The King, being provoked, put me under the charge of another of those personal attendants of his own, who was called Monsignior lo Iscontro d'Orbech. This man, with as much amiability as it is possible to imagine, provided me with all my requirements. When I had made all the arrangements of the house and workshop most convenient for my use and most honorably for the service of my establishment, I immediately set to work to make three models of the exact size that they had to be in silver: these were *Jove, Vulcan,* and *Mars.* I made them of clay, well mounted upon an iron (framework); then I went to the King, who directed to be given to me, if I remember right, three hundred pounds weight of silver, so that

I might begin work. While I was giving directions about these things the small vase and oval basin, which had occupied several months, were completed. When I had finished them I had them very thoroughly gilded. This seemed the most beautiful piece of work that had ever been seen in France. I immediately carried them to the Cardinal of Ferrara, who thanked me very much, and then without me carried them to the King and made him a present of them. The King was very delighted, and praised me more immeasurably than any man such as I had ever been praised; and for this present he bestowed upon the Cardinal of Ferrara an abbey producing seven thousand *scudi* of revenue; and he wanted to make me a present. Whereat the Cardinal stopped him, telling His Majesty that he was going too rapidly, since I had not provided him with any work yet. The King, who was most generous, said: "Therefore I want to inspire him with courage that he may be able to provide it for me." The Cardinal, put to shame by this, said: "Sire, I pray you to leave the doing of this to me; for I will make him an allowance of at least three hundred *scudi* directly I have obtained possession of the abbey." I never had it, and it would take too long to attempt to relate the devilry of this Cardinal; but I want to reserve myself for matters of greater importance. I returned to Paris. Along with such favor as was shown to me by the King I was admired by every one. I received the silver and began the said statue of *Jove*. I employed many workmen, and with greatest application day and night I never rested from my labors; in such fashion that having completed in clay *Jove, Vulcan* and *Mars,* when I had already commenced to proceed a good way with *Jove* in silver, the workshop soon showed a very rich appearance. At this juncture the King appeared in Paris: I went to visit him; and directly His Majesty saw me, he gladly summoned me to him, and asked me if there was anything beautiful in my dwelling to show

him, for he would come thither. Upon which I recounted to him
all that I had done. There immediately came to him a very great
desire to come thither; and after his dinner, he made arrangements
with Madama de Tampes, with the Cardinal of Lorraine, and with
certain other of those nobles, who were the King of Navarre, the
brother-in-law of King Fran^{co} and the Queen, the sister of the said
King Francescho; the Dauphin and the Dauphiness came (also);
so that upon that day there came all the nobility of the Court.
I had gone ahead to my house; and had set myself to work. When
the King appeared at the door of my château, upon hearing the
blows of several hammers, he commanded everyone to stay quiet.
In my house every one was at work; in such a way that I found
myself taken by surprise by the King, whom I had not expected.
He entered my saloon; and the first thing that he saw was myself
with a great plate of silver in my hand which I was using for the
body of *Jove*: another piece formed the head, another the legs, in
such a way that the noise (of the work) was very great. While I was
working, I had a little French lad of mine assisting me, who had
committed I don't know what trifling offense, for the which reason
I had launched a kick at him, and by my good fate my foot entering
the fork of his legs, I had driven him forward (a distance of) more
than four *braccia,* in such a way that at the King's entrance this
child was precipitated against the King: at which the King laughed
loudly, and I remained much embarrassed. The King began to
question me as to what I was doing, and wished me to go on working; then he told me that I would cause him much greater pleasure
if I never labored myself, but that I should rather employ as many
men as I wanted, and make them do the (hard) work; for he
wanted me to keep myself in good health so as to be able to serve
him the longer. I answered His Majesty that I should at once
fall ill if I did not work; neither would my works be of that

quality that I desired to make them for His Majesty. The King thinking that what I was saying was said for braggadocio, and not because it was the truth, made me repeat it to the Cardinal of Lorraine, to whom I explained my reason so fully and clearly that he remained quite convinced. Therefore he advised the King to let me work little or much according to my own will. The King being satisfied with my work, returned to his Palace, and left me loaded with so many favors as it would take a long time to relate. The next day at dinner-time he sent to summon me. The Cardinal of Ferrara was present who was dining with him. When I came in the King was still at the second course. Upon my approaching His Majesty, he immediately began to chat with me, saying that since he had so fine a basin and so beautiful an ewer of my workmanship, as company for these things he demanded a fine salt-cellar, and that he wished that I would make a design for it; but that he would like to see it soon. Thereupon I rejoined, saying: "Your Majesty shall very quickly indeed see such a design as You ask of me; for while I was making the basin I thought that as a match for it one ought to make the salt-cellar, and such a thing has already been made, and if it pleases You I will exhibit it to You immediately." The King roused himself with much spirit, and turning to those lords (present), who were the King of Navarre, the Cardinal of Lorraine, and the Cardinal of Ferrara, he said: "This truly is a man to make himself liked and desired by everyone who knows him." Then he told me that he would very gladly see the design which I had made for such an object. Setting off, I hastily went and returned, for I had merely to cross the river, that is to say the Seine. I brought (back) with me a wax model which I had made already in Rome at the request of the Cardinal of Ferrara. When I reached the King, I uncovered the model; and the King, in astonishment, said: "This is a thing one hundred times more divine than I could ever have imagined. This man is indeed a great genius! (*questa è gran cosa di quest' uomo*); he ought never to leave off his working." Then he turned to me with a very joyful expression, and told me that that was a work which pleased him very much, and that he desired that I would execute it in gold. The Cardinal of Ferrara, who was present, looked me in the face, and reminded me that he recognized that this was the model which I had made for him in Rome. At this I said that I had already told him that I would execute that work for whoever was to have it. The Cardinal recalling those same words, as if insulted, for it seemed to him that I wanted to revenge myself, said to the King: "Sire, this is a very great work; however I would not be suspicious of anything except that I do not believe that we shall ever see it finished; for these brilliant men who have these great inspirations in this art, cheerfully commence them, but never consider carefully when they will have them completed. Therefore, were I ordering so great a work as this to be carried out, I would wish to know when I should be able to have it." To this the King replied saying, that whoever looked so narrowly after the end of a work would never begin anything; and he said this in a special manner, indicating that such works as these were not suited to men of small enterprise. Thereupon I said: "All princes who encourage their servants after that fashion in which Your Majesty acts and speaks, succeed in facilitating great undertakings; and since God has granted me so splendid a patron, I hope to succeed in completing many great and splendid works." "And I believe it," said the King, and rose from the table. He summoned me into his chamber, and asked me how much gold would be necessary for that salt-cellar: "One thousand *scudi*," said I. The King immediately summoned one of his treasurers, who was called Monsignior lo Visconte di Orbeche, and commanded him that he should then and there provide me with one thousand old *scudi* of full weight in gold. Leaving His Majesty, I sent to summon those two notaries who had provided me with the silver for the *Jove* and many other things, and crossing the Seine (to my house) I took a very small basket (*sportellina*), that one of my first cousins (*sorella cugina*), a nun, had given me on my passage through Florence; and (it was) by my good fortune that I took that basket and not a small bag: and thinking that I could hasten the business by daylight, for it was still full early, and I did not wish to disturb my workmen, still less did I want to take a servant with me. When I reached the treasurer's house, he already had the coins laid out before him, and was selecting them as the King had told him. From what I seemed to observe that thief of a treasurer skillfully contrived to delay the counting of the said money for me until the third hour of the night. I, for I was not lacking in diligence, sent to summon certain of those workmen of mine, to come to accompany me, because it was a matter of considerable importance. When I saw that these said men did not come, I demanded of that messenger if he had delivered my message. A certain thievish servant said that he had done so, and that they had said that they could not come; but that he would willingly carry that money for me; to whom I replied that I wished to carry the money myself. Meantime the contract was completed, the money counted out and everything. I put it into the said basket, and then thrust my arm through the two handles; and since it passed through them with some considerable effort it (the money) was well closed in, and I carried it more conveniently than if it had been a small bag. I was well armed with coat and gauntlets of mail, and with my small sword and dagger at my side I hastily set out upon my way on my own legs. At that moment I saw certain servants, who whispering together also hastily left the house, appearing to be going by another route to that upon which I was going. I, as I was walking along steadily, having passed the Exchange Bridge, came out upon the embankment of the river, which led me to my house at Nesle. When I had come exactly to (the Convent of) the Augustines (*Austini*), a very dangerous spot—for although but five hundred paces distant from my own house, the residential portion of the château was so far away again that my voice would not have been heard inside if I had begun to call out; but making up my mind in an instant, when I saw four men appear behind me with four swords, I hastily covered that basket with my cloak, and clapping my hand upon my sword, when I saw that they were pressing upon me with determination, I said: "From soldiers one can gain nothing but a cloak and a sword; and before I give up this one to you, I hope you will have but little gain of your own." And encountering them boldly I spread myself out many times, so that if they had been set on by those servants who had seen me take the money, they might suppose with some reason that I had not such a sum of money upon me. The skirmish lasted but a short time, for little by little they retreated; and they said to themselves in their own tongue: "This is a brave Italian, and he is surely not the man that we are looking for; or more truthfully, if it be him, he has nothing upon him." I addressed them in Italian, and continually with blows of cut and thrust I sometimes came near aiming at their bodies; and since I was very well skilled in arms, they concluded that I was a soldier rather than anything else; and closing up together little by little they withdrew from me, always murmuring in a low voice in their own tongue; and I kept on saying continually (quietly however) that whoever wanted my arms and my cloak should not have it without some trouble. I began to hasten my steps, and they always came at a slow pace behind me; whereat there grew up in me a fear, thinking that I might fall into some ambuscade of several more (fellows) like them, who would have set me between them; so that when I was one hundred paces off, I set off at full speed, and cried out with a loud voice: "To arms! To arms! Out! Out! For I am being murdered." There immediately ran up four young men with four halberds (*pezzi d'arme in aste*); and when they wanted to follow after those men, whom they could still see, I stopped them, saying very loudly: "Those four cowards have not known how to plunder one man alone of one thousand gold *scudi* in gold, which have almost broken his arm (by their weight); therefore let us first go and put it away, and afterwards I will, with my great two-handed sword, accompany you wherever you like." We went to deposit the money; and those young men of mine, lamenting much the great peril that I had run, chiding me at the same time, said: "You put too much trust in yourself, and one of these days you will give us all cause to weep." I made many remarks (upon the point), and they also replied. My adversaries fled; and we all supped gaily and cheerfully, laughing at those great chances that fortune creates, as much for good as for bad; and which when they do not come off are as if nothing had occurred. It is very true that one says to oneself: "You will learn for another time." But this goes for nothing, for things always fall out in some different fashion, and not as one ever expects.

Chapter Four 1540-1543

THE following morning I immediately began upon the great salt-cellar, and with application I made it proceed along with the other works. I had already taken (into my service) many workmen, as much for the Art of Sculpture as for the Art of the Goldsmith. These workmen were Italians, French, Germans; and sometimes I employed a great number, according as I found good ones; for I changed them from day to day, selecting from those who knew the most; but I endeavored to secure those of a kind whose health, seeing that they were working for me, would serve me rather better in continuous labor, than those who, unable to endure great fatigue, thought to restore it by drinking and eating a great deal; some of those Germans who had more (practical) knowledge than the others, when I wished them to imitate me (*i.e.,* my energy) their constitution would not support such a strain, for it killed them.

While I was proceeding with the silver *Jove,* when I saw that there was a good deal of silver left over, I set to work without the King's knowledge to fashion a large silver vase with two handles of the height of about a *braccio* and a half. A desire also came to me to cast in bronze that large model that I had made for the silver *Jove.* Setting my hand to this new experiment, which I had never tried before, and consulting with certain of those old Parisian master-workmen, I described to them all those methods by which we in Italy are accustomed to carry out such a job. They told me that they had never proceeded in that way, but that if I would let it be done according to their methods, they would hand it over to me made and cast as sharp and beautiful as was that (figure) in clay. I wanted to make a bargain with them, laying (the responsibility) of this work upon them: and beyond the price which they demanded from me I promised them several *scudi* in addition. They set to work upon this job: and when I saw that they were not going the right way to work, I hastily commenced a head of *Julius Caesar,* with his bust, in armor, much larger than life, which I copied from a small model that I had brought from Rome, a reproduction of a very wonderful antique head. I also set to work upon another head of the same size, which I copied from a very beauteous girl, whom I was keeping with me for my sexual satisfaction. Upon this bust I conferred the name of *Fontana Belio,* which was the name of that place which the King had chosen for his own special enjoyment. Having constructed a most beautiful little furnace (*fornacetta*) for melting the bronze, and having prepared and baked our molds, they (*i.e.* the Parisian master-workmen) the *Jove,* and I my two heads, I said to them: "I do not believe that your *Jove* will come out (successfully), because you have not given enough draft from below to enable the air to circulate: wherefore you are losing time." They said to me that if their work did not succeed, they would give me back in full all the money that I had given them, and would make good to me all the lost expenditure; but that I must keep a good lookout, for those fine heads of mine, which I wanted to cast after my Italian method, would never succeed for me. At this discussion there were present those treasurers and other nobles who, by the directions of the King, had come to watch me: and everything that I did or said they reported it all to the King. Those two old master-workmen who wanted to cast the *Jove* made some delay in giving directions for the casting: because they said that they would have liked to prepare those two molds of my heads: for according to that method by which I was making them it was impossible that they should come to anything, and it was a great pity to lose such fine works. When they let the King hear of this, His Majesty answered that they must wait to learn, and not seek to try to teach the master. With a loud laugh they set up their piece of work in the furnace (*fossa*): and I steadily, without any exhibition either of laughter or of passion (though I felt it), set my two molds on either side of the *Jove*: and when our metal was thoroughly well melted, with very great satisfaction we made a passage for the said metal, and it completely filled the mold of the *Jove*: at the same time it filled the mold of my two heads: to such purpose that they were overjoyed and I content: for I was glad to have given the lie to their work, and they showed that they were very glad to have given the lie to mine. They demanded, however, after the French fashion with great rejoicing, something to drink: I very willingly had a handsome breakfast prepared for them. Then they claimed from me the money that they had bargained to have, and that extra sum which I had promised them. Upon which I said: "You are laughing over a matter regarding which I have great fear lest you may yet have occasion to weep: for I consider that much more material has run into that mold of yours than should have done: wherefore I do not want to give you more money of that which is due to you until to-morrow." These poor men began to think over what I had told them, and without saying anything they went home. When morning came they began gently to dig out the furnace-pit: and since they could not uncover their own large mold without first digging out those two heads of mine, which they dug out and they were very excellent: and they set them up so that they could be very well seen. Then beginning to uncover the *Jove* they had not got two *braccia* down, when together with their four workmen they uttered so loud a cry that I heard it. Thinking that it was a shout of joy, I set to running, for I was in my chamber more than five hundred paces away. When I reached them I found them in that attitude wherein are represented those who guarded the Sepulcher of Christ, despairing and terrified. Casting my eyes over my own two heads, and seeing that they were all right, I combined my pleasure with regret: and they excused themselves by saying: "It is our ill luck!" At which remark I said: "Your luck has been most excellent, but your small amount of knowledge has been very bad indeed. If I had seen you put the soul into the mold I could have shown you in one single word that the figure would have come out most excellently, by which means that thing would have resulted to my very great credit, and would have been very useful to you: but (now) owing to my credit I shall be able to find excuse for myself, while you have no escape either in credit or profit. Another time therefore learn to work, and do not learn to jeer." They besought me however, saying that I was right, and that I if I did not help them, by having to defray that great expense and that loss, they along with their families would have to go begging. Upon this I said that when the King's treasurers wanted to make them pay that (sum) for which they were bound, I would promise them to pay it out of my own pocket, for I had seen clearly that they had in good faith done all that they knew. These acts acquired for me such good will from those treasurers, and from those ministers of the King, as was unbounded. Everything was communicated in writing to the King, who, unique in his great liberality, commanded that I should carry out all that I said (I would). At this time there arrived that most marvelously brave Piero Strozzi: and when he reminded the King of his own Letters of Naturalization, the King immediately commanded that they should be made out; and at the same time with them, said he, should be made out those for *mon ami* Benvenuto, and carried immediately on his behalf to my dwelling, and presented to me free of all expense. Those of the great Piero Strozzi cost him many hundreds of ducats: one of those principal secretaries of his (the King's) who was named Messer Antonio Massone, brought me mine. This nobleman handed me the Letters, on behalf of His Majesty, with extraordinary ceremony, saying: "The King makes you a present of these, in order that you may be able to serve him with greater courage. These are Letters of Naturalization;" and he related to me how they had been bestowed upon Piero Istrozi at his own request after a long delay, and as a great favor; but that these had been sent to me as a present by (the King) himself of his own accord: that such a favor had never before been conferred in that Realm. At these words I thanked the King with much feeling; then I begged the said secretary that he would of his kindness tell me what these Letters of Naturalization meant. This secretary was very accomplished and agreeable, and spoke Italian very well; giving vent first to a loud laugh, he then, recovering his gravity, told me in my own language (that is to say in Italian), what the Letters of Naturalization meant, which (letters) were one of the highest dignities that could be conferred upon a foreigner, and he said: "This is a far greater matter than to be made a Venetian noble." On leaving me, and returning to the King, he reported the whole matter to

His Majesty, who laughed awhile and then said: "Now I want him to know why I sent him Letters of Naturalization. Go and make him lord of the Château of *Petit Nesle,* in which he dwells, which belongs to my private estate. He will comprehend what this means much more easily than he understood what my Letters of Naturalization were." A messenger came to me with this said gift, whereat I wished to show him some hospitality: he would accept nothing, saying that such was His Majesty's command. The said Letters of Naturalization, together with those (documents) concerning the gift of the château, I brought with me when I came to Italy: and wherever I go, and wherever I may end my life, there I will endeavor to keep them. I now continue the tale of my life already begun. Having on my hands the above-mentioned works, that is to say the silver *Jove* already begun, the said gold salt-cellar, the said great silver vase, and the two bronze heads, I labored assiduously upon these works of art. I gave orders besides to cast the base of the said *Jove,* which I fashioned most richly in bronze, overlaid with decorations, amid which ornaments I sculptured in low relief the *Rape of Ganymede,* and then upon the other side *Leda and the Swan;* I cast this (base) in bronze and the result was most excellent. I made moreover another similar one, upon which to place the statue of *Juno,* waiting to begin this also, until the King should give me the silver to enable me to carry out such a work. By working assiduously I had put together the silver *Jove:* I had besides put together the gold salt-cellar; the vase was very advanced; the two bronze heads were already finished. I had also executed several small jobs for the Cardinal of Ferrara: besides a small silver vase richly decorated. I had made this to present to Madama de Tampes. For many Italian nobles, that is to say, for the lord Piero Strozzi, the Conte dell' Anguillara, the Conte di Pitigliano, the Conte della Mirandola, and many others, I had carried out many commissions.

Returning to my great King, as I have said, when I was very well
forward with these commissions of his, at this time he returned to
Paris, and the third day (after his return) he came to my house
with a great number of the principal nobility of his Court, and he
marveled greatly at the vast number of works that I had in hand
and had brought to so excellent a result: and since his Madama di
Tampes was with him they began to talk about Fontana Beliò.
Madama di Tampes told His Majesty that he ought to direct me to
make something fine as a decoration for his Fontana Beliò. The
King immediately said: "It is a good idea that you put forward, and
here and now (*adesso adesso*) I want to make up my mind as to
what fine thing he shall make." And turning to me he began to ask
me what it seemed to me should be done for that beauteous fountain. Upon this I proposed some fanciful ideas of my own: His
Majesty also gave his opinion: then he told me that he wanted to go
for an excursion of fifteen or twenty days to San Germano dell Aia,
which was twelve leagues distant from Paris, and that during this
time I must make a model for this beautiful fountain of his with the
richest devices that I knew of, for that spot was the (place of) greatest refreshment that he possessed in all his kingdom: therefore he
commanded and besought me that I would make an effort to create
something handsome: and this I promised him I would do. When
the King saw so many things in hand he said to Madama de Tampes:
"I have never had a man of this profession who pleased me more,
nor one who more deserves to be rewarded than this one: therefore
it is necessary to think how to secure him. Since he spends a great
deal and is a good comrade, and yet labors a great deal, it is necessary that we should keep him in our mind: for, consider, Madama,
how many times he has come to me, and how many times I have
come here, and he has never asked anything of me; his heart it may
be seen is entirely centered upon his work; and we must needs do

something very quickly, in order that we may not lose him." Madama de Tampes said: "I will remind you of him." They departed: I set myself with great assiduity to the works that I had begun, and turned my hand besides to the model of the fountain, and I urged it forward with close interest. At the end of a month and a half the King returned to Paris: and, since I had labored day and night, I went to see him, and I carried with me my model sketched out so well that it could be clearly understood. At that date there had begun to revive the devilries of the war between the Emperor and him, in such fashion that I found him much disturbed. Wherefore I spoke with the Cardinal of Ferrara, telling him that I had with me certain models which His Majesty had commissioned of me: I therefore begged him if he saw an opportunity to put in some word whereby these models might be exhibited to him, for I believed that the King would derive much pleasure from them. Such the Cardinal did. He suggested the said models to the King: and the King immediately came to the place where I had the models. First of all I had fashioned the gateway of the Palace of Fontana Beliò. In order to alter as little as possible the arrangement of the doorway which had been erected to the said palace, which was wide and dwarfed after that ugly French style of theirs: the opening of it was little more than a square, and above that same square was a half-circle crushed down after the manner of a basket handle: in this half-circle the King desired to have a figure which should represent Fontana Beliò; I gave a very fine proportion to the said opening. Then above the said opening I placed a correct half-circle: and for the sides I made certain charming excrescences, beneath which in the lower section, so as to come into correspondence with the part above, I placed a bracket, and a similar one above: and instead of the two columns which it clearly required, according to the fashioning employed above and below, I had constructed a satyr in each of the sites for the columns. The one was in more than half-relief, and with one of his arms appeared to support that portion (of the doorway) which rests upon the columns; in the other arm he held a thick staff, and with his bold and fierce expression he struck terror into the beholder. The other figure was similar in attitude, but was different and varying in expression and in some other such respects: it had in its hand a scourge with three balls attached by certain chains. Although I say "satyrs," these figures had nothing about them of the satyr, except certain small horns and a goatish head: all the rest was in human form. In the half-circle I had fashioned a woman in a beautiful recumbent attitude; this figure held her left arm upon the neck of a stag, which was one of the King's devices. On one side I had fashioned in half-relief little wild goats and some wild boars and other woodland creatures in lower relief. On the other side hunting-dogs and hounds of many kinds, for thus teems that most beauteous wood wherein rises the fountain. I had then confined the whole of this work into a rectangular oblong, and in the angles of the composition above, in each I had fashioned a *Victory* in low relief, with a torch in its hand as the ancients are accustomed to (represent them). Above the said composition I had placed the *Salamander,* the personal device of the King, with many other most charming adornments appropriate to the said work, which was expressed in the Ionic order (of architecture). When the King saw this model, it immediately caused him to recover his spirits, and it diverted him from those weary discussions in which he had been involved for more than two hours. When I saw him cheerful to my satisfaction, I uncovered the other model, which he had by no means expected; for it seemed to him that he had seen enough work in the first one. This model was more than two *braccia* in height, and in it I had fashioned a fountain in the form of a perfect square, with most beautiful flights of steps around it, which intersected one another, a thing that had never been seen in those parts (France), and very rarely in these (Italy). In the center of the said fountain I had set a base, which rose a little higher than the said basin of the fountain: upon this base I had placed a nude figure of very charming grace, of a size to correspond. This (figure) held a broken lance raised aloft in its right hand, and the left hand was placed upon the hilt of a scimitar fashioned in a most beautiful shape: it was poised upon its left foot, and the right rested upon the crest of a helmet as richly decorated as it is possible to imagine: and at the four corners of the fountain, I had placed upon each a seated figure raised up (from the base), each bearing many charming emblems of their own. The King began asking me to tell him what that fine conception which I had executed meant, telling me that all that I had prepared for the doorway he had understood without asking for any explanation, but with regard to this (Model of the) fountain, although it seemed to him most beautiful, he understood nothing whatsoever: and he knew well enough that I had not made it like those other fools, who if they succeed in making things with some small amount of charm, make them without any sort of meaning. To this end I prepared myself: for since he was pleased with the work itself, I wanted very much that he should be pleased as much by my account of it. "Know then, Sacred Majesty, that the whole of this small work is very carefully measured out in small dimensions (*piccoli piedi*) so that on subsequently putting it into execution it will result with the same beauty that you see it now. That figure in the middle is to be fifty-four feet high." At this remark the King gave signs of very great astonishment: next it is made to represent the God *Mars*: these other four figures are designed for the *Talents* in which Your Majesty delights and favors so much. This one on the right hand is intended for the Science of all *Literature*: you see that it holds its own distinguishing attributes, which display

Philosophy with all its accompanying merits. This second (figure) expresses the whole Art of *Design*: that is to say Sculpture, Painting, and Architecture. This next is intended for *Music,* which it is right should accompany all these Sciences. This last figure which looks so charming and benign is intended for *Liberality,* for without her none of these splendid Virtues which God Himself displays to us can be demonstrated. This huge statue in the middle is intended for Your Majesty's self, who art a God *Mars;* for you alone in the world are brave, and this bravery you employ in a just and pious fashion in the defense of your own glory." He had scarcely enough patience to let me finish speaking, before, raising his voice loudly he said: "Truly I have found a man after my own heart": and he summoned the treasurers appointed to supply me, and told them that they should provide me with all that I had need of, let the expense be as much as it would. Then he tapped me upon my shoulder, saying to me: *"Mon ami"* (that is to say "my friend") "I do not know which is the greater pleasure, whether that of a prince who has found a man after his own heart, or that of the man of talent who has found a prince who provides him with so much support that he can express his great and brilliant conceptions." I replied that if I were that man of whom His Majesty spoke, by far the greater good luck were mine. He answered laughing: "We will say that it is equal." We separated with great good spirits, and I returned to my labors.

My evil fortune willed that I was not warned to make a similar comedy with Madama de Tampes, for on hearing that evening, from the King's own mouth, all these things that had occurred, it begot in her breast so much poisonous rage that she said with indignation: "If Benvenuto had shown his fine works to me, he would have given me cause to remember him at the proper time." The King wanted

to make excuse for me, but secured nothing from her. Wher
heard of this circumstance, at the end of their fifteen days' t
through Normandy to Rouen, and to Dieppe, after that they h
returned to the above-mentioned San Germano del' Aia, I took th
handsome little vase which I had made at the request of the s
Madama di Tampes, thinking that by presenting it to her I sho
regain her favor. I therefore took it with me: and having ma
myself known to a certain nurse of hers, and shown to that s
person the handsome vase that I had fashioned for her mistress, a
(told her) that I wished to present it to her, the said nurse show
me unbounded civilities, and said that she would speak a word
Madama, who was not yet dressed; and that directly she had t
her I should be admitted. The nurse told Madama everything, w
angrily answered: "Tell him to wait." When I heard this I cloth
myself with patience, the which thing is very difficult for me: ho
ever, I kept my patience until after her dinner hour. And whe
saw then the lateness of the hour, hunger aroused in me so mu
wrath that, being unable to stand it any longer, devoutly invoki
plagues upon her in my heart, I departed thence, and going to fi
the Cardinal of Lorraine, I made him a present of the said va
begging him only to keep me in the King's good graces. He sa
that it was not necessary, but that when there was need for it
would do so gladly. Then summoning a treasurer of his he spo
in his ear. The said treasurer waited until I had left the presence
the Cardinal; then he said to me: "Benvenuto! Come with me,
I will give you a glass of good wine to drink." I replied to him, n
knowing what he meant: "Thanks! My Lord Treasurer! let the
give me a single glass of wine and good mouthful of bread, 1
truly I am fainting, since I have been from this morning at an ea
hour up to this time of day that you see, fasting at Madama di Ta
pes' door in order to present to her that handsome little silver-g

vase. And I let her know the whole matter, but she, in order to continually mock me, caused me to be told to wait. Hunger has now
supervened and I feel faint. And since, as God has willed it, I
have presented the object and the result of my labors to one who is
much more deserving of it, I ask nothing more than a little something to drink, for, since I am somewhat over choleric by nature,
fasting upsets me in such a way as to make me fall fainting to the
ground." While I was struggling to utter these words, there appeared some wonderful wine and other agreeable materials to form
a meal, so that I refreshed myself excellently: and having recovered
my vital spirits my anger departed from me. The kind treasurer
handed to me one hundred gold *scudi*: to which I offered resistance,
as not wishing by any means to accept them. He went to report the
matter to the Cardinal, who, showering upon him a great deal of
abuse, commanded him to make me take it by force, or otherwise
he must not come again into his presence. The treasurer came to
me in wrath telling that he had never before been so scolded by the
Cardinal: and when, upon his wishing to give me (the money), I
made some slight resistance, he told me very angrily that he would
force me to take it. I took the money. When I wanted to go and
thank the Cardinal, he let me know by one of his secretaries that
he would always heartily do whatever he could to give me pleasure.
I returned to Paris the same evening. The King was made cognizant of everything. They laughed at Madama de Tampes, which
was the cause of making her still more poisoned (in her desire) to
injure me, wherefore I ran great peril of my life, a circumstance
which shall be related in its own place.

I ought to have recorded some time earlier the friendship that I
acquired of the most talented, the most lovable and the most companionable man of worth that I have ever known in this world: this
was Misser Guido Guidi, an excellent physician and doctor, and a

noble Florentine citizen, who, on account of the infinite troubles brought upon me by a perverse destiny, I have had to leave somewhat in the background. Although this is not of great importance, for I thought that it would suffice to have him continually in my heart: but perceiving afterwards that the story of my life is not complete without him, I have inserted his name here amid these my greatest trials in order that, since he was there a comfort and help to me, I may here record that benefit. The said Messer Guido arrived in Paris: and our acquaintance having begun I took him to my château, and there provided him with an apartment free for his own use: thus we enjoyed several years together. The Bishop of Pavia also arrived, that is to say Monsignior de' Rossi, brother of the Conte di San Sicondo. This lord I took out of the inn and housed in my château, giving to him also a separate apartment, where he was excellently accommodated, together with his servants and horses, for the space of many months. Another time also I took in Misser Luigi Alamanni with his sons for some months: indeed God granted me the grace to be able to give some pleasure also to men both great and talented. With the above-mentioned Misser Guido I enjoyed a friendship as many years as I stayed up there (*i.e.* in Paris), glorying often together that we were learning each day some fresh talent in our own (respective) professions at the expense of that very great and wondrous prince. I can say with truth that what I am, and whatever of the excellent and of the beautiful I have accomplished, all has been owing to that wondrous King. However I pick up again the thread of my discourse regarding him, and the fine works executed by me for him. I had in this château of mine a court for playing tennis (*un giuoco di palla da giucare alla corda*), from which I drew much profit while I made use of it. There were in that said place some tiny chambers, where dwelt different sorts of people, among whom there was a very clever printer of books: this man had almost his entire workshop within my château, and he it was who printed that first fine book on Medicine by Misser Guido. Since I wanted the use of these chambers, I turned him out, but with no little difficulty. There still remained a merchant in saltpeter (*maestro di salnitri*): and when I wanted to use these little chambers for certain of my excellent German workmen, this said merchant of saltpeter would not dislodge. I courteously told him many times that he must give me the use of my apartments, for I wanted to use them for the housing of my workmen in the service of the King. The more gently I addressed him, the more impertinently this beast (of a man) replied to me: then at last I gave him three days' notice. He laughed at me and told me that at the end of three years he would begin to think about it. I did not know that he was the favored servant of Madama di Tampes: and if it had not been that that trouble with Madama di Tampes caused me to ponder a little more upon these matters than I should have done previously, I would have turned him out then and there: but I wished to wait patiently for those three days. And when they had expired, without saying anything further, I took Germans, Italians and French, with weapons in their hands and many journeymen whom I employed: and in a short time I dismantled the entire house, and cast his goods outside my château. And this action I performed somewhat rigorously, because he had told me that he knew of no Italian who possessed sufficient spirit to remove one ring (of his) from its place. However, after it was over, the man arrived; to whom I remarked: "I am the least of Italians in Italy, and I have done nothing in comparison to what I have the courage to do to you, and that I will do if you speak a single word"; with other abusive words that I said to him. The man, astonished and terrified, put his goods in order as best he could: then he ran to Madama de Tampes, and depicted to her a very Hell: and that great enemy of mine painted to the King one as much the greater as she was the more eloquent and of more weight: who twice, I was told, was inclined to be furious with me, and to give cruel orders against me; but since Arrigo the Dauphin his son (now King of France) had received some insults from that too haughty lady, he, together with the Queen of Navarre, the sister of King Francesco, took my part with so much skill that the King turned everything into ridicule: for the which reason, by the true help of God, I survived a great danger.

I HAD to do the same thing to another similar person, but I did not destroy his home: I threw all his property, however, out of doors. For the which reason Madama de Tampes had so much impudence as to say to the King: "I believe that this devil will one day sack Paris." At these words the King in a rage replied to Madama de Tampes, telling her that I was doing very right in defending myself from that rabble who wanted to prevent me from being in his employ. Rage ever waxed greater in this cruel woman: she summoned to her a painter, who dwelt at Fontana Beliò, where the King resided almost continually. This painter was an Italian and from Bologna, and was known as *Il Bolognia*: for his proper name he was called Francesco Primaticcio. Madama di Tampes told him that he should ask of the King that commission for the fountain, which His Majesty had conferred upon me, and that she would help him in the matter with all her power. Thus they agreed among themselves. This Bologna experienced the greatest happiness that he had ever had, and he thought the matter quite sure, although it was not his line of work. But since he had a rather fine skill in design, and had contracted with certain workmen who had been trained under the direction of *Il Rosso,* a Florentine painter of ours, a truly and most wondrously able man, whatever of merit he executed he had acquired from the splendid example of the said Rosso, who was already dead. Those crafty arguments together with the great assistance of Madama di Tampes, and with the continual hammering day and night, now of Madama, and now of Bologna, prevailed in the ears of that great King. And that which was the potent cause of making him yield was that she and Bologna with one accord said: "How is it possible, Sacred Majesty, for Benvenuto, according to your wish, to make twelve silver statues? wherefore he has not yet completed one? And if you employ him in so great an undertaking as this (*i.e.,* the fountain) it is necessary that of these other (objects), which you desire so much, you must certainly be deprived: for one hundred most able men could not complete such vast works as this clever man has planned out. It is very clear that he has a great desire for work: the which very thing will be the cause of Your Majesty's losing both him and the commissions at one blow." These with many other similar works chancing to find the King in the humor he consented to all that they had asked of him; although at that time neither the designs nor models for anything by the said Bologna's own hand had ever been shown to him. At this same time in Paris that second tenant, whom I had driven from my château, had taken action against me, and he had commenced a law-suit against me, saying that I had stolen a great quantity of his goods when I had dislodged him. This law-suit

gave me very great annoyance, and took up so much of my time
that many times I wanted in despair to prepare to go right away.
They have a habit in France of making very great capital out of
any law-suit that they commence with a foreigner, or with any
other person whom they see may be somewhat careless about litigation: and directly they begin to see any advantage to be gained out
of the said suit, they find means of selling it: and some give up the
privilege to those who make a regular practice of this trade of
buying causes. They have another ugly custom, that the men of
Normandy, almost the larger number of them, have for their profession the giving of false evidence: to such purpose that those
persons who buy the causes, immediately instruct four of these witnesses, or six, according to their need, and by means of these the
man who is not warned to produce as many on the opposite side—
one who does not know the custom—immediately has the case
given against him. And to me these said chances befell: and since
it seemed to me a very dishonorable thing, I appeared at the Great
Hall (of Justice) of Paris to defend my rights; where I saw a
Judge, the King's Lieutenant, of Civil Causes, raised aloft upon a
great tribune. This man was big, gross and fat, and of most austere aspect. He had around him upon the one side and upon the
other many proctors and advocates, all set in rank to the right and
to the left; others kept coming in, one at a time. And they were
stating a case to the said Judge. Those advocates, who were at
the side, I noticed sometimes talking all at once; wherefore I stood
in astonishment how that marvelous man, the true image of
Pluto, bent his ear with evident attention, now to this one, and now
to that, and skillfully replied to them all. And since I have always
delighted in observing and testing every kind of skill, this seemed
to me so admirable that I would not have liked to have missed
seeing it for anything in the world. It chanced that that Hall was

very large and was filled with a vast number of people. They also used care that no one should enter in who had no business there, and they kept the door locked and a guard at the said door: which guard sometimes in resisting someone whom he did not want to enter, disturbed with his great noise that wonderful Judge, who angrily poured out abuse upon the said guard. And this occurred in my sight many times, and I noticed the circumstance: and the particular words which I heard were those which the Judge himself spake when he observed two noblemen who came to look on: and this porter offering a very great resistance (to their entry), the Judge scolding him said in a loud voice: " Be quiet! Be quiet! Limb of Satan (*Sotanasso*)! Get out of this! Be quiet!" These words in the French language sounded after this fashion: PHE SATAN PHE PHE SATAN ALÈ PHE. To me, who had learned the French language very well, on hearing this expression, there came in mind what Dante meant to say when he in company with his master Virgil entered within the portals of the Infernal Regions. For Dante, at the time of the painter Giotto, was together with him in France, and especially in Paris; wherefore for the said reasons one might say that that place where they carry on litigation was an Infernal Region. Dante therefore also, understanding thoroughly the French language, employed this expression: and it seemed to me a remarkable thing that it has never been understood after this fashion. Wherefore I declare and believe that the commentators make him say things of which he never even thought.

Returning to my own affairs, when I saw them pass certain judgments upon me through the medium of these lawyers, not seeing any means of being able to help myself, I had recourse for my assistance to a great dagger that I had, for I always delighted in possessing fine weapons; and the first (man) that I began my attack upon was that principal who had set in motion against me the unjust suit: and one evening I inflicted upon him so many wounds, taking care however not to kill him, in the legs and in the arms, that I deprived him of the use of both legs. Then I sought out that other person who had purchased the suit and wounded him also in such a way that he abandoned that suit. Thanking God always for this and every other thing, thinking from that time to remain awhile without being molested, I told the young men of my household, especially the Italians, that for the Love of God everyone of them should attend to his own jobs, and assist me for some time, in order that I might be enabled to finish those works of mine that had been begun; for I should soon complete them. Then I would return to Italy not being able to bear with the rogueries of those French people: and if that good King was once enraged against me, he would have made it bad for me, for I had done in my own defense many things of such a kind. These said Italians were, the first and dearest, Ascanio, from a placed called Tagliacozze in the Kingdom of Naples: the second was Pagolo, a Roman, a person born of a very humble origin, and whose father was unknown: these two were the men whom I had brought from Rome, who were with me in that said (city of) Rome. Another Roman had also come from Rome on purpose to find me. This man was also called Pagolo by name, and he was the son of an impoverished Roman noble of the family of the Macharoni. This young man did not know much about the profession but he was very handy with his weapon. Another I had who was a Ferrarese, and by name Bartolommeo Chioccia. I had also another man; this man was a Florentine and had the name of Pagolo Miccieri. And his brother, who was called by the nickname of *Gatta,* was clever at keeping accounts, but had spent too much when managing the property of Tommaso Guadagni, a very wealthy merchant. This Gatta set in order for me certain books wherein I kept the accounts of the great and most Christian King, and of others. Pagolo Miccieri having acquired from his brother the method (of keeping) these my account-books continued his work for me and I gave him a very handsome salary. And since he seemed to me a very good sort of youth, for I noticed that he was devout, overhearing him continually, sometimes murmuring Psalms, sometimes with his rosary in his hand, I counted very much upon his feigned piety. Calling him aside alone, I said to him: "Pagolo, my very dear brother, you see that you are well off with me, and you know that you had no other means of livelihood, and besides you are also a Florentine: therefore I trust you above all, since I see you very devout in your religious duties, which is a circumstance that pleases me very much. I pray you to help me, for I have not so much faith in any one of these others: wherefore I pray you to have a care upon these two principal matters, which would give me much anxiety: the one is that you very carefully guard my property in order that it be not taken from me, and also not touch it yourself: and you see also that poor girl of a Caterina, whom I maintain principally for the service of my profession, since I could not do without her: and whom I also, since I am a man, have employed for my carnal satisfaction, and it is possible that she may present me with a child: and since I do not want to provide expenses for other people's children, still less would I endure that such an insult should be shown to myself; if any member of this household were so impudent as to do such a thing, and I were to find it out, I believe for certain that I should slay both her and him. Wherefore I pray you, dear brother, to assist me: and if you see anything, tell me at once, for I will send her and her mother and whoever should do such a thing to the gallows; therefore, take care of your own self first." The rogue made a sign of the cross which extended from his head to his feet, and said: "Oh Blessed

Jesu! God keep me that I should ever think of such a thing; principally because I am not given to such wicked practices: besides do you not believe that I recognize the great benefit that I receive from you?" At these words, which I saw him utter with an appearance of simplicity and affection towards myself, I believed that the matter stood exactly as he said. Two days later, a feast-day occurring, Messer Mattio del Nazaro, also an Italian and a servant of the King, a most able man of the same profession (as my own), invited me with those young men of mine to disport ourselves in a garden. Wherefore I got myself ready and I told Pagolo also that he ought to come out of doors to enjoy himself, for it seemed to me that that tiresome law-suit had somewhat quieted down. The young man replied to me saying: "Truly it would be a great mistake to leave the house so unprotected: you see how much gold, silver and precious stones you have here. Since we are in this respect in a city of thieves, it is necessary to be on our guard by day as by night: I will attend to the repetition of certain of my prayers, and meantime I will guard the house. Go with a calm mind to give yourself pleasure and a good time. Another time someone else will perform this duty." Since it appeared to me that I could go with my mind at rest, together with Pagolo Macharoni, Ascanio and Chioccia we went to the said garden to enjoy ourselves, and we passed a great portion of that day happily. When it began to turn towards evening, after midday I became thoughtful, and I began to think of those words which with feigned simplicity that villain had said to me. I mounted my horse and with two of my servants I returned to my château, where I found Pagolo and that wretched Caterina almost in the very act of sin: for when I arrived that French bawd her mother shouted with a loud voice: "Pagolo! Caterina! Here is the master." When I saw them both come to me, terrified, surprised, and all in disorder, not knowing either what they said or, like idiots, whither they were going, the commission of their offense was clearly evident. Wherefore reason giving place to rage, I drew my sword, resolved to slay them both: the one (the man) fled, the other (the woman) flung herself upon her knees on the ground, and clamored for all the mercies of heaven. I, since I had wanted to strike the male first, not being able thus to catch him at once, when subsequently I caught him, I came meantime to the conclusion that it were better for me to drive them both away: for, with so many other things that had taken place so close upon this one, I should with difficulty have saved my own life. Nevertheless I said to Pagolo: "If my eyes had seen what you, you scoundrel, make me believe (has occurred) I would run you ten times through the belly with this sword. Now begone from my presence, so that if you ever say a Paternoster again, know that it is that of San Giuliano." Then I drove out the mother and the daughter with violent blows (*colpi di pinte*), both kicks and thumps. They meditated how to revenge themselves for this injury, and having consulted a Norman lawyer, he instructed them that she (Caterina) should assert that I had had intercourse with her after the Italian fashion: by which he meant contrary to nature, that is to say by sodomy, saying: "At least when this Italian hears of this kind of accusation, and understands how great is the danger he runs, he will immediately give you several hundreds of ducats, in order that you may speak no more of it, recollecting the great penalty that they exact in France for this species of crime." Thus they entered into agreement. They laid this information against me, and I was summoned. The more I sought for rest, so much the more did tribulations spring up for me. Injured by fortune every day in varying fashion, I began to think which of the two things I ought to do; whether to go right away and leave France to her own perdition, or truly to fight this battle also, and see for what end God had created me. For a long time I was troubled upon this point. Then at last I took the resolution to go right away, since I did not wish to tempt so far my perverse fortune till she should cause me to break my neck. When I had arranged matters in all things and for all things, and had taken steps for the hasty disposal of those goods which I could not carry with me, and for packing those other light articles upon my own persons and that of my servants in the best way that I could, with much heavy distress I set off on such a departure. I remained alone in a private studio of mine: for to those young men of mine who had advised that I ought to depart right away, I said that it were well that I should take counsel with myself a little while, although I knew well that they were to a great extent speaking the truth: for as long as I should be out of prison, and could allow a little space (of time) for this storm to pass over, I could much better justify myself to the King, telling him by letters how this attack had been made upon me out of envy alone. And as I have said, I had resolved to do this: and in moving (from my seat) I was taken by the shoulder and turned round, and a voice said to me encouragingly: "Benvenuto! be like yourself, and have no fear!" Having immediately taken the contrary opinion to that which I had done, I said to those young Italians of mine: "Take good weapons and come with me, and obey whatever I tell you, and think of nothing else, for I wish to face it. If I were to depart, the next day you would all vanish into smoke. Therefore obey and come with me." All those young fellows said with one accord: "Since we are here, and we live of his substance, we ought to go with him and help him as long as life lasts, according to whatever he shall propose: for he has uttered more of the truth than we thought of. Directly he had gone out of this place, his enemies would have us all driven away. Let us consider carefully all the great works that are in course of construction here, and of how great an importance they are. We should not have the courage to finish them without him, and his enemies would say that he had gone away himself because he had not the spirit to finish such tasks as these himself." Besides these they uttered many other remarks of weight. That young Roman of the family of the Macharoni was the first to infuse courage into the others. He also summoned several of those Germans and French (workmen), who liked me. We were ten in all: and I took the way I had planned for myself, resolved not to let myself be imprisoned alive. When I arrived in the presence of the criminal (*cherminali*) judges, I found there the said Caterina and her mother. As I came upon them they were laughing with their attorney. I entered within (the Court), and boldly called for the judge, who, swollen out gross and fat, sat raised up above the rest upon a tribune. When this man saw me, shaking his head furiously at me, he said in a subdued voice: "Although you have the name of Well-come (*Benvenuto*) this time you will be Ill-come (*mal venuto*)." I heard him, and called out again, saying: "Despatch me quickly. Tell me what it is that I am come here to do." Then the judge turned to Caterina and said to her: "Caterina! Tell us all that occurred in your relations with Benvenuto." Caterina said, that I had had intercourse with her after the fashion of Italy. The judge turning to me said: "You hear what Caterina says, Benvenuto?" Thereupon I said: "If I had intercourse with her after the Italian fashion, I should have done so solely with the desire of having a child, just as you (French) all do." Then the judge rejoined, saying: "She means that you have had connection with her by another method than the natural one." To this I replied that that was not the Italian fashion; rather it must be the French fashion, since she knew it and I did not: and that I would like her to describe exactly in what fashion I had had intercourse with her. This shameless whore wickedly stated openly and clearly the disgusting fashion that she meant. I made her repeat it three times in succession: and when she had said it, I cried in a loud voice: "My Lord Judge! Lieutenant of the Most Christian King, I demand justice. For I know that the laws of the Most Christian King ordain the stake for this crime, for both agent and patient. She confesses to the crime: but I know nothing about it in any way whatsoever. Her bawd of a mother is here (also), who for the one crime and the other deserves the stake. I demand justice." And I repeated these words so frequently and in a loud voice, always demanding the stake for her and for her mother: telling the judge that if he did not put her in prison in my presence I would hasten to the King and tell him of the injustice that a lieutenant of his in criminal affairs was exercising towards me. At this great noise of mine they began to lower their voices: thereupon I raised mine the more: the young whore along with her mother (began) to weep, and I kept shouting to the judge: "To the stake, to the stake" (*fuoco, fuoco*). That great coward (of a judge), when he saw that the matter had not come off in the fashion that he had planned, began with many soft words to excuse the weak female sex. At this I thought that it seemed I had won a great battle, and muttering and threatening, I gladly went away: but I certainly would have paid five hundred *scudi* not to have ever appeared there. On issuing from that ocean (of trouble) I thanked God with all my heart, and joyfully returned with my young men to my château. When perverse fortune, or rather we should truthfully say that contrary star of ours, takes to persecuting a man it is never wanting in fresh methods of taking the field against him. Since it seemed to me that I had escaped from an immeasurable ocean, I thought that for some small space of time this perverse star of mine ought to let me rest; but although

I had not yet recovered my breath from that extreme danger it set two more in my way at one blow. At the end of three days two events happened to me: in each of the two my life was poised upon the turn of the balance. The one was that I went to Fontana Beliò to discuss (a matter) with the King, who had written me a letter, in which (he had said that) he wished me to execute the dies for the money of his entire realm. And along with that same letter he had sent me some sketches, to show me what his wishes were: but nevertheless he gave me permission to make whatsoever thing was pleasing to myself. I had made new designs according to my own opinion and according to the beauties of my art: so when I arrived at Fontana Beliò, one of those treasurers who held the King's commission to provide for me (this man was called Monsignor della Fa) immediately said to me: "Benvenuto! The painter Bolognia has received a commission from the King to fashion your great *Colossus,* and all the commissions that our King had given to us for you he has taken them all away from us, and transferred to him. To us it has seemed very wrong indeed, and it appears to us that this Italian of yours has behaved himself most daringly towards you: for you had already got the commission by virtue of your models and your hard work. He takes it from you solely through the favor of Madama di Tampes: and it is now many months that he has had this job and yet it has not appeared that he has given directions for anything." I, astonished, said: "How is it possible that I have never known anything of this?" Then he told me that he (Bologna) had kept it very secret, and that he had got it with very great difficulty, because the King did not wish to give it to him: but the active interest of Madama di Tampes alone had causd him to get it. Having heard that I had been injured in this fashion and thus greatly wronged, and seeing a work taken away from me which I had earned by my own great exertions: proposing

to myself to do something serious, I went with my weapon straight
to see Bolognia. I found him in his chamber and at his studies.
He had me called within; and with certain of his Lombardic expressions of welcome he asked what good business had brought me
thither. Thereupon I said: "A very good and important business."
The man directed his servants to bring us something to drink, and
said: "Before that we discuss anything I desire that we drink together, for thus it is the custom in France." Thereupon I said:
"Messer Francescho, you must know that these discussions that we
have to enter into together do not call for drinking first. Perhaps
afterwards we shall be able to drink." I began to argue with him,
saying: "All men who make a profession of being honest men
execute their works in such fashion that by them one may know
them to be honest men: and if they do the contrary they have no
more the name of honest men. I know that you were aware that
the King had commissioned me to make that great *Colossus,* of
which we had been talking for eighteen months; and that neither
you nor anyone else came forward to say anything upon the subject. Wherefore by my important works I had become known to
the great King, who, being pleased with my models, gave this great
work to me to carry out: and for many months past I have heard
nothing further. This morning only have I heard that you had
got it, and had taken it from me: the which work I had earned
by my wondrous efforts, and you take it from me merely by your
empty words." To this Bolognia answered and said: "Oh! Benvenuto! Everyone seeks to do his business in all the ways that he
can. If the King wishes it thus, what would you like to say in
opposition? You will throw away your time, for I have hastened
it on, and it is mine. Now tell whatever you like and I will listen
to you." I spoke thus: "Know, Messer Francesco! That I should
have many words to say to you, whereby with admirable reasoning

and true I would make you confess that such methods as those which you have said and done are not customary among rational creatures. However I will come with a few words quickly to the point of the matter; but open your ears and listen well to me, for the matter is important." He wanted to rise from his seat, for he saw me flushed in countenance and greatly changed. I said that it was not yet time to rise: wherefore he should remain seated and listen to me. Then I began speaking thus: "Messer Francesco! You know that the job was mine first, and that by common sense the time had passed in which anyone should speak further regarding it. Now I tell you I shall be content if you make a model, and I, besides that which I have (already) made, will make another for it. Then we will quietly carry them to our great King: and whichever of us shall gain by that means the merit of having worked the best that man will be deservedly worthy of (making) the *Colossus*. And if it shall fall to you to do it, I will set aside all this great injury that you have done me, and will invoke a blessing upon your hands, as more worthy than mine of so great a triumph. Therefore let us remain thus, and we shall be friends. Otherwise we shall be enemies; and God, who always assists the right, and I, who am making the way for it (the right) would demonstrate to you in how great an error you were." Said Messer Francesco: "The job is mine, and since it has been consigned to me, I do not wish to put my title to it in question." To him I replied: "Messer Francesco! Since you will not take the good line, which is just and reasonable, I will show you the other one, which shall be like your own, that is to say, ugly and disagreeable. I tell you thus, that if I ever hear in any sort of way that you are speaking about this job of mine, I will immediately slay you like a dog: and since we are neither in Rome, nor in Bologna, nor in Florence, for here one lives after another fashion, if I ever learn that you have spoken about it to the King or to any one else, I will slay you at all costs. Think which way you prefer to take; either that first good one which I have told you of, or this latter bad one of which I speak now." The man did not know either what to say or what to do: and I was prepared to produce more willingly that result then and there, than to put it off to another opportunity (*mettere altro tempo in mezo*). The said Bologna uttered no other words than these: "When I do the things that an honest man ought to do I shall have no reason in the world for fear." To this I replied: "You have well said. But in doing the contrary beware, for the matter concerns you." And I immediately departed from him and went to the King. And I discussed with His Majesty a long time the making of the coins, a subject whereon we were not much in accord. For his Council being there present, they persuaded him that the coins ought to be made after the fashion of France, according to which they had been made up to that time. To them I replied that His Majesty had caused me to come from Italy in order that I should carry out commissions that should be good: and if His Majesty ordered me to the contrary, I should never compose my conscience to doing it. The discussion was put off to another occasion: I immediately returned to Paris. I had scarcely dismounted, when a kind person, one of those who take pleasure in spying out evil, came to tell me that Pagolo Miccieri had taken a house for that vile strumpet of a Caterina and for her mother, and that he was continually going thither, and that in speaking of me he always kept saying with disdain: "Benvenuto gave the lettuce into the charge of the geese, and thought that I would not eat of it. It is sufficient to say that he is now going about swaggering, and he believes that I am afraid of him. I have girt this sword and this dagger at my side to let him see that my sword also cuts, and that I am a Florentine as well as he, and of the Miccieri family, a much greater house than are his Cellini." The rascal, who brought me such a message, told it to me with such force that I felt a fever immediately leap upon me—I say a fever not speaking merely for (the purposes of) comparison. And since perhaps so bestial a passion would have slain me, I took a remedy by giving it that outlet which such an opportunity afforded me, according to the mood that I was laboring under. I told that Ferrarese workman of mine, who was called Chioccia, to come with me, and I had my horse brought behind me by the servant. And when I reached the house where this scoundrel was, finding the door half-closed, I entered. I saw that he had his sword and his dagger at his side, and was seated upon a chest, and he had his arm around the neck of Caterina; and I just as I was coming in heard him chatting mockingly with her mother regarding my affairs. Pushing open the door, and at the same time drawing my sword, I placed its point at his throat, without giving him time to remember that he also had a sword; and I said to him at the same moment: "Vile coward! Commend yourself to God, for you are a dead man!" Keeping still, he cried out three times: "Oh mother mine, help me!" Though I had the desire to slay him anyhow, when I heard him utter such silly words as those, half my wrath passed away. Meanwhile I had told that workman of mine, Chioccia, not to let either her or her mother escape, for, when I had done with him, I wished also to punish those two whores. Keeping continually the point of my sword at his throat, I sometimes pricked him a little, ever with terrifying words, till I pereceived that he made no defense in the world; and since I knew not what more I could do,—it did not seem to me that that threatening of mine had any object,—the fancy came to me as the lesser evil to make them marry, with the design of taking my revenge upon them afterwards. Having thus resolved, I said: "Take off that ring that you have upon your finger, you coward, and marry her, so that then I can take the revenge that you deserve." He immediately said: "So long as you do not slay me, I will do anything." Then I said: "Put the ring upon her (finger)." When I removed the sword a little way from his throat he put the ring on (her finger). Then I said: "This is not enough, for I want two notaries to come here, so that this thing may pass as a contract." Telling Chioccia to go for the notaries, I immediately turned to her (Caterina) and to her mother. Speaking in French I said: "The notaries and other witnesses are coming here: the first of you that I hear speaking anything of this matter, I will immediately slay, and I will slay you all three. Therefore keep your heads." To him (Pagolo) I said in Italian: "If you oppose anything to all that I shall propose, at the smallest word that you say, I will give you so many dagger thrusts as to make you void all that you have in your stomach." To this he replied: "It is sufficient for me that you do not kill me, and I will do whatsoever you wish." The notaries and the witnesses arrived; they made a binding (*attentico*) contract, and the wrath and fever miraculously passed from me. I paid the notaries and went away. The next day Bolognia came to Paris on purpose, and caused Mattio del Nasaro to summon me: I went and saw the said Bolognia, who with a cheerful countenance came to meet me, begging me that I would hold him as a good brother, and that he would never more speak of that work: for he recognized very well that I had reason. If I did not say that in some of these adventures of mine I realize that I did wrong, those others wherein I know I did right would not pass for truth: I know, however, that I made a mistake in wishing to revenge myself so extravagantly upon Pagolo Miccieri. Although, if I had thought that he had been a man of such weakness of character, there would never have come into my mind so shameful a revenge as that which I wrought upon him: for it was not sufficient for me to have made him take

to wife so vicious and low a strumpet, but yet further, in my desire
to complete the remainder of my revenge, I had her summoned
and modeled her likeness. Every day I gave her thirty soldi:
and since I made her pose naked she first wanted me to give her
her money in advance: secondly, she wanted very much to break her
fast: thirdly, out of revenge I had intercourse with her, jeering
all the while at her and her husband for the various horns that
I was providing him with. The fourth circumstance was that I
made her pose to her great discomfort for many many hours at a
time: and since posing in this discomfort became very irksome to
her, so much the more did I delight in it, for she was of most beautiful form and brought me greatest credit. And since it seemed to her
that I had not that consideration for her that I had before she was
married, becoming greatly annoyed she began to grumble: and in
that French fashion of hers she kept boasting in words, quoting her
husband, who had gone to live with the Prior of Capua, the brother
of Piero Strozzi. As I have said she kept quoting this husband
of hers: and when I heard her talking about him there immediately
came upon me unmeasured wrath. However I bore it unwillingly
in the best way I could, considering that for (the purposes of) my
profession I could not find a thing (a model) more suited to that
purpose (of mine): and I kept saying to myself: "I am here executing two sorts of vengeance: one through her being a wife: these
are no empty horns such as were hers when she played the whore
upon me: wherefore if I am taking this revenge upon him, and
employing towards her also such extravagance by making her pose
here with so much personal discomfort; besides the pleasure that
it affords me, it results for me in so much honor and so much
profit. What more could I desire?" While I made this calcula-
tion for myself, this wretch of a woman redoubled those insulting
words of hers, speaking moreover of her husband. And she kept

doing and saying so much that she led me beyond the bounds of reason: and giving myself a prey to fury, I took her by her hair and dragged her about the room, administering to her so many kicks and blows that I was tired out. And no one could come in thither to her assistance. Having been very thoroughly pounded, she swore that she would never come back to me again: for the which reason it appeared to me at first that I had done very wrong, for I seemed to be losing an admirable opportunity of doing myself credit. And seeing her besides all torn, bruised and swollen I thought that, even if she were to return, she must of necessity be treated for fifteen days before I could make any use of her. Returning to her I sent a woman servant of mine to help her dress; which servant was an old woman who was called Ruberta, a most kindly creature. And when she came to this wicked woman she brought her again a drink and food. Then she anointed with a little cooked bacon-fat those severe bruises that I had given her; and the remainder of the fat that was left over they ate together. When clad she went away abusing and cursing all Italians, and the King who harbored them: thus she went weeping and muttering all the way to her home. It is true that this first time it seemed to me that I had done very wrong, and my Ruberta rebuked me, and said to me: "You are very cruel to treat so roughly so handsome a girl." Wishing to excuse myself to this Ruberta of mine, I related to her the wickedness that she and her mother had practiced upon me when they were in my house. At this Ruberto scolded me saying that it was nothing, for it was the custom of France, and that she knew for certain that there was not a husband in France who was without his own small horns (*cornette*). At these words I was provoked to laughter, and then I told Ruberta that she must go and see how Caterina did, for I would have had great pleasure in being enabled to finish that work of mine by making use of her. My Ruberta rebuked me, telling me that I did not know how to live: "for that as soon as it is daylight, she will come here of her own accord: whereas if you should send to ask after her, or to visit her, she will do the grand, and will not come here." When the following day came, this said Caterina came to my door, and knocked at the said door with great fury; to such purpose that I, who was down below, ran to see if it was some mad-man or (some-one) belonging to the house. On my opening the door this animal laughingly flung herself upon my neck, embraced and kissed me, and asked of me if I was angry with her any more. I said: "No!" She said: "Give me then a good breakfast." I gave her a good breakfast (*ben d'asciolvere*), and ate with her in sign of peace. Then I set to work to model from her, and during that operation there happened the (usual) sexual amusements; and then at that same hour as on the past day she incensed me so much that I had to give her the same blows. Thus we went on for several days, doing every day all these same things as a matter of course (*come che a stampa*): it varied little from more to less. Meantime I, having acquired very great credit and having finished my figure, I gave orders to cast it in bronze: in the which operation I experienced some difficulty, so that it would be most valuable for the purposes of my profession to narrate such a matter: but because I should go into too much length over it, I will pass it over. It is sufficient that my figure turned out most beautiful, and was as finely cast as any that has ever been accomplished.

W HILE this work was proceeding I set aside certain hours
of the day, and worked therein upon the Salt-Cellar, and
sometimes upon the (statue of) *Jove*. Since the Salt-Cellar was
worked upon by many more men than I had sufficient convenience
for to work upon the *Jove,* by this time I had already completely
finished it. The King had returned to Paris, and I went to see him,
carrying with me the said completed Salt-Cellar: which as I have
said above was oval in shape, and was of the size of about two-thirds
of a *braccio,* all of gold, chased with the aid of the chisel. And as I
said, when I described the model, I had represented the *Sea* and the
Earth, both seated; and they intertwined their legs, just as certain
arms of the *Sea* run up into the *Earth,* and the *Earth* (juts out into)
the said *Sea*: I had therefore appropriately given them that charming
attitude. And in the right hand of the *Sea* I had fixed a trident, and
in his left I had placed a boat, delicately chased, in which was to be
placed the salt. There were beneath this said figure his four sea-
horses, which as far as the breast and front hoofs were like a horse:
all the remaining part from the middle backwards was (like) a
fish: the fishes' tails were interlaced together in charming fashion:
above that group there sat in a very haughty attitude the said *Sea*:
he had around him many varieties of fishes and other sea-beasts.
The water was represented with its waves; it was moreover most
excellently enameled in its own proper color. For the *Earth* I had
presented a very beauteous woman, with the *Horn of Abundance* in
her hand, entirely naked exactly like the male figure: in the other,

her left hand, I had made a small temple in the Ionic style, most delicately fashioned: and in this I had arranged the pepper. Beneath this female (figure) I had placed the handsomest animals that the *Earth* produces: and the rocks of *Earth* I had partially enameled and partially left of gold. I had then posed this work and set it up upon a base of black ebony. This was of a certain suitable thickness and had a small bevel, upon which I distributed four golden figures, executed in more than half-relief: these represented *Night, Day, Twilight* (*graprusco*), and *Dawn*. There were also four other figures of the same size, made for the *Four Chief Winds,* contrived with as much finish as it is possible to imagine, and partly enameled. When I placed this work before the eyes of the King, he uttered an expression of astonishment (*stupure*), and could not sufficiently gaze at it. Then he told me to carry it back to my house, and that he would tell me in due time what I was to do with it. Carrying it back home I immediately invited several of my special friends, and in their company I dined with greatest enjoyment, setting the Salt-Cellar in the middle of the table: and we were the first people to use it. Then I pursued the completion of the silver *Jove,* and of a large vase, already spoken of, worked all over with many very charming decorations and with a number of figures.

At this period the above-mentioned painter Bolognia gave the King to understand that it would be well for His Majesty to let him go to Rome and to give him letters of recommendation, by which he might be enabled to make casts from those fine early antiques; that is to say the *Laocoön* (Leoconte), the *Cleopatra,* the *Venus,* the *Commodus* (Comodo), the *Zingara* and the *Apollo.* These truly are the finest things that there are in Rome. And he told the King that after His Majesty had seen those wondrous works he would then know how to judge regarding the art of design; for all that he had seen by us modern (artists) was very far removed from the splendid work of those ancient ones. The King was agreeable, and granted him all the recommendations he asked for. So this beast went away with his own ill-luck. Not having the courage to enter with his own handiwork into competition with me he took that other Lombardesque expedient of seeking to belittle my work by becoming a copyist of the antique. And although he executed the casting very well, he produced an effect altogether opposite to that which he had imagined: which thing shall be related later in its own place. Having driven away altogether the said wretch Caterina, and that poor unfortunate youth of a husband of hers having departed right away from Paris, since I wanted to finish completely (*nettare*) my *Fontana Beliò* (*sic*), which was already cast in bronze, and also to execute properly those two *Victories,* which were to go in the angles beside the half-circle of the doorway, I took a poor little girl of about the age of fifteen years. She was very beautiful in the shape of her body and was somewhat swarthy: and since she was a little savage and spoke seldom (*di pochissime parole*), quick in her movements, with frowning eyes, all these circumstances caused me to impose upon her the name of "Scorzone": her proper name was Gianna. With (the aid of) this said girl I completed very thoroughly in bronze the said *Fontana Beliò,* and those two said *Victories* for the said doorway. This young girl was intact and a virgin, and I got her with child: She brought forth to me a daughter on the seventh day of June at the thirteenth hour of the day 1544, which was exactly the 44th year in the course of my own life. To the said daughter I gave the name of Constanza: and she was godfathered by Messer Guido Guidi, the King's physician, my very great friend, as I have written above. He was the only godfather, for a single godfather is the custom in France, and two godmothers, one of whom was the Signiora Maddalena, wife of Misser Luigi Alamanni, Florentine noble and wondrous poet: the other godmother was the wife of Messer Ricciardo del Bene, our Florentine (fellow) citizen and an important merchant there: she was a French gentlewoman of rank. This was the first child that I ever had, as far as I remember. I consigned to the said girl as much money for her portion as contented an aunt of hers, to whom I handed her over: and never more afterwards did I know her. I gave my attention to my commissions and progressed much with them: the (statue of) *Jove* was almost at its completion; the vase likewise; the door began to display its beauties. At this time the King arrived in Paris: and, although I have mentioned 1544 in connection with the birth of my daughter, we had not yet passed 1543: but because it occurred to me as opportune to speak of this daughter of mine now, so as not to hinder me in connection with other matters of greater importance, I will say nothing further about her until the proper time. The King came to Paris, as I have said, and immediately came to my house: and finding so many works before him, such as could most excellently satisfy the eyes as (in fact) they did those of the wondrous King, the works satisfied him as much as one who had endured the labor as I had done could desire, and he immediately remembered of his own accord that the above mentioned Cardinal of Ferrara had given me nothing, neither pension nor anything else of that which he had promised me: and in a whisper to his Admiral he said that the Cardinal of Ferrara had done very ill not to give me anything; and he wished to remedy such an unhandsome act, for he saw that I was a man to say few words but that some day presently (*da vedere a non vedere*) I should be gone right away without saying anything further. On going home, after His Majesty had dined, he told the Cardinal that he must tell the treasurer of the Exchequer by his orders to pay me as soon as he could seven thousand gold *scudi* in three or four instalments, according as it was convenient to him, so long as he did not fail to do it: and he added moreover saying: "I

gave Benvenuto into your charge and you have forgotten him."
The Cardinal said that he would willingly do all that His Majesty
told him. The said Cardinal of his own evil nature allowed this
wish of the King's to be neglected. Meanwhile the Wars increased:
and it was at this period that the Emperor with his very great army
marched towards Paris. When the Cardinal saw that France was in
great need of ready money, having taken one day the opportunity of
speaking about me he said: "Sacred Majesty! It is for the best that
I have not caused money to be given to Benvenuto. For one reason
is that there is now too great need of it. Another reason is that so
great a sum of money would very soon have caused us to lose Benvenuto: for imagining himself to be wealthy he would have with it
purchased property in Italy, and one day when the fancy took him
he would the more readily have departed from you. Wherefore I
have thought that it would be best for Your Majesty to confer upon
him something within your kingdom, since you have a desire that
he remain a longer time in your service." The King agreed to
these arguments, since he was in need of money: nevertheless in
accordance with his most noble soul, truly worthy of such a King
as he was, he thought that the said Cardinal had done this thing
more to gratify himself than from necessity, for he would certainly
have thought of that long before the needs of so great a kingdom.
And although, as I have said, the King showed that he approved of
these said reasons, privately he did not interpret it thus: for, as I
have said above, he returned to Paris, and the next day, without my
going to urge him, he came of himself to my house: where, going
forward to meet him, I conducted him through various chambers,
wherein there were different kinds of works of art, and beginning
with the inferior works, I exhibited to him a vast quantity of works
in bronze, of which he had not seen so many for a long time past.
Then I took him to see the silver *Jove,* and I exhibited it to him as

though complete with all its very beautiful decorations: which appeared to him a much more admirable thing than it would have done to another man, on account of a certain disastrous chance that had happened to him a few years before. For when after the capture of Tunis the Emperor passed through Paris by agreement with his brother-in-law King Francesco, the said King desiring to make him a present worthy of so great an Emperor, caused a silver *Hercules* to be made of precisely the size that I had made the *Jove*: which *Hercules* the King admitted to be the ugliest work of art that he had ever seen, and had therefore condemned it as such to those brilliant Parisian craftsmen, who pretended to being the ablest men in the world in that profession, having given the King to understand that that was the best (*tutto*) that could be done in silver, and nevertheless wanted two thousand ducats for that dirty (piece of) work of theirs. For this reason when the King saw that work of mine, he perceived in it such finish as he would never have believed. He therefore made a fair judgment, and wanted my work upon the *Jove* to be valued also at two thousand ducats, saying: "I did not give those men any salary: this man, to whom I give about one thousand *scudi* of salary can certainly make this thing for me for the sum of two thousand gold *scudi,* since he has the said advantage of his salary." I afterwards took him to see the other works in silver and in gold, and many other models for the fashioning of fresh objects of art. Then at the very moment of his departure, I exhibited to him on my château green that huge *Giant,* which caused the King greater astonishment than he had ever experienced at any other thing: and turning to the Admiral, who was called Monsignior Aniballe, he said: "Since nothing has been provided for this man by the Cardinal, it is necessary (for us to do it), since he also is slow in asking: without saying anything further I wish him to be provided for; for in the case of men of this sort, since they are not accustomed to ask for anything, their works would seem sufficient to demand their due (recompense). Wherefore look out for the first abbey that falls vacant, which may amount to the value of two thousand *scudi* of revenue. And should it not amount (to that sum) in one benefice alone arrange that it be in two or three; for that will be the same thing to him. Being present, I heard everything, and I immediately thanked him as if I had already had it; telling His Majesty that when this gift came to me I wanted to labor for His Majesty without any other reward, either (in the form of) salary or in any other valuation of my works, until such time as constrained by old age, being unable to work any longer, I could repose my weary life in peace, living honorably upon this same revenue, and recalling how I had served so great a King as was His Majesty. At these words of mine the King with much merriment (turning very cheerfully towards me), said: "And let it be so!" And satisfied with me His Majesty departed from me, and I remained behind.

Madama di Tampes, on learning of these doings of mine, became more violently poisoned against me, saying to herself: "I rule the world nowadays, and an insignificant man like this values me at naught." She prepared the shop entirely in order to act in opposition to me. And a certain man falling into her hands, who was a clever distiller (he supplied her with certain perfumed liquids which were admirable for improving the skin, a thing never previously employed in France): she presented him to the King: the man proffered some of these distilled preparations, which much delighted the King: and while in this state of pleasure she made him ask of His Majesty a tennis court (*un giuoco di palla*) that I had in my château, with certain small chambers adjoining which he said that I was not using. That excellent King, who recognized whence the matter came, gave him no answer. Madama di Tampes set herself to soliciting by those methods that women are able (to employ) with

men, in so much that this design of hers was easily successful; fo
finding the King in an amorous mood, to which he was very pron
he was complacent to Madama to as great an extent as she desire
This said man came in company with the Treasurer Grolier, a ve
great French noble; and since this Treasurer spoke Italian very we
he came to my château, and entering therein into my presence a
dressed me in Italian in a jesting manner. When he saw the oppo
tunity (*Quand e' vidde il bello*) he said: "On behalf of the King
put this man here in possession of that tennis court together wit
those small buildings that belong to the said court." To this I r
plied: "Everything belongs to the sacred King: therefore you cou
have entered in here more freely. Wherefore a matter done in th
fashion by means of notaries and the Law Court looks more like
way of deceit than an honest commission from so great a King.
protest therefore that before I go to complain to the King, I wi
defend myself in that fashion that His Majesty the day before ye
terday commissioned me to do, and I will fling this man whom yo
have put here out of the windows unless I see another express wa
rant under the King's own hand." At these words of mine the sa
Treasurer went away threatening and murmuring; and doing th
like I remained behind, nor did I want at that time to make ai
other demonstration. Subsequently I went to see those lawye
who had put that man in possession. These men were very we
known to me, and they told me that it was a formal act proper
done by the King's commission, but that it was not of much impo
tance; and that if I had made the slightest resistance, he would n
have taken possession, as he had done; and that these were acts ai
customs of the Court, which in no way affected the King's obec
ence. So that when it seemed well to me to oust him from posse
sion in that same way wherein he entered, it would be well don
and there would be no further trouble. It was sufficient for me

be advised of this, for the next day I began to use my weapons; and although I experienced some difficulty in the matter, I took it as a great pleasure. Every day I made all of a sudden an assault with stones, with pikes, with arquebuses, firing however without ball. But I inspired them with so much terror that no one wanted any more to come to his assistance. Wherefore finding one day that his defense was weak, I entered the house by force, and drove him out; flinging outside everything (*tutto tutto*) that he had brought with him. Then I repaired to the King, and told him that I had done everything (*tutto tutto*) that His Majesty had commissioned me to do, defending myself from all those persons who wanted to hinder me in the service of His Majesty. At this the King laughed and sent me fresh letters, under which I was not to be molested any more. Meanwhile with great application I completed the fine silver *Jove* together with its gilded base, which I had mounted upon a wooden plinth, which was scarcely visible. And in the said wooden plinth I had embedded four small balls of hard wood, which were more than half hidden in their sockets after the fashion of the nuts of crossbows. These things were so neatly contrived that a small boy could easily, without any exertion in the world, push backwards and forwards the said Statue of *Jove,* and turn it in all directions. Having fixed it up in my own way, I went with it to Fontana Beliò, where the King was. At this time the above-mentioned Bolognia had brought from Rome the above-mentioned statues; and had had them with great care cast in bronze. I knew nothing of this, because he had carried out this business of his very secretly, and since Fontana Beliò is more than forty miles distant from Paris, I therefore could not know anything (about it). When I endeavored to learn from the King where he wished that I should place the *Jove,* Madama di Tampes, who was present, told the King that there was no place more appropriate for placing it than in his handsome gallery. This

was, as we should say in Tuscany, a *loggia,* or more accurately a
wide corridor (*androne*): more correctly could it be called "a wide
corridor," because we call a *loggia* those chambers which are open
upon one side. This long room was much more than one hundred
ordinary paces (*passi andanti*) in length, and was adorned and very
rich with paintings by the hand of that wondrous Rosso, our Florentine (fellow-citizen); and below the paintings were arranged very
many pieces of sculpture, some in whole (*tonde*) and some in half
relief (*basso rilievo*); it was in width about twelve ordinary paces. The
above-mentioned Bolognia had transported into this said gallery all
the above-mentioned antique works of art, executed in bronze and
very well done; and had set them out after a very fine plan, raised
up on their own bases: and as I have remarked above they were
most beautiful objects copied from the antiques in Rome. Into this
said chamber I conveyed my *Jove,* and when I saw that fine show
all arranged with skill, I said to myself: "This is like passing
through the pikes. Now may God assist me." Having set it (the
statue) in its place, and as far as I was able, arranged it very satis-
factorily, I waited till the great King should come. The said *Jove*
held his thunder-bolt in his right hand, contrived in an attitude as
if desirous of hurling it, and in the left I had placed the World.
Amid the flames I had with much skill inserted a piece of a white
torch. And Madama di Tampes had entertained the King until
nightfall in order to do me one of two evil turns; either that he
should not come at all, or that my work on account of its being
night would truly show to less advantage: but as God protects those
of his creatures who have Faith in Him, it turned out quite the
opposite; for when I saw that night had come, I lighted the said
torch that was in the hand of the *Jove;* and since it was somewhat
raised above the head of the said *Jove,* the light fell from above, and
made a much more beautiful effect than it would have done by day.

The said King appeared, together with his Madama di Tampes, with the Dauphin, his son (now King), and with the Dauphiness, with the King of Navarre his brother-in-law, with Madama Margherita his daughter and with several other great lords, who were instructed for the purpose by Madama di Tampes to speak against me. When I saw the King enter I caused it (the statue) to be pushed forward by Ascanio (that workman of mine already mentioned), so that the handsome *Jove* moved gently towards the King. And since I had also executed it with some small amount of skill, the slight motion that was given to the said figure, from its being so well fashioned, made it seem to be alive: and the said antique figures being left by me somewhat in the rear, the great charm of my work came first to the eyes. The King immediately said: "This is much the most beautiful thing that was ever seen by any man, and I, although I delight in and understand these things, could never have imagined the hundredth part of it." Those lords, who were to have spoken against me seemed to be unable to say enough in praise of the said work. Madama di Tampes impudently said: "It seems very clear that you have no eyes. Do you not see how many fine antique bronze figures are placed further back: in them exist the true merits of this (branch of) art, and not in these modern tricks?" Thereupon the King moved on, and the others with him. And when he had given a glance at the said figures which, since they were in an inferior light, did not show to advantage at all, the King said: "Whoever wished to do this man a bad turn has actually done him a great service. For by means of these admirable figures one can see and recognize this work of his to be a long way more beautiful and more wondrous than they are: wherefore to make a full reckoning of Benvenuto, not only do his works stand comparison with antique ones, but also surpass them." Upon this Madama di Tampes said that when one saw such a work by day it would not appear by one

thousand times as beautiful as it appeared by night; besides it mu
be observed that I had put a veil over the said figure to conceal i
faults. This was a very thin veil which I had draped with cor
siderable grace round the said *Jove,* in order to increase its majesty
the which at those words I removed, lifting it from below, uncovei
ing thereby its handsome genital organs; and with some sma
amount of visible annoyance I tore it all off. She thought that I ha
uncovered that portion as a personal affront to her. When the Kin
perceived her wrath, and that I too, overcome with passion, wante
to begin speaking, the wise monarch immediately pronounced thes
sober words in his own language: "Benvenuto, I cut short you
speech. Therefore be quiet, and you shall have more treasure
thousand times than you desire." I, being unable to speak, writhe
with violent rage, a reason for her growling more furiously: and th
King departed much sooner than he would have done, saying alouc
in order to encourage me, that he had drawn from Italy the greates
man that was ever born, and one full of so much ability. Havin
left the *Jove* there, and desiring to depart in the morning, I mad
them give me one thousand gold *scudi*: part of it was my salary, an
part for the accounts of what I showed that I had spent of my ow
money. Taking the cash, joyful and content I returned to Pari
and directly I arrived, reveling in my home, after dining I mad
them bring me all my clothing, which consisted of a vast quantit
of silken (articles), of handsomest fur, and likewise of very fin
cloth. From these I made a present to all those workmen of min
allotting them to these same servitors according to their deserts, eve
down to the maid-servants and stable-boys, giving to all of ther
courage to assist me with brave hearts. Having recovered m
strength, with greatest care and attention I set about finishing tha
great statue of *Mars,* which I had contrived of pieces of wood ver
well fitted together (*tessuti*) to form a prop; and over this his fles

was a crust an eighth of a *braccio* thick, made of plaster, and skillfully modeled. Then I next prepared to cast the said figure in many pieces, and afterwards to dovetail (*commetterla . . . a coda di rondine*) them together as the art directs: (an operation) which I did very easily. I do not wish to omit relating a tale (*dare un contra segnio*) regarding this huge work, a thing truly worthy of laughter. I had given orders to all those in my employ (*a chi io davo le spese*) that they should not bring into my house and into my château any prostitute: and I gave close attention to this point that such a thing should not occur. That youth of mine Ascanio was enamored of a very handsome young girl, and she of him: wherefore that said young woman escaped from her mother, and came one night to visit Ascanio. And when she did not want to go away, and he did not know where to hide her, being an ingenious person, as a last resource, he put her inside the figure of the said *Mars,* and arranged a sleeping place in the very head itself. And there she remained some time, and at night he used at times quietly to bring her out. Since I had left that head very nearly complete, and out of a little vainglory on my part I used to leave the said head uncovered, it could be seen by the greater part of the city of Paris: the nearest neighbors had begun climbing upon the roofs, and very much people went on purpose to see it. And since there was a report throughout Paris, that in that château of mine there had dwelt from ancient times a spirit (of which thing I never saw any sign to make me believe that such was the truth), the said spirit was by the common folk of Paris universally called by the name of *Lemmonio Boreo*: and since this young girl who inhabited the said head could not at times prevent a certain small amount of motion being seen through the eyes: at this some of those foolish people asserted that the said spirit had entered into the body of that great figure, and that it caused the eyes to move in the head, and the mouth, as if it wanted to speak.

Many departed terror-stricken, and some clever ones, who came to look and could not disbelieve that flashing of the eyes which the said figure made, also affirmed that there was a spirit there, not knowing that there was (indeed) a spirit there, and sound flesh as well.

MEANWHILE I gave my attention to the putting together of my beautiful doorway with all the (other) objects described below. And since I do not want to trouble to indite in this my Autobiography matters which appertain to those persons who write chronicles, I have therefore omitted the advent of the Emperor with his vast army and the King with all his armed forces (*sforzo*). And at that time he (the King) sought my advice in order to fortify Paris in haste. He came to me to my house on purpose, and conducted me all round the City of Paris: and when he understood that I would with good judgment fortify Paris for him quickly, he gave me express directions that I should immediately carry out whatsoever I had said: and he gave orders to his Admiral that he should command those people to obey me under the pain of his displeasure. The Admiral, who had been appointed to such a post through the favor of Madama di Tampes, and not on account of his own valiant deeds—being a man of but small talent; and bearing the name of Monsignior d'Anguebò, which in our tongue means Monsignior d'Aniballe, in that language of theirs it sounds in such a way that most of those people called him Monsignior *Ass-Ox* (*asino bue*)—this beast having talked it all over with Madama di Tampes she commanded him that he should hastily summon Girolimo Bellarmato. This man was a Sienese engineer, and he was at Diepa, a little more than a day's distance from Paris. He came immediately, and having put in operation a longer method of fortification, I withdrew from that undertaking:

and if the Emperor had pressed forward he would have captured Paris with great ease. It was indeed said that in the agreement made subsequently, Madama di Tampes, who interfered more than any one else, betrayed the King. Nothing further occurs to me to say upon this point, because it is not part of my present object. I set myself with close application to the putting together of my bronze doorway and to finishing that large vase and two other moderate-sized ones made of my own silver. After these troubles the excellent King came to take some rest in Paris.

This accursed woman (Madame d'Estampes) having been born as if for the destruction of the universe, it seemed to me that I might consider myself of some importance, since she reckoned me as her principal foe. (The subject) of my affairs chancing to arise with that good King, she spoke so ill of me that that good man in order to pacify her took an oath that he would never more in this world take any notice of me, as if he had never known me. These words a page of the Cardinal of Ferrara, who was called Villa, came immediately to repeat, and he told me that he himself had heard them from the King's mouth. This circumstance put me into such a rage that, flinging all my tools in different directions, and likewise all my works of art, I got myself in readiness to depart right away, and I immediately went to seek the King. After his dinner I entered a chamber where His Majesty was with a very few attendants; and when he saw me enter, and I had made that due obeisance which is due to a King, he immediately bent his head toward me with a cheerful expression of countenance. Wherefore I regained hope and approaching His Majesty by degrees, for they were exhibiting to him certain objects belonging to my own trade, when we had talked awhile about these said things, His Majesty asked of me if I had any thing beautiful to show him in my house. Then he asked when I would like him to come and see them.

Thereupon I said that I was in readiness to show him something at once if he greatly desired it. He immediately told me to go away home and that he wished to come directly. I went away, in expectation of this excellent King, who went to take leave of Madama di Tampes. Upon her wishing to know whither he was going—for she said that she would keep him company—when the King told her whither he was going, she told His Majesty that she did not wish to go with him; and that she besought him to do her so much kindness as not even himself to go that day. She had to repeat her request more than twice in her desire to dissuade the King from that purpose: but for that day he did not come to my house. The next day after I returned to the King at that same hour: directly he saw me, he swore that he wanted to come immediately to my house. Having gone according to his wont to obtain leave from his Madama di Tampes, when she saw that with all her power she was unable to deter the King, with her biting tongue she set herself to saying as much evil of me as could possibly be said of a man who was the mortal enemy of that worthy Crown (of France). Upon this that excellent King said that he wanted to come to my house merely to scold me after such a fashion as would terrify me. And so he gave his word to Madama di Tampes that he would do. And he came immediately to my house, where I conducted him into certain large lower chambers into which I had put together the whole of that great door of mine. And when the King came to it he remained so stupefied (with astonishment) that he could not find the way to express to me that violent abuse which he had promised Madama di Tampes. Nevertheless upon this occasion he did not want to miss finding an opportunity for uttering that promised abuse, and he began by saying: "It is indeed a very important thing, Benvenuto, that all of you, even though you be talented, ought to know, that you cannot exhibit those great talents by your own efforts: and that you only show yourselves to be great through the medium of the opportunities that you receive from us. Now you ought to be a little more submissive, and not so haughty and headstrong. I remember having ordered expressly that you should fashion for me twelve silver statues: and that was all that I wished for. You wanted to make me a Salt-cellar, and vases and busts and doorways, and so many other things that I am much disappointed, seeing you neglecting all the desires of my heart and attending to the satisfaction of all your own wishes. If then you are thinking of acting in this way, I will presently let you see how I am accustomed to act when I wish people to act in my way. Wherefore I say to you: attend to obeying me in as much as I have told you; for by sticking obstinately to these fancies of your own, you will run your head against the wall." And while he was speaking these words all those lords stood attending to him, observing how he was shaking his head, contracting his eyes and gesticulating, now with one hand, now with the other; in such a way that all those men who were there present trembled with fear on my behalf, though I was resolved to harbor no fear whatsoever. And directly he had finished giving me that scolding which he had promised his Madama di Tampes, I bent one knee to the ground, and kissing the robe upon his knee, I said: "Sacred Majesty! I admit that all that you say is true. My only reply to you is that my heart has been continuously day and night, with my vital energies, intent alone upon obedience and service. And regarding all that which may appear to Your Majesty in contradiction to what I say, may Your Majesty understand that it has not been Benvenuto, but one may say my evil fate or adverse fortune, which has wished to make me unworthy of serving the most wondrous prince that the earth ever possessed. Wherefore I beg you to pardon me. Only it appeared to me that

Your Majesty had given me silver sufficient for but one statue only: and not having any of my own I was unable to fashion more than that one. So of that small amount of silver that was left over from the said figure, I made that vase to demonstrate to Your Majesty the fine taste of the ancients: a thing of such a kind as perhaps Your Majesty has never seen before. As for the Salt-Cellar, it would seem to me, if I remember well, that Your Majesty ordered it of me of your own accord one day; entering (upon the subject) in connection with one (a salt-cellar) that had been brought to your notice. Wherefore having shown you a model that I had already made in Italy, at your own suggestion alone you directed one thousand gold ducats to be given to me immediately in order that I might make it, telling me that you were much obliged to me for such an idea: and it seemed to me that you thanked me very specially when I handed it over to you completed. As regards the doorway it seemed to me that, discussing it by chance, Your Majesty gave the commission to Monsignor di Villurois, your First Secretary, who commissioned Monsignor di Marmagnia and Monsignor dell' Apà that they should keep me at such a work and provide me with supplies: and without these directions I should never have been able on my own account to carry out such great undertakings. As for the bronze busts and (the decorations on the base (*le base*)) of the *Jove*, and the rest, the busts in truth I made of my own accord in order to make experiments with these French clays, of which I as a foreigner knew nothing at all: and without making trial of the said clays I should never have attempted to cast such large works of art as these. As for the base-(decorations) I made them, because it seemed to me that such a thing was most excellently suitable to accompany such figures as those: nevertheless all that I have done or thought most of doing is never to separate myself from the will of Your Majesty. It is certainly true that I have completed that great Colossus up to the point which it has now reached, by the expenditure of my own funds; thinking only that since you are so great a king and I so insignificant an artist, I ought to create for your glory and my own a statue such as the ancients never had. Having realized now that it does not please God to make me worthy of so honorable a service, I beseech you that instead of that honorable reward that Your Majesty intended for my works, you will merely grant me a little of your good favor, and with it kindly permission (to depart); for at this juncture, if you make me worthy of such favors, I will depart, and returning to Italy, continually thank God and Your Majesty for those happy hours that I have passed in your service." He seized me with his own hands and with great kindness raised me from my knees: then he told me that I must be content to serve him; and that everything that I had done was excellent, and that he was very grateful. And turning to those lords, he uttered these exact words: "I certainly believe that if Paradise had gates, it would never have a finer one than this." When I saw that he had paused a little in the ardor of these words, which were all in my favor, with a very profound reverence I thanked him again, repeating, however, my desire for my permit; for my irritation had not yet passed away. When that great King perceived that I had not given that value to those unaccustomed and great courtesies of his that they deserved, he ordered me in a loud and fearsome voice not to say another word, for it would be woe to me; and then he added that he would drown me in gold, and that he would give me the permit, for, beyond the works of art commissioned to me by His Majesty, with all that I had done in the meantime upon my own account he was most satisfied, and that I must never more have any differences with him, for he understood me: and that I must also endeavor to understand His Majesty as my duty directed. I said that I thanked

God and His Majesty for everything. Then I begged him to come
and see the huge figure, how I had progressed with it: so he
came along with me. I caused it to be uncovered: the which
object caused him as much astonishment as one could ever have
imagined: and he immediately commissioned one of his Secretaries
presently to pay me back all the money of my own that I had
expended; and let the sum be what it would, it sufficed that I
should give him the account under my own hand. Then he departed and said: "Good-bye, *mon ami*": a fine expression such as
is not usual in a king. When he returned to his palace, he chanced
to recall the fine words so wondrously humble and so haughtily
proud that I had employed to His Majesty, words which caused
him much irritation, and he recounted some of the details of those
expressions in the presence of Madama di Tampes, where was
Monsignor di Sanpolo, an influential French Baron. This latter
had in the past made a very great profession of being a friend of
mine: and certainly he showed it at this time very brilliantly, "after
the French fashion." For after much discussion, the King lamented
that the Cardinal of Ferrara, to whom he had given me in charge,
had never thought any more about my affairs, and that it was no
thanks to him (*non era manchato per causa sua*) that I had not
gone right away from his kingdom: and that he should in fact
think about putting me into the charge of some person who would
understand me (*i.e.,* my value) better than the Cardinal of Ferrara
had done, for he did not wish to give me any more occasion of
losing me. At these words Monsignior di Sanpolo immediately
offered himself, telling the King that he should put me into his
charge, and that he would take good care that I should never more
have cause to depart from his kingdom. At this the King said that
he would be very pleased if San Polo would tell him the means
that he proposed to employ so that I should not depart. Madama,

who was present, was much displeased, and Sanpolo stood on his dignity (*stava in su l'onorevole*), not wishing to tell the King the method that he wanted to employ. When the King asked him again, he, to please Madama di Tampes, said: "I would hang him by the neck, this Benvenuto of yours: and in this way you would not lose him from your kingdom." Madama di Tampes immediately raised a loud laugh, saying that I well deserved it. At this the King for good-fellowship's sake joined in the laugh, and said that he was very willing for Sanpolo to hang me, if he would first find another man equal to me; for although I had never deserved such a fate, he gave him full permission. After this said fashion the day ended, and I remained sound and safe: for which may God be praised and thanked. The King had at this period settled the war with the Emperor, but not with the English (*inghilesi*), so that these devils kept us in much tribulation. The King, having something other than pleasures to occupy his head, had commissioned Piero Strozi that he should command certain galleys in those English waters: the which matter was very great and difficult of accomplishment even for that wondrous soldier, unique in his own times in such a profession, and as unique in ill-fortune. Several months had passed, during which I had received neither money nor any orders for work: so that I sent away all my workmen except those two Italians whom I directed to make two large vases of my own silver, because they did not know how to work in bronze. When I had completed the two vases I went with them to a city which belonged to the Queen of Navarre: this place is called Argentana, and is many days distant from Paris. I arrived at the said place, and found the King, who was unwell. The Cardinal of Ferrara told His Majesty that I had arrived in that place. At this the King answered nothing: which was the reason why I had to remain for many days in discomfort (*a dis-*

agio). And in truth I never suffered greater annoyance. However, at the end of several days I presented myself one evening, and placed before his (the King's) eyes those two fine vases: and they pleased him excessively. When I saw the King in a very good humor, I begged His Majesty that he would be pleased to grant me so much favor that I might walk off (*andare aspasso*) as far as Italy, and that I would forgo seven months of salary for which I was creditor: the which money His Majesty would deign to have paid to me afterwards, so that it might serve me for my return journey. I besought His Majesty to grant me this particular favor, because it was in truth then a time for fighting and not for statue making. Besides, since His Majesty had granted a similar thing to his painter Bolognia, I therefore most devoutly besought him that he would be pleased to make me also worthy of it. The King, while I uttered these words, regarded with very close attention those two vases, and from time to time pierced me with a terrible look: I, however, to the best of my power and knowledge besought him that he would grant me this particular favor. All of a sudden I saw that he was in a violent rage, and, rising from his seat, he said to me in the Italian language: "Benvenuto, you are a great fool. Carry those vases to Paris, for I want them gilded:" and giving me no other answer, he departed. I approached the Cardinal of Ferrara, who was present and I begged him that, since he had done me so great a kindness as to free me from the prison of Rome, together with so many other benefits besides, he would also oblige me in this matter that I might go as far as Italy. The said Cardinal told me that he would very willingly do all that he could to give me that satisfaction, and that I might freely leave the charge of it to him; and also, if I wished I might go freely, for he would arrange it very well on my behalf with the King. I told the said Cardinal that since I knew that His Majesty had given me into the charge of His Most Reverend Lordship, if he gave me permission I would gladly depart, to return upon the slightest hint from His Most Reverend Lordship. Thereupon the Cardinal told me to go to Paris, and stop there eight days, and that during this period he would obtain the favor from the King that I might go: and in case the King were not willing that I should depart, without any fail he would inform me. Wherefore if he did not write to me to the contrary, it would be a sign that I might freely go.

Chapter Eight   *1545*

G OING to Paris, as the Cardinal had told me (to do), I made
some admirable packing cases for those three silver vases.
When twenty days had passed by I got myself in readiness, and I
put the three vases in the pack of a mule which the Bishop of Pavia,
who was lodging again in my château, had lent me as far as Lyons.
In an evil hour I departed in company with the Lord Ipolito Gonzaga (which lord was in the King's pay, and entertained by Count
Galeotto della Mirandola), and with certain other noblemen in the
service of the said Count. There accompanied us besides Lionardo
Tedaldi, our Florentine (fellow-citizen). I left Ascanio and Paolo
in charge of my château, and of all my belongings, among which
were certain small vases that had been begun, which I left behind so
that those two youths might not be at a standstill. There was besides much household furniture of great value, for I was very handsomely lodged: the value of these said properties of mine was more
than fifteen hundred *scudi*. I told Ascanio that he must remember
how many great benefits he had received from me, and that up to

that time he had been a lad of but small judgment: and that it was now time for him to have the judgment of a man; wherefore I wished to leave him in charge of all my belongings, along with the whole of my credit; and that if he should hear one thing more than another from those beasts of Frenchmen he was immediately to let me know, for I would take post and fly (back) from wherever I was, whether on account of the great obligation that I was under to that excellent King or for the sake of my own credit. The said Ascanio with feigned and thievish tears said to me: "I have never known any other better father than you, and all that a good son ought to do towards his own good father I will always do towards you." Having agreed thus I departed with one servant and with a little French urchin. When midday had passed there came to my château certain of those treasurers, who were by no means my friends. This scoundrelly crew immediately said that I had gone off with the King's money, and they told Messer Guido and the Bishop of Pavia to send quickly for the King's vases, lest they themselves should send after me for them with great annoyance to myself. The Bishop and Messer Guido felt much more fear than the matter warranted, and hastily sent after me by the post that traitor of an Ascanio, who appeared (before me) at midnight. And I,—for I could not sleep,—was condoling with myself saying: "To whom have I left my belongings, my château? Oh! what destiny is this of mine, that forces me to take this journey? For the Cardinal may be in league with Madama di Tampes, who desires no other thing in the world except that I should forfeit the favor of that good King." While I was holding this discussion with myself, I heard myself called by Ascanio; and at once I rose from my bed, and demanded from him whether he brought me good or bad news. The thief said: "I bring good news. Merely that you must send back the three vases; for those scoundrels of treasurers are crying out, 'Stop Thief' (*achor-*

ruomo), in such fashion that the Bishop and Messer Guido say that anyhow you must send them back. And for the rest give yourself no further annoyance, and go and enjoy this journey happily."

I gave up the vases immediately, although two of them were my own, together with the silver and everything else. I was conveying them to the Cardinal of Ferrara's abbey in Lyons: for although they spread a report about me that I wanted to take them into Italy, it was well known to everyone that one could not remove either money, or gold or silver, without full permission. They ought indeed to have considered whether I were able to take out those three great vases, which with their cases loaded one entire mule. It is very true that because those objects were very handsome and of great value, and I was afraid of the King's death, (for I certainly left him very unwell), I said to myself: "If such an event (as his death) were to happen, if I had them in the hands of the Cardinal, I should not lose them." Now, to settle the matter (*in conchlusione*), I sent back the said mule with the vases and the other things of value, and with the said company I set forward the following morning upon my way; nor ever throughout the whole journey could I refrain from sighing and weeping. Sometimes however I comforted myself by addressing God, saying: "Oh Lord God! Thou knowest the truth. Thou knowest that this journey of mine is solely to carry alms to six poor wretched little maidens and to their mother, my very own sister; for although these (girls) have their father, he is very old, and his trade brings him in nothing, so that they might easily turn to evil courses: wherefore in doing this pious work, I hope for aid and counsel from Your Divine Majesty." This was as much recreation as I took while journeying forward. When we were one day's journey from Lyons, it was nearly twenty-two of the clock, when the heaven commenced to emit certain sharp claps of thunder (*tuoni*), but the air was very

clear. I was a bolt's distance in front of my companions. After t
thunder the heaven emitted a noise so loud and so terrifying that
reckoned to myself that it was the Day of Judgment. And as
stopped for a moment there began to fall a shower of hail without
drop of water. This (hail) was larger that the pellets of a blo
pipe, and when it struck me, it hurt me very much. And little
little this hail began to grow bigger in such fashion that it was li
the bullets of a crossbow. Observing that my horse was very ter
fied, I turned back at a tremendous gallop (*con grandissima furia
corso*) until I rejoined my companions, who on account of the sar
terror had halted within a pinewood. The hailstones increased
the size of large lemons. I intoned a *Miserere*: and while I w
communing thus devoutly with God, there came one of those ha
stones so large that it broke in pieces a very thick branch of th
pine whereunder I had fancied myself to be safe. Another mass
those hailstones struck my horse upon the head, which show
signs of falling to the earth; one struck me also, but not with fu
force, for it would have killed me. Likewise one struck that po
old fellow Lionardo Tedaldi in such fashion that, since he was li
me upon his knees, it made him set his hands upon the ground (*i.
go upon all fours). Then I, when I saw that that branch could :
longer protect me, and that along with my *Misereres* it was needf
that I should take some action, began to fold my garments arou
my head: and so I said to Lionardo, who was crying out for he
(*acquoruomo*) "Jesu, Jesu," that He would help him if he help
himself. I had a great deal more trouble to save this man than m
self. This business lasted a while, then it ceased, and we, who were
pounded, as best we could remounted our horses: and while we we
in the direction of our lodging, showing to each other our scratch
and bruises, we found, a mile further on, so much greater a destru
tion than ours as it seems impossible to describe. All the trees we

stripped and broken, while as many animals as happened to be there were dead: and many shepherds were also dead. We saw a vast quantity of those hailstones which could not be contained in two hands. It seemed to us that we had had a lucky escape (*havere un buon mercato*), and we knew then that our appeal to God and those *Misereres* of ours had served us more than we could have been able to do for ourselves. Thus thanking God we journeyed on to Lyons the next day after, and there we remained for eight days. When eight days had passed, being well refreshed we continued our journey, and passed the mountains very comfortably. I bought there a little pony, because certain of our small baggage had somewhat fatigued my horses. After we had been one day in Italy, Conte Galeotto della Mirandola joined us, who was traveling along by post, and while he was stopping with us, he told me that I had made a mistake in taking my departure, and that I ought not to proceed further, for by returning at once my affairs would prosper better than ever but if I went on I would make room for my enemies and an opportunity of doing me harm; whereas if I returned immediately I should stop the way of that which they had planned against me: and that those in whom I had most faith were just those who were deceiving me. He would not tell me anything else but that he knew this very surely: and that the Cardinal of Ferrara had entered into an agreement with those two scoundrels of mine whom I had left in charge of all my property. The said count (*contino*) repeated to me many times that I ought to return at all costs. Mounting into the post-wagon he proceeded on his way, and I, on account of the above-mentioned traveling companions, resolved also to move forward. I endured a struggle in my heart: now to arrive as quickly as possible in Florence, and now to return to France; I was in such great personal distress, irresolute in this way, that finally I resolved that I would

mount the post-wagon to reach Florence quickly. I had made
no agreement with the first post (that started); for this reason I
was strengthened in my fixed determination of coming to face my
difficulties in Florence.. Having left the company of the Lord
Ipolito Gonzaga,—who took the road to go to Mirandola, and I
that to Parma and Piacenza,—when I reached Piacenza I met in one
of the streets the Duke Pier Luigi, who scrutinized me closely and
recognized me. And to me, who knew that of all the evil which
I had endured in Castel Santagniolo in Rome he had been the
whole cause, it gave me great rage to see him: but, not knowing
any help for escaping out of his hands, I determined to go and
visit him. And I arrived just as they had removed his dinner, and
there were with him those members of the House of Landi, who
were afterwards the men who slew him. When I reached the
presence of His Excellency, the man showed me the most unbounded civilities that one could ever possibly imagine. And amid
those same civilities fell himself upon the subject, saying to those
who were present, that I was the first man in the world in my
own trade, and that I had been a great while in prison in Rome.
And turning to me he said: "Benvenuto mine. That suffering
which you endured grieved me very much: and I knew that you
were innocent, but I could not help you otherwise, because my
father imprisoned you to satisfy certain enemies of yours, who had
besides given him to understand that you had spoken ill of him
(*sparlato di lui*): a thing which I know for very certain was never
true; and it grieved me very much on your account." And to
these words he added so many other similar ones that it seemed as
if he demanded pardon of me. Next he asked me about all the
works of art that I had executed for the most Christian King:
and while I described them to him, he listened attentively, giving
me the most kindly hearing that could possibly be imagined. Then

he enquired of me if I would like to serve him: to this I replied
that I could not do so with honor to myself: that if I had left
complete those many great works which I had commenced for
the great King, I would have deserted every other great Lord solely
to serve His Excellency. Now here may be recognized how the
Great Power of God never leaves unpunished any sort of man
who commits wrongs and injustices towards the innocent. This
man as much as demanded pardon of me in the presence of those
men who, a short time later, executed vengeance upon him for me
as well as for those many other persons who had been injured by
him: therefore no lord, be he ever so great, should scoff at the
Justice of God, as do some of those whom I know, who have injured me so cruelly, whereof I shall speak in their own place.
And I do not write of these affairs of mine out of worldly arrogance;
but solely to give thanks to God, who has brought me out of so
many great trials. Besides of those (trials) that present themselves
before me day by day, in all of them I appeal to Him and claim
Him as my very own Defender, and I commend myself to Him.
And ever, besides the fact that I aid myself as much as I am able,
when afterwards I lose courage at the point to which my feeble
strength cannot reach, that great Might of God is immediately
made manifest to me: which descends unexpectedly upon those
who do wrong to others and upon those who pay but slight attention to the great and honorable position which God has conferred
upon them. I returned to my inn, and I found that the above-
mentioned Duke had sent me most abundantly very splendid gifts
both for to eat and to drink: I derived good courage from my meal.
Then, mounting my horse, I came on towards Florence, where,
when I arrived I found my own sister with six young daughters,
one of whom was of marriageable age and one still at nurse.
I found her husband, who, from various chances in the city, was

working no more at his trade. I had forwarded more than a y
previously precious stones and French goldsmiths' work to
value of more than two thousand ducats, and I had brought w
me to the value of about one thousand *scudi*. I found that althou
I gave them regularly four gold *scudi* per month, they also conti
ally received great sums from those gold objects of mine, wh
they sold day by day. That brother-in-law of mine was such
honest man, that, for fear lest I should have reason to be an
with him,—since the money that I sent for their allowance, gi
them out of charity, had proved insufficient,—had pawned alm
everything that he had in the world, letting himself be eaten
by interest, merely in order not to touch those sums which l
been entrusted to him. From this I realized that he was a v
honest man, and my desire increased to offer him a larger al
and before I departed from Florence, I wanted to make arran
ments for all his daughters. Our Duke of Florence at this ti
(for we were in the month of August in (the year) 1545) be
at Poggio a Caiano, a spot ten miles distant from Florence, I w
to seek him there, merely to pay my duty, since I also was a Fl
entine citizen, and because my ancestors had been great friends
the House of Medici, and because I more than any of them lo
this Duke Cosimo. As I say I went to the said Poggio, merely
pay my respects, and never with any intention of stopping w
him, as it pleased God, Who does all things well: when the s
Duke seeing me, thereupon showed me the most unlimited ci
ities, and he and the Duchess asked of me concerning the wo
of art that I had executed for the King: whereupon I willingly a
in full detail described them. When he had heard me out,
said that he had understood as much, and that such was the fa
and he added afterwards in a tone of sympathy, and said: "C
How small a reward for so many fine and splendid efforts! B

venuto mine! If you are willing to make something for me, I will pay you after a very different fashion than that King of yours has done, whom out of your good nature you praise so much." To these remarks I added the great obligations that I was under to His Majesty, for, having withdrawn me from so unjust an imprisonment, he had afterwards given me the opportunity of executing more wonderful work than any other craftsman of my standing who had ever been born. While I spake thus my Duke twisted himself about, and seemed as if he could not stop to listen to me. Then when I had finished he said to me: "If you are willing to make something for me, I will show you such favors that you will perchance remain in astonishment, provided that your work pleases me: of that I have no doubt." I, poor unlucky creature, anxious to demonstrate in this wondrous School (of Florence), that since I had been away from it I had labored in another branch of it than that which the said School held in esteem, answered to my Duke that willingly, either in marble or in bronze, I would make a large statue for that fine Piazza of his. To this he replied that he would like from me for a first work merely a *Perseus*: this was what for some time past he had greatly longed; and he begged me to make a small model of it. I gladly set myself to make the said model, and in a few weeks I had completed it of the height of about a *braccio*: it was of yellow wax, very suitably finished; it was excellently executed with very great care and skill. The Duke came to Florence, and before I was able to show him this said model several days passed by, when it seemed exactly as if he had never seen nor known me, in such fashion that I formed a bad omen in regard to my relations with His Excellency. Later, however, one day after dinner, when I had conveyed it (the model) into his Wardrobe chamber, he came to inspect it, together with the Duchess and a few other lords. Directly he saw it, it pleased

him, and he praised it extravagantly; whereby he inspired me with
a little hope that he might really understand it to some extent.
After he had gazed at it for some time, his pleasure greatly increasing, he spake these words: "If you, Benvenuto mine! carry out thus
upon a large scale this little model, it will be the most beautiful
work in the Piazza." Thereupon I said: "My most excellent lord!
There are in the Piazza works by the great Donatello and the wondrous Michelagniolo, who were two of the greatest men from
ancient times until now. Nevertheless Your Most Illustrious Excellency inspires a great spirit to my model, wherefor I have sufficient courage to make the (completed) work more than three
times finer than the model." At this there arose no small debate,
because the Duke kept saying continually that he understood (the
matter) very well, and that he knew exactly what could be done.
Upon this I said that my works would decide that question and his
doubts; and that most certainly I would fulfil for His Excellency
much more than I was promising him; but that he must, however, provide me with the conveniences whereby I could carry out
such a matter, for without those conveniences I could not complete
the great undertaking that I was promising him. To this His Excellency replied that I must make a Petition for the amount that
I was asking for, and I must include in it all that I needed, for he
would give most ample orders to that effect. Certainly if I had
been clever enough to secure by contract all that I had need of
for these works of mine, I should not have had such great troubles
as came upon me through my own fault: for he showed the greatest willingness in his desire to carry out the works and to give
proper orders with regard to them. I, however, not realizing that
this lord had a great desire to carry out very important undertakings, went to work most liberally with His Excellency as a Duke
and not as a merchant. I presented the Petitions, to which His

Excellency responded most liberally. Wherein I said: "Most rare (*singularissimo*) patron of mine! My real petitions and our real contracts do not depend upon these words, nor upon these writings, but they depend altogether upon how I succeed in the work that I have undertaken: and if it succeeds then I reckon that Your Most Illustrious Excellency will very clearly remember how much he has promised me." His Excellency, charmed by these words and by my manner and speech, both he and the Duchess, showed me the most unlimited favors that could possibly be imagined. Having the greatest desire to begin working, I told His Excellency that I had need of a house, of such a kind as would enable me to accommodate myself in it together with my furnaces, both for the manufacture of works in clay and in bronze, and besides, separately, in gold and in silver: for I was aware that he knew how well adapted I was to serve him in such branches of my profession as these: and I had need of chambers suitable to enable me to carry out such things. And in order that His Excellency might see how great was my desire to serve him, I had already found the house which was to my purpose, and it was in a locality that pleased me very much. And since I did not want to impose upon His Excellency as regarded money or anything else before he had seen my work, I had brought with me from France two jewels, with which I begged His Excellency that I might purchase the said house, and that he would keep them until such time as I might with my own work and my own labors earn it for myself. The said jewels were very finely executed by the hands of my own workmen, after my own designs. When he had examined them sufficiently, he spake to me these inspiring words, which endued me with false hopes: "Take, Benvenuto! your jewels, for I want you and not them, and you can have your house free." After this he made me out a Deed (*reschritto*) in accordance with my petition, which I have always preserved. The said Deed ran as follows: "Let the said house l examined, and who it is who sells it and the price that he asks fe it; for we wish to please Benvenuto." It seemed to me that l this Deed I was sure of the house: for I promised myself assured that my work would be much more satisfactory than that whic I had undertaken. After this His Excellency had given expre commission to a certain major-domo of his, who was called S^r Pi Fran^{co} Riccio. He was from Prato, and had been tutor to the sa Duke. I spoke with this animal, and told him all the things which I had need: how that where there was a kitchen-garde (*orto*) attached to the said house I wanted to erect a worksho This man immediately gave the commission to a certain lean an thin agent (*pagatore*) who was called Lattanzio Gorini. This litt wisp of a man (*homiciattolo*) with his small spidery hands and tiny mosquito-voice, as rapidly as a snail (*presto come una lum cuza*), in an evil hour, indeed, had brought for me to the hous stones, sand and lime, as much as would have served with difficul to build a pigeon cote. When I saw matters beginning to procee with such inauspicious coldness (*tanto malamente fredde*) I beg; to be dismayed, or rather I kept saying to myself: "Little beginnin, sometimes have great endings," but I also gave myself some sm; amount of hope at the sight of the many thousands of ducats th the Duke had thrown away over certain ugly monstrosities (*ope accie*) in sculpture executed by the hand of that beastly Buacc Bandinello. Recovering therefore my own courage, I kept stirrir up that Lattanzio Gurini to make him move along: I kept grur bling at a number of lame asses and a blind youth who direct them; and under these difficulties (eventually by employing my ow money), I marked out the site of the workshop and razed the tre and vines. Nevertheless, according to my custom, I boldly, with son small amount of impetuosity, proceeded with my business. C the other hand I was in the hands of Tasso the joiner, who was most friendly to me, and I directed him to make certain wooden frameworks for the commencement of the large *Perseus*. This Tasso was a most excellent clever man; I believe the greatest that there ever was in his profession. Moreover he was pleasant and gay, and every time that I went to see him, he met me laughing with a little song in falsetto (*con un canzoncino in quilio*); and since I was already more than half desperate—for I was beginning to hear that matters were going badly in France, and I foresaw little good from these affairs (in Florence) on account of their life-lessness—he compelled me to listen always to at least half of that song of his. In the end, however, I used to cheer up somewhat in his company, forcing myself to forget (*smarrire*) the best I could, some (*quattro*) of those desperate thoughts of mine. Having given orders with regard to all the above-mentioned matters, and having begun to proceed to prepare more quickly for this above-mentioned undertaking, part of the lime was already exhausted, when I was suddenly summoned by the above-mentioned major-domo: and on going to him I found him, after His Excellency's dinner, in the Hall called (the Hall) of the Clock; and when I went up to him— I showing him the utmost courtesy, and he towards me the great-est haughtiness (*rigidità*)—he asked me who it was that had put me into that house, and with what authority I had begun to build inside it: and he (said) that he marveled much at me that I had been so presumptuously bold. To this I replied that His Excel-lency had put me into that house, and that His Lordship in His Excellency's name had given the commission to Lattanzio Gurini: and that the said Lattanzio had brought stone, sand, lime, and had given orders regarding the things that I had asked of him, and for which he (*di tanto*) kept telling me that he had had directions from His Lordship. When I had said these words that said beast turned upon me with greater sharpness than before, and told me that neither I nor any one of those to whom I referred was speaking the truth. Thereupon I roused up and said to him: "Oh! Major-domo! As long as Your Lordship speaks in accordance with that most noble position with which you are endued, I will respect it, and will address you with that submission that I employ towards the Duke: but when you do otherwise I shall address you as Ser Pier Franco Riccio." This man flew into such a rage that I thought that he would go mad there and then, in advance of the time which the celestial Powers (*i cieli*) had determined upon; and he told me, together with certain insulting expressions, that he wondered much that he had deigned to let me address him as one of his equals. At these words I was moved (to wrath) and said: "Now, listen to me, Sr Pier Fran^{co} Riccio, for I will tell you who are my equals, and who are yours: masters to teach children to read." When I uttered these words the man with countenance distorted (with rage) raised his voice, repeating more furiously those same expressions. At which I, still looking daggers (*acconciomi con'l viso de l'arme*) at him, assumed towards him a little presumption, and said that my equals were worthy to address Popes and Emperors and a great King; and that of persons equal to me there was perhaps but one in the (whole) world, but of those equal to him there were ten upon every doorstep. When he heard these words he mounted upon a little window-seat (*un muricciuolo di finestra*), which is up in that Hall. Then he told me to repeat another time the words which I had spoken: the which I repeated more boldly than I had (done before), and I said besides that I did not care to serve the Duke any more, and that I would return to France, whither I could freely go back. The beast remained stupefied, and the color of clay; and I boiling with rage (*arrovellato*) departed with the intention of going right away. Would to God that I had carried out (my intention)! His Excellency the

Duke cannot thus have known of this diabolical occurrence at first, for I remained some few days having dismissed all thoughts of Florence, except as regards my sister and my nieces, for whom I went about making arrangements: for with that small (sum of) money that I had brought with me I wanted to leave the best arrangements that I could; and then I wanted to return to France as quickly as possible, since I never wanted to see Italy again. Being resolved to hasten by the most rapid means that I could, and to go without the leave of the Duke or anyone else, one morning that above-mentioned major-domo of his own accord summoned me most humbly, and commenced a certain pedantic oration of his, in the which I could perceive neither method, nor grace, nor wit, nor beginning, nor ending: I only understood that he told me that he made profession of being a good Christian, and that he did not want to cherish hatred against any one, and he asked me on behalf of the Duke what salary I wanted for my support. At this I stood thoughtful for a while, and did not answer, with the full intention of being unwilling to stop. When he saw that I remained without speaking, he had sufficient cleverness to say: "Oh! Benvenuto! One answers Dukes: and what I am saying to you is on behalf of His Excellency." Thereupon I said that since he spoke to me on behalf of His Excellency, I would very willingly answer: and I told him to tell His Excellency that I was not willing to be second to anyone of those of my profession who were in his employ. The major-domo said: "To Bandinello he gives two hundred *scudi* for his support; therefore, if you are content with this, your salary is agreed upon." I answered that I was content, and that whatsoever I merited further should be given after my work had been seen, and the whole submitted to the good taste of His Most Illustrious Excellency. Thus, against my will I picked up again the thread and set myself to work, the Duke showing me continually the most boundless favors that it is possible to imagine in the world.

I HAD very frequently received letters from France from ⅎ
most faithful friend of mine Messer Guido Guidi: these let
up to now had told me nothing but what was good: that Asca
of mine also sent me advices telling me to see to giving my
a good time, that if anything occurred he would have me inforn
of it. It was reported to the King that I had set myself to w
for the Duke of Florence: but since this man was the best (man)
the world, he said many times: "Why does not Benvenuto retur
And when he specially asked those young men of mine tl
both replied that I had written to them that I was doing so v
and that they thought that I had no more desire to return
serve His Majesty. The King broke into a rage, and on hear
these hasty words (which never came from me myself) he sa
"Since he left us without any cause whatsoever, I will never
him (to come back) again. Therefore let him stay where he
These thievish scoundrels were leading the matters up to that pc
which they desired: for whenever I should return to France tl
would become workmen again under me as they were at fil
so that if I did not return they would remain free and my s
stitutes: wherefore they exerted all their powers so that I sho
not return. While I was making them build the workshop wher
I was to commence the *Perseus,* I labored in a ground floor cha
ber; in the which I fashioned the *Perseus* in plaster, of the size tha
was to be, with the idea of casting it from that plaster one. Wł
I saw that by executing it in this fashion it would take me a lit

long, I chose another expedient, for there was already set up, brick upon brick, a small portion of a workshed, made so miserably that it pains me too much to recall it. I began the figure of *Medusa*, and I made a framework (*ossatura*) of iron. Then I began to make it of clay, and when I had fashioned it in clay, I baked it. I was alone with certain work-lads, among whom there was one very handsome (boy): he was the son of a prostitute named Gambetta. This lad served me to sketch from, for we have no other books which teach us art except nature (*i.e.* the human body). I sought to engage workmen in order to hasten quickly this work of mine and I could not find any, and by myself alone I could not carry out anything. There were indeed some in Florence who would willingly have come to me, but Bandinello immediately hindered me so that they should not come; and while causing me to delay thus for a while, he kept telling the Duke that I was going about hunting after his workmen, because it was impossible for me by myself to know how to put together a large figure. I complained to the Duke of the great annoyance that this beast was giving me, and begged that he would enable me to have some of those workmen from the Opera (*del Duomo*). These requests of mine were the reason for making the Duke believe what Bandinello kept telling him. Perceiving this I disposed myself to do by myself as much as I could. And while I set myself to it with the most extreme exertions that one can possibly imagine, and in this way I was laboring night and day, the husband of my sister fell ill, and in a few days he died. He left my sister still young with six daughters between little and big. This was the first great trial that I experienced in Florence: to remain father and guide in such a disaster. Being anxious that nothing should go wrong, my kitchen-garden (*orto*) being filled up (*carico*) with much rubbish, I called in two laborers, who were brought by me from the Ponte Vechio:

of these, one was an old man of sixty years, the other a young one of eighteen. When I had kept them about three days the young man told me that the old man did not want to work, and that I should do better to send him away, for, not only did he not want to work himself, but he hindered the young man from working: and he told me that what little there was to do, he could do by himself, without throwing away money upon other people. This (youth) bore the name of Bernardino Manellini of Mugello. When I saw that he labored so willingly, I asked him if he would like to make an arrangement with me as servant. At once we came to an agreement. This young man looked after my horse for me, worked in my kitchen-garden, and afterwards endeavored to assist me in my workshop, so that little by little he began to learn the Art with so much goodwill (*gentileza*) that I never had a better assistant than he. And resolving to carry out everything with the help of this man, I began to demonstrate to the Duke that Bandinello was telling lies, and that I should do very well without Bandinello's workmen. At this period there came upon me a slight malady of the kidneys; and since I was not able to work, I gladly stayed in the Duke's Wardrobe in company with certain young goldsmiths, who were named Gianpagolo and Domenico Poggini, whom I caused to make a little vase of gold, all worked in low relief with figures and other fine ornaments. This was for the Duchess, the which His Excellency had made for her to drink water out of. She further requested me to make her a golden girdle: and this work also most richly, with precious stones and with many pleasing devices of small masks and other things I made for her. The Duke came every now and then into this Wardrobe, and took very great pleasure in seeing us work, and in chatting with me myself. When I began to get better in my kidneys, I had some clay brought to me, and while the Duke stood there to pass the time, I took his portrait, making a head much larger than life. In this work His Excellency took very great pleasure, and conferred upon me so much affection, that he told me that it would give him very great pleasure if I could be accommodated to work in the Palace, looking out for myself in the self-same Palace chambers large enough the which I might fit up with furnaces and with whatsoever I might have need of: for he took very great pleasure in such matters. To this I replied to His Excellency that it was not possible, for I would not have finished my works in a hundred years. The Duchess showed me boundless favors, and wanted me to attend to working for her, and not to care about either *Perseus* or anything else. I, when I saw these empty favors, knew for certain that my perverse and biting fortune could not cease causing me some fresh disaster, although there continually came to my mind the great injury that I had done myself while seeking to do myself so great a good: I speak with reference to the affairs of France. The King could not swallow that great annoyance that he experienced at my departure, and would have liked me to have returned, though with the saving of his own credit (*con ispresso suo honore*): but it seemed to me that I had very many excellent reasons, and I did not want to submit, because I thought that if I were to submit to writing humbly, those men would after their French fashion have said that I had been an evil doer (*peccatore*), and that certain faults that had been wrongfully laid to my charge were the truth. For this reason I stood upon my honor, and as a man in the right, I wrote with haughtiness; which gave the greatest satisfaction that they could have to those two traitorous pupils of mine. For I boasted in writing to them of the great courtesies that were shown to me in my own country by a lord and by a lady, absolute masters of the City of Florence, my native place. When they had received one of these sorts of letters, they went to the King, and constrained I Majesty to make over to them my château, in the same way that had given it to me. The King, who was a good and admira person, never wished to consent to the hardy demands of these gr thieves, for he began to perceive at what they were malignan aiming: and in order to give them a little expectation and me occasion of returning immediately, he caused me to be written somewhat wrathfully by one of his treasurers, who was call Messer Giuliano Buonaccorsi, a Florentine citizen. The letter c tained the following (statement): "that if I wanted to uphold th name of honest man that I had borne (hitherto), since I had parted without any reason, I was truly bound to render an accou of all that I had administered and done for His Majesty." Whe received this letter it gave me so much pleasure, that even had asked with my own tongue (*che a chiedere a lingua*) I should ha asked neither more nor less. Setting myself to write, I filled ni sheets of ordinary paper; and in them I set out distinctly all t works that I had accomplished, and all the chances that had befall me in (connection with) them, and all the amount of money th had been expended over the said works, which had all been giv to me under the hand of two notaries and of one of his treasure and countersigned by all those individual persons who had receiv them, which had been given to some for their materials and others for their labor; and how out of that same money I had put one single *quattrino* into my own purse, and that for my co pleted works I had not received anything at all. I had only broug away to Italy with me certain favors and most royal promises, tru worthy of His Majesty. And although I could not boast of havi derived any other (reward) for my work except certain salar ordered by His Majesty for my maintenance; and of those the still remained due to me more than seven hundred gold *scu* which I left behind on purpose, for they were to be sent to me for my comfort on my return journey (*per il mio buon ritorno*). Nevertheless, since I was aware that some malignant persons out of very envy had done me some bad turn, the truth will always come uppermost. I glory in His Most Christian Majesty, and avarice moves me not. Although I know that I have performed for His Majesty much more than that which he offered to me to do: and although the recompense promised to me has not followed, I care for nothing else in the world except to remain in His Majesty's opinion an honest and upright man, such as I always was. And if His Majesty should have any doubt upon this point, at the slightest signal I will come flying to render an account of myself with my very life: but, perceiving that I am held in so little account, I have not wished to return to offer myself, knowing that there will always be sufficient bread to spare for me wheresoever I go: but when I am summoned I will immediately respond. There were in the said letter many other details worthy of that wondrous King and for the saving of my credit. I carried this letter, before I sent it, to my Duke, who experienced much pleasure in seeing it: afterwards I immediately sent it into France, directed to the Cardinal of Ferrara. At this period, Bernardone Baldini, agent in precious stones to His Excellency had brought from Venice a large diamond of more than thirty-five carats in weight. Antonio di Vittorio Landi was also interested with him in inducing the Duke to buy it. This diamond had been already (cut) to a point, but since it did not yield that lustrous clearness which should be desired from such a precious stone the owners of that same diamond had razed off this said point, which truly made it of no value either flat or pointed (*né per tavola né per punta*). Our Duke who greatly delighted in precious stones, though he did not understand them, however, gave sure hope to that rascal of a Bernardaccio that he would buy this said diamond.

And because this Bernardo sought to secure to himself the sole credit of this fraud which he wished to practice upon the Duke of Florence, he never conferred at all with his partner, the said Antonio Landi. This said Antonio was a very great friend of mine from boyhood; and since he saw that I was on very intimate terms (*tanto domestico*) with my Duke, one day among the rest he called me apart. It was near midday, and it was at the corner of the Mercato Nuovo; and he spake to me thus: "Benvenuto! I am certain that the Duke will exhibit you a diamond, which he shows that he has the desire to buy: you will see (that it is) a large diamond. Help me in the sale of it; and I tell you that I can give it for seventeen thousand *scudi*. I am certain that the Duke will want your advice: if you see him well-inclined to want it, the matter shall be arranged that he can take it." This Antonio showed that he had a great certainty of being able to make an agreement regarding the stone. I promised him that if it were shown to me and my opinion then asked, I would say everything that I thought of it, without injuring (the value of) the stone. So, as I have stated above, the Duke came every day into the Goldsmiths' Shop (*oreficeria*) for several hours; and more than eight days after that day when Antonio Landi had spoken to me, the Duke one day after dinner showed to me this said diamond, which I recognized by those marks which the said Antonio Landi had described to me, and by its shape and weight. And since this said diamond was, as I have stated above, of a rather muddy (*torbidiccia*) water, and that for that reason they had razed off the point, when I observed that it was of that kind, I certainly would not have advised him to go to such an expense: however, when he showed it to me, I asked His Excellency what he wished me to say about it, for there was a difference in (the custom of) jewelers in the valuation of a stone after that a lord had bought it and the setting of a price upon it in order that he should buy it.

Thereupon His Excellency told me that he had bought it, and that I was merely to say what I thought about it. I did not want to abstain from hinting modestly what a small opinion I had of that stone. He told me to consider the beauty of those great facets that it had. Thereupon I told him that that was not such a great beauty as His Excellency imagined, and that it was due to a point which had been razed off. At these words my lord, who perceived that I was telling the truth, gave an ugly grunt (*mal grugnio*), and told me that I must attend to the valuation of the stone and to judging what it seemed to me to be worth. I thought that, since Antonio Landi had offered it to me for seventeen thousand *scudi* I might suppose that the Duke would have got it for fifteen thousand at the most, and for the reason that I saw that he would take it ill if I told him the truth, I thought of maintaining him in his false opinion. So handing him the diamond I said: "You have spent eighteen thousand *scudi* upon it." At these words the Duke gave a shout, uttering an "O" bigger than the mouth of a well, and said: Now I believe that you understand nothing at all about it." I said to him: "My Lord! you certainly believe wrong. Do you attend to maintaining the reputation of your precious stone, and I will attend to understanding my own business. Tell me at least what you have spent upon it, so that I may learn to understand matters according to Your Excellency's ideas." The Duke rising with a slightly scornful sneer said: "Twenty-five thousand *scudi* and more, Benvenuto! it cost me": and went away. At this discussion there were present Gianpagolo and Domenico Poggini, the goldsmiths; and Bachiacca the embroiderer, he also, for he worked in an apartment near to ours, ran up at that noise. Whereupon I said: "I should never have advised him to buy it. But if he had had a desire for it, Antonio Landi offered it to me eight days ago for seventeen thousand *scudi*; I believe that I could have got it for him for fifteen or less. But the Duke wishes to maintain the reputation of his stone: for since Antonio Landi offered it to me at such a price, how the devil has Bernardone put upon the Duke such a shameful fraud?" And never believing that such was the truth—as it was—we laughingly passed over that simplicity of the Duke.

Having already constructed the figure of the large *Medusa,* as I have said, I had fashioned its framework (*ossatura*) of iron. Afterwards having made it in clay, like an anatomical specimen (*notomia*), and thinner by half a finger, I baked it most thoroughly, then I put wax over it and finished it off after the fashion in which I wanted it to be. The Duke, who came many times to see it, had such a fear (*gelosia*) lest I should not succeed with it in bronze, that he would have liked me to have called in some master to cast it for me. And because His Excellency kept talking continually and with very great favor of my conceits, his Major-domo was continually seeking for some snare by which to make me break my neck. And since he had authority to command the *bargelli* and all the officers of the poor unhappy City of Florence—to think that a native of Prato, our enemy, the son of a cooper, a most ignorant person, because he had been the rotten tutor (*pedante fradicio*) of Cosimo de' Medici, before he became Duke, should have now come into so great authority:—so as I have said while he stood watching how much he could do to injure me, when he saw that upon no side could he fasten fetters upon me, he thought out a method of doing something. And going to seek out the mother of that work-lad of mine (who bore the name of Cencio, and she Gambetta), they made a plan, that rascally tutor and that blackguardly whore to give me a fright so that in consequence of it I might go right away. Gambetta drawing (her ideas) from her own profession went along under the direction of that mad scoundrelly tutor-major-domo: and since they had also drawn in the Bargello, who was a certain Bolognese (who for doing these very things the Duke subsequently dismissed), it chanced one Saturday evening, at the third hour of the night, the said Gambetta came to see me with her son, and told me that she had kept him shut up several days for my safety. To which I replied that she need not have kept him shut up on my account: and laughing at her whorish arts, I turned to her son in her presence and said to him: "You know, Cencio, whether I have sinned with you?" who weeping answered "No!" Thereupon the mother, shaking her head, said to her son: "Ah! little scamp! Do you think I don't know how these things are done?" Then she turned to me, telling me that I must keep him hidden in the house, for the Bargello was seeking for him, and that he would have him arrested at all costs outside my house; but that inside my house they would not touch him. To this I replied that in my house I had a widowed sister with six saintly young daughters, and that I did not want any one in my house. Thereupon she said that the Major-domo had given orders to the Bargello, and that I should be arrested anyhow; but since I would not take her son into my house, if I gave her one hundred *scudi* I might be sure of hearing nothing more about it, for, since the major-domo was a very great friend of hers, I might rest assured that she would make him do everything that was pleasing to her, provided that I gave her the one hundred *scudi*. I had arrived at such a pitch of fury; in which I said to her: "Get out of my presence! You infamous whore! For if it were not for my credit with the world, and the innocence of that unhappy child that you have there, I would have already cut your throat with this dagger, upon which I have two or three times laid my hands." And with these words, together with many ugly thrusts, I pushed her and her son out of the house. When I subsequently thought over the villainy and power of that evil tutor, I judged that it would be better for me to give a little place to that devilry; and the next morning at an early hour, having consigned to my sister precious stones and articles to the value of nearly two thousand *scudi,* I mounted upon horseback and departed towards Venice; and I took with me that Bernardino of Mugello of mine. And when I reached Ferrara, I wrote to His Excellency the Duke, that although I had departed without being sent away, I should return without being summoned. Afterwards when I arrived in Venice, thinking over in how many different methods my cruel fortune kept harassing me, finding myself nevertheless healthy and strong, I resolved to battle with her according to my wont. And while I went about thinking thus of my affairs, passing my time in that beautiful and very wealthy city, having saluted that wondrous painter Titiano, and Jacopo del Sansovino, the brilliant sculptor and architect, one of our Florentines, (who was) very well entertained by the Signoria of Venice, and—as one of our Florentines we had been acquainted in our youth in Rome and Florence—these two talented men showed me many civilities. The next day after I met Messer Lorenzo de Medici, who immediately took me by the hand with the warmest welcome that one could see in the world, for we had been acquainted in Florence (at the time) when I was making the coins for Duke Lessandro, and afterwards in Paris when I was in the service of the King. He was lodging in the house of Messer Giuliano Buonacorsi, and since he had nowhere else to go to pass away the time without (running the) greatest danger to his life, he remained most of the time in my house, watching me laboring at my great undertakings. And as I say on account of this past acquaintance, he took me by the hand and led me to his own house, where was the Lord Prior delli (*sic*) Strozzi, brother of the Lord Pietro, and while welcoming me they asked me how long I intended to stop in Venice, believing that I wished to return into France. To which lords I replied that I had departed from Florence on account of a matter such as has been mentioned above, and within two or three days I intended to return to Florence to serve my great Duke. When I spoke these words the Lord Prior and Messer Lorenzo turned to me with so much severity that I experienced very great fear, and they said to me: "You would do better to return to France, where you are rich and well known; for if you return to Florence, you will lose all that you have gained in France, and from Florence you will derive nothing but unpleasantnesses." I did not reply to their remarks, but setting out the next day as secretly as I could, I returned towards Florence. Meanwhile the devilries had come to a head and burst (*maturato*), for I had written to my great Duke the whole circumstance wherefor I had removed myself to Venice. And I visited him with his accustomed prudence and sternness without any ceremony. Assuming somewhat that said sternness (of demeanor), he afterwards turned cheerfully to me, and asked me where I had been. To which I replied that my heart had never been turned the distance of one finger from His Most Illustrious Excellency, although for some just reasons it had been necessary for me to take my body on the ramble (*a zonzo*) for a little while. Then making himself more agreeable he began to talk about Venice, and so we chatted for a space: then at the end he told me to attend to my working, and that I must finish his *Perseus*. So I returned home joyful and gay; and I cheered up my family, that is to say, my sister with her six daughters, and having taken up my work again, with as much diligence as I could, I urged it forward.

Chapter Ten 1546-1547

A ND the first work that I cast in bronze was that large head, the portrait of the Lord Excellency (*sic*), which I had fashioned in clay in the Goldsmiths' Shop while I had that malady in my back. This was a work which pleased me, and I did it for no other reason except to experiment in the clays for bronze casting. And although I saw that that wondrous Donatello had executed his works in bronze, which he had cast with Florence clay, it seemed to me that he had carried them out under greatest difficulty. And thinking that they might have arisen from some defect in the clay, before I set about casting my *Perseus* I wanted first to make these researches, by means of which I discovered that the clay was good enough, but that it had not been well understood by that wondrous Donatello; wherefore I perceived that he had achieved his works under greatest difficulty. So, as I say above, with skill in art I compounded the clay, which served me most admirably; and, as I say, I cast with it the said head; but since I had not yet constructed my own furnace, I used the furnace of M° Zanobi di Pagno, the bell-founder. And when I saw that the head had come out extremely well defined, I immediately set to work to construct a small furnace, after my own direction and design, in the workshop that the Duke had built for me, in that very house which he had bestowed upon me. And directly I had constructed the furnace, with as much diligence as I could, I got myself in readiness to cast the statue of *Medusa,* which is the contorted female figure that lies beneath the feet of *Perseus.* And because this casting is a most difficult operation, I did not want to be lacking in all those details of skill (*diligentie*) that I had learned, in order that no mistake should happen to me. And thus the first casting that I made in my said small furnace resulted to a very superlative degree, and was so very clearly defined, that it did not seem to my friends that there would be any need that I should further retouch it; the which thing certain Germans and French (workers) have discovered, who say and boast themselves of very fine secrets for casting bronzes without retouching; a statement truly of mad folk, because bronze, after that it has been cast must be worked over (*riserarlo*) with hammers and with chisels, just as did those most wonderful antique (craftsmen), and as the moderns have also done (I speak of those moderns who have understood how to work in bronze). This casting pleased His Most Illustrious Excellency so much that he came many times to my house to see it, giving me the greatest encouragement to progress. But that rabid envy of Bandinello was so powerful with so much persistency about the ears of His Most Illustrious Excellency, that he caused him to think that, although I was casting some of these statues, I should never be able to put them (the parts) together because the art was a new one to me; and that His Excellency ought to take good care not to throw away his money. These words had such influence in those august ears that some of the allowance for my workmen was diminished: in such fashion that I was obliged to complain hotly to His Excellency. Wherefore lying in wait for him one day in the Via de' Servi I said to him: "My Lord, I am not supported in my needs: wherefore I suspect that Your Excellency has no confidence in me: whence I tell you again that I have sufficient courage as I have promised you to complete this work three times better than was the model." When I had spoken these words to His Excellency and had realized that they produced no result, for I drew no response from him, there immediately sprang up in me a fury, together with an intolerable torture. I began once more to address the Duke, and I said to him: "My Lord, this city truly has always been the School of the Greater Talents: but when a man who, having learned something, has made a name for himself desires to add to the glory of his native city and of his glorious Prince, it is wise to go and labor elsewhere. And that this, my lord, is the truth I know that Your Excellency knew what sort of man Donatello was and what the great Leonardo da Vinci, and what is now the Wondrous Michelagnol Buonarroti. These men by their talents bring fresh glory to Your Excellency: wherefore I also hope to do my share. Therefore, my Lord, let me depart. But let Your Excellency be well advised not to let Bandinello go. Rather give him always more than he asks for; for if he goes abroad his ignorance is so presumptuous that he is qualified to bring shame upon this most noble School. Now, give me leave, my lord: nor do I ask any other reward for my labors up to now, except Your Most Illustrious Excellency's goodwill." When His Excellency saw me resolved after this fashion, he turned to me, with some little irritation, saying: "Benvenuto! If you have a desire to finish the work, nothing shall be lacking to you." Thereupon I thanked him and said that no other desire was mine except to show those envious persons that I had sufficient courage to carry out the promised work. After I had thus departed from His

Excellency, but a small amount of assistance was given me: wherefore I was obliged to put my hand into my own purse, for I wanted my work to proceed at something more than a foot's pace. And in the evening I always went for recreation (*andavo a veglia*) to His Excellency's Wardrobe, where were Domenico and Gianpavolo Poggini his brother, who were working for the Duchess upon a gold vase, which has been mentioned further back, and upon a golden girdle. His Excellency had moreover caused me to made a sketch-model of a pendant, wherein was to be set that large diamond which Bernardone and Ant° Landi had made him purchase. And although I would have avoided it, since I did not want to do such a thing, the Duke with so many charming blandishments made me work upon it every evening until the fourth hour. He sought me also with the most charming devices to induce me to work also at it by day; to which I never would consent. And on this account I believed as a certain fact that His Excellency was enraged with me; for one evening among the others, when I arrived somewhat later than was my custom, the Duke said to me: "You are Ill-come (*Malvenuto*)." To this remark I replied: "My Lord! That is not my name, for I bear the name of Welcome (*Benvenuto*), and because I suppose that Your Illustrious Excellency is joking with me I will not enter further into the matter." To this the Duke replied that he was speaking in solemn earnest (*maladetto senno*), and was not joking, and that I must pay careful attention to what I was doing, for it had come to his ears that, trusting in his favor, I was taking in first this person and then that. At these words I besought His Most Illustrious Excellency to deign to tell me of one single man in the world whom I had ever defrauded. Immediately he turned upon me in wrath and said: "Go and give back that which you have belonging to Bernardone: Behold one person!" To this I replied: "My Lord, I thank you, and I pray you to deign to listen to four words from me. It is true that he lent me a pair of old scales, two anvils and three small hammers, the which harness fifteen days ago this very day I told his (workman) Giorgio of Cortona to send for. Wherefore the said Giorgio came for them himself: and if ever Your Most Illustrious Excellency finds, from the day that I was born until now, that I have ever had anything from anyone in this fashion, whether it be in Rome or in France, let him enquire about it from those who have reported these things, or from others; and on finding out the truth let him punish me without measure (*a misura di carboni*)." When the Duke saw that I was in a very great rage, like a most discreet and kind prince he turned to me and said: "One is not speaking to those who make no mistakes. Therefore if it be as you say, I will always receive you gladly, as I have done heretofore." To this I replied: "Your Excellency must know that the evil-doings of Bernardone compel me to demand and pray that Your (Lordship) will tell me what was the cost of that large diamond, with the point razed off; for I hope to demonstrate why this evil wretch (*homaccio*) is seeking to get me into disgrace." Thereupon His Excellency said to me: "The diamond cost me 25 thousand ducats. Why do you ask me about it?" "Because, My Lord! On such a day, at such and such an hour, at the corner of the New Market, Ant° di Vettorio Landi told me that I must try to make a bargain with Your Most Illustrious Excellency, and at the first demand he asked sixteen thousand ducats for it. Your Excellency now knows what he bought it for. And that this is the truth, ask Sr Domenico Poggini and Gianpavolo his brother, who are here! For I told them immediately; and since then have said no more about it, for Your Excellency told me that I did not understand it, whereat I thought that Your Excellency wanted to keep up its reputation. Know (then), my

Lord! that I do not understand it; and as to the other question
I make profession of being an honest man as much as any other
man that may be born into the world, whoever he may be. I shall
not seek to rob you of eight or ten thousand ducats at a time,
rather I shall endeavor to earn them by my labors. And I stayed
to serve Your Excellency as sculptor, goldsmith, and master of
coinage; but to report upon the business of others, never. And
this that I say now, I say in my own defense, and I do not want
a fee (for my information); and I say it in the presence of so
many honest men who are here, in order that Your Excellency
may not believe what Bernardone says." The Duke rose immediately in a fury, and sent for Bernardone, who was obliged to
run away as far as Venice, he and Ant° Landi: which Ant° told
me that he had not (in speaking to me) meant that particular
diamond. They went and returned from Venice; and I sought
out the Duke, and said (to him): "(My) Lord! What I told you
is true, and that which Bernardone told you about his tools was
not true: and you will do well to put it to the proof, and I will
betake me to the Bargello." At these words the Duke turned to
me, saying: "Benvenuto! Attend to being an honest man, as you
have done in the past, and never doubt about anything." The
matter went off in smoke, and I never more heard any mention of it.
I paid attention to completing his jewel: and on carrying it one
day completed to the Duchess, she herself told me that she valued
my workmanship as much as the diamond that Bernardaccio had
made her buy, and she desired me to fasten it upon her bosom
with my own hand; and she gave into my hand a large pin
(*grossetto spilletto*), and with it I fixed it, and took my departure
with much good favor on her part. Subsequently I heard that
they had had it (the diamond) set by a German or some other
foreigner—if I am not mistaken (*salvo il vero*)—because the said

Bernardone told them that the said diamond would show up better set with less elaboration.

Domenico and Giovanpagolo Poggini, goldsmiths and brothers, labored, as I believe I have said, in the Wardrobe of His Most Illustrious Excellency, after my designs, upon certain small vases of gold engraved with scenes of figures in low relief, and other things of great interest. And since I said many times to the Duke: "My Lord! If Your Most Illustrious Excellency would pay several workmen for me, I would make the coinage for your mint and the medals bearing the head of Your Most Illustrious Excellency; the which I will make in rivalry with the ancients, and shall have the hope of surpassing them. For since the time that I made Pope Clemente's medals, I have learned so much that I can make them much better than those. And in the same way I will do better with the coins than I did for Duke Alessandro, which are indeed still held to be fine. And so too will I make for you large vases of gold and silver, just as I made so many for that admirable King Francescho of France, solely by means of the great conveniences that he afforded me, nor was time ever lost on the great *Colossi* nor from the other statues."

At these words of mine the Duke said to me: "Do so and I will see:" nor did he ever provide for me any convenience or assistance. One day His Most Illustrious Excellency caused me to be given several pounds of silver, and he said to me: "This is some silver from my own mines. Make me a handsome vase of it." And since I did not want to let my *Perseus* fall into arrears, and yet had a great desire to oblige him, I gave the making of it, together with my own designs and sketch-models in wax, to a certain rascal, who was called Piero di Martino, the goldsmith: who began it badly and moreover did not work at it; in such a way that I lost more time than if I had done it all with my own hands. Having thus wasted for me several months, when I saw that the said Piero did not work, nor even less set some one else to work at it, I made him give back to me—and went through great trouble to recover —along with the body of the vase badly begun as I have said— the rest of the silver that I had given to him. The Duke, when he heard something about these disturbances, sent for the vase and for the models, and never spoke to me any more about it, neither why nor wherefore. It is 'sufficient that he directed various people to make it after my designs both in Venice and in other places, and was very badly served. The Duchess told me often that I must execute some goldsmith's work for her: to whom I said many times that the world and all Italy knew very well that I was an excellent goldsmith; but that Italy had never seen works by my hand in sculpture. And throughout the profession certain furious sculptors, ridiculing me called me "the new sculptor"; to whom I hoped to demonstrate that I was an old sculptor, if God should afford me sufficient grace to be able to exhibit my completed *Perseus* in that noble Piazza of His Most Illustrious Excellency. And retiring home, I attended to working day and night, and never allowed myself to be seen at the Palace. But thinking, however, to maintain myself in the good graces of the Duchess I had made for her certain small silver vases as large as a little two-penny stew-pan, with handsome little masks in very rare style, after the antique pattern (*all' antica*). And when I conveyed these said little vases to her, she gave me the most grateful reception that it is possible to imagine in the world, and paid me back my silver and gold that I had expended upon them. But I however recommended myself to Her Most Illustrious Excellency, begging her that she would inform the Duke that I was receiving but little assistance for so great a work, and that Her Most Illustrious Excellency should say to the Duke that he should not put so much

credence in that evil tongue of Bandinello's, with which he was
hindering the completion of my *Perseus*. At these tearful words of
mine the Duchess shrugged her shoulders, and said to me: "It is
certain that the Duke ought to know that this Bandinello of his is
worth nothing." I remained at home and rarely presented myself
at the Palace, and I labored with great assiduity to finish my work.
And I agreed to pay my workmen out of my own (pocket): for
the Duke having caused certain of my workmen to be paid by
Lattanzio Gorini for the space of about eighteen months, and becoming bored at doing so, directed him to take the commission
away from me, wherefore I asked the said Lattanzio Gorini why
he did not pay me. And he answered me, waving his spider-
claws, with the squeaking gnatlike voice (*vocerellina di zanzara*),
"Why don't you finish this work of yours? It is believed that you
never will finish it." I immediately answered him furiously, and
said: "May a plague (*canchero*) fall upon both you and all those
who believe that I shall not finish it." And thus in despair I returned home to my unfortunate *Perseus*, and not without tears, for
I recalled to memory the splendid position that I had left behind
me in Paris under the service of that wondrous King Francesco,
wherein he provided me with everything, while here I lacked everything. And several times I was tempted to throw myself into
despair. And upon one occasion among others I mounted upon
my handsome little nag, and put one hundred *scudi* in my purse
(*accanto*), and betook myself to Fiesole to see a little natural son
of mine, whom I was keeping at nurse with a gossip of mine, the
wife of one of my workmen. And when I reached my little son,
I found him in good health, and I so unhappy kissed him; but
when I wished to depart he would not let me go, for he held me
firmly with his little hands and with a passion of tears and screams,
which at that age of about two years was a thing more than mar-

velous. And since I was resolved that if I met Bandinello, who was accustomed to go every evening to that farm of his above San Domenico, like a desperate man I would cast him to the earth, I departed thus from my baby-boy, leaving him to his broken-hearted weeping. And coming towards Florence when I reached the Piazza di San Domenico, at that moment Bandinello entered the Piazza from the opposite side. Immediately resolving to commit that bloody act, I met him; but when I raised my eyes I saw that he was unarmed, (mounted) upon a mule (*muluccio*) like a donkey, and he had with him a little boy of ten years old: and directly he saw me he became the color of the dead, and trembled from head to foot. I, recognizing that the emotion was a most vile one, said: "Fear nothing, vile coward, for I will not consider you worthy of my blows." He gazed at me, having recovered himself, and answered nothing. Then I regained my self-respect, and thanked God, that by His True Grace He had not permitted me to commit such a crime. Having thus freed myself from that devilish rage, my courage increased, and I said to myself: "If God grant me sufficient grace to finish my work, I hope with it to confound all my scoundrelly enemies, whereby I shall make my revenge much greater and more glorious, than if I had vented it upon one alone"; and with this excellent resolution I returned home. At the end of three days I heard that that gossip of mine had smothered my only little son, which gave me so great a sorrow as I have never felt a greater. Consequently I knelt down on the ground, and not without tears, according to my custom I gave thanks to my God, saying: "My Lord! Thou gavest him to me, and now Thou hast taken him away. But in all things with all my heart I thank Thee." And although that great sorrow had as it were crushed me, however, according to my custom, having made a virtue of a necessity I set about accommodating myself to it as best I could.

There had at this time left the employment of Bandinello a young man, who bore the name of Francescho, the son of Matteo the blacksmith. This said young man made a request to me that I would give him some work; and I was glad to do so, and set him to cleaning the figure of *Medusa,* which had already been cast. This youth after 15 days told me that he had spoken with his master—that is to say, Bandinello—and that he was to tell me from him, that, if I wanted to make a figure in marble, he was sending to offer to present me a fine piece of marble. I immediately said to him: "Tell him that I accept it; and may it be bad marble for him, for he goes about irritating me, and does not remember the great danger that he escaped from me upon the Piazza di San Domenico. But tell him that I want it anyhow. I never speak about him, but that beast is always causing me annoyance: and I believe that it may be through his sending you that you have come to work with me, merely to spy upon my affairs. Oh! Go and tell him that I will have the marble in spite of him; and return yourself with it."

As it had been many days since I had permitted myself to revisit the Palace, I went one morning when that fancy took me, and the Duke had almost finished dinner, and from what I heard His Excellency had that morning talked and spoken very kindly of me, and among other things had much praised me in the matter of setting jewels; and for this reason when the Duchess saw me, she had me summoned (to her) by Messer Sforza: and when I approached Her Most Illustrious Excellency she begged me to set a small pointed diamond (*diamantino in punta*) into a ring. And she told me that she wanted to wear it always upon her finger, and she gave me the measure and the diamond, which was worth about one hundred *scudi,* and begged me to make it quickly. The Duke immediately began to discuss the question with the Duchess, and said to her: "It is certain that in this art Benvenuto was without equal: but now that he has given it up, I believe that to make a little ring such as you want, will be too great a labor for him. Therefore I beg that you will not weary him in this trifling matter, which would be a great one for him since he has let it fall into disuse." At these words I thanked the Duke, and then I begged that he would allow me to perform this small service for the Lady Duchess. And having set my hand to it immediately, in a few days I had completed it. The ring was for the little finger of the hand: so I made four tiny cherubs in relief with four small masks, which formed the said little ring: and I also inserted some fruit and enameled settings, so that the precious stone and the ring together exhibited a very beautiful effect. I immediately carried it to the Duchess: who with kindly words told me that I had made a very fine job of it, and that she would remember me. The said ring she sent as a gift to King Filippo, and after that was always ordering something of me: and so persuasively that I was always compelled to serve her, although I saw but little money for it, and God knows that I had great need of it, for I wanted to finish my *Perseus.* I had found certain young men to assist me whom I paid out of my own (funds): and I again began to allow myself to be seen (at the palace) more often than I had done for some time past.

One feast day among others I went into the Palace after dinner, and when I came up into the Hall of the Clock I saw the door of the Wardrobe open; and when I approached it a little, the Duke called to me, and, with a kindly greeting, said to me: "You are welcome indeed. Look at this chest which has been sent as a present to me by the lord Stefano of Pilestina! Open it, and let us see what the thing is." Having immediately opened it, I said to the Duke: "My Lord! this is a figure in Greek marble, and a wondrous thing. I tell you that for a boy's figure I do not recollect that I have ever seen among the antiques so fine a work, nor one of so beautiful a fashion. Wherefore I offer to Your Most Illustrious Excellency to restore it, and the head and the arms and the feet. And I will make an eagle in order that it may be labeled as a *Ganymede.* And although it is not customary for me to patch up statues—for that is the art of certain bunglers, who do it very badly—yet the excellence of this great master calls me to assist him." The Duke was pleased that the statue was so beautiful, and asked me many questions, saying to me: "Tell me distinctly, my Benvenuto! in what consists the great talent of this master, which causes you so much admiration." Thereupon I demonstrated to His Most Illustrious Excellency after the best method that I knew in order to make him understand such beauty, and the intellectual skill, and the rare manner (of the fragment); upon which questions I discoursed very much and I did it the more willingly, realizing that therein His Excellency took very great pleasure.

While I was thus agreeably entertaining the Duke, it chanced that a page went out of the Wardrobe, and as the said (page) went out Bandinello entered. When the Duke saw him he was half disturbed, and with a severe expression he said to him: "What are you doing here?" The said Bandinello, without making any other reply, immediately cast his eyes upon that chest, wherein lay the said uncovered statue, and with one of his evil chuckles, shaking his head, he said, turning towards the Duke: "My Lord! These are some of those things of which I have so often spoken to Your Most Illustrious Excellency. Know that these ancient (sculptors) understood nothing at all about anatomy, and for this reason their works are quite full of faults." I remained quiet and paid no attention to anything that he was saying; rather I had turned my back on him. Directly that this animal had finished his disagreeable chatterings, the Duke said: "Oh! Benvenuto! This is exactly the opposite to that which you with so many fine arguments have but now so well demonstrated to me. Therefore defend it a little." At these words of the Duke (*Ducal parole*), conveyed to me with so much charm, I immediately responded, and said: "My Lord! Your Most Illustrious Excellency ought to know that Baccio Bandinelli is composed entirely of evil, and so he always has been: in such a way that whatever he gazes upon, to his disapproving eyes immediately, although the thing may be altogether good in a superlative degree, it is immediately converted into the worst evil. But I who am drawn only towards the good, perceive the truth more divinely; in such a fashion that what I have said to Your Most Illustrious Excellency about this most beautiful statue is altogether the simple truth, and that which Bandinello has said is altogether that evil of which alone he is composed."

The Duke stood listening to me with much pleasure; and while I was saying these things Bandinella fidgeted and made the ugliest grimaces of his countenance—which was (itself) the most ugly— that it is possible to imagine in the world. The Duke immediately moved away, proceeding through certain lower chambers (*basse*), and the said Bandinello followed him. The Chamberlains took me by the cloak and led me after him. And thus we followed the Duke, so that when His Most Illustrious Excellency reached a certain chamber he sat down, and both Bandinello and I stood, one upon the right, and the other upon the left, of His Most Illustrious Excellency. I remained silent, and those who were around us— several servants of His Excellency—all gazed fixedly at Bandinello, somewhat sniggering one with another at those words which I had uttered in that chamber above. So the said Bandinello began to chatter, and he said: "My Lord! When I uncovered my *Hercules and Cacus* I certainly believe that more than one hundred ballads (*sonettacci*) were made upon me, which they say were the worst that one could possibly imagine in the world from this mob (*popolaccio*)."

I thereupon answered and said: "My Lord, When our Michelagniolo Buonaroti unveiled his Sacristy, where may be seen so many beautiful figures, this admirable and talented School, the friend of truth and of the excellent, made more than one hundred sonnets upon him, competing with one another which could speak the best of him. And so just as that work of Bandinello's deserved so much ill said as he says has been spoken about it, so that of Buonaroti deserved as much good as was said of him." At these words of mine Bandinello fell into such a fury that he was bursting, and he turned to me and said: "And what do you know that you can say about it?" "I will tell you if you have sufficient patience to know how to listen to me." Says he: "Speak up then now." The Duke and the others who were there, all listened eagerly. I began, and in the first place I said: "Do you know that it pains me to have to tell you of the defects of that work of yours; but I will not speak of such things, rather I will tell you all that this most talented School says about it." And because this wretched man (*huomaccio*) kept now saying something disagreeable, and now moving about his hands and his feet, he caused me to fall into such a rage that I began in a much more unpleasant manner that I should have done if he had acted otherwise: "This talented School says that if one were to shave the hair off *Hercules,* there would not remain noddle (*zucca*) sufficient to contain his brain; and that as regards that face of his one would not know whether it was the countenance of a man or of a lion-ox (*lionbue*): and that he is not paying any attention to what he is doing: and that it is badly attached to its neck, with so little skill and with so bad a grace, that one has never seen anything worse: and that those two ugly shoulders of his resemble the two pommels of an ass's pack-saddle; and that his breasts and the rest of his muscles are not copied from those of a man, but are drawn from an old sack full of melons, which has been set upright propped against a wall. So (also) the loins seem to be copied from a sack full of long gourds: one does not know by what method the two legs are attached to that ugly body; for one does not know upon which leg he is standing, or upon which he is making any display of pressure: still less does he appear to be resting upon both, as it is customary sometimes for those masters who know something about the representation (of figures). It is easy to see that he is falling forward more than a third of a *braccio*; for this alone is the greatest and most intolerable fault that those wretched masters of the common herd (*maestracci di fozzini plebe!*) commit. Of the arms they say that they are both stretched downwards without any grace: nor is there any artistic sense to be perceived in them, as if you had never seen living nudes: and that the right leg of *Hercules* and that of *Cacus* make a mixture in the calves of their legs; so that if one of the two were removed from the other, not only one of them, but rather both would remain without calves at that point where they touch: and they say that one of the feet of *Hercules* is buried and the other appears to have fire under it."

The man could not restrain himself to be patient, so that I might tell him also the great defects of *Cacus*. For one thing was that I was speaking truly, and another was that I was making it known clearly to the Duke and to the others who were in our presence, so that they made very great expressions and acts of astonishment, and then realized that I was telling the very truth. All at once this wretched man said: "Ah! you wicked lying tongue (*cattiva linguaccia*)! Oh! where do you leave my design?" I replied "that he who designs well can never work out that design badly. Consequently I can believe that your design is like your work." Now when he saw from those ducal and other countenances that with their looks and with their gestures they were despising him, he allowed himself to be too much overcome by his insolence, and turning towards me with his most hideous ugly face, he all of a sudden said to me: "Oh! be silent! You b . . . . . b . . . . . you!"

The Duke at this remark contracted his brow angrily at him, and the others pursed their lips, and frowned their eyes at him. I, for I felt myself thus grossly insulted, was provoked by fury; but all at once I plunged at a remedy, and I said: "Oh! Madman! You are exceeding all bounds. Though would to God that I did know how to practice so noble an art, for we read that Jove practiced it with Ganymede in Paradise, and here upon earth it is practiced by the greatest Emperors and the greatest Kings in the world. I am but a low and humble scrap of humanity (*homicciattolo*), who neither could, nor would know how to perplex myself with so wondrous a thing." At this no one could contain themselves; in so much that the Duke and the others raised a shout of the loudest laughter that can possibly be imagined in the world. But although I made myself appear so amiable about it, know, Kind Readers, that within me my heart was bursting when I thought that one, the dirtiest ruffian that was ever born into the world, should be so daring as, in the presence of so great a prince, to utter to me so great and such an insult. But you know that he insulted the Duke and not me. For if I had been outside so great a presence, I would have struck him dead. When this dirty scoundrelly blockhead saw that the laughing of those lords did not cease, in order to divert them from so much mockery, he began to enter upon a new subject, saying: "This Benvenuto goes about boasting that I have promised him a piece of marble." At these words I im-

mediately replied: "How! Did you not send to tell me by Francesco, (the son) of Matteo the blacksmith, your shop-lad, that if
I wanted to work in marble you were willing to give me a piece
of marble? And I have accepted it and I wish for it." Thereupon
he said: "Oh! Make up your mind that you will never get it."
Immediately I, for I was brimful of wrath at the unjust insults
uttered to me first, laying aside reason and forgetting the presence
of the Duke, with great fury said: "I tell you plainly that if you
do not send the marble to my house, look out for another world;
for I will bring you down (*sgonfiero*) in this one at all costs."
Recalling immediately that I was in the presence of so great a Duke,
I turned humbly towards His Excellency, and I said: "My Lord!
One madman makes a hundred. The madnesses of this man caused
me to forget the respect due to Your Most Illustrious Excellency
and to myself. Therefore pardon me." Thereupon the Duke said
to Bandinello: "Is it true that you have promised the marble?"
The said Bandinello said that it was true. The Duke said to me:
"Go to the Opera (del Duomo), and take a piece to your liking."
I said that he had promised to send it me to my house. Our alter-
cation was terrible; and I would not take it in any other way. The
following morning a piece of marble was brought to my house. I
demanded who had sent it; and they told me that Bandinello had
sent it me, and that this was the piece of marble that he had
promised me.

I immediately had it carried into the workshop, and began to
chisel at it: and while I labored at it I made the model. And so
great was the desire that I had to work in marble, that I could
not wait to resolve upon the fashioning of a model with that judgment that is appropriate to such an art. But when I heard the
whole piece ring false (*crocchiare*), I repented many times that I had
ever begun to labor upon it. However I carved out what I could

from it, which is an *Apollo and Hyacinth,* that may still be seen in my workshop incomplete. And while I was working upon it the Duke came to my house; and he said to me many times: "Let the bronze stand aside for a little while, and work a little in marble, so that I may see you." Immediately I took up the tools for marble working, and worked away with assurance. The Duke asked me about the model that I had made for the said marble, to which I replied: "My Lord! This piece of marble is all broken, but in spite of that I shall carve something out of it. Consequently I am not able to make up my mind about the model, but I shall proceed in this way doing the best that I can." With much haste the Duke caused a piece of Greek marble to come to me from Rome, in order that I might restore his antique *Ganymede,* which was the cause of the said quarrel with Bandinello. When the piece of Greek marble arrived, I thought that it was a sin to break it into pieces to form the head and the arms and the other portions for the *Ganymede*: so I provided myself with other marble, and for that piece of Greek marble I made a little sketch-model in wax, to (which) I gave the name of *Narcissus.* And since this piece of marble had two holes in it which went into it more than a fourth of a *braccio,* and as wide as two good fingers, for this reason I fashioned it in the attitude that may be still seen, to avoid these holes: in such a way I had cut them out from my figure. But for so many decades of years it had been rained upon, whereby those holes had been always filled with water, and the said (water) had penetrated so much that the said marble had been weakened, and as if rotted away in that upper part of the hole; a fact which was afterwards demonstrated when there came that great flood of the Arno water which rose in my workshop more than a *braccio* and a half. And because the said *Narcissus* was placed upon a square of wood, the said water caused it to fall down, whereby it was broken above the breasts: and I joined it together; and in order that that fissure of the joining might not be perceived, I fashioned that garland of flowers that may be seen over the breast: and I went on finishing it at certain hours before daybreak, or truly on feast-days, merely not to lose time from my work upon the *Perseus*. And while one morning among others I was preparing certain small chisels for my working, I prised off a very fine splinter of steel into my right eye. And it was so much embedded in the pupil, that by no method could it be extracted. I thought for certain that I should lose the sight of that eye. I summoned at the end of several days Maser Raffaello de' Pilli, the surgeon, who took two live pigeons, and making me lie upon my back (*stare rovescio*) upon a table, he took the said pigeons and with a small knife pierced a small vein which they have in their wings, in such a way that their blood poured right into my eye; by the which blood I immediately felt relief, and in the space of two days the splinter of steel came out, and I remained free (from pain) and improved in vision. And the Feast of Santa Luscia, chancing to happen, which was three days after, I fashioned an Eye of gold from a French *scudo,* and I caused it to be offered by one of my six nieces, the daughters of my sister Liperata, who was about the age of ten years, and with it I thanked God and Santa Luscia: and for a while I did not want to work upon the said *Narcissus,* but pressed forward the *Perseus* under the above-mentioned difficulties. And I prepared myself to finish it, and then go right away.

Chapter Eleven   *1548-1549*

HAVING cast the *Medusa* with a successful result, with great
hopes I brought my *Perseus* toward completion, which I had
already made in wax, and I promised myself that it would result as
well for me in bronze as the said *Medusa* had done. And because
he saw it so well finished in wax that it appeared most beautiful,
when the Duke saw it after that fashion and it seemed to him beautiful—whether it happened that some one had caused the Duke to
believe that it could not result so well in bronze, or that the Duke
imagined such a thing of his own accord—coming more often to
my house than he was accustomed to do, on one occasion among
the others he said to me: "Benvenuto! This figure of yours cannot
succeed in bronze, for the art does not admit of it." At these words
of His Excellency I was very greatly roused, and replied: "My Lord!
I know that Your Most Illustrious Excellency has very little faith in
me in this matter; and I believe that this happens because Your Most
Illustrious Excellency trusts too much to those persons who speak
so much ill of me or verily that you do not understand the matter."

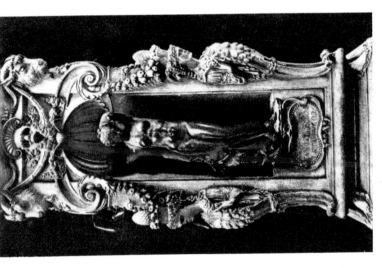

Danae and Perseus, left, and Mercury, right, are two of the four statues on the pedestal of Cellini's Perseus. His installation of them there raised the ire of the Duchess of Florence, who said that "those exquisite figures" would be "wasted on the pedestal down there in the piazza" and wanted Cellini to "fix them in one of my apartments."

He hardly allowed me to complete my words before he said: "I make it my business to understand the matter, and I understand it very well." I answered immediately and said: "Yes, as patron (*Signiore*), but not as artist; for if Your Most Illustrious Excellency understood it after the fashion that he believes he understands it, he would trust in me after the example of the fine bronze head that I have made for him, the very large portrait of Your Most Illustrious Excellency which was sent to Elba; and by the example of the restoration that I have made of the fine marble *Ganymede,* with such extreme difficulty, whereon I expended much greater labor than if I had made it entirely afresh; and besides through my having cast the *Medusa,* even here in the presence of Your Excellency, a casting so difficult, wherein I have accomplished something that no other man has ever done before me in this devil's-own (*indiavolata*) art. See! My Lord! I have erected the furnaces afresh after a method different from the others, for I, besides many other variations and skillful arrangements such as you see in it, have made two outlets for the bronze, since this difficult and twisted figure could never possibly result in any other way; and by these intelligent ideas of mine alone has the result been good; a thing none of those practiced in this art ever believed. And know, My Lord! for very surety that all the great and very difficult works that I executed in France under that most wondrous King Francesco, all resulted very well, solely by reason of the great courage with which that good King always inspired me by that vast amount of provision (for my necessities) and by his obliging me with as many workmen as I asked for; for it sometimes happened that I was served by more than forty workmen, all chosen by myself. And it was by these means that I executed so vast a quantity of works of art in so short a time. Now, My Lord! trust me, and supply me with the assistance that is needful to me, for I hope to conduct to a termination a work of art that will please you. But if Your Most Illustrious Excellency lower my spirits and do not provide me with the assistance of which I have need, it is impossible for me or any other man whatsoever in the world to be able to carry out anything that may be good." With great difficulty the Duke contained himself to listen to these arguments of mine, for now he veered (*voggievo*) in one direction and now in another; and I in despair, poor wretch! (for I recalled the fine position that I occupied in France) thus grieved myself. Suddenly the Duke said: "Now tell me! Benvenuto! How is it possible that that fine head of *Medusa,* which is raised up on high in the hand of *Perseus* can ever result properly?" Immediately I said: "Now observe, My Lord! that if Your Most Illustrious Excellency had that knowledge of art which you profess to have, you would have no anxiety that the fine head of which you speak would not succeed; but rather you would have had anxiety regarding this right foot, which is so hidden at the bottom." At these words of mine the Duke half-angrily turned suddenly to certain lords who were with His Most Illustrious Excellency, and said: "I believe that Benvenuto here does this out of self-conceit for the sake of contradicting everything;" and turning suddenly upon me half in derision, whereupon all those who were present did the same, he began to say: "I want to have sufficient patience with you to listen to such arguments as you are able to devise to present to me, so that I may believe you." Thereupon I said: "I will give you so true a reason, that Your Excellency will be most capable (of understanding it)"; and I began: "Know, My Lord! that it is of the nature of fire to go upwards, and for this reason I promise you that the head of *Medusa* will result extremely well; but because the nature of fire is not to go downwards, and since one has to drive it downwards six *braccia* by force of art, for this essential reason I tell Your Most Illustrious Excellency that it is impossible for that foot to be a success. But it will be easy for me to remake it." The Duke said: "Oh! Why did not you think that the foot would succeed in the same way that you say that the head will?" I told him: "It was necessary to make a much larger furnace, wherein I should be able to make a casting-pipe (*ramo di gitto*) as thick as this leg of mine, and with that weight of hot metal I would have compelled it to move by force; whereas my pipe, which as I say traverses those six *braccia* as far as the feet, is no thicker than two fingers. However it was not worth the expense; for it will easily be repaired. But when my mold is more than half full, I expect that from that half-way point upwards, upon the fire mounting according to its own nature, this head of *Perseus* and that of *Medusa* will succeed most excellently. Therefore be sure of that."

When I had explained that I had these excellent reasons with very many more, which since they would be too long I will not write down, the Duke shaking his head went away.

Having made security for myself with a good courage, and having chased away all those thoughts, which now and again presented themselves before me, which often made me weep bitterly with regret for my departure from France in order to return to Florence, my sweet native land, merely to perform a charity to my said six young nieces, and I saw clearly that by having done so I had exposed myself to the beginning of so much evil; in spite of all this I promised myself for certain that when I had finished the work of *Perseus* that I had begun, all my tribulations ought to be converted into highest pleasure and glorious well-being. And so having recovered my energy, with all my forces both of body and of purse,— although only a few coins remained to me,—I began to endeavor to procure several loads of pine-wood, which I got from the pine groves of the Seristori near Monte Lupo. And while I was waiting for them I clad my *Perseus* in those clays that I had prepared several months previously, in order that they might be in their proper condition (*avessino la loro stagione*). And when I had made his clay tunic (*tonaca di terra*)—for they call it *tonaca* in the profession —and had very thoroughly supplied and girdled it round with great care with iron supports, I began with a slow fire to withdraw the wax, which issued through the many vents that I had made: for the more one makes so much the better do the molds fill. And when I had finished removing the wax I made a funnel around my *Perseus;* that is to say, around the said mold, of bricks interlacing one above the other, and I left many spaces, through which the fire could the better emerge. Then I began to arrange the wood cautiously, and I kept up the fire two days and two nights continuously; to such purpose that when all the wax had been extracted, and the said mold was afterwards well baked, I immediately began to dig the ditch wherein to bury my mold, with all those skillful methods that this fine art directs us. When I had finished digging the said ditch, I then took my mold and with the assistance of windlasses and strong ropes I set it carefully upright: and having suspended it a *braccio* above the level of my furnace, holding it very carefully upright, in such a fashion that it hung exactly in the middle of the ditch, I caused it to descend very gently as far as the bottom of the furnace; and I set it down with all the care that it is possible to imagine in the world. And when I had completed this excellent job I began to prop it up with the selfsame clay that I had dug out of it; and hand over hand as I piled up the earth, I put into it air-holes which were tubes of baked clay such as they use for water and other similar purposes. When I saw that it was thoroughly firm, as well as that method of filling it in, together with the placing of those conduit pipes properly in their places and that those workmen of mine had well understood my plan, the which was very diverse from that of all the other masters in such a profession; being assured that I could put my confidence in them, I turned to my furnace, which I had made them fill with many lumps of copper and other pieces of bronze. And having piled the one upon the top of the other after the fashion that our profession indicates to us, that is to say raised up, so as to make a way for the flames of the fire, whereby the said metal derives its heat quicker, and by it melts and becomes reduced to liquid (*riduciesi in bagnio*), I then cheerily told them to set light to the said furnace. And laying on those pieces of pine wood, which from the greasiness of that resin which the pine tree exudes, and from the fact that my little furnace was so well built, it acted so well that I was obliged to run about now upon one side and now upon the other with so much fatigue as was insupportable to me: but nevertheless I kept it up. And it chanced to me besides that the workshop took fire, and we were afraid lest the roof should fall upon us. From the other side towards the kitchen garden the heaven projected upon me so much water and wind, that it cooled my furnace. Combating thus for several hours with these perverse chances, employing so much more effort than my strong vigor of constitution could possibly sustain; in such a way there sprang upon me a sudden fever, the greatest that can possibly be imagined in the world, by reason of which I was forced to go and throw myself into my bed. And thus very ill-content, being compelled to go there by force, I turned to all those who were assisting me, who were about ten persons or more, including the masters in bronze-founding, the laborers, the peasants and the work-people belonging to my own shop (among whom was a certain Bernardino Mannellini of Mugello, whom I had trained for several years): and to the said (Bernardino) I said (after that I had besought them all): "Look! My dear Bernardino! Observe the rule that I have demonstrated to you, and do quickly as much as you can, for the metal will soon be in readiness: you cannot make a mistake, and these other worthy men will make the channels quickly, and you will surely be able with these two mallets to drive in the two plugs, and I am certain that my mold will fill most excellently. I feel more ill than I have ever felt since I came into this world; and I believe for certain that in a few hours this great suffering will kill me." So very ill-content I departed from them and went to my bed.

When I was laid in bed I ordered my women servants to carry food and drink to all in the workshop; and I told them: "I shall not be alive to-morrow morning." They however encouraged me, telling me that my great suffering would pass, and that it had arisen through my over fatigue. Thus two hours passed in this great contest with fever, and I felt it continually increasing, and I kept always saying: "I feel that I am dying." My servant who looked after my entire household, who bore the name of Mona Fiore of Castel del Rio: this woman was the cleverest that was ever born and also the most kindly; and she kept continually scolding me, saying that I was frightening myself; and on the other hand she showed me the greatest kindnesses in the way of attention that could ever possibly be done in the world. Consequently, seeing me in such boundless distress and so terrified, in spite of all her brave heart she could not restrain a certain quantity of tears which fell from her eyes; but nevertheless she, as far as she could, she kept herself that I should not see them. Being in this boundless tribulation, I saw enter into the chambers a certain man, who in his appearance seemed to be as crooked as a capital S; and he began to say with a certain doleful tone of sadness (*un certo suon di vocie mesto*), like to those who give spiritual comfort (*il commandamento dell' anima*) to those who have to undergo capital punishment (*andare a giostizia*), and he said: "Oh, Benvenuto! Your work is spoiled; and there is no more help for it in this world." Directly I heard the words of that wretch, I uttered a cry so loud that it might have been heard from the firmament of fire: and raising myself from the bed I seized my clothes and began to dress myself. And to the maid-servants, and my boy, and every one who approached to assist me, to all I gave kicks or blows; and I lamented saying: "You traitors, and envious ones! This is a betrayal made on purpose. But I swear by God that I will understand it thoroughly, and that before I die I will leave such a proof of myself to the world that more than one of you will remain in astonishment." Having fin-ished dressing myself I went in an angry spirit towards my work-shop, where I saw all those people whom I had left with so much courage: all stood astonished and terrified. I began by saying: "Up! Listen to me! And since you have not either known how, nor wanted to obey me after the fashion that I instructed you, obey me now that I am with you in the presence of my own work, and do not let any one contradict me, for such cases as these have need of help and not of advice." To these words of mine there replied a certain Alessandro Lastricati, and he said: "See here! Benvenuto! you want to set about an undertaking, which the Profession does not allow of; nor can it be done by any means whatsoever." At these words I turned round with such fury, resolved on mischief, so that he and all the others all with one voice said: "Up! Give us your orders, for we will all help you as much as you can order us, as long as we can endure it with our lives": and I think that they uttered these kindly words supposing that I must after a very little time fall down dead. I went immediately to look at the furnace and saw the metal all congealed; a thing which they call "being made into a cake" (*l'essersi fatto un migliaccio*). I told two laborers to go opposite into the house of Capretta, the butcher, for a load of young oak boughs, that had been dried for more than a year, the which wood Mª Ginevra, the wife of the said Capretta, had offered me; and when the first armfuls had come I began to fill the grate.

And because oak of that kind makes a fiercer fire than any other
sort of wood (wherefore they employ alder and pine wood for
founding artillery, because it makes a gentle fire), oh! when the
cake began to feel that tremendous fire it began to clear, and it became luminous. On the other hand I was looking after the channels: and I had sent others (workmen) up on to the roof to keep off
the flame, which on account of the greater force of that fire had
kindled more violently; and on the side of the kitchen garden I
caused to be erected certain boards and some carpets and coarse
cloths, which sheltered me from the water. After that I had provided
a remedy for all these great disasters, with a very loud voice I kept
shouting, now to this man, and now to that: "Bring this here!" and
"Take that away!" in such a way that, when they saw the said cake
begin to liquefy, all that troop obeyed me with such goodwill that
each one did the work of three. Then I made them take half a pig
of pewter (*pane di stagnio*), which weighed about sixty pounds, and
I threw it in upon the cake within the furnace, which, together with
the other ingredients and the wood, by stirring it up, now with
irons, and now with bars, in a short space of time became liquid.
Now seeing that I had restored the dead to life, against the belief of
all those ignorant people, there returned to me so much vigor that
I did not perceive that I had any more fever, or any more fear of
death. All of a sudden I heard a loud noise with a very great flash
of flame, which seemed exactly as if a bolt had been discharged
there in our presence; by the which unaccustomed appalling fright
every one was terrified, and I more than the others. When that
great noise and flash had passed, we began to look one another in
the face again; and when we saw that the cover of the furnace had
burst, and had been lifted in such a way that the bronze was over-
flowing, immediately I made them open the mouths of my mold,
and at the same time I made them drive in the two plugs. And

when I saw that the metal did not run with that rapidity that it was accustomed to do, having recognized that the cause was perhaps that the alloy had been consumed by virtue of that terrible heat, I made them take all my plates and bowls and platters of pewter, which were in number about two hundred, and one by one I set them in front of my channels, and part I made them throw into the furnace; in such a way that when every one saw that my bronze had very thoroughly liquefied, and that my mold kept filling, they all assisted and obeyed me cheerfully and with joy; and, now here, now there, I kept giving orders, kept helping, and kept saying: "Oh God! Who with Thy immense Power hast raised Thyself from the dead, and hast ascended glorious into Heaven; in the same way that in a moment my mold has filled itself. For the which reason I kneel to you and thank God with all my heart." Then I turned to a plate of salad that was there on a low bench, and with a great appetite I ate and drank together with all that troop. Afterwards I went to bed healthy and joyful, for it was two hours before daybreak; and as if I had never had any ailment in the world, so peacefully did I repose. That excellent servant-maid of mine, without my saying anything to her, had provided me with a fat young capon; in such a way that when I arose from my bed, which was near the dinner-hour, she met me cheerfully, saying "Oh! Is this the man who felt like dying? I believe that those blows and kicks that you gave to us last night, when you were so infuriated, with that diabolical temper which you showed that you had, perhaps struck terror into that so inordinate a fever that you had, so that, lest you should attack it also, it took to flight." And thus I sent my poor establishment, relieved from so much fear and such inordinate efforts, immediately to purchase, in the place of those plates and bowls of pewter, as many earthen pots, and we dined so agreeably that I never remember in all my life eating with a greater joy, nor with a better appetite.

After dinner there came to see me all those who had assisted me, who joyously congratulated me, thanking God for all that had occurred. And they kept saying that they had learned and seen how to do things which by other masters were held to be impossible. I too, somewhat puffed up—fancying myself rather talented—prided myself about the matter: and putting my hand into my purse I paid everyone and satisfied them.

That evil man, my mortal enemy, Messer Pierfrancesco Ricci, the Duke's Major-domo, sought with much diligence to learn how the matter had passed off: in such fashion that those two of whom I had always had my suspicions that they had caused that cake to come about said that I was not a human being: rather I was certainly some powerful fiend, for I had done that which Art could not accomplish; as well as many other important matters, which would have been too much for any ordinary fiend. And since they kept saying much more than had (actually) occurred, perhaps to excuse themselves, the said major-domo wrote immediately to the Duke, who was at Pisa, yet more alarmingly about it, and full of greater marvels than they had told him.

When I had let my (newly) cast work cool for two days I began to uncover it by slow degrees. And I found, the first thing, the head of *Medusa*, which had come out most excellently by reason of the air vents, just as I had told the Duke that the nature of fire was to go upwards. Afterwards I proceeded to uncover the rest, and I found the other head, that is to say, that of *Perseus*, which had likewise resulted very well. And this gave me much more astonishment, because as may be seen it is very much lower than that of *Medusa*. And, since the outlets of the said work were placed up above the head of *Perseus*, and behind his shoulders, I found that all the bronze that there was in my furnace was entirely exhausted in the completion of the head of *Perseus*. And it was a wonderful thing, that in the mouth of the casting not a scrap remained, nor however was anything lacking (to the statue): and this caused me so much astonishment, that it seemed really a miraculous thing, verily guided and directed by God Himself. I went happily forward in completing my uncovering, and always kept finding everything had resulted very excellently, till at length I arrived at the foot of the right leg upon which the statue stands, where I found that the heel had come out, and proceeding onward I saw that it was all complete, in such a way that I rejoiced over it much in one respect, while on the other hand I was half discontented, merely because I had told the Duke that it could not come out. However on completing the uncovering I discovered that the toes of the said foot had not come out, and not only the toes, but there was wanting a small portion above the toes, to such an extent that almost half was wanting; and, although that little would increase my labor, I was very pleased if only to demonstrate to the Duke that I did understand what I was doing. And although there had resulted much more of that foot than I had expected, the cause of it had been that, on account of the said so many divers accidents, the metal was hotter than the rules of our profession prescribe; and also because I had had to supplement the alloy after that fashion that has been described with those plates of pewter, a thing that has never been done by any one else. Now seeing my work so successfully accomplished, I immediately went to Pisa to see my Duke; who gave me as extremely cordial a reception as it is possible to imagine in the world; and the Duchess did likewise: and although that major-domo of theirs had informed them of everything, it seemed to Their Excellencies another thing more stupendous and more wonderful still to hear me relate it by word of mouth. And when I came to

that foot of *Perseus,* which had not succeeded as I had previousl
warned His Most Illustrious Excellency, I saw him filled with aston
ishment; and he recounted to the Duchess how I had told him o
it beforehand. Now when I saw these lords of mine so agreeabl
towards me, I thereupon begged the Duke to permit me to go t
Rome. So he kindly gave me permission, and told me that I mus
return speedily to finish his *Perseus,* and he wrote me letters o
recommendation to his Ambassador, who was Haverardo Serristori
And these were the first years of Pope Julio de' Monti.

B EFORE I started I gave orders to my workmen that they should continue according to the methods which I had shown them. And the reason why I went was that I had made a representation of Bindo d'Antonio Altoviti's head, exactly as large as life, in bronze, and when I sent it to him in Rome, he set this portrait of himself up in his study, which was most richly adorned with antiquities and other fine things; but the said study was not adapted for sculptures, still less for pictures, because the windows came below the said fine works in such a way that these sculptures and paintings, having the light opposite to them, did not show as well in that way as they would have done if they had had their proper lighting. One day it chanced that the said Bindo was at his own door, and as Michel-agniolo Buonaroti the sculptor happened to be passing by, he besought him that he would deign to enter his house to see his study; and so he took him in. Immediately on entering and looking round it he said: "Who is this master who has portrayed you so well, and in such fine style? Know that that head pleases me as much and somewhat more than do those antiques; and yet there are some good things to be seen among them; and if those windows were above them, instead of below them, they would show off so much better; so that great honor would be done to that portrait of yours among these many fine works of art."

Directly the said Michelagniolo had left the house of the said Bindo he wrote me a most amiable letter, which ran as follows: "Benvenuto mine! I have known you for so many years as the greatest goldsmith regarding whom we have ever had any information: and now I shall recognize you to be a sculptor of a similar (renown). Know that Messer Bindo Altoviti took me to see a portrait head of himself in bronze, and told me that it was your handiwork. I received much pleasure from it. But I took it very ill that it was placed in a bad light, for if it had been in its proper light it would show what a fine work it is." This letter was full of the most kindly words and most complimentary expressions toward me: so that before I left to go to Rome I showed it to the Duke, who read it with much interest and said to me: "Benvenuto! If you are writing to him and could cause him to be willing to return to Florence I would make him one of the Forty-Eight." So I wrote him such a kindly letter, and in it I said on behalf of the Duke one hundred times more than I had had directions to do. And since I did not want to make a mistake, I showed it to the Duke before I sealed it; and I said to His Most Illustrious Excellency: "My Lord! I have perhaps promised him too much." He answered and said: "He deserves more than you have promised him; and I will moreover keep to it." To this letter of mine Michelagniolo never made any reply, for the which reason the Duke showed me that he was very indignant with him. Now when I arrived in Rome, I went to lodge in the house of the said Bindo Altoviti: and he immediately told me that he had shown his portrait in bronze to Michelagniolo, and that he had praised it very much. So we discoursed upon this matter a very long time. But because he had in hand one thousand two hundred gold *scudi* in gold belonging to me, the which the said Bindo had held for me, together with five thousand similar *scudi,* which he had lent to the Duke: that is four thousand were his own and my money was in his name, and he gave me the income (*hutile*) of my part as it became due to me; which was the reason for my setting myself to make the said portrait (bust). And since, when the said Bindo saw the wax (model) he sent to me as a gift 50 gold *scudi* by Ser Giuliano Paccalli, one of his notaries, who lived with him: which money I did not want to take, and sent it back by the same person, and afterwards said to the said Bindo: "It is sufficient for me that you keep my money alive, so that I may gain something out of it." And I perceived that he had an evil disposition, for instead of performing courtesies to me, as he had been accustomed to do, he behaved haughtily towards me; and, although he kept me in his house, he never showed himself sincere to me, rather he was surly. However we settled it in a few words: I lost my labor (*fattura*) upon his portrait and the bronze also: but we agreed that he should keep my money at fifteen per cent. during my natural life. First I went to kiss the feet of the Pope: and while I was conversing with the Pope there came in Messer Haverardo Serristori, who was the Ambassador of our Duke. And since I had raised certain discussions with the Pope, by which I believe that I should easily have come to an agreement with him, I would willingly have returned to Rome, on account of the great difficulties that I experienced in Florence; but I perceived that the said Ambassador had worked in opposition to me. I went to see Michelagniolo Buonaroti and I repeated to him that letter which I had written him from Florence on behalf of the Duke. He replied that he was employed on the

Fabric of St. Peter's, and for such a reason he could not depart thence. Thereupon I told him that as soon as he had resolved upon the model for the said Fabric, he could leave his (pupil) Urbino, who would obey very excellently whatever he might order him; and I added many other promises (*parole di promesse*) speaking on behalf of the Duke. He immediately gazed fixedly at me, and said slily: "And how are you satisfied with him?" Although I said that I was very content, and that I was very well treated, he showed that he knew the greater part of my annoyances; and so he answered that it would be difficult for him to be able to leave. Thereupon I rejoined that he should do best to return to his own country, which was ruled over by a most just lord and a greater lover of talent than any other lord that was ever born in the world. As I have said above he had with him an apprentice of his, who was from Urbino, who had been with him for many years and had served him more as a personal attendant (*ragazzo*) and housekeeper (*serva*) than anything else, which was evident, as it could be seen that the said youth had not learned anything about the profession; and because I had constrained Michelagniolo with many so excellent arguments that he knew not how to answer me at once, he turned to his Urbino for the purpose of asking him how the matter appeared to him. This Urbino of his immediately, with one of his rustic gestures, in a very loud voice spake thus: "I do not want ever to separate myself from my Messer Michelagniolo, until either I shall flay him, or he shall flay me." At these silly words I was compelled to laugh, and without saying "Good-bye," with lowered shoulders I turned and departed.

Since I had conducted my business with Bindo Altoviti so badly, with the loss of my bronze head and the giving him my money for (the term of) my life, I learned clearly of what sort is the faith of merchants, and so discontentedly I returned to Florence. I went

immediately to the Palace to visit the Duke, and His Most Illustrious
Excellency was at Castello, above the bridge at Rifredi. I found in
the Palace Messer Pierfrancesco Ricci, major-domo, and when I
wished to address my accustomed salutations to the said man, he
immediately said with unbounded astonishment: "Oh! So you are
returned!" and with the same (air of) astonishment, striking his
hands together he said: "The Duke is at Castello": and turning
his back upon me he departed. I could neither understand nor
imagine the reason why that beast had performed such acts. I went
immediately to Castello, and having entered into the garden where
the Duke was, I saw him for a distance, so that when he saw me he
made a gesture of astonishment, and gave me to understand that I
must go away. I, for I had promised myself that His Excellency
would show me the same courtesies and even greater ones than he
had displayed towards me when I went away (to Rome), now seeing such strange conduct returned to Florence very ill content; and
having taken up my business again, endeavoring to bring my work
to an end, I could not think of any chance from which that circumstance could proceed: noticing however in what way Messer Sforza
and certain others of the Duke's special intimates regarded me, the
desire came to me to ask Messer Sforza what was the meaning of it;
who smiling meaningly (*cosi*), said: "Benvenuto! Attend to being
an honest fellow, and take no notice of anything else."

A few days after I was given the opportunity of speaking to the
Duke, and he showed me certain troubled (*torbide*) civilities, and
asked what I had been doing in Rome: so that the best I knew how
I kept up the conversation and told him of the head that I had made
in bronze for Bindo Altoviti, with all that followed. I saw that he
was listening to me with great attention: and I told him likewise
all about Michelagniolo Buonaroti. He showed some annoyance
and at the words of his Urbino, which he had said about the flaying,

he laughed loudly. Then he said: "So much the worse for him (*suo danno*)"; and I departed.

It is certain that that S. Pierfrancesco, the major-domo, must have done me some evil office with the Duke, which did not succeed: because God, the Lover of Truth defended me, as always up to this period of my life He has saved me from so many countless perils, and I hope that He will save me up to the end of this my life of mine, troubled though it be: nevertheless I go boldly forward, in His Strength alone, nor does any rage of fortune or of perverse planets terrify me; so God only maintain me in His Grace.

Now listen, most kindly reader, to a most terrible mishap. With as much diligence as I knew and was able, I kept my attention to the completion of my work, and in the evening I went to pass the time in the Duke's Wardrobe, assisting those goldsmiths who were laboring for His Most Illustrious Excellency; for the greater part of those works which they were carrying out were after my designs. And, since I saw that the Duke took great pleasure in it, as much in seeing us work as in chatting with me, it seemed to me appropriate to go thither also some times by day.

Being one day among the others in the said Wardrobe, the Duke came according to his custom; and much more willingly, because His Most Illustrious Excellency knew that I was there. And directly he arrived he began to discourse with me on many divers and most agreeable matters; and I answered accordingly, and I charmed him in such a manner that he showed himself more amiable towards me than he had ever shown himself in the past. All of a sudden one of his secretaries appeared, who speaking in His Excellency's ear (for it was perhaps a matter of much importance) the Duke rose directly and went into another chamber with the said secretary. And since the Duchess had sent to see what His Most Illustrious Excellency was doing, the page reported to the Duchess: "The

Duke is chatting and laughing with Benvenuto, and in an amiable mood." When she heard this, the Duchess immediately came into the Wardrobe, and not finding the Duke, sat herself down near us. And when she saw that we had a piece of work on hand, with much amiability she turned to me and showed me a necklace of large and really very rare pearls; and on asking me what I thought of it, I told her that it was a very beautiful thing. Thereupon Her Most Illustrious Excellency said to me: "I want the Duke to buy it for me. Therefore, Benvenuto mine! Praise it to the Duke as much as ever you know how and can." At these words I, with as much courtesy as I knew, confessed myself to the Duchess, and said: "My Lady, I thought that this necklace of pearls belonged to Your Most Illustrious Excellency; but now that I know that it does not belong to Your Most Illustrious Excellency, since reason does not compel me to refrain from saying anything that it occurs to me to say, rather it is necessary for me to say it. Your Most Illustrious Excellency must know that, since it is my own particular profession, I recognize in these pearls very many defects, on account of which I should never advise Your Excellency to purchase it." At these words of mine she said: "The merchant offers it to me for six thousand *scudi;* but if it had not had some of those small defects, it would be worth more than twelve thousand." Thereupon I said, that even if that necklace had been of entirely complete quality I would never advise anyone to go up to five thousand *scudi* for it. For pearls are not precious stones; pearls are a kind of fish-bone and in course of time must deteriorate; but diamonds and rubies and emeralds and sapphires do not grow old. These four are (real) precious stones, and these one ought to buy. At these words of mine the Duchess said to me somewhat indignantly: "I have a desire now for these pearls, and therefore I beg you to carry them to the Duke, and praise them as much as ever you can and know how to; and although it may seem to you that you are uttering some small amount of falsehood, say it to do me service, for it will be well for you."

I, who have always been most devoted to the truth and the enemy of lies, being (compelled) by necessity, anxious not to lose the favor of so great a princess, thus ill-content took those accursed pearls, and went with them into that other chamber, whither the Duke had retired. Directly he saw me he said: "Oh! Benvenuto! What are you doing here?" Displaying those pearls I said: "My Lord! I am just come to show you a very beautiful necklace of pearls, a most rare one and truly worthy of Your Most Illustrious Excellency. And for eighty pearls I do not believe that there were ever so many put together that showed off better in a necklace. Therefore purchase them, My Lord! for they are miraculously (fine)." The Duke immediately said: "I do not want to buy them, for they are not such pearls, nor of that excellence of which you say they are; and having seen them they do not please me." Thereupon I said: "Pardon me, My Lord! These pearls exceed in infinite beauty all the pearls that were ever arranged for a necklace." The Duchess had risen up, and was standing behind a door, and she heard all that I was saying: in such a way that when I had said more than a thousand things—more than I write down here—the Duke turned to me with a benign expression, and said to me: "Oh! Benvenuto mine! I know that you understand the subject very well; and if these pearls were possessed of so many of those rare merits that you attribute to them, there would not appear to me to be any difficulty about purchasing them, whether to please the Duchess, or merely in order to possess them; for I have need of these things, not so much for the Duchess, as for my other arrangements for my sons and daughters." And I at these words of his,—since I had begun to tell lies,—with yet greater boldness continued to utter them, giving them greater color of truth in order that the Duke might believe me, trusting to the Duchess that at the proper time she would help me. And although I anticipated for myself more than two hundred *scudi* for making such a bargain, and the Duchess had hinted as much to me, I had resolved and determined to be unwilling to take a single *soldo,* merely for my own security, in order that the Duke should not think that I had done (the job) out of avarice. Again the Duke, with most amiable expressions, began saying to me: "I know that you understand these things very well. Consequently if you are that sort of honest man that I have always thought that you were, now tell me the truth." Then, reddening up to my eyes, which became somewhat suffused with tears, I said: "My Lord! If I tell the truth to Your Most Illustrious Excellency the Duchess will become my most mortal enemy; for the which reason I shall be obliged to depart at once and my enemies will immediately revile the credit of my *Perseus,* which I have promised to this most noble School of Your Most Illustrious Excellency: therefore I commend myself to Your Most Illustrious Excellency." The Duke having understood that all that I had affirmed I had been made to say as if under compulsion, said: "If you have faith in me have no doubt about anything in the world." Again I said: "Alas! My Lord! How can it be possible that the Duchess will not hear of this?" At these words of mine the Duke took an oath, and said: "Count upon having buried this in a casket of diamonds." At these noble words I immediately related the truth as I understood it about those pearls, and that they were not worth very much more than two thousand *scudi.*

The Duchess having heard us stop talking, for we were speaking, as far as it was possible to speak, in a low voice, came forward, and said: "My Lord! Will Your Excellency of your kindness buy me this necklace of pearls, for I have a very great desire for it, and your

Benvenuto has said that he never saw a more beautiful one." Thereupon the Duke said: "I do not want to buy it." "Why, My Lord! does not Your Excellency wish to please me by buying this necklace of pearls?" "Because it does not please me to throw away the money." The Duchess again said: "Oh! How do you throw away the money; for your Benvenuto, in whom you deservedly put so much faith has told me that it would be cheap at more than three thousand *scudi?*" Thereupon the Duke said: "My Lady! My Benvenuto has told me that if I buy them I shall be throwing away my money, for these pearls are neither round nor equal in size, and many of them are old. And that this is the truth now look at this and at this other, and see here, and there. Therefore they are not in my way."

At these words the Duchess looked at me with a most malevolent expression, and threatening me with her head, departed thence in such a fashion that I was tempted to go away at once and disappear from Italy. But because my *Perseus* was almost finished I did not want to lose the chance of exhibiting it: nevertheless let every man consider in what serious tribulation I found myself. The Duke ordered his porters in my presence that they should always permit me to enter the chambers and to wherever His Excellency might be; and the Duchess commanded those very same persons that every time that I arrived at the Palace they should drive me away; in such a way that when they saw me, they immediately came out of those doors and drove me away. But they watched that the Duke should not see them; for if the Duke saw me before these wretches did, he either summoned me or made a signal to me that I should come to him. The Duchess summoned that Bernardone, the agent, of whose roguery and vile worthlessness she had so often complained to me, and commended herself to him, as she had done to me; who said: "My Lady! Leave the matter to me." This big villain went into the Duke's presence with this necklace in his hand. The Duke, directly he saw him, said that he must take himself off. Thereupon that said big villain with that great ugly voice of his, which he sounded through his big ass's nose, said: "Pray! My Lord! Buy this necklace for that poor lady, who is dying of desire for it, and cannot live without it." And adding many other stupid ugly expressions, and becoming a nuisance to the Duke, he said: "Oh! Go away from here, or puff yourself out at once." This big ugly villain, who knew very well what he was doing, for, whether by way of puffing out, or by singing *La Bella Franceschina,* he could contrive that the Duke should make that purchase, he would gain the thanks of the Duchess, and his brokerage besides, which amounted to several hundreds of *scudi;* and so he puffed and the Duke gave him several heavy slaps on those big ugly chaps of his, and in order to get rid of him, he gave them a little more violently than he was accustomed to do. At these heavy blows on those ugly chaps of his, not only did they become over red, but the tears rolled down. With these he began saying: "See! My Lord! I am a faithful servant of yours, who seeks to do right, and is content to endure every sort of discomfort, in order that that poor lady may be happy."

Since this wretched fellow had become such a nuisance to the Duke, and on account of the slaps in his face, and for love of the Duchess, whom His Most Illustrious Excellency always wanted to please, he (the Duke) immediately said: "Get away with the evil luck (*malanno*) that God may bring upon you, and go make the bargain, for I am content to do all that the Lady Duchess desires." Now here may be seen the wrath of evil fortune against a poor man, and the shameful luck that favors a scoundrel. I lost all the favor of the Duchess, which was good cause for taking from me also that of the Duke; and he (Baldini) gained that large brokerage and their favor. Therefore it is not sufficient to be an honest and virtuous man.

AT this time there broke out war with Siena. And since the Duke desired to fortify Florence, he distributed the gates among his sculptors and architects. Wherefore to me was assigned the gate towards Prato and the postern leading to the Arno ,which is in the meadow as one goes to the Mills; to Cavaliere Bandinello the gate at San Friano; to Pasqualino d'Ancona the gate at Sanpier Gattolini; to Giuliano di Baggio d'Agniolo, the joiner, the gate at San Giorgio; to Particino, the joiner, the gate at Santo Niccolo; to Francesco da Sangallo, the sculptor, called *Margolla,* was assigned the Porta alla Crocie; and to Giovanbatista,

called *il Tasso,* was given the Porta a Pinti; and similarly various
other bastions and gates were allotted to different engineers whom
I do not remember, nor does it make any difference to my argument. The Duke, who really was always of excellent ability, of
his own accord went around his own city. And when His Most
Illustrious Excellency had well examined it, and made up his
mind, he summoned Lattanzio Gorini, who was one of his pay-
masters. And since this man also dabbled somewhat in this profession, His Most Illustrious Excellency directed him to design all
the methods wherewith he desired the said gates to be fortified, and
to each one of us he sent the design for his gate; in such a way
that when I saw that (design) which was allotted to me, and it
seemed to me that the manner of it was not in accordance with
common sense, rather that it was most incorrect, I immediately
with this design in my hand went to see my Duke; and being desirous of pointing out to His Excellency the defects of that design
which had been given to me, no sooner had I begun to talk, than
the Duke infuriated turned upon me and said: "Benvenuto! In
the making statues most excellently I will yield to you, but in this
profession I wish you to yield to me. Therefore carry out the design that I have given to you!" To these bullying (*brave*) words
I answered as gently as I knew how in this world, and I said:
"Even, My Lord! in the fine method of making statues I have
learned something from Your Most Illustrious Excellency, wherefore we have always disputed together to some small extent; so in
this matter of fortifying your city,—a matter of far greater importance than the making of statuary,—I beseech Your Most Illustrious Excellency that you will deign to listen to me. And discussing
thus with Your Excellency, you will be the better able to demonstrate to me the manner in which I can serve you." Whereupon,
at these most courteous words of mine, he kindly began a discus-

sion with me; and on demonstrating to His Most Illustrious Excellency with vivid and clear reasonings that it would not be satisfactory (to fortify) according to the method which he had designed for me, His Excellency said to me: "Oh! Go and make a design yourself, and I will see if it pleases me." So I made two designs for fortifying those two gates according to the correct rule, and I took them to him; and when he had recognized the true from the false, His Excellency said to me courteously: "Oh! Go and do it in your way, for I am content." Thereupon with great diligence I commenced. There was on guard at the Porta al Prato a Lombard captain. This man was a fellow of tremendously robust figure and of very coarse speech; but he was presumptuous and very ignorant. This man immediately began asking me what I wanted to do; upon which I courteously exhibited to him my designs and with extreme trouble I gave him to understand the method in which I wanted to carry them out. Then this vulger beast, now shook his head, now turned this way, now that, frequently changing the position of his legs and twisting the ends of his moustache, which he wore very long; and he kept frequently pulling down the peak of his cap over his eyes, repeatedly saying: "Plague upon it! I don't understand this business of yours." Wherefore, the beast becoming an annoyance to me, I said: "Let me then do it for myself, for I do understand it": but as I turned my back to him to go to my work, the man began threatening me with his head; and with his left hand, which he placed upon the pommel of his sword, he raised the point of it somewhat and said: "Ho there! Master! So you want to bring me to the point of bloodshed (*che io facci quistion teco al sangue*)." I turned me round in great wrath, for he had aroused my anger, and I said: "It will seem less trouble to me to fight with you than to build a bastion for this gate." In a moment we both laid hands upon our swords, but we had not entirely unsheathed them, when there immediately came upon us a number of honest men, some being our Florentine fellow-citizens and others courtiers. And the greater number of them scolded him, telling him that he was in the wrong, and that I was a man able to pay him back, and that if the Duke were to know of it, woe to him. So he went about his business; and I began upon my bastion. And when I had given my directions for the said bastion, I went to the other postern on the Arno, where I found a captain from Cesena, the most courteous man of worth that I ever knew in such profession: and he appeared to be like a charming young maiden, and yet in time of need he was the bravest of men and the most bloodthirsty that can be imagined. This agreeable person watched me so attentively that many times he made me bashful; and he desired to understand (what I was doing), and I courteously explained it to him. It is sufficient that we endeavored which of us could show the greater courtesies to one another; in such a way that I made this bastion much better than that other one. When I had almost completed my bastions, in consequence of an attack having been made by certain soldiers of those troops of Piero Strozzi's, the district of Prato was so terrified that (the inhabitants) all deserted their homes, and on this account all the carts in that district came laden, every one conveying their property to the city. And since the carts jostled each other, for there was a very great number of them, when I saw such a disorder I warned the sentries at the gates that they must take heed lest there should occur at that gate a disturbance such as happened at the gates of Turin; for if it were necessary to have recourse to the portcullis (*saracinesca*), it could not do its duty, since it would remain suspended upon the top of one of those wagons. When that great beast of a captain heard these words of mine, he turned upon me with insulting expressions, and I answered him accordingly; in such fashion that we were about to enter upon a much worse (quarrel) than the first time. Wherefore we were separated, and I, having finished my bastions, unexpectedly received several *scudi,* which delighted me, and gladly returned to finish my *Perseus.*

During these days there were found in the district of Arezzo certain antiques, among which was the *Chimaera,* which is that bronze lion which may be seen in the chambers adjacent to the Great Hall of the Palace. And along with the said *Chimaera* there were found a number of small statuettes, also of bronze, which were covered with earth and rust; and since to each of these there was wanting either the head or the hands or the feet, the Duke took great pleasure in cleaning them himself with certain small goldsmith's chisels. It chanced that I happened to speak to His Most Illustrious Excellency, and while I was chatting with him, he handed me a little hammer, with which I struck those little chisels that the Duke was holding in his hand, and in that way the said little figures were cleared from the earth and from the rust. When several evenings had thus passed away, the Duke set me to work, whereupon I began to remake those limbs which were wanting to the said little figures. And since His Excellency took so much pleasure in that small matter of these little things, he made me work also by day, and if I delayed in going to him His Most Illustrious Excellency sent for me.

Many times I made His Excellency understand that if I diverted the day time from the *Perseus,* several inconveniences would follow. And the first of these which terrified me most was that the vast amount of time which I saw that my work was taking up would be a reason for causing annoyance to His Most Illustrious Excellency, as subsequently did happen to me; the other was, that I had a number of workmen, and when I was not present they committed two notable abuses. And the first of these was that they ruined my work, and the other that they worked as little as possible; therefore the Duke was satisfied that I should go to him only from twenty-four of the clock onwards. And thus I had pacified His Most Illustrious Excellency so marvelously that, when I came to him in the evening, he kept increasing his courtesies towards me. In these days he was building those new rooms towards the (Via dei) Leoni; so that, when His Excellency wished to retire apart more privately, he had fitted up for him a certain small chamber in these newly built apartments, and he directed me that I should come to him by way of his Wardrobe, whereby I passed very privately across the gallery of the Great Hall, and by way of certain small closets (*pugigattoli*) I used to go to the said small chamber most privately: of which (privilege) in the space of a few days the Duchess deprived me, causing all those conveniences for me to be closed up; in such a way that every evening when I arrived at the Palace I had to wait a long time for the reason that the Duchess for her private convenience (*comodità*) remained in those ante-chambers, through which I had to pass; and since she was ailing I never arrived at any time when I did not incommode her. Now for this and for another cause she conceived for me so much dislike, that for no reason could she bear to see me; but in spite of all this my great discomfort and infinite trouble, I continued patiently to go thither. The Duke had however given express commands upon the point, so that directly I rapped upon those doors they were opened to me, and without saying anything to me I was allowed to enter anywhere; in such a way that it happened sometimes that, entering quietly thus unexpectedly by way of those private apartments, I found the Duchess employed upon her own private affairs (*comodità*); who immediately burst out upon me with so much angry fury that I was terrified, and she kept always saying to me: "When will you ever finish repairing those little figures?

For I am now excessively annoyed at this coming and going of yours." At which I gently answered: "My Lady! My sole patroness! I wish for nothing else but to serve you faithfully and with the utmost obedience. But since these commissions which the Duke has ordered of me will last for many months, will Your Most Illustrious Excellency tell me if you do not wish me to come here any more. I will not come for any reason whatsoever, let who will summon me. And although the Duke should summon me I will say that I am ill, and in no sort of way will I ever come here." To these words of mine she replied: "I do not tell you not to come here, and I do not tell you not to obey the Duke. But it appears plainly to me that these works of yours will never have an end." Whether the Duke received some information about it, or that it fell out in some other way, His Excellency began again; as soon as it drew near to 24 of the clock he used to send to summon me; and the person who came to summon me said to me: "I warn you not to fail to come, for the Duke is waiting for you": and thus I continued under the same difficulties for several evenings. And upon one evening among the others, on entering according to my custom, the Duke, who must have been talking with the Duchess, perhaps upon private matters, turned upon me with the greatest fury in the world; and when I, somewhat terrified, wished to withdraw quickly, all of a sudden he said: "Enter, Benvenuto! and go on with your work, and in a little while I will come and join you." As I was passing along, there seized me by the cloak the Lord Don Gratia, a little boy of a few years of age, and he played with me in the most charming manner that such a child could possibly do: whereat the Duke marveling said: "Oh! What a charming friendship is this that my children have for you." While I was occupied in these articles of small importance, the Prince and Don Giovanni and Don Hernando and Don Gratia used to station themselves behind me every morning, and unseen by the Duke keep poking at me: whereat I used to keep begging them of their kindness to leave off. They used to answer me, saying: "We cannot." And I said to them: "That which is impossible no one expects. Now do as you please! Go on!" All of a sudden the Duke and Duchess burst out laughing. Another evening, when I had finished those four small bronze figures, which are inserted into the base—which are *Jove, Mercury, Minerva* and *Danae (the mother of Perseus) with her little Perseus (suo Perseino) seated at her feet* —having had them brought into the said chamber where I worked in the evening, I set them in a row a little higher than the point of vision, in such a way that they made a most beautiful effect. The Duke having heard of this, came thither somewhat sooner than was his custom. And since that individual who informed His Most Illustrious Excellency must have reckoned them much higher than what they were (for he told him that they were better than antiques and such similar things), my Duke came, along with the Duchess, chatting cheerily about my work; and I rising immediately went to meet them. He, with those Ducal and fine manners of his, raised his right hand in which he held a pear-shoot as large as it is possible to see, and very fine, and said: "Do you, Benvenuto mine! plant this pear in the kitchen-garden of your house!" To these words I replied pleasantly: "Oh! My Lord! Does Your Most Illustrious Excellency in very truth tell me to plant it in the kitchen-garden of my own house?" Again the Duke said: "In the kitchen-garden of the house which is yours. Have you understood me?" Thereupon I thanked His Excellency, and likewise the Duchess, with greatest ceremony that I knew how to show in the world. Then they both sat down opposite the said statuettes, and for more than two hours they talked of nothing else but these beautiful little figures; in such a way that there came to the Duchess so immoderate a desire that she thereupon said to me: "I do not want these beautiful little figures to go and be lost upon that base down in the Piazza, where they will run the risk of being injured. Rather do I wish you to arrange them for me in one of my apartments, where they will be preserved with that reverence which their very rare merits deserve." To these words I raised opposition with many elaborate arguments, and when I saw that she was resolved that I should not place them in the base where they now are, I waited until the following day. And I went into the Palace at 22 of the clock, and finding that the Duke and Duchess were out riding, having already prepared my base, I had the little figures brought down and immediately soldered them in as they were intended to be. Oh! When the Duchess heard of it her anger grew so violent, that if it had not been for the Duke who skillfully assisted me, I should have caused her much harm: and on account of that anger in connection with the pearl necklace and of this matter she worked so hard that the Duke was deprived of that little bit of pleasure; which was the reason why I went thither no more, and I immediately fell back into the same difficulties that I was in before regarding my access to the Palace. I returned to the Loggia whither I had already conveyed the *Perseus,* and I went on finishing it under the difficulties already spoken of: that is to say, lack of money: and with so many other misfortunes, that the half of them would have terrified a man clad in adamant (*armato di diamanti*). Pursuing my way however according to my customs, one morning among the others, having heard Mass in San Piero Scheraggio, there came into my presence Bernardone, the agent, that worthless goldsmith (*horafaccio*): and through the kindness of the Duke he was purveyor to the Mint. And suddenly, as he was just outside the door of the Church, the ugly pig let fly four blasts of wind (*coreggie*) which you might have heard up at San Miniato.

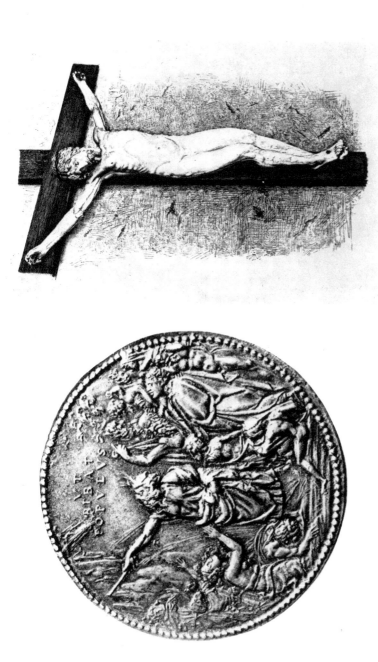

Left, a medal by Cellini showing Moses striking the rock. Right, Cellini's white marble crucifix which was bought by the Duke of Florence who presented it to Philip II of Spain, where it hangs in the Escorial.

At which I said: "Oh! you pig, coward, and ass! Is this the voice of your filthy talents?" and I ran for a stick. He quickly retired into the Mint, while I stood on the threshold of my door, and kept outside a little boy of mine, who should give me a signal when this pig should come out of the Mint. Now when I saw that I had waited some considerable time, becoming bored, and that small amount of irritation having subsided, when I remembered that blows are not given by contract, whereat some inconvenience might ensue, I resolved to take my revenge in another way. And since this event happened about the time of the Feast of our San Giovanni,—within a day or two,—I made these four lines and affixed them upon the corner of the church, at the place where they performed the necessities of nature, and they ran as follows:

> Here lies that donkey Bernard, called the Big,
> Pandora's heir, spy, broker, robber, pig:
> All her worst ills are his, and handed on
> By him to Buaccio, his block-head son.

The story and the lines found their way to the Palace, and the Duke and the Duchess laughed at them: and before he (Baldini) had perceived them himself, there had halted there a great many people, and they made the greatest merriment in the world. And as they were gazing in the direction of the Mint, and fixing their eyes upon Bernardone, his son Master Baccio perceiving (the lines) immediately tore them down in a great rage, while he (Bernardone) bit his thumb, pouring out threats with his great ugly voice, which issued through his nose: he made a great display of bravado.

When the Duke heard that all my work on the *Perseus* could be exhibited as complete, he came one day to see it, and showed by the most clear signs that it satisfied him greatly; and turning to certain lords who were with His Most Illustrious Excellency, he said: "Although this work may appear to us very beautiful, it has also to please the people. Therefore, Benvenuto mine! before you give the last touch to it, I would like you out of affection for me to uncover a little of this part (of the screen) on the side of my Piazza, for half a day, in order to see what the people say about it. For there is no doubt that from seeing it in this enclosed fashion to seeing it in an open space it will produce a different effect from that which it displays shut up thus." To these words I replied humbly to His Most Illustrious Excellency: "Know, My Lord! that it will show half as well again. Oh! how is it that Your Most Illustrious Excellency does not remember having seen it in the kitchen-garden of my house, wherein it showed so well in such a wide space that from the kitchen-garden of the Innocenti Bandinello came to see it; and in spite of all his bad and very evil nature he was compelled to, and has spoken highly of it in such a way as he has never spoken well of any one in his life? I perceive that Your Most Illustrious Excellency believes too much in him." At these words of mine, sneering with a little irritability, with many kindly words he said: "Do it, Benvenuto! if merely to give me a small satisfaction." And when he had departed I began to give directions for uncovering it. And since it was lacking in a little gold and certain varnishes and other such trifles, that belong to the completion of the work, I kept murmuring angrily and complaining, cursing that unlucky day which was the occasion of bringing me back to Florence; for I had already seen the very great and certain loss that I had made by my departure from France, and I did not see nor know besides in what way I could hope for prosperity with this Lord of mine in Florence. Since from the commencement to the middle, and to the end, everything that I had done was always accomplished with much destructive loss: and thus ill content I unveiled it the following day. Now as it pleased God, directly it was seen, so immoderate a cry arose in praise of the said work as was the cause of consoling me somewhat. And the people did not cease from continually attaching (sonnets) to the posts (*spalle*) of the door, at which was kept a little drapery, while I gave it its finishing touches. I say that the same day, during which I kept it unveiled for several hours, there were more than twenty sonnets attached (to my door), all in most unmeasured praise of my work. After that I had covered it up again, every day there were affixed a quantity of sonnets, and of verses in Latin and verses in Greek; for, since it was the vacation at the University of Pisa, all those most excellently learned persons and scholars vied with each other (upon the subject). But that which gave me greater content with hope of greater prosperity for myself as regards my Duke was the fact that those members of the profession, that is to say, sculptors and painters, also vied with each other as to who could speak best about it. And among the others, the one whom I esteemed the most was the clever painter, Jacopo da Puntorno, and besides him his excellent (pupil) Bronzino the painter, to whom it was not sufficient to cause several to be affixed (to the door), but he sent them by his boy Sandrino to my house, speaking so well (of it) with that charming style of his, which is very rare, that this was the occasion of consoling me somewhat. And so I covered it up again and made haste to finish it. My Duke, although His Excellency had heard of the favor which had been shown to me at that short inspection by this most excellent School, said: "It gives me great pleasure that Benvenuto has had this small piece of satisfaction, which will be the occasion for his bringing the work to its desired completion with more speed and with more diligence. But don't let him think that later, when it shall be seen all unveiled, and one can see all round it, that the people will speak of it after this same fashion; rather there will be discovered all the defects that there are in it, and many will be attributed to it which are not there. Therefor let him provide himself with patience." Now these were words of Bandinello addressed to the Duke, along with which he quoted the works of Andrea del Verocchio, who made that fine *Christ and Santommaso* (*sic*) in bronze, which may be seen on the façade of Horsamichele (*sic*); and he cited many other works down to the wonderful *Davitte* (*sic*) of the divine Michelagniolo Buonaroti, saying that that figure only showed off well when seen in front; and then he spoke about the numerous and abusive sonnets which had been attached to his *Hercules and Cacus* and abused this public (of Florence). My Duke, who believed in him very much, had induced him to utter those expressions, and he thought that for certain the event must come out to a great extent in that way; for that envious (creature) of a Bandinello never left off speaking evil. And upon one occasion among many others when that great scoundrel (*manigoldo*) Bernardone, the agent, was present, in order to support the words of Bandinello, he said to the Duke: "Know, My Lord! that to make large figures is another species of dish (*minestra*) to making little ones. I don't want to say that he has not made the small figures well enough; but you will see that that one (the large one) will not succeed." And with these evil words he mingled many others, carrying out his business of spy, in the which he mingled a mountain of lies.

Now as it was pleasing to My Glorious Lord and Immortal God I finished it entirely; and one Thursday morning I unveiled the whole of it. Immediately, though it was not yet daylight, there assembled so vast a number of people, as it is impossible to describe; and all with one voice kept striving which could say the best things about it. The Duke stood at a lower window of the Palace, which is above the door, and thus half-hidden within the window-frame, listened to all that was said about the said work. And after he had listened for several hours, he rose with so much courage, and so satisfied, that, turning to his Messer Sforza, he spake thus: "Sforza! Go and find Benvenuto, and tell him on my behalf that I am much more pleased with it than I expected. And tell him that I will satisfy him in such a fashion as will make him marvel. Therefore tell him to be of good courage." So the said Messer Sforza brought me this splendid message, which heartened me; and that day for this good news and because the people kept pointing with the finger, now to this merit, now to that, as a thing wonderful and new. . . . Among the rest were two noblemen who had been sent on business by the Viceroy of Sicily to our Duke. Now these two amiable personages encountered me in the Piazza, for I was pointed out to them as they were passing by; so that they came up to me hurriedly, and immediately, with their caps in their hands, made me one of the most ceremonious of speeches, such as would have been too much even for a Pope. I, however, as much as I was able, belittled myself: but they overwhelmed me so much that I began to beg them that of their kindness they would leave the Piazza, for the people were stopping to gaze at me more closely than they were doing at my *Perseus*. And amid these ceremonies they were so pressing that they invited me to go to Sicily, and would have made such a contract with me as would content me; and they told me that Fra Giovanagniolo de' Servi had made for them a fountain, complete and adorned with many figures, but that they were not of that excellence which they perceived in *Perseus*; and that they had made him very rich. I did not allow them to finish all that they would have liked to say, for I said to them: "I marvel much at you that you should seek to make me leave such a patron, a lover of talent more than any other prince that ever was born, and when I am besides in my native country, the School of all the greatest talents. Oh! If I had an appetite for great gains I could have remained in France in the service of that great King Francesco, who gave me one thousand gold *scudi* for my maintenance (*piatto*), and paid me besides for the cost of production of all my works, in such fashion that every year I gained more than four thousand gold *scudi per annum*; and I have left behind in Paris my labors of four entire years." With these and other words I cut short their ceremonies, and I thanked them for the great praises that they had bestowed upon me, which were the greatest rewards that can be given to one who has labored conscientiously. And (I told them) that they had increased so much my desire to do well that I hoped in a few years' time to exhibit to them another work, which I hoped would please that wondrous Florentine School much more than the (present) one. The two noblemen wanted to recommence their string of ceremonies; whereat I lifting my cap with a low bow wished them "Good-bye."

After that I had allowed two days to pass by, and I saw that the great praises (of my work) kept on continually increasing, I thereupon prepared myself to go and show myself to my Lord the Duke; who with great amiability said to me: "Benvenuto mine! you have satisfied and pleased me. But I promise you that I will content you in such a fashion as will make you marvel. And I tell you besides that I do not wish to delay beyond to-morrow (*che e' passi il giorno di domane*)." At these wonderful promises, I immediately turned all my highest powers both of soul and body in a moment to God, thanking Him in very truth; and at the same moment I approached my Duke, and thus half-crying with joy, I kissed his robe. Then I rejoiced, saying: "Oh! My Glorious Lord! True and most liberal lover of the arts, and of those men who labor upon them! I beseech Your Most Illustrious Excellency to do me the favor of allowing me first to go for eight days to thank God. For I know well the boundless extent of my great toil, and I recognize that my great faith has moved God Himself to come to my aid. For this and for every other miraculous assistance, I want to go an eight days' pilgrimage, continually giving thanks to my Immortal God, Who always helps those who truly call upon Him." Thereupon the Duke asked me whither I wished to go. To which I replied: "To-morrow morning I will depart and will go to Valle Hombrosa; then to Camaldoli and to the Eremo. And I will go as far as the Bagni di Santa Maria, and perhaps as far as Sestile; for I hear that there are some fine antiquities there! Afterwards I will return by San Francesco della Vernia, and always giving thanks to God I will return content to serve you." The Duke immediately said to me cheerfully: "Go and return! For you truly please me. But leave me a couple of lines to remind me, and leave the matter to me." I at once wrote four lines, in the which I thanked His Most Illustrious Excellency; and I gave them to Messer Sforza, who gave them on my behalf into the Duke's hand; who took them. Afterwards he gave them into the hand of the said Messer Sforza, and said to him: "Arrange every day to set the matter before me; for if Benvenuto should return and find that I had not hastened it, I believe that he would murder me." And laughing thus His Excellency said that he must be reminded of it. These positive words were repeated to me in the evening by Messer Sforza laughingly, and wondering moreover at the great favor that the Duke was displaying towards me; and he said to me pleasantly: "Go! Benvenuto! And come back again, for I envy you."

Chapter Fourteen   *1554-1556*

I SET out from Florence in the Name of God constantly chanting
psalms and prayers to the Honor and Glory of God throughout
the whole of that journey. In the which I took very great pleasure,
for the season of summertime was very beautiful and the journey
and the country, wherein I had never before been, appeared to me
so beautiful that I was both astonished and pleased at it. And because there had come as my guide a young workman of mine, who
was from Bagnio and was called Cesere, I was much welcomed by
his father and by all his household: among whom there was a vet-
eran of more than 70 years of age, a most agreeable man. He was
uncle to the said Cesere, practised the profession of a surgeon
(*medico cerusico*) and had in him something of the Alchemist.
This good man pointed out to me how that this (place) Bagni(o)
possessed a mine of gold and silver, and he enabled me to see many
very fine things in that district; in such a way that I experienced as

great enjoyment as I ever had. When I had become intimate with him to his liking, one day among others he said to me: "I do not wish to omit telling you an idea of mine, to which if His Excellency should lend an ear, I believe it would be a most useful piece of information. And it is this, that in the vicinity of Camaldoli is to be found a pass so unprotected (*scoperto*), that Piero Strozzi could not merely pass through it safely, but he would be able to plunder Poppi without any opposition." And together with this piece of information, having pointed it out sufficiently in words, he took a sheet (of paper) from his wallet, upon which this good old fellow had sketched out all that district in such a fashion that it could be most excellently seen, and it could be clearly understood that the great danger was a real one. I took the plan and departed immediately from Bagnio, and, proceeding as fast as I could by the road through Prato Magnio and San Francesco della Verni, I returned to Florence; and without stopping except to draw off my riding-boots I went to the Palace. And as I was by the Badia I met my Duke, who was coming along the street of the Palace of the Podestà: who directly he saw me gave me a most gracious welcome together with some surprise, saying to me: "Oh! Why have you come back so soon? For I did not expect you for these eight days or more to come." To which I replied: "I have returned on Your Most Illustrious Excellency's service; for I would gladly have spent several days wandering through that most beautiful country." "And what good business brings you?" said the Duke. At which I said: "My Lord! It is necessary that I should speak to you and point out to you matters of great moment." So I went with him to the Palace. When we were arrived in the Palace he took me into his room privately, where we were alone. Then I told him everything, and I exhibited to him that sketch plan, which he showed himself most pleased to have. And when I told His Excellency that it was necessary to remedy such a matter quickly, the Duke remained thus a little while in thought, and then he said to me: "Know that we are in agreement with the Duke of Urbino, who has to look after this matter. But keep it to yourself." And with very great demonstration of his good will I returned to my home. The next day I presented myself, and the Duke after a short chat, said to me cheerfully: "To-morrow without fail I want to hurry up your affair. Therefore be of good cheer." I, who reckoned the matter as most certain, awaited the next day with great longing. When the longed-for day arrived I went to the Palace: and as by custom it seems that it always happens that evil news pass with greater rapidity than do the good, Messer Jacopo Guidi, His Most Illustrious Excellency's Secretary called to me with his pursed-up mouth and haughty voice, and drawing himself all up into himself, with an appearance all stiffened like a ramrod, he began to speak after this fashion: "The Duke says that he wishes to know from you how much you ask for your *Perseus.*" I remained bewildered and astonished; and I answered immediately that I was never in the habit of fixing prices for my labors, and that this was not what His Excellency had promised me two days before. Immediately this man in a louder voice said to me that he commanded me expressly on behalf of the Duke, to tell him what I wanted, under pain of His Most Illustrious Excellency's total displeasure. I, for I had promised myself, on account of the great courtesies shown to me by His Most Illustrious Excellency, not only to have gained something, but I had even greatly anticipated that I had acquired the whole favor of the Duke, because I never asked for any other greater reward than merely (some portion) of his good will; now this method, so unexpected by me, caused me to fly into such a rage; and even more at the manner in which that poisonous toad presented it to me. I said that if the Duke were to give me ten thousand *scudi,* he would not pay me, and that if I had ever thought that I should come to these straits, I would never have stopped here. This spiteful fellow immediately uttered to me a number of insulting remarks, and I did the same to him.

The next day following, when I made my bow to the Duke, His Excellency beckoned to me: whereat I approached him; and he said to me angrily: "Cities and great palaces are built with tens of thousands of ducats." To which I immediately replied, that His Excellency would find a vast number of men who might know how to build cities and palaces; but that for *Persei* he would perhaps not find a single man in the world who knew how to carry out such a work. And I immediately departed without saying or doing anything more. A few days later the Duchess sent for me, and told me that I must consign the difference that I had with the Duke to her, for she boasted herself that she could arrange the matter so that I should be satisfied. To these kind words I replied, that I had never demanded any other reward for my labors than the good favor of the Duke, and that His Most Illustrious Excellency had promised it to me. And that there was no need that I should refer to their Most Illustrious Excellencies that which from the first days in which I began to serve them I had already freely committed to them. And I added besides, that if His Most Illustrious Excellency only gave me for my labors one single penny, which has but the value of five *quattrini,* I should call myself content and satisfied, so long as His Excellency did not deprive me of his good favor. At these words of mine the Duchess smiling somewhat, said: "Benvenuto, you will do better to do what I tell you": and turning her back upon me she departed from me. I, for I thought that I was doing the best for myself by employing those humble words, chanced to have produced the worse effect for myself: for, although she had had a certain amount of wrath against me, she had afterwards a certain measure of conduct in her, which was kindly disposed. At this period I was very intimate with Girolimo degli Albizi, who was Commissary of the troops of His Excellency. And one day among the others he said to me: "Oh! Benvenuto! It would be a good thing to set to rights this small difference that you have with the Duke. And I tell you that, if you have faith in me, I will put my heart into arranging it, for I know what I am talking about. If the Duke should become enraged in earnest, you will fare very badly in the matter. Let this be sufficient; I cannot tell you everything." And since I had been told by someone—perhaps a mischievous person, after that the Duchess had spoken to me—who told me that he had heard it said that the Duke,—upon I don't know what specified occasion,—had said: "For less than two *quattrini* I would throw away *Perseus,* and thus end all these differences." Now on account of this jealousy I said to Girolimo degli Albizi, that I would entrust the whole matter to him, and that with whatever he did I should be most entirely satisfied, so long as I might remain in the Duke's good graces. This honest man, although he understood most excellently the art of soldiering, especially that of those troops who are all peasant-folk, took no interest in the art of making pieces of sculpture, and therefore understood nothing at all about it; in such a fashion that in talking with the Duke he said: "My Lord! Benvenuto has put himself into my hands, and has besought me to commend him to Your Most Illustrious Excellency." Then the Duke said: "And I also commit myself to you, and I shall be content with all that you adjudicate." Thereupon the said Girolamo composed a very clever letter, and one greatly in my favor, and awarded that the Duke should give me three thousand five hundred gold *scudi* in gold, which should not be taken as payment for such a fine work, but merely as a small sum towards my support; it sufficed that I was to be satisfied; with many other words, which entirely fixed the said price. The Duke agreed to this letter as gladly as I was dissatisfied with it. When the Duchess heard it, she said: "It would have been much better for that poor man if he had committed the matter to me; for I would have made them give him five thousand gold *scudi*." And one day when I went to the Palace the Duchess repeated the same words in the presence of Messer Alamanno Salviati, and she made sport of me, saying that all the evil that I had received was good for me. The Duke directed that I should be paid one hundred gold *scudi* in gold per month, up to the said amount, and thus several months passed by. Afterwards Messer Antonio de' Nobili who had had the said commission, began by giving me fifty, and then sometimes he gave me twenty-five, and sometimes he gave me nothing; in such a way that when I saw the matter thus so long drawn out I asked the said Messer Antonio civilly, begging him that he would tell me the reason why he did not complete my payments. He also replied to me courteously; in the which reply it seemed to me that he wandered from the point a little too much, as let him judge who understands the matter. He first of all told me that the reason why he did not continue my payments was on account of the very great shortness (of money) that they were suffering from at the Palace, but he promised me that when money came to him he would pay me; and he added, saying: "Alas! If I do not pay you I shall be a great scoundrel." I was astounded to hear him make such a speech, but on that account he promised me that when he could I should be paid. Wherefore when it turned out exactly the opposite, in such a fashion that I saw myself being ill-used, I was enraged with him; and I uttered many fierce and furious words to him; and I recalled to him all that he had told me should happen. Eventually he died and I remain yet up to this present hour, with five hundred gold *scudi* still due to me, which is nearly the end of the year 1566. I was entitled besides to have the remainder of my salary, which it seemed to me that they would pay no more attention to paying me, because about three years had already passed. But there fell upon the Duke a dangerous illness, for he passed forty-eight hours without being able to make water; and when he recognized that the doctors' remedies were of no avail, he perhaps turned himself to God, and on this account wished that everyone should be paid his arrears of salary, and I also was paid. But I was not paid the balance upon my *Perseus.*

I was almost half-disposed to say nothing further about my unlucky *Perseus;* but so notable an event occurred that I am forced to do so, therefore I will take up again the thread for a little, turning somewhat back. I thought I was acting to my best advantage when I told the Duchess that I could no further compromise that which was no longer in my power, for I had told the Duke that I was satisfied with all that His Most Illustrious Excellency might be willing to give me. And this I said, thinking to gain some favor for myself. And with that little display of humility I sought every likely means of somewhat placating the Duke, for a few days before that he had come to an agreement with Albizi the Duke had shown himself to be much provoked with me, and the reason was that when I was complaining to His Excellency of the most disgraceful injustices that Messer Alfonso Quistello and Messer Jacopo Polverino, the Fiscal, were committing upon me, and more than all of them Ser Giovanbatista Brandini of Volterra. When I explained these arguments of mine thus with some display of passion, I saw the Duke getting into as great a rage as it is possible ever to imagine. And when His Most Illustrious Excellency had come to this pitch of fury he said to me: "This case is like that of your *Perseus,* for which you have demanded ten thousand *scudi.* You allow yourself to be too much overcome by your greed; therefore I wish to have it valued, and I will give you for it all that may be awarded against me." To these words I immediately responded to some small extent too hotly and half furiously, a thing which is not suitable to do with great lords, and I said: "Oh! How is it possible for the value of my work to be reckoned when there is no man to-day in Florence who knows how to do it?" Thereupon the Duke waxed more furious still, and uttered many passionate expressions, among which he said: "There is a man in Florence to-day who should know how to do a thing like that, and therefore he will know very well how to judge it." He wished to allude to Bandinello, Knight of S^{to} Jacopo. Then I said: "My Lord, Your Most Illustrious Excellency has given me the privilege of executing in the greatest School in the World an important and very difficult work, which has been praised more than any work that was ever unveiled in this most divine School. And that which makes me more proud is that of those brilliant men who understand, and who belong to the profession, like Bronzino the painter, this man has gone to work, and has written upon me four sonnets, using the most well-chosen and glorious words that it is possible to employ; and on account of this wondrous man almost the whole city is moved to so great an excitement *(rumore)*. And I say well that, if he had devoted himself to sculpture as he does to painting, he would have understood well how to do it. And I say moreover to Your Most Illustrious Excellency that my master Michelagniolo Buonaroti, although he would have executed such a thing when he was younger, would not have endured less labor than I have done; but now that he is very old he could certainly not have done it at all. So that I do not believe that at the present day we have knowledge of a man who would understand how to accomplish it. So that my work has achieved the greatest reward that I could desire upon earth. And more than all that Your Most Illustrious Excellency, not only expresses yourself content with my work, but rather that you have praised it more than any other man. Oh! What greater or more honorable reward could a man desire? I say for very surety that Your Excellency could not have paid me more in more glorious coin: nor could he with any wealth whatsoever equal this. Therefore I am overpaid and I thank Your Most Illustrious Excellency with all my heart." To these words the Duke replied and said: "Rather you think that I have not sufficient to be able to pay you. But I tell you that I will pay you much more than it is worth." Thereupon I said: "I did not expect to have any other reward from Your Excellency; but I call myself most well paid by that first (reward) that the School has given me, and with this I will go right away this very moment *(adesso adesso)*, without ever returning any more to that house which Your Most Illustrious Excellency presented to me, nor do I ever care to see Florence again." We were just at Santa Felicita, and his Excellency was returning to his palace. At these angry words of mine the Duke immediately turned in great wrath and said to me: "You are not to go, and take care that you do not go"; in such a fashion that half terrified I accompanied him to the Palace. When His Excellency arrived at the Palace he called Bishop De' Bartolini, who was Archbishop of Pisa, and summoned Messer Pandolfo della Stufa, and told them to tell Baccio Bandinelli on his behalf that he must consider carefully that work of mine of *Perseus,* and that he must value it, because the Duke wished to pay me its just value. These two worthy men immediately found the said Bandinello, and when they gave him the message, he told them that he had very carefully considered that work, and that he knew too well what it was worth; but since he was at discord with me regarding other past matters, he did not want to be mixed up with my affairs in any way whatsoever. Thereupon these two noblemen rejoined and said: "The Duke has said to us that, under pain of his displeasure, he commands you to fix the value, and if you desire 2 or 3 days' time for careful consideration, do you take them: and then tell us what it seems to you that the labor deserves." The said man replied that he had very carefully considered it, and that he could not neglect the commands of the Duke, and that that work had turned out very splendid and fine, to such a point that it appeared to him that it was worth sixteen thousand gold *scudi* and more. Those excellent noblemen immediately reported this to the Duke, who was greatly irritated; and they likewise repeated it to me. To whom I responded that in no way whatsoever would I accept the praises of Bandinello, since this evil man spoke ill of every one. These words of mine were repeated to the Duke, and for this reason the Duchess wanted me to entrust the matter to her. All this is the pure truth: it is sufficient to say that I did my best to leave myself to the Duchess' judgment, in order that I might shortly be paid, and I should have had that reward besides.

The Duke let me know through Messer Lelio Torello, auditor, that he wanted me to make certain histories of his on bas-reliefs of bronze around the Choir of Sᵃ Maria del Fiore; and since the said Choir had been undertaken by Bandinello I did not want to embellish his trashy work with (the results of) my labor; but for all that the said Choir was not after his design, for he did not understand anything in the world about architecture: the design was made by Giuliano di Baccio d'Agniolo the joiner, who spoiled the Cupola. It is sufficient that there was no talent in it; and for the one reason and the other I did not want in any way whatsoever to execute such a work. But I always kept politely telling the Duke that I would do all that His Most Illustrious Excellency might command of me; so that His Excellency commissioned the Directors of the *Opera* (*operai*) *di Sᵗᵃ Maria del Fiore* that they should make an agreement with me: that His Excellency would merely provide my allowance of two hundred *scudi* per annum, and that he desired that the said Directors of the *Opera* should furnish every other thing from the Fund of the said *Opera*. So that I appeared before the said Directors, who informed me of all the orders that they had received from the Duke: and since it seemed to me that with them I could more safely explain my arguments, I began by pointing out to them that so many histories in bronze would be a very great expense, which was entirely thrown away: and I gave them all the reasons; by which they were fully convinced. The first (reason) was that that arrangement of the Choir was altogether incorrect, and was made without any judgment, nor could one see in it either art, or convenience, or grace, or design; the other was that the said histories were to go into too low a position, that they would come too much below the line of vision, that they would be a place for dogs to make water upon (*un pisciatoi' da cani*) and would be continually covered with all sorts of filth, and that for the said reasons by no means whatsoever did I want to execute them. It was only in order not to cast away the remainder of my best years without obliging His Most Illustrious Excellency, whom I desired so much to please and serve. Therefore if His Excellency wanted to make use of my labors he would allow me to make the central door of Sta Maria del Fiore, which would be a work that would be conspicuous, and would be much more to the glory of His Most Illustrious Excellency. And I would bind myself by a contract that if I did not make it better than that which is the most beautiful of the doors of S° Giovanni, I wanted nothing for my labor; but if I carried them out according to my promise, I would content myself that they should make a valuation, and afterwards give me one thousand *scudi* less than the price at which it was valued by the men of the profession.

These Directors were much pleased by the thing which I had proposed to them, and they went to speak of it to the Duke. There was one among the rest, Piero Salviati, who thought that he was saying something that would be most agreeable to the Duke, and it was quite the opposite; for (the Duke) said that I was always wanting to do the exact opposite to that which it pleased him that I should do: and without any other decision the said Piero departed from the Duke. When I heard this I immediately went to see the Duke, who showed himself somewhat angry with me. I begged him that he would deign to listen to me, and so he promised to do. So that I commenced from the beginning; and with so many fine arguments I gave him to understand the truth of the matter, pointing out to His Excellency that it was a great expense thrown away; in such fashion that I much soothed him by saying that, if His Most Illustrious Excellency was not pleased that I should make that door, there was need of executing for that Choir two pulpits, that they would be two important works, and would be to the glory of His Most Illustrious Excellency, and that I would fashion a great number of histories in bronze in low relief with much decoration: thus I soothed him, and he commissioned me to make the sketch-models. I made many models and endured very great fatigue; and among the others I made one with eight panels, with much greater study than I expended upon the others, and it seemed to me that it was much more convenient for the purpose for which it had to serve. And since I had carried them many times to the Palace, His Excellency gave me to understand by Messer Cesere, the Wardrobe-Keeper, that I must leave them. After that the Duke had seen them I perceived that His Excellency had chosen the less beautiful. One day His Excellency had me summoned, and in discussing these said models, I told him and pointed out to him with many arguments that the one with the eight panels would be much more suitable for such a purpose, and much more beautiful to look at. The Duke answered me that he wanted me to make it square, because it pleased him much more after that fashion; and so he discussed it with me a long time very pleasantly. I did not hesitate to tell him all that occurred to me in defense of the art (in my work). Oh! That the Duke could have known that I spoke the truth; but nevertheless he wanted it made in his own way: and it was a long time before anything more was said to me about it.

AT this period the great piece of marble for *Neptune* had been conveyed up the river Arno, and then transported by way of the Grieve along the road by Poggio a Caiano, so as to enable it to be more easily conveyed to Florence by that level road, whereon I went to see it. And that although I knew for very certain that the Duchess by her own special favor had caused Cavaliere Bandinello to obtain it; not out of any envy that I bore to Bandinello, but rather inspired by pity for the poor unlucky piece of marble. Observe that, whatever the object may be, if it be subject to an evil destiny, though one may seek to avoid some obvious ill, it happens that one falls into one much worse, as did the said marble at the hands of Bartolomeo Ammannato, regarding whom I will tell the true story in its own place. When I had seen this most beautiful piece of marble, I immediately measured its height and its width from all points, and returning to Florence I made several appropriate models. Afterwards I went to Poggio a Caiano, where were the Duke and the Duchess, and the Prince their son; and finding them all at table—the Duke and the Duchess were eating apart—I set myself to amuse the Prince. And when I had entertained him for some considerable time, the Duke who was in an apartment close by, heard me, and with much courtesy had me summoned. And when I reached the presence of Their Excellencies, with many polite words the Duchess began to chat with me: and in the course of that conversation little by little I commenced to talk about that very beautiful piece of marble that I had seen; and I began by reminding them that their ancestors had made their most noble School so very brilliant solely by causing all the talented men in their profession to enter into competition; and that after that ingenious fashion had been created the wondrous Cupola, and the very beautiful doors of S^{to} Giovanni and the so many other fine temples and statues, which formed a crown of such brilliance for their city, which from the older masters onwards has never been equaled. Immediately the Duchess said to me irritably that she knew very well what I wanted to imply, and she told me that I was never again to mention that piece of marble in her presence, for I was causing her displeasure. I said: "Then I cause you displeasure by wishing to act as proctor for Your Excellencies, arranging everything in order that you may be better served? Consider, My Lady! if Your Most Illustrious Excellencies were pleased that every one should make a model of a *Neptune,*—although you are resolved that Bandinello should have (the commission),—it would be a reason that Bandinello for his own credit should employ greater care in making a fine model, which he would not do if he knew that he had no competitors: and in this way you, our patrons (*signiori*), would be better served, and would not take away the courage of the talented School; and you will see who excels,—I speak of the fine methods of this wondrous Art,—and Your Lordships will show that you delight in it and understand it." The Duchess in great wrath told me that I was wearying her, and that she wished that that piece of marble should be Bandinello's; and she said: "Ask the Duke about it, for His Excellency also wishes that it should be Bandinello's." When the Duchess had spoken, the Duke who had continually kept silent, said: "It is twenty years since I had that fine piece of marble quarried expressly for Bandinello, and so I wish Bandinello to have it and it shall be his." I turned at once to the Duke and said: "My Lord! I beg serves to have it (*i.e.*, the commission)." Then the said men both spoke highly in my favor, and more especially the Ambassador from Lucca, who was a well-read person, and a doctor (*dottore*). I, for I had gone a little way off, in order that they might be able to say all that seemed good to them, hearing them speak in my favor, immediately drew near, and turning to the Duke I said: "My Lord! Your Most Illustrious Excellency ought again to give another special (*mirabil*) trial: to give orders that whoever wants to may make another model in clay of the same size exactly as (the statue) is to result out of that marble; and in that manner Your Most Illustrious Excellency will see much better who deserves it. And I tell you, that if Your Excellency gives it to one who does not deserve it, you will not wrong the one who does deserve it, rather you will wrong your own self, for you will acquire injury and shame: whereas by doing the opposite, by giving it to him who does deserve it, you will, in the first place, acquire very great glory, and you will spend your treasure well, and talented persons will then believe that you do like and understand these things." Directly I had uttered these words, the Duke shrugged his shoulders, and as he was starting to go away the Ambassador of Lucca said to the Duke: "My Lord! This Benvenuto of your[s] is a formidable man." The Duke replied: "He is much mor[e] formidable than you say he is, and it would be well for him if h[e] were not so formidable, because he would at this present time hav[e] had commissions that he has not had." These particular words th[e] same Ambassador repeated to me, as if reproving me that I oug[ht] not to act thus. To whom I replied, that I loved my lord as his lo[v]ing faithful servant, and I did not know how to act the flattere[r.] After several weeks had passed Bandinello died: and it was b[e]lieved that, over and above his ailments, this disappointment

Your Most Illustrious Excellency that you will grant me the favor that I may speak to Your Excellency four words in your service." The Duke told me that I might say all that I wished, and that he would listen to me. Thereupon I said: "You know, My Lord, that that marble out of which Bandinello made *Hercules and Cacus* was quarried for that wondrous Michelagniolo Buonaroti, who had made a model of a *Samson* (*Sénsone*), (a group of) four figures, which would have been the finest work (of art) in the world, and your Bandinello extracted from it but two figures only, badly executed and entirely botched; wherefore the talented School still complains of the great wrong that was done to that fine piece of marble. I believe that there were attached to it more than one thousand sonnets in abuse of that abominable work, and I know that Your Most Illustrious Excellency remembers that very well. And therefore, My Noble Lord! if those men who had such a charge were so unwise that they took from Michelagniolo that fine piece of marble which was quarried for him and gave it to Bandinello, who spoiled it as may be seen, oh! will you ever tolerate that this still much more beautiful piece of marble should, although it does belong to Bandinello who will spoil it, not be given to some other talented man who will use it befittingly? Direct, My Lord! that every one who will, shall make a model, and then all shall exhibit them to the School and Your Most Illustrious Excellency will hear what the School says. And Your Excellency with that excellent judgment of yours will know how to choose the best, and in this way you will not throw away your money, nor even less take away the desire for merit from so admirable a School, which is to-day unique in the world: for the entire glory of it belongs to Your Illustrious Excellency." The Duke when he had listened to me very kindly, immediately rose from the table, and turning to me said: "Go, Benvenuto mine! and make a model, and earn that fine piece of marble, for you are telling me the truth and I recognize it." The Duchess, threatening me with her head, indignantly began murmuring I don't know what. And I made my bow to them and returned to Florence, for it seemed to me a thousand years ere I set my hand to the said model. When the Duke came to Florence, without letting me hear anything further, he came to my house, where I displayed to him two small models, differing one from another. But although he praised them both to me, he told me that one pleased him more than the other, and that I must finish thoroughly that which pleased him, for it would be to my advantage. And since His Excellency had seen the one which Bandinello had made, and also some of the others, His Excellency praised mine at much greater length, for so was I informed by many of his courtiers who had heard him. Among other remarkable things to be remembered, and to make special note of, it happened that there came to Florence the Cardinal of Santa Fiore. And as the Duke was taking him to Poggio a Caiano, on the way thither in passing, on seeing the said piece of marble, the Cardinal praised it greatly, and then asked to whom His Excellency had consigned it to be worked upon. The Duke immediately answered: "To my Benvenuto, who has made a most beautiful model for it." And this (statement) was repeated to me by men of credit. For this reason I went to visit the Duchess, and I carried her some pretty little examples of my trade, which Her Most Illustrious Excellency liked very much. Then she asked what I was laboring upon; to which I replied: "My Lady! I have undertaken for pleasure to carry out one of the most laborious tasks that was ever done in the world. And this is a Crucifix of very white marble, upon a cross of very black marble; and it is of stature large (*grande*) as a living man." She immediately asked me what I wanted to do with it. I said: "Know, My Lady! that I would not give it to any one for

two thousand gold ducats in gold. For into such a work no man has ever put so vast an amount of labor. Still less would I have contracted to make it for any lord whatsoever, for fear lest I should be shamed by it. I bought the pieces of marble with my own money, and I have kept a lad for about two years, who has assisted me; and, what with the pieces of marble and the irons upon which it is kept steady, and wages, it has cost me more than three hundred *scudi*. Therefore I will not give it up for two thousand gold *scudi*. But if Your Most Illustrious Excellency wants to confer upon me a very reasonable favor, I will willingly make you a free present of it. Only I beg Your Most Illustrious Excellency that you will not show disfavor to me,—still less not favor me,—with regard to the models of *Neptune* that His Most Illustrious Excellency has commissioned to be made for the great block of marble." She said with much wrath: "Then you do not value my help nor my opposition at all?" "Rather, I do value it, My Lady! or why do I offer to present to you an object that I value at two thousand ducats? But I put my trust so much in my own laborious and painstaking studies that I anticipate winning the prize for myself, even though it had been against that great Michelagniolo Buonaroti, from whom, and never from any other, have I learned all that I know: and it would be much more pleasing to me if he should make a model, who knows so much than these others who know so little; for with that so great a master of mine I could profit very much, whereas with these others one cannot profit anything." When I had spoken these words she half-angrily rose, and I returned to my work, putting forward my model as much as I was able. And when I had finished it the Duke came to see it, and there were with him two Ambassadors, the one from the Duke of Ferrara and the other from the Signioria of Lucca, and they were thus greatly pleased; and the Duke said to these lords: "Benvenuto really de-

witnessing the loss of the piece of marble was the principal cause of it.

The said Bandinello had heard that I had made that *Crucifix* of which I have spoken above. He immediately set his hand to a piece of marble and made that *Pietà* that may be seen in the Church of the Nunziata. And since I had destined my *Crucifix* for Santa Maria Novella, and I had already fixed the staples for setting it up, I only asked leave to make in the ground beneath the feet of my *Crucifix* a little sepulcher to enter into after I was dead. The said monks told me that they could not grant me such a thing without asking the Directors of their Fabric (*Operai*). To whom I said: "Oh! my brothers! why did you not ask the Directors at first, when providing a place for my beautiful *Crucifix,* for which without their permission you have allowed me to fix the staples and other things?" And for this reason I would not any more give the results of my so severe labors to the Church of Santa Maria Novella, although subsequently those Directors came to see me, and besought me for it. I immediately turned to the Church of the Nunziata, and when I proposed to give it to them on those terms which I wanted to make at Santa Maria Novella, those pious monks of the said Nunziata all with one accord told me that I might set it up in their church, and that I could make my sepulcher in any way that seemed good to me and pleased me. Bandinello having got wind of this, set to work with great diligence to finish his *Pietà,* and demanded of the Duchess that she should enable him to have that chapel which belonged to the Pazzi; the which he got with difficulty. And directly he got it, with great haste he set up his piece of work there; the which was not completely finished when he died. The Duchess said that she had assisted him in life, and that she would aid him still in death; and that although he was dead, I must never cherish any idea of securing that piece of marble. Wherefore Bernardone the agent told me one day, on meeting me in the country, that the Duchess had given away the piece of marble. To whom I said: "Oh! Unfortunate marble! It is certain that it would have come off badly in the hands of Bandinello, but in the hands of Ammanato it has come off one hundred times worse." I had received orders from the Duke to make the clay model, of the size that it would result in marble, and he had caused me to be provided with the wood and the clay; and directed them to make me a little screen in the Loggia, where is my *Perseus,* and he paid for a laborer for me. I set to work with all the diligence that I could, and I made the skeleton of wood according to my excellent rule; and I brought it happily to its termination, not caring about making it in marble, for I knew that the Duchess was determined that I should not have it, and for this reason I did not trouble about it. It merely pleased me to endure that labor with which I promised myself, so that when I had finished it, and the Duchess, who was after all a person of intelligence, might chance later to see it I promised myself that she would be very distressed that she had inflicted upon the piece of marble and upon herself so unmeasured a wrong. And Giovanni the Fleming made a model in the cloisters of Sta Crocie, and Vincentio Danti of Perugia made one in the house of Messer Ottaviano de' Medici; another the son of Moschino began at Pisa, and another Bartolomeo Ammannato made in the Loggia, which we had divided between us. When I had well sketched it all out, and I wanted to begin finishing the head, to which I had already given a small part of its first touches, the Duke came down from the Palace, and Giorgetto the painter took him into the apartment of Ammannato, to show him the *Neptune,* upon which the said Giorgino had labored with his own hand for many days, along with the said Ammannato and with all his workmen.

While the Duke was looking at it I was told that he was very little satisfied with it; and although the said Giorgino wanted to fill him up with those chatters of his, the Duke shook his head, and turning to his Messer Gianstefano, he said: "Go and ask Benvenuto if his giant is sufficiently advanced that he will be willing to give me a glimpse of it." The said Messer Gianstefano very briefly and most courteously gave me the message on behalf of the Duke; and he told me besides that if my work did not seem to me to be yet fit to exhibit I must freely say so, for the Duke knew very well that I had had very little help in so vast an undertaking. I told him that he might come with pleasure, and although my work was little advanced the intelligence of His Most Illustrious Excellency was such that he could very well judge how it would result when finished. So the said nobleman took my message to the Duke who came gladly; and directly His Excellency entered the apartment, having cast his eyes over my work, he showed that he found much satisfaction therein. Afterwards he went all round it, stopping at the four points of view, in no other way than one most expert in the profession would have done. After that he showed many great signs and indications of exhibiting great pleasure, and he merely remarked: "Benvenuto! You have only to give it a last coat." Then he turned to those who were with His Excellency and spoke very highly of my work, saying: "The little model, which I saw in his house pleased me very much, but this work of his has surpassed the excellence of the model."

As it was pleasing to God, who does everything for our advantage:—I speak to those who recognize and believe in Him, God always defends them:—at about this time there fell in my way a certain scoundrel from Vicchio, called Piermaria d'Anterigoli, and (he bore) for his nickname *Sbetta* ("the Wedge") (*sic*): the trade of this man was that of a shepherd, and since he was a near rela-

tive of Messer Guido Guidi, the physician, and to-day Provost of
Pescia, I inclined my ear to him. This man offered to sell me one
of his farms for the term of my natural life. The which farm I
did not care to see because I had a desire to finish my model for the
Giant Neptune, and also because there was no need that I should
see it, because he sold it me for the income only: the which the
said man had noted down for me in so many bushels of wheat,
and of wine, oil, and corn and chestnuts and other profits; the which
said produce I reckoned at the period in which we were as worth
more than one hundred gold *scudi* in gold, and I gave him six
hundred and fifty *scudi,* including the taxes. So that, since he left
me a writing in his own hand, that he would always, for as long
as I lived, keep up for me the said income, I did not trouble myself
to go to see the said farm. But, nevertheless, in the best way that
I could, I made enquiries whether the said Sbietta, and Ser Filippo
his very own brother, were sufficiently well off to make me secure.
Thus by many different persons, who knew them, I was told that
I was most secure. We summoned by agreement Sr Pierfrancesco
Bertoldi, notary to the Mercatantia; and first of all I gave into his
hand all that the said Sbietta was willing to keep up for me, thinking that the said writing would have been set out in the contract.
However the said notary, who attested it, was attending to the
twenty-two boundaries, which the said Sbietta was reciting to him;
and, according to my opinion, he did not remember to include in
the said contract that which the said vendor had offered me; and
I, while the notary was writing, kept on working. And since it took
several hours to write out, I did a great piece of the head of the
said *Neptune.* So having completed the said contract, Sbietta began to show me the greatest civilities in the world, and I did the
like towards him. He presented me with kids, cheese, capons,
curds (*ricotte*) and many sorts of fruit, in such fashion that I be-

gan to be more than half (*mezzo mezzo*) ashamed; and in return
for these courtesies I took him, every time that he came to Florence away from the inn. And many times he was accompanied
by some one of his relatives, who came also: and in a pleasant way
he began saying to me that it was a shame that I had bought a
farm, and that now so many weeks had passed and I had not
arranged to leave my business a little for three days to my workmen and to go to see it. He succeeded so well in alluring me that
in my evil hour indeed I went to see it. And the said Sbietta received me into his house with so many courtesies and with so much
honor, that he could not have done more for a Duke. And his
wife showed me more civilities than he did. And in this way we
continued for a while, until there came to pass all that he and his
brother Sʳ Filippo had plotted. I did not leave off busying myself
about my work upon the *Neptune,* and I had already sketched it
all out, as I said above, upon a most excellent rule, such as has
never been employed, nor known by any one before me; to such
purpose that although I was sure of not having the piece of marble,
for the reasons given above, I believed that I should soon have
finished it (the model) and immediately allowed it to be seen in
the Piazza,—merely for my own satisfaction. The season was
warm and pleasant, in such a way, that being made so much of
by these two rascals, I started one Wednesday, which was a double
festival, from my villa at Trespiano and I made there a good
luncheon, so that it was more than twenty of the clock when I
arrived at Vicchio, and I immediately found Ser Filippo at the gate
of Vicchio; who seemed to know that I was coming. He showed
me many civilities and escorted me to the house of Sbietta, where
was his shameless wife. She also showed me unlimited courtesies;
to whom I gave a very fine straw hat; for she said she had never
seen one more beautiful. Sbietta himself was not there then. As

it drew near evening we all supped together very agreeably. Afterwards there was allotted to me a splendid bedroom, wherein I reposed myself in a very clean bed; and to my two servants were given the like according to their rank. In the morning, when I arose, there were shown to me the same courtesies. I went to see my farm, which pleased me: and there was handed over to me so much wheat and other (kinds of) corn (*biade*). And after that I had returned to Vicchio, the priest Sr Filippo said to me: "Benvenuto! Do not be uneasy. For if indeed you have not found everything entirely such as has been promised to you, be of good courage, for it will be kept up to your profit, because you are dealing with honest people. And know that we have dismissed this laborer because he was a rogue." This laborer was named Mariano Rosegli, who had told me many times: "Look well after your affairs, for in the end you will know which of us is the greater rogue." This rustic, when he spoke these words to me, smiled in a certain suspicious way, jerking his head, as if to say: "Go thither! that you will see for yourself." I formed rather an evil opinion of the matter, but I never imagined anything of what did happen to me. Having returned from the farm, which is two miles distant from Vicchio towards the Alps, I found the said priest, who with his accustomed courtesies was waiting for me. So we went to take luncheon all together: this was not a dinner, but it was an excellent luncheon. After that, I went walking about in Vicchio. The market had already begun; I found myself gazed at by all those inhabitants of Vicchio as a thing unusual to see, and more than all the others by an honest man who lived many years ago in Vicchio, and whose wife makes bread for sale. He has at nearly a mile from there certain excellent properties belonging to him: he is however content to live in that way. This honest man lives in one of my houses in Vicchio, which had been consigned to me with the said farm, which is called the Farm of the Fountain; and he said to me: "I am living in your house, and at the proper time I will give you your rent. Or if you want it beforehand I will do in all ways as you wish. It is sufficient if you will always be in agreement with me." And while we were talking together I observed that this man was fixing his eyes upon me: in such a way that I, constrained by such a circumstance, said to him: "Pray tell me, my dear Giovanni! why have you gazed at me many times so fixedly?" This worthy man said to me: "I will tell you willingly, if you being such a man as you are promise me not to say that I have told it you." So I promised him. Thereupon he said to me: "Know that that wicked priest Ser Filippo not many days ago went about boasting of the abilities of his brother Sbietta, saying that he had sold his farm to an old man for his life who would not survive the whole year. You are mixed up with a party of rogues; therefore contrive to live as long as you can, and open your eyes, for you have need to do so. I don't wish to say any more." While strolling through the market, I met Giovanbatista Santini, and he and I were taken to supper by the said priest. And as I said further back it was about twenty of the clock, and I was supping at so early an hour for my convenience, because I had said that I wanted to return that evening to Trespiano: so that they hastily prepared for it, and the wife of Sbietta worked hard, and among others a certain Cechino Buti, their bravo (*lancia*). When the salads were made and as we began to sit down to table, that said evil priest, making a certain wicked little laugh of his, said: "You must needs pardon me, for I cannot sup with you, because there has occurred to me a matter of great importance on behalf of my brother Sbietta: and since he is not here, it is necessary that I supply his place." We all besought him, but we could not prevail upon him at all. He departed and we began to sup. When we had eaten the salads out of certain common platters, in commencing to serve us with boiled meat, a soup-plate appeared for each person. Santino, who was at the table opposite me, remarked: "To you they are giving all the crockery different from these others. Did you ever see anything handsomer?" I told him that I had not noticed such a matter. He also suggested to me that I should summon to the table Sbietta's wife, who, she and that Cechino Buti, were running backwards and forwards, both extraordinarily busy. At length I begged that woman so much that she came. And she complained, saying to me: "My fare does not please you, wherefore you eat so little." When I had praised the supper several times over, telling her that I had never eaten with more willingness nor better, at last I said that I had eaten quite as much as I had need of. I should never have imagined why that woman put so much pressure upon me that I should eat. When we had finished supping it was already past 21 of the clock, and I had a desire to return that evening to Trespiano, so as to be able to go the next day to my work in the Loggia. So I said "Good-bye" to all; and having thanked the woman I took my departure. I had not gone three miles, when it seemed to me that my stomach was on fire, and I felt in such torment that it seemed to me a thousand years ere I arrived at my farm at Trespiano. As God willed, I arrived at nightfall with great difficulty, and at once made arrangements to go to bed. That night I could not sleep at all, and besides my bowels were disturbed which forced me several times to go to the closet, so much so that when daylight came, feeling that my genital organs were on fire, I wanted to see what could be the matter. I found the sheet covered with blood. At once I imagined that I had eaten something poisonous, and over and over again I turned over in my own mind what the thing could have been. And there returned to my memory those plates and bowls and saucers differing from the others allotted to me by the said wife of Sbietta, and (the reason) why that evil priest, the brother of the said Sbietta, who had been laboring so hard to do me such honor, did not then want to remain at supper with us himself. And there returned to my memory besides that the said priest had said that his (brother) Sbietta had done such a fine stroke (of business) in having sold a farm to an old man for life, who would never survive a year. For such words had been repeated to me by that honest man Giovanni Sardella. So that I concluded that they had given me in a bowl of sauce, which had been very well made and was very pleasant to the palate, a dose of sublimate (*silimato*); because sublimate causes all those symptoms that I observed that I had. But since I am accustomed to eat few sauces or condiments with meat, other than salt, I consequently chanced to eat but two small mouthfuls of that sauce, because it was so good to the taste. And I went on to remember how many times the said wife of Sbietta kept urging me in divers fashions, telling me that I must eat that sauce: so that I knew for very certain that with that said sauce they had administered me that small dose of sublimate. Though I was suffering in that way I went anyhow to work upon my *Giant* in the said Loggia, so much so that a few days later a violent illness overcame me so entirely that I was confined to my bed. Directly the Duchess heard that I was ill she caused the commission for that unlucky marble, now at liberty, to be given to Bartolomeo dell' Amannato, who sent to tell me by Messer . . . that I could do what I liked with the model which I had begun, for he had earned the piece of marble. This Messer . . . was one of the lovers of the wife of the said Bartolomeo Ammannato: and because he was the most favored, since he was polite and discreet, this said Ammanato gave him every opportunity, upon which subject there would be much to say of importance. However I do not want to act as did Bandinello his master, who in his arguments wandered away from the question of art. It is sufficient that I said . . . I had always foreseen it; and therefore I told Bartolomeo that he should strive that he might demonstrate his acknowledgments to the fortune which had conferred upon him so undeservedly so great a piece of luck. So ill-content I remained in bed, and I had to attend me that most excellent man Master Francesco da Monte Varchi, the physician, and along with him there treated me in surgery Master Raffaello de' Pilli; for that sublimate had in a way burned the gut of my genital organs, so that I could in no way retain my excrement. And when the said Master Francescho recognized that the poison having done all the evil that it could, had not been sufficient to overcome the strength of the sound constitution which he found in me, he said to me one day: "Benvenuto! Thank God! For you have gained the day; and do not doubt that I want to cure you to spite the scoundrels who have wished to do you harm." Then master Raffaellino added: "This will be one of the finest and most difficult cures that has ever been heard of. Know, Benvenuto! that you have swallowed a mouthful of sublimate." At these words Master Francesco interrupted him and said: "Perhaps it was some venomous caterpillar." I said that I knew for very certain what the poison was, and who had administered it to me: and here every one of us kept silence. They attended to my cure more than six whole months; and more than a year passed before I could enjoy my life.

AT this period the Duke went to make his (State) Entrance into Siena, and Amannato had gone several months in advance to erect the triumphal arches. A bastard son, that Ammannato had, had remained in the Loggia, and he removed some of the curtains which were around my model of *Neptune,* which, since it was unfinished I kept covered up. I immediately went to complain to the Lord Don Francesco, the son of the Duke, who displayed a liking for me, and I told him that they had unveiled my figure, which was incomplete, for if it had been complete I should not have minded. Upon this the said prince answered me, threatening me somewhat with his head, and said: "Benvenuto! Do not mind that it has been uncovered, for it does them so much the more injury. But if however it pleases you that I have it covered up again I will have it covered up": and with these words His Most Illustrious Excellency added many others very favorable to me, in the presence of many lords. Thereupon I said that I besought His Excellency to afford me the means whereby I might be able to finish it, since I would make a present of it, along with the small model, to His Excellency. And he answered that he gladly accepted both, and that he would afford me all the assistance that I should ask. So I fed myself upon this small amount of favor, which was the cause of saving my life; for since there had come upon me so many inordinate evils and unpleasantnesses at one blow, I saw myself collapsing; through that small amount of favor I comforted myself with some hope of life. A year having already passed, since I had held that farm of the

Fountain from Sbietta, and besides all the injuries done to me both by poison and their other extortions, when I saw that the said farm did not produce for me half of that which they had offered me, and I had regarding it, over and above the deeds of contract, a writing under the hand of Sbietta, who had bound himself to me before witnesses to keep up the said income, I went to the Lords of the Council: for at that time there was living Messer Alfonso Quistello, and he was the Fiscal, and he was assembled with the Lords of the Council, and among those Councillors was Haverardo Serristori and Federigo de' Ricci: I do not remember the names of them all. There was also one of the Alessandri: it is sufficient that they were a set of men of high account. Now having recounted my arguments to the Court, all with one voice desired the said Sbietta to restore to me my money, except Federigo de' Ricci, in whose service at that time the said Sbietta was: in such fashion that every one condoled with me that Federigo de' Ricci was keeping them back from summarily treating my case. And among the others Haverardo Serristori with all the rest; although he made an extraordinary disturbance about it, and likewise that member of the Alessandri family: but the said Federigo having delayed the matter so much, until the Court was dissolved, the said nobleman (Serristori) met me one morning, as they were coming out upon the Piazza della Nunziata, and without considering anyone said in a loud voice: "Federigo de' Ricci has so much more force than all of us, that you have been ruined against our wishes." I don't want to say anything more upon this point, because it would be offensive to the supreme power of the Government; it is sufficient that I was ruined designedly by a wealthy citizen, merely because that shepherd was in his service.

The Duke being at Livorno, I went to see him, merely to demand my dismissal. Feeling my strength return and observing that

I was employed upon nothing, it grieved me to do so great a wrong to my studies: so that having made up my mind I went to Livorno, and I found my Duke there, who made me a most kindly welcome. And since I stayed there several days I went riding every day with His Excellency and had much opportunity of being able to tell him all that I wanted to, for the Duke went outside Livorno, and he went four miles along the seashore, where he was having a small fort built; and in order not to be disturbed by too many people, it pleased him that I should chat with him: so that one day, when I saw that he was showing me certain special favor, I intentionally began to talk about Sbietta, that is to say Piermaria d'Anterigoli, and I said: "My Lord, I want to relate to Your Most Illustrious Excellency an amazing circumstance, by which Your Excellency may know the reason that hindered me from being able to complete my *Neptune* in clay, which I was working upon in the Loggia. Your Most Illustrious Excellency must know that I had bought a farm for my life from Sbietta."—It is sufficient that I related to him the whole matter minutely, not ever tarnishing the truth with the false. Now when I came to the poison, I said that if I had ever been an acceptable servant in the sight of His Most Illustrious Excellency, he should, instead of punishing Sbietta or those who gave me the poison, give them some reward; because the poison was not sufficient to kill me; but nevertheless was quite enough to purge me of a deadly slime that I had suffered from in the stomach and intestines: which has operated in such a way that, whereas, had I remained as I was, I could have lived three or four years, this kind of medicine has acted in such a way that I believe I have gained life for more than twenty years: and for this, with greater devotion than ever, I thank God still more. And therefore that is true which I have heard said sometimes by certain people, who say: "God sends us evil that we may turn it to advantage." The Duke remained listening for more than two miles of our journey, continually giving great attention. He merely remarked: "Oh! wicked people!" I concluded that I was under an obligation to them and entered upon other agreeable subjects. I watched for an appropriate occasion, (*ungiorno approposito*) and finding him agreeable to my mood, I besought His Most Illustrious Excellency that he would grant me honorable dismissal, so that I might not throw away any year as long as I was still fit to carry out any work; and as regarded that portion of the (sum) which I was still entitled to receive for my *Perseus,* His Most Illustrious Excellency might give it to me when it pleased him. Along with this proposition I proceeded with many elaborate ceremonies to thank His Most Illustrious Excellency, who answered me nothing at all, rather it appeared to me that he showed that he had taken it in bad part. The next day following Messer Bartolomeo Concino, the Duke's Secretary,—one of the first of them —sought me out; and half bullyingly, said to me: "The Duke says that if you want your dismissal he will give it to you; but if you want to work, he will set you to work: and may you be able to carry out all that His Excellency will give you to do." I answered him that I did not desire any other thing than to have work to do, and especially for His Most Illustrious Excellency, more than all the rest of the people in the world; and were they even Popes, or Emperors or Kings, I would more gladly serve His Most Illustrious Excellency for one *soldo* than any other person for a ducat. Thereupon he said to me: "If you are in this frame of mind you are in agreement without saying anything further. Therefore return to Florence and be of good cheer, for the Duke likes you." So I returned to Florence.

Directly I was in Florence there came to see me a certain man named Raffaellone Scheggia, a weaver of cloth of gold, who spake to me thus: "Benvenuto mine! I want to put you in agreement with Pier Maria Sbietta"; to whom I replied that no one but the Lords of the Council could put us in agreement, and that in this Council, now in power, Sbietta will not find a Federigo de' Ricci, who for a present of two fat kids, without caring either for God or his own honor, is willing to support so wicked a struggle, and to do so ugly a wrong against Holy Justice. Having spoken these words, together with many others, this Raffaello with continued civility told me that a thrush was much better for him, with power to eat it in peace, than was a very fat capon, although you were certain of securing it but to have it after so much fighting. And he kept telling me that it was the way with lawsuits that sometimes they extend over so long a period, that I should much better expend that time in some fine work, whereby I should acquire much more honor and much greater advantage. I, for I recognized that he was telling the truth, began to incline my ears to his words; so that in a short time he put in an agreement after this fashion: that Sbietta should take the said farm on lease from me at seventy gold *scudi* in gold per annum for the whole period of my natural life. When we were making the contract (the which was attested by Sr Giovanni di Sr Matteo da Falgano), Sbietta said that in that fashion in which we had made our computation, it would involve the larger tax; but that he would not fail me; and therefore it would be well that we make this lease for five years at a time; and that he would keep his faith to me without ever reviving any other lawsuits. And so also that scoundrel of a priest brother of his promised me; and after that said arrangement of five years the contract was completed.

Though I want to enter upon another subject, and to leave babbling regarding this unbounded roguery for a while, I am first of all bound to speak of the consequences of the five years' lease. For when it had been completed those two scoundrels did not want to keep any of the promises made to me; rather they wanted to give me back my farm, and did not want to hold it any longer on lease. For which reason I began to complain, and they threw back the contract upon me; so that in consequence of their bad faith I could not help myself. When I saw this I told them that the Duke and the Prince of Florence would not suffer that in their city men should be ruined so wickedly. Now the terror of this threat was of such force that they sent back to me that same Raffaello Scheggia, who made that first agreement; and they said that they did not want to pay me the seventy gold *scudi* in gold as they had said for the five years past. I replied to them that I would take nothing less. The said Raffaello came to see me, and said to me: "Benvenuto mine! You know that I am on your side. Now they have handed over everything to me." And he showed me a writing in their hand. To me, for I did not know that the said man was a close relative of theirs, it seemed to be very right, and so I put myself entirely and altogether in the said man's hands. This worthy man came to me one evening at half an hour after sunset (*a mezza hora di notte*), and it was in the month of August, and with very much talking (*tante suo' parole*), he constrained me to have the contract attested: solely because he knew that if he had delayed until the morning, the fraud which he wanted to practice upon me would not have succeeded. So the contract was made, by which they were to give me sixty-five *scudi* in cash per year for the lease in two payments each year during the whole of my natural life. And although I pro-tested (*scotessi*), and on no account did I want to stay quiet under it, the said (Raffaello) exhibited my signature, with which he com-pelled everyone to lay the blame upon me. And the said man said that he had done everything for my advantage, and that he was on my side. And the notary and the others, not knowing that he was their (*i.e.* the other side's) relative, all laid the blame upon me. For which reason I soon yielded and I shall endeavor to live as long as possible. After this I made another mistake in the month of December 1566 following. I bought half the farm of the Poggio from them, that is to say from Sbietta, for two hundred *scudi* in cash, which adjoined that first one of mine of the Fountain, with a reversion at the end of three years, and gave it to them on lease. I did this for the best. It would necessitate too much for me to dilate at length upon it in writing in my desire to describe the great cruelty that they have inflicted upon me. I wish to refer it entirely and altogether to God who has always defended me against those who have wished to do me evil.

Having finished my marble *Crucifix,* it appeared to me that by raising it upright and setting it some *braccia* lifted up from the ground, it would show off much better than if I kept it upon the ground. And although it showed off well already, when I had set it upright it showed very much better, at which I was very satisfied. And so I began to exhibit it to whoever wanted to see it. As God willed it was mentioned to the Duke and the Duchess; so that when they had come back from Pisa one day unexpectedly both Their Most Illustrious Excellencies with all the nobility of their Court came to my house merely to see the said *Crucifix*: which pleased them so much that the Duke and the Duchess did not cease giving me infinite praise, and so consequently did all those lords and noblemen who were present. Now, when I saw that they were much satisfied, I began to thank them so courteously, telling them that the fact of their taking from me the trouble of the piece of marble for the *Neptune* had been the real cause of my having executed such a work as no other person had ever attempted before me; and that although I had endured the greatest labor that I ever endured in the world, it seemed to me to have been well expended, and especially since Their Most Illustrious Excellencies praised me so much. And since I could never believe myself able to find any one who could be more worthy of it than Their Most Illustrious Excellencies I would gladly make them a present of it; I only begged them that before they departed they would deign to come into the ground floor of my house. At these words of mine, courteously rising at once, they left my workshop, and entering into my house they saw my small model of *Neptune,* and of the fountain, which the Duchess had never seen before that time. And it achieved so much power in the eyes of the Duchess that she at once raised a cry of indescribable astonishment: and turning to the Duke she said: "In the course of my life I have never imagined anything a tenth part of such beauty." At these words the Duke kept saying many times: "Oh! did I not tell you so?" And so among themselves they discoursed about it for some time to my great credit. Then the Duchess summoned me to her, and after many praises conferred upon me by way of excuse—for in the course of those words of hers she appeared as if to ask pardon—she afterwards said to me that she wished that I should have a piece of marble excavated after my own fashion, and would like me to set to work upon it. To these kind words I replied that if Their Most Illustrious Excellencies gave me the convenience, gladly, for love of them, would I set about such a laborious undertaking. Upon this the Duke immediately answered and said: "Benvenuto! To you shall be given all the conveniences that you know how to ask for, and beyond that I will give you on my own account what will be of very much greater value." And with these pleasant words they departed and left me very content.

Many weeks passed away and nothing more was said about me. So that, when I saw that no orders were given me to carry out anything, I was half desperate.

At this period the Queen of France sent Messer Baccio del Bene to our Duke to ask for a loan of money. And the Duke kindly assisted her, for so it was said. And since Messer Baccio del Bene and I were very intimate friends, recognizing each other in Florence we saw one another very gladly: so that the said man related to me all those great favors which His Most Illustrious Excellency had shown him; and in course of conversation he asked me if I had any great works on hand. Wherefore I told him all the matter, as it had fallen out, of the great *Neptune* and of the fountain, and the great wrong that the Duchess had done me. At these words he said to me on behalf of the Queen that Her Majesty had a very great desire to complete the tomb of King Henry her husband, and that Daniello da Volterra had undertaken to make a great bronze horse, and that the time during which he had promised her to make it had expired, and that to the said tomb there were to be added very important decorations. Therefore, if I wanted to return to my château in France, she would have me supplied with all the conveniences that I could ask for, provided that I had the desire to serve her. I told the said Messer Baccio that he should ask (leave) for me from my Duke; and that if His Illustrious Excellency was satisfied I would gladly return to France. Messer Baccio joyfully said: "We will return together"; and reckoned upon it as settled. So the day after, while the said man was talking with the Duke, the subject came up of discussing me, so that he said to the Duke that, if it were with his good favor, the Queen would like my services. To this the Duke replied and said: "Benvenuto is a brilliant man whom the world knows of, but now he does not want to work any more;" and he turned to other subjects. The next day I went to see the said Messer Baccio, who repeated it all to me. At this I could no longer restrain myself, and I said: "Oh! Since His Most Illustrious Excellency gave me nothing to do, I on my own account have executed one of the most difficult works that have ever been done by any other person in the world, and it cost me more than two hundred *scudi,* which I have expended out of my indigence. Oh! What would I not have done if His Most Illustrious Excellency had set me to work. I tell you truly that he has done me a great wrong."

The excellent nobleman repeated to the Duke all that I had answered him. The Duke said that he was joking, and that he wanted me for himself; so that I was several times goaded to go right away. The Queen, so as not to cause displeasure to the Duke, did not wish to argue further; and so I remained very ill-content.

At this time the Duke went away, with all his Court and with all his children, except the Prince who was in Spain. They went by way of the marshes of Siena; and by that route they went to Pisa. The Cardinal first of all the others, imbibed the poison of that bad air; so that after a few days a pestilential fever attacked him and in a short time slew him. This (son) was the Duke's right eye: he was handsome and good, and it was a very great loss. I allowed several days to pass, until I thought that their tears were dried: then I went to Pisa.—

Epilogue

"THEN I went to Pisa." Thus abruptly ends Cellini's own account of his adventures and "laborious life"; but neither the student nor the general reader will be satisfied to leave in this fashion the Life-Story of so interesting a personality; and a natural desire must arise to know something of the years that remained to him between 1562, when his own narrative ends, and February 1st, 1570 (1571 *st. com.*), when he breathed his last. Although in these later years we miss the elaboration and wealth of detailed fact that we learn from the *Autobiography,* a certain amount of information more or less interesting may still be gleaned from the *Memoranda* left by himself—now in the Riccardian Library in Florence—and from other documentary evidence preserved in the Public Archives of that city. Moreover from these same sources we gather certain facts of considerable interest not recorded by our hero himself.

From a *Minute* in the Public Records we learn, for example, that on December 12th, 1554, his claim to be admitted into the ranks of Florentine nobility was officially recognized; and on June 2nd, 1558, he received the tonsure of an ecclesiastic, and was admitted into the first grade of Holy Orders. Two years later he married a wife, who in a number of documents and in his Last Will and Testament bears the name of *Piera di Salvatore Parigi.* Whether—as some critics have suggested—this Piera may be identified with the woman (*serva*) whom he names in his narrative as *Mona Fiore,* and who was managing his household at the time of the casting of his *Perseus,* is uncertain and more than doubtful. We learn, however, from his *Supplica* to the Grand Duke, dated June 12th, 1570, that this marriage was the result of a vow made during the illness produced by the poison of the infamous Sbietta that he would wed *una sua pura ancilla* who had nursed him devotedly at this time; and the *Entries* of the births of at least three children before that date, two of whom are definitely stated to have been the offspring of this very *Piera,* would tend to confirm this conjecture. This woman appears to have belonged to a family of *Parigi* from the Mugello, and not to the Pratese family, distinguished by the talents of the two celebrated architects, Giulio and Alfonso; and she may perhaps (as TASSI suggests) have been a cousin or other relative of that very Domenico Parigi, surnamed *Sputasenni,* whose son, Antonio, Cellini subsequently adopted. We learn from the following *Entry* in the Archivio di Stato in Florence that Mona Piera died in 1588: *1588, 24 aprile, Monna Piera donna fu di messer Benvenuto Cellini rip͡ nella Nunziata.*

Of Benvenuto's children, born in and out of wedlock, two are alluded to in the course of his own *Autobiography*; *i.e. Costanza,* the daughter born to him in Paris by his model Gianna; and the little boy, to whose untimely death he so feelingly alludes in Book II, Chapter Ten. Besides these we find record of no less than six others, as follows: *Jacopo Giovanni,* born November 27th, 1553, and legitimatized in 1554; *Giovanni,* born in 1561, March 22nd, legitimatized the following November, whose death in May, 1563, was the occasion of a very touching letter to Benedetto Varchi from the broken-hearted father; *Elisabetta,* born October 29th, 1562, died September 21st, 1563; *Liberata* or *Reparata,* born January 15th, 1564; *Maddalena,* born· September 3rd, 1566 (married to ser Noferi di Bartolomeo Maccanti) and *Andrea Simone,* born March 21st,

1569. Of these children only the last three appear to have been legitimate.

Besides these children of his own, Cellini, out of a feeling of mistaken kindness, adopted, in November 1560, the son of his model Dorotea and of her husband, Domenico Parigi, commonly known as *Sputasenni*. This Sputasenni was a most worthless fellow, who, being arrested for some brawl, was condemned to serve a term of imprisonment in the Stinche. Cellini, who had already bestowed a dowry of one hundred *scudi* upon the wife, finding her left without means of support, received her with her two children, *Antonio* and *Margherita,* into his own house on July 8th, 1559; and eleven months later—having at that time no surviving son of his own— undertook to adopt the boy (under the name of *Nutino*—diminutive of Benvenuto) into all the rights of a legitimate son, settling upon him the sum of one thousand *scudi* when he reached the age of eighteen, provided that he embraced the profession of sculptor. The lad, however, turned out so idle and troublesome that there was nothing for it but to make a monk of him; and he entered upon his noviciate in the Convent of the SS. Nunziata under the name of *Fra Lattanzio.* Meanwhile Cellini continued to watch over the interests of the lad and endeavored to keep him away from the bad influences of his father, who was then residing in Pisa. In 1568—1569 Sputasenni appears to have revisited Florence, and, complaining loudly that his son had been compelled to enter religion without his consent, attempted to withdraw him from Cellini; who in return forbad any intercourse between Lattanzio and his father. The youth, however, disobeyed his benefactor, and absconded from his convent, so that Cellini early in 1569 renounced the whole connection, and formally disinherited him. This however was, alas! not the end of the matter, for Sputasenni brought an action against Cellini to compel him to provide maintenance for Lattanzio, who had resumed the name of *Antonio,* and to secure to him part of the artist's estate under the *Articles of Adoption.* Sentence was actually pronounced against our hero on June 2nd, 1570, upon which he petitioned the Grand-Duke, and, although he succeeded in freeing his estate, he himself was condemned to pay an annual allowance to the boy for his sustenance.

This circumstance, and the grief that Cellini exhibited on the occasion of the deaths of his two little boys, point to a strong, and not unnatural, desire on the part of the artist to leave behind him some one to carry on his artistic labors and traditions: and it is somewhat pathetic to think that his only legitimate son died without heirs, and that even his daughter's line failed in the next generation.

In March 1561 (*st. com.*) the Grand-Duke, by a *Deed* in which he speaks in high praise of the artist's talents, formally presented to Cellini his house in the Via del Rosaio: a gift subsequently confirmed on February 5th, 1563 (*st. com.*) with reversion to his heirs. But during the last years of his life he seems to have been involved in constant disagreements with the Grand-Duke in the matter of payment for work done; and for one reason or another he appears to have gradually dropped out of public employment. In 1569 (*st. com.*), he was concerned in the valuation of a picture painted by Girolamo Macchietti: and he seems to have devoted a good deal of his attention to various speculations in land.

On March 16th, 1564, at the solemn obsequies prepared by the citizens of Florence in the Church of Santa Croce to do honor to Michelangelo Buonarroti, Cellini was chosen, in company with Ammanato to represent the Art of Sculpture among the other Arts which followed that mighty genius to his last resting-place: but Vasari tells us that, to our hero's bitter disappointment, he was prevented by ill-health from attending that ceremony. Among other ailments that plagued him none was perhaps more persistent than the gout, from which he suffered severely.

During some four years previous to his death Cellini made a variety of Wills, but his actual *Last Will and Testament* bears date December 18th, 1570. To it, however, he added *Codicils* on January 12th, February 3rd and February 6th in the following year. On the 13th of this latter month he expired; and on the 15th was buried with public honors in the Church of the Nunziata. After his death a *List* of his goods and an *Inventory* of his artistic possessions, to which reference has frequently been made already, were drawn up on behalf of his heirs.

GREAT ILLUSTRATED CLASSICS

Adam Bede—*Eliot*
Afloat and Ashore—*Cooper*
The Arabian Nights
Around the World in Eighty Days—*Verne*
Ben-Hur—*Wallace*
The Black Arrow—*Stevenson*
Black Beauty—*Sewell*
The Call of the Wild and Other Stories—*London*
Captains Courageous—*Kipling*
Christmas Tales—*Dickens*
The Cloister and the Hearth—*Reade*
A Connecticut Yankee in King Arthur's Court—*Clemens*
The Cruise of the Cachalot—*Bullen*
David Copperfield—*Dickens*
The Deerslayer—*Cooper*
Emma—*Austen*
Famous Tales of Sherlock Holmes—*Doyle*
Great Expectations—*Dickens*
Green Mansions—*Hudson*
Gulliver's Travels—*Swift*
Henry Esmond—*Thackeray*
The House of the Seven Gables—*Hawthorne*
Huckleberry Finn—*Clemens*
The Hunchback of Notre-Dame—*Hugo*
Ivanhoe—*Scott*
Jane Eyre—*Brontë*
A Journey to the Centre of the Earth—*Verne*
Kenilworth—*Scott*
Kidnapped—*Stevenson*
King Arthur—*Malory*
The Last Days of Pompeii—*Bulwer-Lytton*
The Last of the Mohicans—*Cooper*
Little Dorrit—*Dickens*
Lord Jim—*Conrad*
Lorna Doone—*Blackmore*
The Luck of Roaring Camp and Other Stories—*Harte*
The Man in the Iron Mask—*Dumas*
Martin Chuzzlewit—*Dickens*
The Mill on the Floss—*Eliot*

The Moonstone—*Collins*
The Mysterious Island—*Verne*
Nicholas Nickleby—*Dickens*
The Odyssey—*Homer*
The Old Curiosity Shop—*Dickens*
Oliver Twist—*Dickens*
Our Mutual Friend—*Dickens*
The Pathfinder—*Cooper*
Père Goriot—*De Balzac*
Pickwick Papers—*Dickens*
The Pilot—*Cooper*
The Pioneers—*Cooper*
The Prairie—*Cooper*
Pride and Prejudice—*Austen*
Quentin Durward—*Scott*
Quo Vadis—*Sienkiewicz*
The Red Badge of Courage and Other Stories—*Crane*
The Return of the Native—*Hardy*
Robinson Crusoe—*Defoe*
The Scarlet Letter—*Hawthorne*
Sense and Sensibility—*Austen*
Silas Marner—*Eliot*
The Sketch Book—*Irving*
The Spy—*Cooper*
The Strange Case of Dr. Jekyll and Mr. Hyde And Other Famous Tales—*Stevenson*
A Tale of Two Cities—*Dickens*
Tales—*Poe*
The Talisman—*Scott*
Tess of the D'Urbervilles—*Hardy*
The Three Musketeers—*Dumas*
Tom Sawyer—*Clemens*
Treasure Island—*Stevenson*
Twenty Thousand Leagues Under the Sea—*Verne*
Twenty Years After—*Dumas*
Two Years Before the Mast—*Dana*
Uncle Tom's Cabin—*Stowe*
Vanity Fair—*Thackeray*
Walden—*Thoreau*
The Way of All Flesh—*Butler*
Westward Ho!—*Kingsley*
The Wreck of the Grosvenor—*Russell*
Wuthering Heights—*Brontë*

GREAT ILLUSTRATED CLASSICS—TITANS

Autobiography of Benvenuto Cellini—*Cellini*
Barnaby Rudge—*Dickens*

Bleak House—*Dickens*
Dombey & Son—*Dickens*
Short Novels of Henry James—*James*